A ROAD MORE
or Less
TRAVELED

A Road More or Less Traveled

Madcap Adventures Along the Appalachian Trail

Stephen Otis
Colin Roberts

First printing 2008

Visit the book web site at www.aroadmoreorlesstraveled.com

Jacket design by Benjamin Brezina
Book design by Benjamin Brezina and Jamie Gibson

ISBN 978-0-615-20305-8

LCCN 2008903604

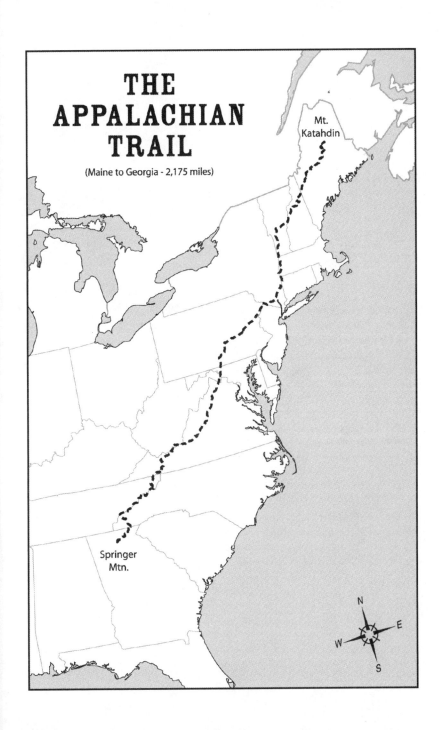

THE APPALACHIAN TRAIL

(Maine to Georgia - 2,175 miles)

Mt. Katahdin

Springer Mtn.

BOOK I

JOIE DE VIVRE

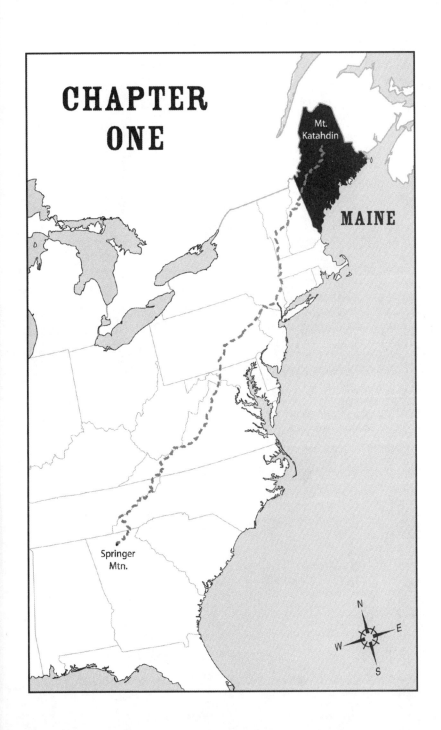

CHAPTER
ONE

Mt.
Katahdin

MAINE

Springer
Mtn.

N
E
W
S

All manner of natural earth – the slopes of hills, branches of trees and foundation veins of nearby mountains – were cast indistinguishable one from another, blue-black against the royal twilight. Light from far away stars burned through their nebulae, spanned incalculable distances and appeared in late June on that small track of earth carved out from the northern wilds. Grace. It shone there on the roof and through the window of an old house with sounding beams and crooked stairs, into a room where three men slept. Early the next morning, as though climbing upward through the black soil, the sun rose white and clear, above the rugged forests of Maine.

I

Applejack woke up. *Daylight. I've missed it. How could I have missed it, today of all days?* Mike was sitting across the room from him, docile, carving the skin off an orange.

"Good morning, sir," Mike said.

"Did we miss it?" Applejack said.

"No, we're good. It's only 4:30."

"What do you mean 4:30? The sun is up."

"We're in Maine. Sun comes up early this far north."

Futureman stirred in a nearby bed but did not wake. A mouthful of dreams clamored in his beard, full and round like his belly. Broken snoring resumed. Leaned against his bunkhouse bed was a glimmering new top-of-the-line backpack, the weight of it nearly bending the struts (you get what you pay for). Futureman had burned the midnight oil in an attempt to purge the thing, yet still it weighed fifty-three pounds. Still it rested there, proud and defiant, ready to drag down the man's dreams.

"I couldn't sleep," Mike said. "Been thinking about her all night."

"We get to see her today. I've been waiting since I was a kid," Applejack said.

"I know you have."

Applejack gripped the edge of the mattress. The 80-year-old hardwood was rough and cold on the balls of his feet as he crossed the room.

"Futureman, get up, buddy. It's time."

Muffled response. *Get up.*

Futureman raked his eyes. *Sunlight.* He sat up quickly. "Did we miss it?"

"We're good. It's early still," Applejack said.

"You sure? The sky is –"

"We're in Maine. Sun comes up early this far north," Applejack said.

Mike smiled from across the room.

A cloud of profanity followed Old Man Shaw wherever he went, most of it censored by a toothless jargon. He was short, hobbled and possessed one outfit of clothes – an undershirt tucked into trousers held up by suspenders. Shaw owned and operated Shaw's, a hiker hostel in Monson, Maine, the first outpost southbound on the Appalachian Trail. It wasn't the only show in town. Pie Lady was just down the road and she was much kinder. She made pies. But Shaw was the legend, and Americans can't accept good behavior in their icons.

Since 5:00 AM, the Old Man had been conducting a maelstrom in the kitchen – pots and pans clanging, wire brushes scraping, bacon sizzling, eggs frying. His wife worked beside him silently, peculiar contentment resting on her face.

"Get up, you little bastud!" Shaw shouted, rapping on the door of an adjacent room.

"Aw right, ole man, don't have a hawt attack," Keith Jr. answered, staggering into the kitchen in sweats, hair poking out like a kindergarten art project.

"Everybody's sittin here waitin' for cawfee," Shaw said, "and ya in there fawtin in ya sheets!"

Keith looked at the floor. A pile of grounds lay underneath the coffee maker. He rolled his eyes and grabbed a broom. "Same thing, every morning at the crack a' dawn. Who needs an alarm clock?"

Mrs. Shaw watched her lover and son grab at each other. There were times when she wanted to tell her men that love is supposed to be more like warm peanut butter cookies and less like dodge ball, but today she remained silent, understanding. This was Maine. They were Mainers.

Applejack, Mike and Futureman waited at the table like curious children, eager for Shaw's breakfast, famous Trail-wide and nearly as mythic as his persona. Across the table flipping through the (very) local paper sat a man named Reed, a dark mix of Victorian dandy and Melungeon, freshly showered and already on his way to being drunk.

"Goin' up the ole bitch today, eh?" Reed asked without taking his eyes off the paper.

"I'm sorry?" Futureman stiffened.

"The bitch. Mount Katahdin. Ya climbin up her today?"

"Yessir," Applejack said, anxious to get on the mountain. "Come all the way from Tennessee. Today's the day."

"Tennessee, eh? I'da got the hell outta there too if I was youse. Probably 'bout time ya got off ya dumps and did something worthwhile with your lives." Reed returned to his reading.

"Sir, I don't believe any of us have had the pleasure of formally meeting–" Mike said, putting his fork down calmly. Reed ignored him and screamed into the other room.

"Old man! You gonna feed me before I die of starvation? And by the way, this coffee's colder than my mutha's glass eye!" A mild grin came over his face. There was history there between the Old Man and he. A durability that spoke of hunting and drinking. Loaning. He looked at Mike. "You wanna say something, guy?"

Mike was Applejack's friend of many years. Before that, he had been a Ranger. Not the perky gentleman in the cupcake-brown hat at the visitor's center. Naw. Army Ranger. Special-ops. Ghost rider. He had seen intimate combat in the Middle East, HALO-jumped into Bagdad at the end of a dishrag-in the dark. Mike understood that a battle has many faces. There is a time to fight and a time to listen, so he held his tongue and nodded. "Good eggs. I was saying these are good eggs."

Shaw emerged with an aluminum pot and slammed it down, mumbling a mix of English curses and Gaelic oaths. Reed grinned as he watched the old man hobble back to his kitchen.

"I just hope you guys aren't quittahs. Seems like every other piece a' monkey dung I run into comes back from Katahdin cryin' about blisters and backaches. Amateurs."

Mike tapped the table with his finger. "Sir, they are not quitters."

Reed piled sausage into his mouth. "I guess we'll see, won't we guy?"

Monson lay around them: white houses and quiet streets. Particles floated slow motion in the aureate sky. Futureman had never been so far north. There was an edge-of-the-world slant to the light here. And in his own obtuse way, each man began to absorb the mystery of Maine, certain of its uncertainty, secretly hoping to run smack dab into the kingdom of hiddenness that was surely waiting in these great woods. This was Maine. Alien Maine. Far-away Maine. Not Tennessee or Virginia or Iowa. This was Maine.

The screen door rattled open. "Load up!" Keith said, throwing backpacks into the bed of his truck.

Born well past the years of reasonable expectation, Keith had been raised under that strange combination of grandparently indulgence and taskmaster scrutiny. He was the last hope to carry on the family business, yet as the baby, fated to struggle for manhood and independence. Out of this, he'd managed to carve out a niche for himself. He gave people rides. The roads, turns, ruts, ditches and jumps on the way to Baxter Park had been whittled into his skull with the dull edge of repetition, but the fixedness of his life was what he loved most. People rattled on about "the world abroad" with its lightning-paced fads and one-night dreams. Keith just drove. Old Man Shaw could snort and holler all he wanted back at the hostel. Keith just drove.

As the engine idled, he pulled out a silver can and pinched a four-finger load of brown tobacco (large enough to kill a donkey) and crammed it into his lower lip. He laid his head back and smiled – first dip of the day. Tobacco seeped into his bloodstream. The meniscus had just started to tingle when Reed interrupted.

"Dumb little punk! I told you not to leave without me! And if ya think for a second I'm sittin between these hicks, you got another thing comin."

"Shut up, ya lazy drunk. You want a ride, get in the back," Keith said.

Reed threw his pack into the truck bed and jumped over the tailgate with surprising agility. But before he had time to situate himself properly, Keith punched the gas. At the sound of the big man's bulk skidding across the truck bed, Keith pulled his hat down, his crooked smile finding the long road that wound toward the mountain.

Last winter's chill had survived in the late-June wind. Reed slumped in the bucket seat and pulled a weathered hood over curly hair.

"What's his deal, anyway?" Applejack asked.

Keith shrugged. "Reed? Aw, he's harmless I guess. Comes around a few times a year, actin' like he owns the place." Keith jerked the truck through a small ravine. "Knows a helluva lot about these pawts, though."

"What does he do for a living?"

"Do for a living?" Keith sputtered, tobacco bouillon dripping. "Drinks bea. Gambles. Dabbles in the mawket. Waits out the winters and then heads back into the woods." Disapproval and envy co-habitated in his voice.

Applejack caught a view of sky through the dark trees. The little track they were on was like dozens of others, all cut in a futile attempt to domesti-cate the Maine wilderness. There were no paved roads this deep into the Great Northern Woods. Only these paths lying still and quiet. A lone plane might grace the sky every week or so.

Futureman's belly bobbed in the ruts. He sucked it in and pulled his legs together, hoping to stay out of Keith's driving space. "So how long you been up here, Keith?"

"Hell, forevuh. That old house is all I've ever known." Spittle cup and coffee cup – both between his knees, both the same consistency and color-sloshed dangerously over the bumps and jolts.

"You ever think about getting out? Going to school or something?"

"Yeah. There's a mechanics school out in Wyoming I was lookin at. But the Old Man got sick, so I stuck around and ran everything til he got better. See, I know every place a road intersects the Trail. Funny thing is, I never got out on the Trail myself. Ironical, ain't it?" He shrugged. "You fellas aren't from New England, ah ya?"

"No. You ever been down south?" Futureman asked.

"Oh, yeah. I been to New Hampshire a shit load a' times," Keith said.

He wasn't joking.

Keith stopped the truck. There were no more roads to drive, only trails to walk.

"You make sure they come out in one piece, Mike," Keith said.

"They'll be alright," Mike said.

"You guys walk hard and keep goin. The Hundred-Mile Wilderness is no joke."

"Moose droppings. Bear dung," Reed muttered, hefting his pack. "That's what they'll be in ten days, I can promise ya that." Applejack watched him disappear into a thicket beside the road. *OK. Reed is a bastard. He is a freeloader. He is a rot-gut sot. He interrupts people and probably pees on their things. He's an all-around shady character. But I kinda like him. He has an honesty that's refreshingly despicable.*

"So, good luck, fellas. I expect to be takin some more of ya money ten days from now." Keith spat his chaw onto the dirt and stepped into his truck.

They watched the pickup disappear down the road southward, dust stirring beneath the mountain.

"This is it." Mike nodded and walked into the forest.

Applejack and Futureman glanced at each other, took a breath and stepped into the trees.

II

The temperament of Maine mirrors the character of Mt. Katahdin. At times the mountain is like a benevolent grandmother, watching over momma moose as they lead their babies to water. Fat rabbits and squirrels play games underneath speckled alder and sumac. Trails winding through gardens of aster, black-eyed Susan, hepatica and Indian pipe. Yet Katahdin is also a judge. She presides over sprawling marshlands and holy mountains with a just jealousy displayed in gray and purple skies, like a train of royal garments. Austere aiguille.

Long ago, the Abenaki people believed the summit to be shrouded by Pamola, a creature with the body of an eagle and a face as large as four horses. They believed this Storm Bird had decreed no mortal would see the hallowed peak, and any who tried would be snatched up into her talons and carried away like carrion into the mist.

As they climbed upward along the Abol Approach trail, the three hikers didn't realize any of this. Didn't know. Didn't care. Their thoughts, arms, hands, legs and heels scattered among the chopped up granite.

Mike's days were numbered. He wouldn't be moving down the Trail past the Hundred Mile Wilderness. He had come to encourage them through the first leg of their journey. His experience in the field had taught him that physical presence has a lasting effect. Time-release. A bond of blood and sweat.

Adrenaline coursed through Applejack's legs, carrying him up steadily. Futureman struggled below, reality hard at work on his fat body. Excitement had towed it along for the first half mile, but now the extra pounds were revolting, taking it out on his right heel where a small blister began to form.

You can't be serious, he thought. *Already?* Refusing early defeat, he pressed on. *Ignore it. It'll go away...maybe.* It didn't.

"Hey, can you guys hold up for a sec?"

"What is it?" Mike said.

"Don't know. Could just be a rock in my shoe." *Mike thinks I'm a baby. He's thinking that I wet the bed.* "But take every precaution, I always say."

"Good idea. If it's a blister, you don't want it to bust open this early in the game."

"I couldn't agree more." *I'm an idiot.*

Futureman slid off his trekking shoe (not broken in properly) to survey the damage – a runny mound of dermis on the crown of his heel. *Not even halfway up the first mountain. Damn this fat body.*

Baxter Peak, the tip of the behemoth, lay several hundred feet above tree-line in a naked world stretching to the sea on one side and locked in a turbine of cloud and bluster on the other. They were eager to gain that highest point, to see the wooden AT sawhorse as notched and weathered as the travelers who clutch it at journey's end. For those coming north from Georgia, 2,160 trail miles to the south, it is a beacon of accomplishment. For the Southbounder, the sign is the mark of a long journey ahead, pregnant with mystery, a dim lamppost at the edge of a clouded future.

Mike found Applejack standing, mouth agape. A small crowd of dayhikers had gathered around to take pictures.

"Can you believe this? There's a line. For the sign."

"At least it's not a long one," Mike said.

Nearby, Futureman spotted an attractive woman seated on an eave of rock. Moving across the ledge to talk to her, he suddenly noticed – *handsome, well-muscled companion at two o'clock.* A retreat would be awkward. *Emasculating.* He soldiered bravely ahead with, "Howdy doody there, hikers."

"Howdy doody there, yourself," the beautiful woman replied. She was exquisite. Magnetic. Electric. Like the Van Allen Belt.

"Ahya va you…what think about this day?"

"I think it's a gorgeous day and a gorgeous mountain, and I can't wait to start this gorgeous hike."

What a woman. You still may have a chance, Futureman thought. *He might be her brother. Don't sell yourself short. You're quite a specimen yourself, fat though you are. Be smooth, smooth, smooth.*

"Yessum agree, is too a pretty dray…today – mean to say – who are the days?" *Your stomach is oozing over the elastic waistline of your baby-blue shorts.*

"Boy, you're a weirdo!" She smiled.

Her man did, too. He had really nice teeth. *Bleached? No. Natural. Bastard.* "I'm Fred Baby. This is my wife, Little Moose. At least I think that's who we are. The names might change."

He and Little Moose spoke with the genteel accents of Old South blue bloods. Pure bred. Fred Baby had just finished doctor school and would soon be practicing in Pennsylvania.

"You alone?" Little Moose said, tenderly.

"No…Applejack and Ranger – who is Mike, who is a Ranger, or was, but not a park, you know – an army Ranger. Applejack and I aren't in the army. We're teachers, of Tennessee children."

They looked a him blankly.

Get it together, Futureman thought. State a fact: "There are many school house children." *Fffff.*

Fred Baby crinkled his brow.

"So are ya'll thru-hiking to Georgia?" Little Moose asked.

"Mike is leaving after the Wilderness. He drove all the way up here from Tennessee just to say goodbye."

"That's quite a goodbye," Fred Baby said.

"Yes, it is. And ya'll? Thru-hiking?"

Fred Baby wrapped his arms around Little Moose. " That's the plan." They connected their foreheads and screamed through their teeth.

It was love – the kind of love that makes it to Georgia.

"That's nice," Futureman said.

"We'll see you around, friend," said Little Moose. "We like you." She tapped him on the shoulder.

Futureman watched them go, poking at each other, popping kisses back and forth. He liked them too, their love and warm Southern charm. He even liked their neato matching outfits.

Waiting his turn in line, Applejack continued to simmer. To his left, he spied two old people walking briskly toward him along the western side of the cordillera. They were really, really old. Old skin. Old hair. Old crooked backs. They had climbed Katahdin too.

Suddenly, a curtain pulled back. Applejack felt naked. Puzzled. This was not the moment of clarity, not the dream-like buzz he had imagined for so many years.

Where's the ancient wisdom floating above the peak? he thought. Where is the silence? The dreaming? Where is the ego-less void?

"What's wrong?" Futureman asked.

"Nothing. What do you want? Let's take these pictures and get down off this mountain."

"Whoa there, buddy. This is it, the start of our long hike," Futureman said.

"So it is."

"Well c'mon. This is what you've been waiting for and now you're here. We're here!" Futureman tugged on his arm like a child. "Look at that wide open sky. We have no clue what we're doing – I know I don't. I just hit on a married woman, and I already got a blister on the way up here." Laughter stirred in Applejack's throat, but he forced it back down.

"Say Georgia!" The old couple said as they snapped a shot.

The trio descended to the pin needle edge of the lower shelf and stood, leaning against the fragments of a gale. Applejack looked out. From there, he could see a red wind rising from the tendrils of the Hundred Mile Wilderness, moving outward. Tierra del fuego. *I'm here at last,* he thought. *I'm actually hiking this thing, and I really don't have a clue what I'm doing.*

"Here goes nothin."

III

Leaves brushed against their shoulders. The transition forest at the base of Katahdin pulled in big tooth aspen from the north and green hawthorn from the south, understory thick with hobblebush and wildflower.

The path was light and level, a cruel deception. It would be short-lived. It skirted a marsh and ran along the edge of a river. The wind blew steadily. The sun glistened on the surface of the water. Warblers and finches followed them through the trees, calling to them. *Spring is here. Summer's near. Windiscalm and skiesareclear. Thiswon'tlast, believemedear, dayslikethis come onceayear. Dontwaistunour, thend izneur. Berooperoo berahberear.*

As they walked, they became aware of a rhythm created by stepping that would soon be as indiscriminate to them as breath – but for now, it required concentration. Soon after, they were interrupted by another, one sure and steady.

Beating strong against the ground, a tap, a click, a jab, echoing, moving fast. Hiking poles (extensions of fingers) vaulted off the roots and grazed across the path. A man appeared out of the green tangle. He stepped fluidly and without effort. His stride had been forged over time. He had long hair and a scratchy beard, eyes intense, far off. His shirt was ragged. His pack was folded and cinched. His black nylon creek-gaiters, torn to shreds, lay loose around his ankles. He was strong. Worn but not haggard.

Folks called him Reggae. Of course, he had a proper Christian name. But on the AT he was and always would be Reggae. [Trailname, galldarnit. It's an AT tradition. Everybody gets one. Bunch of pagan hippy tree-huggers.]

"That's a thruhiker," Applejack said. "He's come all the way from Georgia. He's about to finish."

They stepped aside.

Reggae stopped, barely noticing the greenhorns in front of him. He could see Katahdin above the birch. "There she is."

"Any advice?" Futureman asked.

"Sure. Get rid of the Nalgenes. Use Gatorade bottles instead. Saves a pound."

Not exactly what I was expecting, but, "Alright, thanks," Futureman said.

An hour later Reggae was on the granite holds, clutching the rickety sawhorse and staining it with his tears.

In the early afternoon, in a flat just beyond Abol Bridge, they come upon a simple sign. The entrance to the Wilderness. There is nothing menacing about its appearance, just a piece of wood standing there on a lip of thick forest. But the warning is clear: *You are about to enter one hundred miles of flat-out wilderness. So please, do not proceed unless you're prepared.*

"Are we?"

A shiver migrated across the base of the neck. The weight of their packs pressed down. They felt weak, like sentenced men as they climbed into the forest, doing their best to defy the portent with a weak sneer.

"What choice do we have?"

It would be ten long days inside. On the other side waited Monson, and beyond Monson, the long journey home. With wobbly feet and untested resolve, they began.

IV
Wilderness Day 1

A steamy day. Katahdin, their northern star, was lost behind them in a haze. Morning dew dripped off the fern tail shrubs that lined the trail. Wet moss carpeted the forest. The wind was humid. It moved through the canopy as though the forest was breathing.

Futureman winced. The moleskin he'd put over his blister for padding had slipped off and he was hobbling again. "How much further is it to Georgia, again?"

Applejack looked down as he walked. His boots were making crimson puddles in the soil. "I put a spell on you..." he sang. Tremolo clung to the branches of trees.

"Damnation, it's hot," Mike said, rubbing his forehead. "I'll see you guys at camp tonight." A swarm of oversized deer flies followed him as he disappeared into the trees.

"Mike?" Futureman called.

"I put a spell on you," Applejack echoed, "because you're mine."

Futureman looked at the moss. Was it visibly growing up the stems? "What are we doing here? This doesn't seem like a happy place."

Thunder sounded and sky grew dark.

"No. These woods are clearly not happy."

Thunder and rain pounded the earth all afternoon.

That night at camp, Applejack was relieved to spy a gap in the clouds. Even though the inside of the tent was as slimy as sewage, and even though his fifty-pound pack was soaked through, and even though he and Futureman had never gotten their absurd food bag to stay up in the trees, and even though his feet hurt half as much as his thighs and his thighs hurt half as much as his shoulders, he was relieved to see a gap in the clouds.

Futureman lay beside him, drifting off to sleep, muttering, "Flies can't catch me anymore. Little African children pulled off their wings and boiled them on the fire. And now they're going going going to eat them..."

Approximately 2,150 miles lay ahead of them, but Applejack was relieved for now – to see a gap in the clouds.

Day 2

The daily rains spilled violently into the marshlands and ancient steaming swamps. This constant presence of dank moisture increased the chances for wet rot and testicle chafing. Futureman's opened blister had become infected and was issuing a white puss from its raw epicenter. Its twin was forming on the other heel. *What is this? Blisters are as contagious as loneliness?*

When it wasn't raining, every inch of the forest air swirled with some sort of insect or other floating menace: spores, deadwood particles, mosquitoes, black flies, deer flies, etc.

"I've never met bugs who can bite through bandanas before."

"Hey, where did all the birds go?" Applejack asked.

Futureman looked up into the empty sky. "They must have combusted in the sun."

"I'm serious."

"I don't know, Applejack. How could I know that?"

Futureman hobbled and torqued his ankles out to protect his heels. The path ahead seemed to be forcing them into another long thigh-high bog walk. He tried to stay atop a log, but his foot slipped and disappeared into the decay. Mud-sop gristle filling his shoe, grinding against his raw skin.

"Applejack, I have this cousin. Spawn of the devil. One time he put his cat into a trash heap just because he wanted to see it get squished between the compactors."

"Why are you telling me this?"

"Cats in grinders – don't you see-that's what we are right now – cats in grinders. I'm pretty one hundred percent sure that I hate everything about this. I just went for a poop in the woods…and the flies, they…"

"I know." Applejack looked around at the slow decay of the surrounding forest. Stultified by water. "I'd say plenty of cats have died in here."

Applejack was the first to make the clearing through seven miles of bitter swamp. Around him he saw rocks and roots through his heroin eyes. Didn't matter. Stumbled anyway. His stomach growled angrily, yet he couldn't discern hunger, necessarily. His pack gripped him like an angry raccoon digging claws into his shoulders. His body was becoming one swollen, shapeless mass of flesh, bone, sinew and organ, all allies, all enemies, straining against gravity, begging for a soft landing, but he was too brittle and nothing would bend anymore, so he crashed to the ground like a mangled seesaw. His insides slid forward, an out-of-step cattle car on a ghost train, and smashed into his brain.

"Is that a human?" a hiker named *Speedo* asked, afraid to touch it.

Behind, Futureman lurched on through the swamp, casting his mind over anything other than the pain. *Island, find that island, that one in the middle of the ocean.* He tried to imagine it, but couldn't because the little boy who was dreaming it up somewhere wasn't done dreaming it up: a beautiful island with sunshine and waterfalls and hidden bays and nurse sharks – that seems to make sense in a world that doesn't make any sense. *Maybe the boy is me. Maybe the island is just around the next corner. Maybe the sun is really a devil.*

When Futureman came to the broken seesaw, he bent down to examine it. Eyes darted. It muttered something.

"Applejack, that you?"

"Eeeeeeeeeeeee."

"What's wrong with you? What do you need?" Futureman asked.

"Foooooooooooo."

"That's out of the question in this heat. It's too explosive. You'll blow up and kill us all. How about salvation from your sins?"

"Here. Put this powder in his water. The electrolytes will do him some good." It was Fred Baby, just as cooked as the rest but a doctor first and foremost. Little Moose sat in the shade. Head hung low, her magnificent coloring faded and pale, she forced a question through labored breath.

"Where...how are your feet, Future...are you keeping bandages changed?"

"How far is it to camp?"

"We're getting there buddy. Eight miles now."

Eight more miles? Might as well be eight thousand.

Day 3

A stream cut through the woods. The sound of it drew them to its shore where a tall boy with a shaved head and bright blue eyes was fishing.

"Shhhh," the boy motioned to them. "Watch. He's about to take it."

A large brookie was drifting in the current, eyeing a bait above the rapids. The trout struck. Masterful. Yet it found itself dangling, drowning in the air of another world.

"Anyone hungry for brookie?" the boy said, holding it up through its gill.

He said his name was Colonel. Applejack and Futureman were already wary of several other hikers they'd met who had obviously named themselves. They had asinine names like *Lone Wolf, Gandalf, Spirit Watcher*. One self-namer had pronounced he was to be known as *Restless Wanderer*. The first thing *Restless Wanderer* said to them was, "My name is *Restless Wanderer*." Then *Restless Wanderer* said, "My name is *Restless Wanderer* because...I'm a restless wanderer."

Self-namers are often self-authenticating people.

Are we, then, self-authenticating people? Applejack and Futureman were forced to ask.

They could tell immediately that this Colonel was not such a person. He was an honest Mormon. His friends had given him the noble moniker when he set out just after high school graduation. In his hand he carried a long wooden staff with their signatures on it.

The Colonel's enthusiasm refreshed them, but his eighteen-year-old legs were too fleet for Applejack and Futureman. He was long gone by the time they finally crossed Whitetop Mountain, but Mike's little green pack lay on a rock. They hadn't seen him all day.

"Where has Mike gotten off to?" Applejack asked.

"Maybe he got carried off by one of the prehistoric mosquitoes around here," Futureman said.

"I feel like a cleaved, salted steak," Applejack said, dropping his fifty-pound monster beside Mike's twenty-five pounder.

"How does he get away with carrying thirty pounds less than us?" Futureman asked.

"I don't know. I'm not sure what else I could have gotten rid of," Applejack said.

"Perhaps we should find out."

Then there was singing in the bushes behind them. They turned in time to see Mike emerge with a straw hat on his head, boots on his feet, a tube sock on his penis and pride on his face.

"Mornin' boys," Mike said, arms out, sun burning his shoulders.

"Mike, why are you na…"

"You boys forget? It's *International Hike Naked Day*." The nude man grabbed his things and loped over the crest of the hill, picking up his song where he had left it. In the distance, a special-ops coyote call sounded.

"Do you think he knows Hike Naked Day was a week ago?" Futureman asked.

"I think he's got a fever. Keep an eye on him."

The end of day 4, or is it still day 3?

As they pitched their tent, the clear sound of a flute floated up from Rainbow Stream. A wild, shoeless man wielded it. He lifted his knees as he played. He told them it was a song he had composed for the stream. His dinner was mostly comprised of Indian cucumbers and wild mushrooms he had found in the forest. He was an unbridled earth-worshiper. An extraordinary heathen. A *Tom Bombadil* sort of fellow.

He shared his supper with them and told them a story.

Back in his college days (last year), he and some friends had fashioned a pantheon of little idols and placed it in the middle of campus on account of "we're bored." The next day at dawn, they bowed before the idols as the student body passed by. It didn't take long for the worship circle to grow, causing no small amount of concern among the staunchly irreligious faculty. Some were repulsed. Others were secretly thrilled. Regardless, the issue was "tagged" by the administration, and a missive was sent to the custodial staff: "Please remove PHENOMENOLOGICAL DISTURBANCE from middle of campus." A misstep on their part. Once the holy place was desecrated, protests ensued. The campus was overrun with freethinkers of every size, shape and color. Several days of Bill-of-Rights quoting and psycho-tropic sojourning followed. Class was cancelled.

I like him, this Tom Bombadil fellow. What is he talking about?

It soon grew dark under a clear sky. The temperature dropped. An audible sigh rose to the heavens. Applejack and Futureman came down from their tent on the hill to talk some more with the strange man.

Three hikers named *Krom, Ringleader* and *Lollygag* were sharing a pipe of marijuana with Bombadil, discussing the virtues of a vegetarian lifestyle. "Animals are more innocent than people ever could be." "The human dental structure is clearly adapted for the consumption of plants." Etc.

"I'm a vegan," offered Bombadil. "Don't get me wrong. If I owned a cow, I'd suck milk from her tits, but corporate farming is cruel and irresponsible."

"Yeah, man!" Lollygag squealed. "And these damn state parks raping the land!"

"What are you talking about?" Krom said, taking a fatherly tone. "If it weren't for state parks, loggers would have chewed all this land up by now and you wouldn't be sitting here getting high in the woods."

Lollygag giggled. "Yeah, so thank God*ess* for the parks."

"Isn't Katahdin superb!" Bombadil was unable to contain his joy. "That wind pounding down on the razor ridge was coming so hard I nearly blew right off the trail. At one point, I leaned forward, open-armed, into the wind." He was standing now. " I asked her to take me. Right then and there. *You wouldn't be such a bad way to go!* Better than dying by some disease or getting run over by a train," he said to no one on his way back to the ground.

"Disappearing into the sky *would* be a good way to go," Krom said.

"*Good*, you say?" Ringleader rocked forward, intent on the meaning of words. "A *good* way to go. *GOOD*, way to go, *good*. What does it mean…good…"

Day 4, is this Day 4, who is this Day for?

At 103°, the wooden planks were cooking Applejack's cheeks. Candied apples. He didn't care. He was prostrate on a boat dock on Pemadumcook Lake, forty-five miles into the Wilderness. Mike was beside him, feet in the water, leaning against a post with an air horn and a note attached to it: *Blow the horn. Will come get you.* Opposite the dock sat Whitehouse Landing, a fortress in the middle of the Wilderness, a hidden refuge of bunkhouses and cabins with steaks and hamburgers, drinks and cold showers.

Futureman made his way along the shore, stumbling over the uneven rocks. He watched uncomprehendingly as the outboard approached. A mile back, he'd made the decision to armor himself in full rain gear, preferring to smother in plastic rather than surrender his flesh to the thousands of blood-sucking black flies that lay in wait along the path. *Cunning assassins with their anesthetizing fangs and anti-coagulant venom. No, there will be no more bloodshed today.* But somewhere his vision had blurred. *I don't think I can make it after all. I have to make it.*

Through his salty eyes, Whitehouse looked like a glittering Xanadu sinking into the Pemadumcook depths. *A metaphor of the Self. That's what's sinking. This is my lesson. Whitehouse Landing will be my coffin.*

Mike grabbed his arm. "C'mon, the man is here to take us across."

"To the other side? Alright, I'm ready. Be sure to put the coins on my eyes." Futureman dropped into the boat.

Day 5, or 6, or maybe both

Ho! It is *Little Dave*, sitting on the logging road. An hour ago he had been "cruising along" when he "accidentally" fell over a ledge after "tripping on a rock" that he "didn't know was there" and "before he even knew what was going on" his "already weak (from a climbing [man it was killer!] accident)" left wrist absorbed the impact from all "eighty pounds" of his pack, which caused it to "smash into a million pieces," and now it needs to be "examined by a doctor." "Immediately." And thus it is "unavoidable" that he "must" "get off the Trail."

"Where are you going, Little Dave?" Speedo asks.

"Don't worry, someday I will return, my friends, to finish what we've begun," Little Dave says as he reclines in the dusty bed of the logging truck. His eyes are closed in agony and regret as the driver shifts into second. Or is one eye open?

A yellowish Day with a hint of red and black

Futureman's feet, now wrapped completely in duct tape, are two lumps of throbbing pulp, full of raspberry Jell-o. With every step, they are in danger of bursting under the force of his fat body.

Before they started the Trail, Applejack had given him the advice: *Put on some pounds before you begin. You're going to lose a lot of weight from walking so much, so a little extra will help you in the long run.*

Futureman had used it as an excuse to get as fat as he could in as little time as possible. So while other people were running three or four miles a day, he had eaten bacon and Belgian waffles. While they rode bikes and worked out their legs at the gym, Futureman sampled cake and ice cream between meals. While they ran stairs and took backcountry hikes, he inhaled extra-large tubs of buttered popcorn in local movie theaters. In two months time, he had gone from 168 to 201 pounds.

"Damn my fat body, and damn Applejack for letting me get it so fat," Futureman said to himself, collapsed on the side of a sweeping rock scramble below the peak of Nesuntabunt Mountain. He had been unsuccessful at moving any part of his body for quite some time now. He needed water in a bad way. Dark green clouds roiled above him. Static charges buzzed inside. He didn't know what to say, what to do. He screamed.

These were the words that came out, "God, do you exist?" "I need a miracle!" "You did it for Moses in the desert?" "If you don't, I am going to die!"

"I think."

Applejack couldn't hear his friend. He was on top of the mountain resting, face down in a hollowed-out place that fit the contours of his frame perfectly.

Behind his buried head, a blue-green mist spread out across the great space between the Nesuntabunt and a long black line of thunderheads that had stacked themselves above the northern peaks. If he had turned for even a second, he would have seen the purple form of Mt. Katahdin pushing out from underneath a heap of burnt orange clouds. He would have seen that the distance he had come was so great a beauty that it could not be measured in miles, existing in an almost untouched manner in Maine's northern forests.

Lost Day

"Mike's gone. Went ahead. Note says…something about…spider bite." Applejack knelt in the mud. The scrap of paper fell from his hand. His chest rose weakly with air.

Futureman couldn't hear the talk. His shirt was spread across the rock beside him. It hung in the current of the mountain stream, swaying back and forth irrhythmically. He stared at it, unconcerned about time or spider poison. The sun had been in that one spot for days. One by one, butterflies collected on the warm fabric. There were five of them now, slowly spreading their wings apart and pulling them back together. In this, he became entranced. *Such vivid color,* he thought. *Each wing is like a painted canvas. So beautiful. Why does the Creator care about such tiny details? Strange. I'm breathing as they flap their wings but I'm not trying to. Is this meditation? Am I praying? What comes tomorrow and tomorrow and tomorrow…*

Day 1, 3, 5 (the prime ones have meaning), 7 and so on

Seventy-eight miles into the Wilderness, food running low, they ran into Colonel in a brown bog, liquefying in the hot sun, not so young anymore. He had flown too fast and too close to the sun.

"You need water. We all need water," Applejack said. "We all need water now."

The one and only source was a dirty swamp pool nearby.

"The only thing going on in there are the happy movements of an unadulterated insect orgy," Futureman peered in, remembering the Giardia bug he had caught four years prior from a bush puddle in the Zimbabwean Gwandavale desert. Never having quite recovered, his intestines jiggled, resisting. *Please, not again!*

"Colonel, you got a pump?" Applejack asked.

"Yes."

"This'll do fine."

A mile later, still chewing on grit and particles, they came upon a group of eight French-Canadian teenage girls, planted in the dirt, stewing in their anger, crying in frustration, swatting weakly at the insects. Headed north with seventy-eight miles to go, with nothing left to give the wilderness, they'd handed themselves over to the fantasy that a man, valiant and brave, would come to rescue them. That's when the Colonel – Arian of Arians, blonde and blue eyed, brown and tall – came over the rise. The girls shuddered as he helped them off the forest floor, whimpered sexually under his palms, buzzed to life, giggled, squeezed every last drop of flirtatiousness out of their stinky, nasty skin.

Then they panicked, convincing one another that he was only a mirage, an unreal man-oasis in this, their direst of days. So the young virgins rejected the Colonel as a cruel temptation, and plunged hopelessly back into the throes of despair. Thus, they left the golden young Mormon in a new torment all his own, as though he were only a man made of cellophane.

<u>During the month of July</u>
Applejack began to sing a yuletide song to himself, somewhere on the side of a nameless mountain.

"Why are you singing *White Christmas*?" Futureman asked.

Applejack didn't answer. His thoughts were bending inward.

I love the smell of fall, the breeze and the turning of the leaves. It reminds me of my sisters. They were born in the fall. The World Series is played in the fall, and Thanksgiving is in the fall. My family eats the turkey and the dressing, and then we throw the pigskin that arches across the sky toward December. Christmas is in December. The lights cover the houses during Christmas. The cars swerve in and out of the traffic. The people swerve in and out of the stores. They're wearing jackets, because it's cold in December. It's not like July. Your socks don't soak through your shoes and stick in between your toes and make rashes on the bottoms of your shins. July is dreadful and hot. July is the nemesis. Christmas and snow will be here again. I'll sing until they come.

<u>70 days, 96 nights</u>
Tom Bombadil had been crouched in the lotus position for a full hour, claiming that any second now he would light it by pyro-kinesis. "It's a little bit harder than telekinesis," he said, "but not quite as difficult as astral projection." Finally, he resorted to a primitive method – the match. His downcast expression signified yet another grievance against an ever changing list of false gods.

Futureman laid inside the tent, safe from the bugs, his favorite part of the day. His infirmities were airing out. His blisters could breath. The wet-rot lines on the bottoms of his feet were smoothing out. He watched as a mosquito bumped against the no-see-um netting of the tent. Childishly, he laughed and pointed his finger at this rare triumph over evil, suspecting that, if humans were able to look into the spirit world, he would instead see a massive, leather-winged beast with talons and red eyes and acid breath.

Applejack unzipped the tent to crawl in.

"What are you doing? No!" Futureman yanked him inside, scrambling to get it closed.

"What?!"

"You'll let it in, you idiot! Where is it? Where did it go?" he said, searching frantically while the intruder quietly began to suck the blood from his forehead.

Still Day 1, but it's now 10, because the last are first

"Mike will be there, if he's still alive," Applejack said to himself.

He had not seen his friend in several days, maybe weeks, perhaps years. No, weeks. Mike had shifted into ghostrider overdrive after discovering the brown poison of a recluse spider a couple days after "International Hike Naked Day." His shoulder was beginning to rot when he finally mentioned it to them.

Applejack's throat was almost completely constricted, parched and throbbing. "Mike will bring Keith, and Keith will bring the truck. Gotta be close now," he muttered. "It can't all be like this, can it? It's going to get easier, right?"

He came upon Futureman. Collapsed in a small mud puddle. He was smearing mud all over his legs and arms.

"Man, what are you doing?"

"I jussss'don't care anymore. I jussah, jussah-"

Applejack pitied his friend. *What have I done to him? This is my fault. How did it come to this?*

He searched for words that would snap his friend out of this pathetic state, but even as he began to speak them, he found himself asking instead, "Does it feel good?"

"Oh yes. It's cool, cool, cool on the skin," said Futureman in a sloppy ecstasy.

So Applejack dropped his pack and rubbed the mud on his body too.

An hour later Speedo walked by. Eyeing the two sub humans, he kept his distance and tossed some beef jerky over to them. "Here, eat this, looks like you need the sodium," he said. "Just a few more miles now is all. You can do it."

Mike had been in Monson for two days, full-bellied and recovering. Now he was standing at the edge of the Hundred Mile Wilderness, waiting nervously for his friends. The sun was setting. "They've got to be close now."

The last three miles skirted one of Maine's pristine lakes. The wind was strong. It pushed the leatherleaf over and made great ripples on the surface of the water.

There was nothing left in them. Vile paste streaked their faces and arms. Air was in their veins. As they looked at the sun's reflection on the choppy water, the two lost boys realized how much like the surface they had become, driven lamely by another force, unable to dream anymore, thinking only in steps and moments.

"At last." Mike held his arms open to embrace them. "This is it, where I end and you begin," he said.

"Begin what, Mike?"

V

Life is not predictable. The universe is far too complex to be corralled or cornered. We do not know what is going to happen next. We cannot know what to expect. From another person. From a harmless situation. From a wild animal. From the weather. From a relationship, conversation or ball game. From our mouths, brains or intestines. We never know what is going to come out. We can only make an educated guess. Sure, sure, we try to sound intelligent. We want to be prophetic, clairvoyant. Wise. But – alas – we are not.

So, we make lists and equations and formulate theories and hypotheses. We graph out our expectations, write them down in diaries, on maps, flow charts and NCAA tournament bracket sheets. When we are right we feign assuredness. Perhaps, it's that we want to be like God. We want to have Knowledge, be in Control. But invariably we wake up and find ourselves wandering around in fig leaves, wondering what the hell just happened and why we didn't see it coming.

So the merry band of Wilderness survivors – a dozen or so – gathered in Shaw's front yard. They had eaten, slept, cleaned their stinking, filthy bodies and were milling around in proud silence.

Out of the Pit. We made it.

And yet, after all the preparation, sacrifice and struggle, only a handful of them were leaving by foot. Sure that the Trail was not what they'd thought, the rest were taking cars, buses and planes back home. But, Applejack and Futureman were among those who would remain, busting up the odds – a pathetic ideal proving that the fittest do not always survive and the dumbest sometimes do.

Later that afternoon, around the globe, regimes were being overthrown, marriages annulled, books read, bottles quaffed. In Monson at Shaw's, in the old crooked beamed house, Futureman sat in the den and read an article about the last untouched people groups of the world. Applejack was upstairs, room 13. As he lay on the bed listening to the hum of the fan, watching the last of the daylight drip down the wall, his thoughts swirled together into a cumulus riddle, mixing the past with the present.

Monson would be a good place to live for a few months a year. It's just the right distance from cities, from noise, from doubt, from the jungle gym where Downtown Carla Brown nearly scratched my eyes out for hitting her with that milk carton full of rocks in 2nd grade. And right over there beyond the woodpile is where Mike Croom kicked me in the gut with his big brother's cowboy boots. Three days in a row. I wanted to kill him, and my dad might have let me, but God kept me from it. And in the parking lot if I had said what I wanted to, it would have ruined her. I can smell her still. It's resting on the inside of the red sweater she left in my car, right around the neck where she wore her silver necklace, maybe I should have said goodbye earlier and then maybe that picture of the Grand Canyon wouldn't be so blurred because my grandfather thought it would be better to get to Monterey a day earlier than it would to see the Painted Desert or to stop and talk to Charles Bronson in the Burger King on the edge of the Mojave Desert. Don't they run a marathon through there in July or August or something? Personally, I would rather run the bulls at Pamplona than see the world's largest porcelain doll collection here in a town like...

Memories, polished and stained, half-thoughts and scents of days that had been lived by someone not yet reborn, sorrow, color, hope, regret, music, anxiety, stillness, art, spilled over to be acknowledged, sorted, validated. His body fell into high-speed dormancy. Muscles were regenerating. Ligaments and tendons and bones were being re-aligned, re-stocked and re-assimilated. Applejack's cerebral cortex was beginning to purr like the engine of a '79 Astin Martin. His eyeballs bounced around behind their lids – lottery balls, subconscious usurping consciousness in an extended REM sleep.

Rapid Eye Movement normally lasts from ten to thirty minutes. At best, an adult might enjoy this deep state of dreaming for 100 minutes during the course of an eight-hour sleep. Applejack was now entering into an REM that would cast across ten linear hours. With no real memory of what had taken place in those hundred miles between Katahdin and Monson, he was now going to make sense of it.

It was 2:38 AM when Futureman woke up on the couch in the den. He sat up and winced. *Oh, my knees, my lower back! Will they ever feel normal again?* His mouth was filled with cotton, throat dry and cracked. *Water. I need water.*

The tap water from the kitchen sink was cold. His throat felt like a long, heel-dug canal that connects a boy's sand castle moat to the ocean. *Now sleep, sleep in a bed.*

Sleep is upstairs.

The stairs seemed to be without end. As he climbed upward, to his surprise he began to feel earth between his toes. He looked down. The boards were turning to moss and dirt. *Oh God, I'm in the Wilderness again, in my underwear, climbing another damned mountain?*

Applejack lay on his bed on top of the peak, sheets pulled tight around his neck, eyes moving wildly underneath their lids.

Futureman looked out from the peak. The sky was dark green, filled with deep orange billows of clouds. A red dragon circled above, breathing fire. Down below, Futureman could see the entire Hundred-Mile Wilderness, tierra del fuego. A strand of memories were falling from the underbellies of the clouds like the tail of a wrecked kite. One by one, Futureman set out to collect them.

The next morning, the sun rose high above Monson, burning the world. From Shaw's yard, they watched Mike drive away, back to Tennessee. Their blood and sweat stained brother. What would take him a day was going to take them half a year. *Clues to the mystery of Maine, the beginning.*

By noon, Applejack and Futureman were deep into the woods, digesting the forest. With the Wilderness behind them and a hint of confidence underneath, the rest of the Trail now unfurled ahead. 2,050 miles. Five million steps from home, they began again, one foot in front of the other.

"Here goes something."

VI

"To those who would see the Maine wilderness, tramp day by day through a succession of ever delightful forest, past lake and stream, and over mountains, we would say: Follow the Appalachian Trail across Maine. It cannot be followed on horse or awheel. Remote for detachment, narrow for chosen company, winding for leisure, lonely for contemplation, it beckons not merely north and south but upward to the body, mind and soul of man."

-Myron H. Avery, *In the Maine Woods* (1934)

Bombadil broke free from the understory of Indian pipe and rhodora. He was halfway up a tilted old-growth red oak, stretching to get a view of the high-water Piscataquis River, four miles out from Monson. Steadily flowing, rapid reflection in the light, the sound of it took over all surrounding cares.

"This is where we cross," Bombadil called to Applejack and Futureman below (who didn't know he was there).

"Tom Bombadil?" Futureman looked along the bole of the tree through a scarcity of branches. "How'd you get up there?"

"Hands. Legs." The funny man swung from a tall branch and dropped onto a clump of soft club moss.

"You'll have to show us how to climb like that sometime," Futureman said.

"Okay," Bombadil said and started back up the tree. "C'mon up."

From the top, again (while Futureman and Applejack were chinning the bark at the base), Bombadil sang out a song.

Flow, flow, Old River, life giver,
Indian friend, teacher of men.
Would you allow us through your water?
Go, run from the shore, ask your father.

"These rivers are something else. I like it that Maine makes us ford these rivers, not bothering to build bridges." Futureman was perched on a rock, ringing out his socks on the opposite side of the Piscataquis. "Save for the fact that I have to change out these heel bandages every time."

"Do not fret my bulbous friend. Your rubber tire waist will be gone and your heels calloused over before you know it," Applejack said.

"I hope so."

"Hope is good. Hope is powerful."

Without their notice, Bombadil had slipped off – gone probably chasing after a rabbit, head lodged in a hollow log somewhere.

"That Bombadil's one heck of an interesting guy," Applejack said. "I'm starting to think he's made of dirt."

"Aren't we all?" Futureman said.

That night, they camped on the shores of Bald Mountain Pond, one of Maine's secret swimming holes, surrounded by untouched woods at the base of Moxie Bald. The bluff of bald granite, course-grained gabbro, white feldspar and black hornblend, is inhabited by smooth stone outcroppings called "rock sheep." Once 12,000 feet high above the Hudson, the old ice cover slowly moved north and eroded away the rough parts, sculpting it all these years. Time's razor.

The low-sky sun descended behind the knob, a scarlet-purple backdrop silhouetting the black sheep. As it sunk, shadowed forms of pond creatures skulked from the woods onto the shores – darkness initiating the motions of night. A familiar rhythm settled over water and forest. Applejack and Futureman were beginning to move to its beat, feeling out the quiet agenda of nightfall. Back packs opened, wet clothes slung over branches, tent pitched, food bags emptied, stove hissing, dinner cooked, mummy bags rolled out, food sack slung over the arm of a tree. Varmints scurried, breaking twigs (stalking or escaping). Readying for bed, the wind played its restless tricks with the oaken knots and summer's canopy of dreams.

As it was, Applejack and Futureman happened to be moving into the tent at precisely the same moment, shoulder to shoulder. It was always weird whenever this occurred, but mutual appreciation for weirdness was the glue of their friendship. Celebration of the gauche and awkward side of human relationships – those unseen yet undeniable truths that undulate through the world – were their bread and butter.

Yet, there was something about this particular moment at the end of the day when they met one another, side by side, on their hands and knees at the door of their little kiwi green tent. It was weird…and they didn't like it.

"You first."

"No, you."

"I insist. Please."

"Okay…thank…you."

In the darkness.

"Good night."

"Yep."

Somewhere down the line, someone forgot to tell Maine about switchbacks. Her trails waste no time-they run straight up the eastern crown of the continent, roughshod over shorn rocks and snaky roots. Mid-morning, they began the climb up Moxie Bald with its cemetery of trees.

Sweat, balsam fir needle pricks and black soil consumed skin and lung. Pain shot through Futureman's heels as he climbed, digging into his trekking poles. *At least we're not back in the Pit. Something good. This is good.* Ahead, Applejack took a rest against a boulder. Regaining his breath, he echoed the mockery songs of tiny pinball birds. *Tee-hee-hee, tee-hee-hee.* They called back, correcting his mispronunciations. *Nice try, scarecrow man.*

On top, pain again turned to beauty. The fabric of Maine's patchwork forest – jagged, sloped, rolling and open green, coastal lowlands to the south; the blood red Wilderness to the north – Chairback, White Cap, Big Squaw – still scrambled like a codeine dream on the periphery. More toil and painful adventure awaited to the west. Through strained eyes Futureman saw – days away, atop Mt. Bigelow, the tiny silhouette of himself – waving. *Here! Look here, Self! New legs await you, strong ones. Just keep walking, Self!*

"When will they come?" Futureman called.

"The nobos say it takes three weeks," Applejack assured.

Three weeks to get *Trail Legs*, legs that don't get tired or sore. Robotic, hypnotic, iron man legs that can handle fifteen, twenty, even thirty miles a day.

"I hope they're right," Applejack said.

Futureman looked into the distance. "Hope is good. Hope is powerful."

The descent was painstaking and steep. Tired of the tedium, Futureman was midway through a new joke – *You know what the locals call those piles of moose droppings everywhere* – when he fell headlong over a rocky shelf.

Applejack peered over a eight-foot drop of slickrock. "Oh boy." His friend was folded neatly between a boulder and a fierce-looking root.

"You really oughta watch where you're going. You okay, man?"

Futureman ground his teeth. "Niiibbllllll."

"Nibble?"

Lifting his shirt, they could see that the right nipple was barely clinging to its usual spot on his chest.

"That looks like it stings." Applejack offered a hand. "So – what do they call it?"

"Call what?"

"You were saying – the moose droppings – the Mainers call it…"

Futureman winced, standing to his feet. "Mooseltoe."

In a grove beside Pleasant Pond, they were greeted by a gruff and familiar voice.

"Whaddyuh know, the little bitches made it. And here I didn't think you'd get past Monson."

"Reed." Applejack said. "How pleasant to hear your soothing voice again."

"You tryin' to make a pun, kid?"

"Oh, Pleasant Pond, right. Clever."

"Now there's a good boy, you'll be thinkin whole thoughts in no time. By the way, if youse wanna camp here – forget it. This is my favorite spot, and I don't wanna be disturbed. I'm gonna be fishin. So, take a breather and then get the hell on down the yellowbrick road."

"Thanks for the pep talk but we were planning on sleeping in the shelter."

"Figuhs. That's why they put those goblin boxes up anyway. So every ten miles, weenies like youse can have a place to hide from scary things like dirt and rain."

"So we'll see ya around, Reed," Applejack said over his shoulder.

Futureman swung his legs over the edge of the shelter, kicked the boards and clicked his headlamp on. Couldn't sleep. He pulled out some paper to write his parents a letter. Pen on words on ideas floating above his body and brain, between the lightning bugs and up toward Alpha Centauri – not dense enough to make it past earth's atmosphere, they fell down onto the page. Perhaps for the first time since he left home, he'd caught his breath. He realized that he and Applejack were really doing something – finally – something deranged and fertile and solid, all of it galvanized by the white fire of beauty. *Tomorrow we'll be paddling the Kennebec River to cross over into the rest of Maine,* he began. *Kennebec. A river like a fortress wall. But...is it okay I haven't found the beast yet? Maybe in the morning, maybe later, maybe a thousand miles from now, I will. Who knows...*

His parents never understood his letters, but they read them lovingly anyway. At last, night engulfed him with its noisy peace and quiet. He put away pen and paper. Reed's inebriated snoring carried across Pleasant Pond.

VII

Life with your query,
Death rowing your ferry,
Across the wide black sea,
I see you're coming for me.

In the gray light of early morning, miles ahead of Applejack and Futureman, Bombadil stood on the shore of the Kennebec, judging, gauging the smooth current. Long ago, the Abenaki had given the river its name: "long level water without rapids." They taught their children how to swim in the Kennebec River. That was then.

Here in the 21st century, at any moment the hydro-electric authorities down in Boston can open the dam up in northern Maine. A lethal torrent raises the water level in seconds and the river can't be crossed fast enough. For this reason, the MATC provides safe transport for hikers by canoe.

Even so, longhaired Bombadil waits for dawn to break. Out-of-sight, waist-deep in the water, arms and legs ready, head cocked – listening for the release of the floodwaters. Remembering. Intimating.

Futureman sang to himself, glancing around at tiny birds ricocheting off the branches. A bank of billowy clouds guarded the horizon. A mile past lunch, he came to an abrupt halt. The frayed birches flapped and whirred in the wind. But that was not all. There was a pattering, then a rush of breath that played off the trees, somewhere behind the brush.

"Did you hear that?" Futureman asked.

Applejack paused beside him, putting away his usual idle tune.

"Yeah, what is it?"

Just above the earthworm struggles of the ancient dirt but far below the shrill arc of the birds of prey – somewhere in between – plain as the hair under their noses, they heard little feet drumming, flicking across the forest floor, beating down the mole's tunnel – fairy wind laced with the whispers and giggling of little children – stolen children, W.B. Yeats would have called them.

Spooked now by the silence, they walked on toward the Kennebec, where the Ferryman waited.

He was expecting them somehow, standing there on the bank as they emerged from the sylphish forest. They knew he would not charge them – no coinage for this boatman. Unlike Charon on the Cocytus, he was the servant of any who wished to cross over to the other side. He made no demands. His skillful steady hands were his pride. Trust his fare, safe passage his payment. Abenaki waters flowed under the oars as the Ferryman guided them through the strong current.

When the bow ran aground, the Ferryman tossed their packs onto the bank. It was just as well. They were glad to press on and leave for good this first, most troubled leg of their journey. With knowing, the Ferryman silently watched them go then turned to rejoin his boat to its berth across the water. There, where he has spent his entire life, jealously guarding the anxious and haunted struggles of northern Maine. There, he waits until another comes. Always there, at his lonely outpost, forgotten as the far shore of the River Lethe.

Wet Bombadil sifted through the lincoln sparrows and skulked in the branches of the labrador-tea, sang songs with fluted thrushes and swainsons, found forgotten fields of Indian cucumbers and stood on the tip-topmost top of a pin cherry tree. Detail and shadow ran together. On he went, spinning his world...

Applejack and Futureman found him five miles from the Kennebec in a forest of white pine and spruce on Bates Ridge, going on about the intersection of life and death.

"Wait. Say that again," Applejack said.

"I found it, man – life and death," Bombadil repeated.

"That's what I thought you said. Do you mind explaining?"

"I found a mushroom. I thought it was a Collared Earthstar, so I ate it, but it wasn't. Whatever it was sent me on one hell of a trip, man. Must have been in it for at least ten hours. Ground disappeared and this tundra-like marble carpet rose up, except it was soft. The air became like this heavy liquid. I stopped breathing, but my lungs were warm, like they didn't even have to breathe, man. My hands and legs were weightless, and I floated through the woods. I would have floated away if the vines hadn't grabbed my boots and pulled me back down. And get this – every tree had its own aura of color that explained its personality, and the woods formed, like, this strata that was suspended in a field of pastel colors I've never seen before, swirling like river current. Completely off the spectrum. New colors, man! Have you ever seen new colors?"

"Um…" Sun was shining through Futureman's Nalgene prism onto the ground.

"So about that life and death thing again," Applejack reiterated.

"At the edge of the forest, where the trees end, there was this void spinning around like a spiral galaxy."

"At the edge of the forest was outer space?" Futureman asked.

"No – not outer space. It's Maine, man. These forests, I'm telling you, things we forgot to see in the rest of the country, they're still here, deep in the woods."

"Life. And. Death." Applejack was hung up on this point.

"Choice, man. Leap into the void or return to the forest. To leap is to choose death, to return to the forest is to choose life. I chose life."

Futureman stared. Applejack took a breath. What to say? This was beyond explanation. Like new colors.

And once again Bombadil was gone. Whistling, singing his songs.

VIII

A day for ponds. Pierce Pond. East Carry Pond. West Carry Pond. When there wasn't a pond, there was Sandy Stream, Arnold Swamp and Bog Brook. It was Mr. Beaver's paradise. He had transformed the area into a flood plain with his dams. Following the Trail was difficult in three feet of water.

"Are you sure it runs through here?" Futureman said, standing at the edge of the water.

"I see the white blazes, but the tree trunks are underwater."

Slap goes the tail of the beaver, as he investigates the commotion around his dam.

"I'll be, a beaver," Futureman said, pointing, "straight out of Narnia. Look, he's smiling at us. That little fella's flooded this whole area."

"I guess there's only one way through," Applejack said. "And that's through."

Beaver saluted the thigh-deep hikers as they passed his various homes. Balsam pine cookies were baking inside one of them, complements of Mrs. Beaver.

They found Bombadil on a blanket of smooth stones spread along the southern edge of Flagstaff Lake at the base of the 4,200-foot bald Bigelow Range.

Wind from the north chopped the water into ten thousand angry hands. A greenbacked heron flew low over the water, drawing its wings so slowly that sustained flight seemed a wonder, legs dragging across the surface. She circled back around with a hefty pike dangling from her claws. Back to the nest. *That there is a pretty goodlookin fish. That'll make a good meal.*

Other birds joined, circling before retreating to their nests as night came. The darkness brought the call of the loons, eerily wailing like funeral dirges. Beneath the waters of the lake lay the flooded towns of Dead River and Flagstaff.

In 1949, the Central Maine Power Company closed the locks of Long Falls Dam and flooded the valley's farming communities. They say at low water, the bridges and buildings of the drowned towns appear. Applejack and Futureman could see none of these things. Still, a cadence – some dark magnetism from the past – called to them through the choppy waters of Flagstaff Lake, beckoning them to rest for a while underneath the glassy surface.

Applejack threw what remained of his handful of pebbles into the waves and watched the circles undulate in the moonlight. "We should move on. Find a place to camp."

Sometimes things stretch and bend well beyond their limits. Einstein said so. There in the basin between Roundtop Mountain and Flagstaff Lake, where the rocks and roots twist like spiny fingers and swollen knuckles from the ground, a full moon filled the woods with an azurean veil that seemed to push even the closest things to a great distance. And something happened, a convergence of realms.

Through the blue-green-black tunnels painted with pale moonlit laurel, Applejack and Futureman ran. With their packs on, for minutes – maybe for an hour – for no apparent reason, they ran. Toward midnight. Toward bed. Toward home. Toward Georgia. Tomorrow was going to be a special day. Like tadpoles, they could tell.

IX

A day for becoming. The double arch of Bigelow and Avery framed the sky. Halfway up, they paused on the scaffolding of the twin beasts. Applejack crouched beside the spring to fill their bottles. High-altitude Maine goodness, through the watershed, straight from the deep.

"These are really big mountains. You sure we have to knock both of them out today?" Futureman said.

"Gotta get over this hump if we're ever going to get back to Tennessee."

"Yeah, you're right," Futureman said.

"How do you feel?"

"Good?"

"Is that a question?"

Futureman shrugged.

They paced themselves through the first thousand feet, diligently pressing upward. Two thousand. One rock to another. After three thousand feet of climbing, they had not yet stopped for a rest. They kept going, upward past four thousand.

"This isn't the top. Can't be," Futureman said, looking around. "This is something new. I haven't even hit the wall yet."

(Welcome, Self said quietly. *Ready to do some real Appalachian Trail hiking?)*

"By golly, I think I'm ready to do some real Appalachian Trail hiking," Futureman said, stepping into the summit wind.

"The Northbounders were right. Three weeks exactly." The muscles in Applejack's calves whirred like generators.

They took lunch on a great precipice. The valley spread below, framed by far ranges blurry in the blue-white haze. The hardest stretch of Appalachian Trail lay to the immediate south – fifty thousand feet of climbs – even so, they sat with smiles on their faces, excited by the prospect of so much rugged beauty. Yep, Maine could be a harsh place, but today it seemed a little more welcoming somehow. Their peace was interrupted by a conversation moving up the mountain.

"Harry, it's just a store that sells stuff. This is America. People make small stores, then they make bigger stores. Not a big deal, it's just capitalism."

Harry's mustache twitched, face flushed, a cocktail of exertion and ire. "Just capitalism? John, John. Up here in rural Maine, it is a big deal!"

"I'm just saying –"

"I can't believe you think it's okay for a mega-store bigger than our state capitol to plant a warehouse in – excuse me – *near* our little town." Harry looked into the valley and spread his hands, calling out to the wide world, "Hey, everybody! Superstore's here to save you the frustration of having to go to *different* stores to do your shopping. To save you one tenth of one cent on every item you purchase! Isn't that exciting? But wait, that's not all – we're also here to smash all the private businesses that have supported your pitiful, little bucktooth towns since World War II. And by the way, we're gonna make a flatbed out of your hills so we can pour 800 tons of black, shitty asphalt all over the pure Maine earth!"

"Harry, don't you think that maybe you're over-reacting a little?"

Rocket fuel was leaking from the soles of Harry's feet. He smeared his hand across the canvassed valley. "Asphalt everywhere, all of this, concrete and tar." He turned and headed back down alone.

John toed the granite and saw the boys out of the corner of his eye.

"Harry's a little high strung, fellas."

"Sounds a bit worked up," Applejack said.

"He'll go on till he's blue in the face," John said. "But we need more guys like him. Yep, he's a good fighter and a loyal friend." John switched gears. "So how's it feel to be thru-hiking?"

"How'd you know?"

"Aw, I can just tell. You have that look about you. Always wanted to go myself, but I could never get away for long enough."

"What do you do?" Applejack asked.

"I own a small grocery store. Harry's right. Business is getting a little slow these days. Hard to keep it all going but I still try to get up here every week. Man-oh-man, I love this mountain. Sure puts things into perspective." He looked into the valley, over to the Baldpates. "Getting busy down there. I guess I thought it would never change. How naïve."

"It's just capitalism, John," Applejack said.

John laughed. "I'm overreacting, huh?" He nodded up at Avery. "You guys climbing her today?"

"I believe so," Applejack said.

"Enjoy. And when you get down south, tell Georgia that John from Maine says hi."

"Will do, sir."

The razor arch of Avery Peak cut the sky in two. The mountain was named after Myron H. Avery, chairman of the Appalachian Trail Conference from 1931 to 1952. The first (unofficial) '2000 Miler,' Avery's wide knowledge and love for the woods helped build the Trail. It was his vision that had carried the AT north through the Hundred Mile Wilderness toward Katahdin to plant the sign under the shadow of Pamola.

A colony of stonecrop lichen patched the peak together. Wind blew hard on Futureman's face, streaking sweat sideways across his cheeks. His father's parting words came to mind: "One step at a time." They had seemed trite then, now they had flesh and bone. *All the days of sheer misery up to this point,* he thought. *And today I actually enjoy climbing.*

"Man, this mountain is stunning," Applejack exclaimed. "And I feel good."

"Yeah. It's weird. That cruddy brittle bone feeling is completely gone.

Pride found its way into Futureman's stride as he picked his way down wind-raked Avery, proclaiming to the valley – "I've subdued my belly, yes, yes! Fat be gone, a new man is here. A bona fide thruhiker!" Then it happened. In a blink, his trekking pole caught in a crevice and his wrist gave like a hinge. Momentum snapped the pole in two, slicing his shin and throw-

ing him down (chest open and broken wir
over the handlebars.

"Aww'll!" He moaned, ribs folded aro
Trail! I hate it." Futureman looked at the w
hand and tossed it over the edge.

Applejack cackled.

"Don't say it, man. I don't want to hear it,"
good pole.

"Hey, lest we forget, Maine has a way of…'

"Yeah, yeah. Maine is mighty. Maine is w   ......u respect Maine.
Blah-blah-blah."

"You hurt?"

Twisted wrists. Flayed knees. Bloody shins. Bruised ribs. And a re-torn nipple. "Naw. Well, maybe my pride."

X

An eight-foot wolf sat on top of the marquis, howling above the motel aptly named-The White Wolf Inn. After the challenges of the Bigelow Range, they were in need of a re-supply. Stratton (population 700) had been a short hitch away. Besides, Fred Baby and Little Moose were there. A note taped to the trailhead sign said so,

Hey! All ya'll prancy foots that call yourselves hikers, Fred Baby and I are in Stratton for the night. So come laugh and dance and sing with us. It's a reunion party. We're family!
Heart with Wings,
      Little Moose

"Let's at least check it out," Applejack said as they crossed the street toward the motel.

"Sure. I could go either way," Futureman said.

Applejack pointed toward the mountains, "Tell you the truth, I'm just as comfortable out there as I am indoors."

A bell clanged as the door swung back. "Hey there, fellas. I'm guessing you two wanna get off the Trail for the night," a round-faced woman said from behind the counter.

"We're thinking about it? How much?"

"Twenty-five, not counting tax."

"Do you have no smoking?"

"None available."

"Air conditioning?"

"This is New England, honey. Course not."

"Cable TV?"

u can stand."

e it," they said in unison.

ey wouldn't take. Applejack jiggered it.

"Now that's one big pile of beer cans," Futureman was pointing next door toward an industrial-sized garbage bag bulging with crushed PBR and Natural Ice.

From inside the room, a voice slurred, "I'll be damned. You shit-sacks made it in after all."

That voice. So familiar. So unwelcome.

"Reed," Applejack muttered.

"I see ya friend there's losin some of his baby fat." The big man appeared behind the screened door. "Startin to look more like a person and less like a Tennessee sow."

"Reed, I swear if you weren't so drunk –"

"Let it go," Applejack said, unlatching the lock.

"Yeah, cool it, Futureboy. Just go on in your room and take yourself a little nappie-nap. Heh-heh." Reed tossed an empty can onto the floor. "That's a good boy."

"Enjoy your stay, Reed."

Self-realization often follows trauma. In the diner across the street, Applejack and Futureman began to see the outlines of a new gift forming. A power for good or for ill, one (as yet) uncommitted, untapped, growing with every swallow. Down went the cheese sticks, the fried mushrooms, the salad. Down went the chicken tenderloin, steak and baked potato, the beans, the Texas toast. Down went the apple pies with double whipped cream. Next came the hamburger at the convenience store, then an entire bag of chips, finally topped off by a box of Swiss Cake rolls.

There was no end to their hunger.

They'd been burning ten thousand calories a day, up and down mountains, in constant aerobic motion. *Before long,* the Nobos had said, *you'll have an appetite you can't fathom.* At Shaw's, Applejack and Futureman had watched in wonder as Sunsweep, a 120 pound blonde, put away several of the Old Man's giant-sized breakfast plates.

"She was right. I can actually feel my body metabolizing food, sending energy to my extremities," Applejack said as he gulped down a pint of Ben and Jerry's. Second dessert. "Yep, there goes that Swiss Roll, down my leg. Amazing."

"Remember before we started, when you told me to gain all that weight?" Futureman said, trying to unstick a Reese's chunk from the bottom of his carton.

"Now, I didn't exactly…"

"And I got real fat, remember? Made my life a living hell for the past three weeks."

"No, you misinterpreted…"

"I didn't tell you this, but I got stuck on the side of Chairback in the Wilderness. While you were cavorting around on top."

"Cavorting! I wasn't…"

"I called for you, but you weren't there. My fat got stuck in the cliffs and I couldn't move. I thought I was going to die. A thundercloud was moving in over me, my blubbery fingers losing grip, hundreds of feet of freefall behind me. I asked God for a miracle that day."

Applejack was laughing.

"He didn't answer me. Now what do you make of that?"

"Well you're here, aren't you?"

A shaggy man in a baby-blue shirt waved from across the parking lot, smiling doll of a girl at his side.

"Lookee there," Futureman said. It was Fred Baby and Little Moose.

"Ya'll made it!" Little Moose beamed at Futureman. Fred Baby raised a can in congratulation.

"So, everyone's meeting across the street later," Little Moose said. "Some local band's playing, *Trigger Effect* or something or other. You boys will be there!"

A command. "Yes, ma'am."

The band was *Triggerfinger*. One word. Two men.

They were taking a smoke break when Applejack and Futureman showed up. One played an electric base. The other rocked it acoustic-style. Both wore sunglasses. Firing off watery renditions of some of the most explosive songs in rock history was Triggerfinger's modus operandi. They manhandled the best of Jimmy Hendrix and CCR and slayed some of Zeppelin's most epic material, before plummeting into the dark corners of their own original music. A songwriter's graveyard. But no one seemed to care what they did. It wasn't about the music. It was about the release.

Applejack and Futureman were greeted by a hiker who was busy lining up shot glasses along the bar. "Name's Nico." The dark man turned, quickly dropping two shots down the hatch, one after the other. High five.

He was a New Yorker through and through, Italian, flattop, cut from marble.

"Buncha hotties here tonight." Nico said, taking another shot. "So. Guess how much."

"How much what?" Applejack asked.

"Just guess, guy."

"Uh."

"C'mon. Youse won't believe it."

"T-t-two-fifty?"

Nico slammed down the glass and laughed. "Ha! Two-fifty he says, now dat's some funny stuff. No, my pack weight. Guess how much."

"Oh, I see. Probably...thir..."

"Fifteen pounds! You believe dat? And when I build the new stove this guy told me about, I'm gettin it down to thirteen."

"Wait a second," Futureman said, suddenly very interested. "You said thirteen pounds? For everything? That's unbelievable."

"Yeah, I'm fascinated with how little you can carry out here and still survive. I used to be in the Army. Those clowns pile on the pounds. It's like, *ya gotta be kiddin' me.* So, I broke my back skydivin' a few years ago and gotta carry as few pounds as possible, know what I'm sayin?" Nico spoke with the rapid-fire certainty of crowded city streets.

"What? You mean your chute didn't –"

"Nevuh stopped me from doin what I love, though. I sez 'I wanna hike the Trail' so here I am. My friends all sez 'Yo Nico, yuh crazy, wiv ya broken back.' But I sez 'All youse can go to hell. I can do whatevuh I put my mind to.' Girlfriend's freakin out. The whole Twin Towers thing screwin with her head, so I dumped her ass. Whatcha gonna do? Plus, there's always more where that came from, right? Youse know what I'm talkin about." Nico elbowed Applejack, checked his hair in the bar mirror and scanned the room again. "Yeah, buncha hotties tonight."

"Oh yeah?"

Nico ordered some more shots. "Foxes all ova the place out here on the Trail, no need for conjugals." Shot. Slam. "You guys gotten any yet?"

A fair question. Yet, having been raised in conservative homes where open conversation about promiscuous sex was not going to get you extra dessert, Applejack and Futureman were reluctant to comment.

"C'mon, be honest with Nico. How much sex you had since you been out here?"

"Nico, I can't say that I've had any, really," Applejack said.

"Sorry, bro." Nico put a hand on Applejack's shoulder. "Just be patient. It'll happen for ya." He looked at Futureman. "How 'bout you?"

"Well Nico, I'm still trying to figure out the whole hiking thing, you know. That's where my head is."

"Man, I hear dat!" Shot five. Shot six. "Bet you can't wait till you figure it out." Punch on the shoulder.

"Um." Futureman shot Applejack a self-conscious glance.

"Ah. Oh." Nico backed away. "I see how it is. Sorry. No, that's cool, bros. I can respect that." Then he gave them *The Look*. "This is the 21st century and all."

"Wait a sec, Nico," Futureman said. "We're not – I think you've misunderstood – are you under the impression that we're – that Applejack and I are…"

The crowd erupted. Triggerfinger were back on stage. The dancers coalesced again, three beers looser than before.

Nico checked the mirror one last time. "Got some work to do before closin' time." He strutted off into the smoke like Travolta on a steamy New York night.

Other hikers – Jasper, George, Snot, Ogre, Colonel and Buttercup – had all followed the invitation into town as well. Family. They had taken over a section of the parquet dance floor.

There was Colonel, standing tall in the neon haze. *Mormon dancers, who knew?* There was Jasper, tying ribbons in the air with the tips of her fingers. Nico had found a local ready to lose her innocence for the first time in days. Snot wanted to mosh. Ogre and Buttercup in the corner were trying a slow dance to *Proud Mary*. Dreadlocked George dawned the dance of the hippy, toes kicking air, pants slipping down his bony, briefless buttocks. Some of the meatier local women whistled.

Along the wall, Applejack and Futureman pulled up chairs beside Fred Baby. He was admiring his wife out on the dance floor. Little Moose had lost it completely. She was single-handedly redeeming Triggerfinger's litany of musical heresies. Her hair sprang in all directions, a three-year-old riding the teacups. She whipped her hips back and forth without rhythm, effortlessly fusing multiple forms of dance – salsa, tango, hip-hop, ballroom, shag, jazz, ballet, tap, clog, African tribal, folk, polka, and old school – into what could only be described as *The Little Moose*. She danced everywhere. Everyone wanted to dance with her. But she only had eyes for the man sitting contentedly next to Applejack.

"How'd you manage, Fred?" Futureman asked.

"I got lucky," he said, blinking slowly in the smoky air.

Mercifully, Triggerfinger ran out of steam at long last, and everyone filed out into the parking lot to joke and flirt under the broad Maine sky.

XI

Refueled and resupplied, the hikers dispersed in the morning, each to his own hike. Some hitched out of town early. Some went out late, others not at all, taking a lazy zero (off-days, time away from the world of time).

Applejack and Futureman were on the Trail by late morning. The sun filtered through the canopy holes and expanded the club moss that carpeted the forest floor. The going was slow – vertical labor up the side of Crocker Mountain along a five-mile 4,200-foot toe rope of stones and twisted roots. The crest of the mountain rose like the back of a camel, a north and south peak, both offering unguarded vistas of Maine's hinterland. Their hardy new legs had passed the test. Unfazed, they craved more. Down into the shadows of Caribou Valley and straight up Spaulding Mountain, onward towards glacier-borne Sugarloaf (Maine's second tallest summit). Over to Spaulding Mountain knob, a pinprick spike in the sky, the perfect spot to sit for hours under the changing colors of evening. *No watch, no checking time. Go to bed with the sun, and why not?* The lean-to was close by. They descended to it in the dark.

Futureman woke up late. Across the dusty shelter-boards, Applejack was still sleeping. The sun was at a great height, having already spilt into the valley, creating an illusory bridge of light. Snug in his bag, arms pressed against the inner lining, Futureman's mind began to quicken – ruminating in the quiet. In the quiet.

Black cedars stretched toward the billows. An eagle turned against the wind and hovered in place high above the forest. *I wonder how high that eagle can go? How deep into the ground can the roots of that great oak burrow? God, you say your Spirit is with me always, right? And you say that I can't hide from you? If I could climb to heaven, you'd be there, and if I could swim down to the bottom of the ocean, even there, you'd find me. You say you cradle your children in your hand like a moth in a cocoon...so I don't understand...why are you so silent?*

It had been a while since Futureman had prayed. Earnestly. In large part, that was why he had chosen to come out here – to seek the Divine One. To find a connection not easily grasped in the busy fray, in the world of quick answers and static noise.

Here, now, as he sat in the late morning light below Spaulding Mountain pondering the silence of God, he felt his chest open a bit and his heart begin to grow soft. The seeds of prayer were slowly spreading the roots of an early spring, when – his reverie was broken. The crash of heavy feet in the woods. A bear?

"You two bastuds still lazin' around in the sheltuh, I see."

"Hi Reed. So nice to see you. Again. Already." *How do you manage to drink so late and rise so early?*

"Wake up Applejack. Tell him it's time for his medicine." Reed dumped his monstrous pack out on the ground. A gallon jug of Old Crow whiskey fell out.

Futureman poked Applejack with his trekking pole. "Applejack, Reed's here. He was wondering if you wanted to get drunk with him at ten o'clock in the morning."

"That's another thing. Why do you two wusses prance around out here with those ladies' poles. You look like a couple a fruity skiers." The big man spun the top off his gallon of whiskey.

Applejack rubbed his eyes. "Hey there, Reed. How did you get here? I mean, how are you doing?"

"Whenever you two clowns get ya act together you outta head up to the top of Mt. Abraham. It's a castle up there."

"What do you mean? There's a castle up there? Like a medieval castle?"

"I didn't say there was a medieval castle, ya dumb prick. It's a mountain. I *call* it a castle. That okay with you? It's like a giant fortress. My favorite place in all of Maine." Reed started with a gulp.

"Are you goin' up there?" Applejack rolled off the bed board and walked around the corner of the shelter to water the wildflowers.

"It's my favorite spot in Maine. Of course I'm goin up there."

"Reed, have you ever wondered what it's like to live inside of a cocoon?" Futureman asked, gazing towards the sunlight.

Reed took another swig and closed it up. "I swear, I've about lost my patience with you two shelter sluts." He slipped headphones over his ears and disappeared down a side path toward the castle, the subtle tones of Frederic Chopin soothing his addled spirit.

That afternoon, Applejack and Futureman set foot over the valley across the light bridge to Poplar Ridge. There, a man named WayBack rested – lotus position, alone in the lean-to, unmoved and steady – waiting for his moment today in this life, a Zen meditative smile on his northern white snow face. Applejack and Futureman found him serenely contemplating his existence amongst a particularly hostile cloud of sharp-toothed black flies. (Concocting black-fly repellants is one of Maine's winter pastimes. But with the problem being unresolved, Wayback was holding out.)

"Hello there," WayBack said to the travelers.

"Hey," Futureman swatted at his neck. "The flies haven't been this bad since the Wilderness bogs."

WayBack nodded. "Mmm, I noticed this yesterday. That's why I'm wearing pants today." He lifted a pant leg. From ankle to knee, his white skin was peppered with dozens and dozens of bloody, swollen bites.

"Good grief man!" Futureman said. "Why didn't you put your pants on before they bit you two hundred thousand times?"

"Well, I was working on my water bladder and I guess I just didn't think about it," said WayBack.

"Didn't think about – what was wrong with your water bladder?"

"See, I was hoping to cross the Saddlebacks yesterday, but as I was packing, I noticed that my water bladder had a hole in it."

"And?"

"And I said to myself, 'Well, there goes today.' So I stayed here and fixed it."

Applejack, figuring in all complications, couldn't see it taking more than three minutes to fix a leak in a water bladder. *A strip of duct tape on the hole should do it.*

"I'm a slow hiker," WayBack said, deliberately. "They call me WayBack because I walk my own pace. What's the rush? I've always been like that. I was a paratrooper in the Army for sixteen years. In Basic Training, they were always yelling at me to run faster. That just didn't motivate me. Guess I hike the same way. When I want to go I go, and when I want to stop I stop. Long as I'm enjoying myself, a mile a day is fine with me. I figure I'm only doing this once."

"How long you think it'll take you to finish?"

"About twelve months total. A month to hitch here, ten to hike the Trail and a month to hitch back."

"One month to hitch here!" said Futureman. "Where do you live, Alaska?"

"Good guess," WayBack said.

"Oh…I was just…really?"

"Yep. I drive a school bus there."

"Okay."

"Tried to hike the Trail last year and failed, so I'm back."

"Why'd you quit?"

"Girl problems. Well, ex-girl now." WayBack nodded, a fly chewing on his neck. "The mystery of women. Will we ever understand it?"

Will we ever understand the mystery of Wayback?

"But now I have another girl, who supports my being out here. So, about the time the sun started coming through the windshield at night, she pushed me out of the bus and said, *We're getting married as soon as you come home to me.*" WayBack smiled. "She's quite a girl."

"Sun at night?" Futureman furrowed his brow.

"Windshield – of the bus?" Applejack added.

"Sun cycles are funny in Alaska." WayBack said. "Especially when you live in a bus."

We are children, little, little children with a lot to learn about a lot of things.

"Well, it was nice meeting you gentlemen. You probably won't see me again. I imagine you hike a little faster than I do," WayBack said.

"Yeah," Futureman said, failing to grasp (at all) what kind of human creature this was sitting before him. "Tell your fiancé she is a lucky bus to have a

WayBack like you."

The young grasshoppers pushed on, up into the Saddleback Range.

Leather-horned Saddleback is aptly named, raw granite above tree line, seat of the giant bull rider. Here, fierce storms nearly scrape the rock clean of all living tissue. Nearly. An unusual smattering of survivor species clings to the stone, leaving a scrub forest on the edge of life. Gnarled balsam and eastern larch hunker down in a dwarf meadow. The Saddleback summit makes you wonder if the moon wouldn't be a friendlier place to live.

As Applejack and Futureman crossed the open mountaintop, an ominous storm like a team of gray horses rose in the distance, turning southeast. Hooves thundering over the ground, bolts like stirrups against the static.

"We gotta get down off this mountain," Futureman said, leery of electrocution.

"Little Swift River Pond is just a few miles away," Applejack said. "Believe there's a campground there and thunder's a ways off, yet. We might make it."

They pulled hard into a spot on the north side of the pond. In the shroud of silence that lingers just before downpour, they threw the tent up to slide in on their bellies just as the sky opened. The rain hammered the forest floor. Words drifted, dribbled, drafted through the mind with ease. Raindrops found them dozing at suppertime.

At midmeal, a dark stocky figure emerged from the woods and threw his wet pouch on the ground. He had a thick, pitch-black Hayduke sort of beard.

"Join us."

"Thanks. Helluva storm, huh?"

"Yep. So, where'd you come from, friend?" Applejack asked.

"Resupply in Rangely, a few miles back. I had to walk the entire way into town and back out. Hitchhiking can be a real pain sometimes. It's like they know I'm a New Yorker. Uncanny."

"You from the city, then?"

"No, Hamptons."

"As in *the* Hamptons?" Applejack leaned toward the fire.

"Yeah, I know. But trust me, I'm not a famous millionaire. My family was out there long before the hype." Blackbeard seated himself on a wet log and set to untaping his feet. The outline of a tortoise was etched in black ink on his calf.

"Seems like I just saw a piece on *Headline Tonight* about the Hamptons," Applejack said.

"You did. All about how it's the epitome of American excess, right? That show made us all look like a bunch of pretentious jerks. But isn't that what good journalism is? You see what they want you to see."

"So it's not really like that up there?" Applejack asked.

"Yes and no. Used to be mostly local families like mine, just a beautiful spot to live. But like most things beautiful, people have to buy it and build something on it. Own it. Now, the weekends are insane, Manhattan richies everywhere. My family doesn't belong anymore."

"Why don't you sell it? You could probably get millions." Futureman said.

"Because to hell with the yacht club, that's why." Blackbeard smiled into the fire. "You should see some of the bull I live with everyday."

"Like what?"

"My family has our little twenty-year-old skiff docked right between Puff Daddy and Steven Spielberg. We're talkin' multi-million dollar yachts. See, I'm a house painter, so I meet a lot of people. I get invited to all these parties with celebrities and directors and brokers and stuff. It's a real riot. Everyone just assumes I'm famous. When I say I'm a painter, these Hollywood and Manhattan socialites immediately think hyper-realism or whatever."

"Of course."

"Yeah. It's a perfect set-up. I get to hob-nob with some of the most famous people in all of America and they kiss my shiny white behind, because for all they know, I'm the next Jackson Pollock. Like a fly on the wall, I get to witness the unadulterated American dream in all its glory – the money, the groping and self-congratulation."

"So, you don't care for the Hamptons anymore," Applejack said.

"I'll always love it. It's my home. I still wake up in my shack every morning and go to the coffee shop where I do my writing. I mean, where else can you see Monica Lewinsky getting her cocoa-mocha-frapa-whatever? And when she sees me she comes over and says, 'Hey, Will. Killer party last night, huh?' Man, you can't ask for better material. I love the Hamptons."

"Why'd you come out here?"

"One can only take so much. It's nice to get a little perspective. See, I have a tendency to be negative sometimes." The man showed a sly grin from behind his brooding tangle of beard.

Once the fireglow had faded into the black landscape, they went to bed. As usual, Futureman took his time falling asleep. He listened to the water of Little Swift River Pond. He listened as the trees struggled against the grip of an after-storm wind. He listened as restless waters lapped against the shore, creatures slithering up onto the muddy bank, and he wondered what monsters would one day come to steal his home away.

XII

At first light, Blackbeard packed up and set out, a loner in the revelation of morning. He nodded slightly as he passed. Something told Applejack they would see him again soon.

After breakfast, they made for Bemis Mountain.

Applejack walked briskly ahead. Futureman plodded behind, slow enough to notice – moose! – a giant momma with two calves. Her massive antlers divided the meadow, long snout nudging her wobbly little squirts into the drink. At first, they bawled and squealed in trepidation, but soon began to play, wrestling and running beneath their mother. Futureman stood quietly at the pond's edge opposite the creatures, wonderstruck. He had seen two others in the Wilderness – in flight, frightened by the hairy zombie marching toward them. This was different, natural. She didn't realize he was there. Or did she? Raising her head toward him, eyeing, she dropped low again gulping from the bog, huge and unafraid. Wholly returned to the problem of how to one day set her children.

Sun was getting hot again. *Cool at night. Pleasant in the morning. Intolerable in the afternoon. Untameable Maine – so blasted annoying. I love it.* They made their way up Bates Ledge, down and up Spruce Mountain, down and up First Peak Bemis, down and up Second Peak, and down and up countless other nameless spikes and hills and outcroppings.

A reliable water source is always priority one. So at the end of a draining thirst-mocking day, the stagnated trickle atop Bemis Mountain was a disappointment to say the least. Its only movement was a track meet of microbial fauna. Pieces of what appeared to be snakeskin floated on the surface.

"Can you believe this?" Futureman said.

"This is worse than that hole the Colonel found in the Wilderness," Applejack said.

Whistling diverted their attention, someone else coming to collect water. A tall man, very thin, shaved head covered by a white bandana. He carried a stainless steel bowl, a small hand towel and a bar of peppermint soap.

"Hey boys. Mind if I take a bath?" The slightest lisp attended his speech. "I just hate being dirty. I know, then what the *h* am I doing out here? I also love to hike – so shoot me! Oh. My. Lord! That is the dirtiest water I've seen in like – forever. There has got to be another source!"

"If there was, we'd be there," Applejack said.

"Then this will have to do." He offered a matter-of-fact smile and abruptly disrobed. "I'm 10% by the way." The man filled his basin, threw his clothes on a tree branch and stood unashamedly tall and nude before them, lathering in their drinking water.

Assuredly, it is no big thing to take a bath in the woods. It can be quite liberating, in fact. And yet there is a time for every season.

10%'s timing was a little off.

On their way back to the tent site (peppermint soapwater in their bottles), Applejack and Futureman dealt with the issue head-on. Sort of.

"Perhaps-"

"maybe –"

"I wonder if-"

"Is 10% gay?"

As rosemary steam began to seep from his titanium cooking set, 10% insisted on preparing supper for his new friends, Applejack and Futureman.

It was a lavish affair, indeed. And the dehydrated mussels with jasmine rice, the array of other spices (cayenne, thyme, basil) mounded on a silk towelette beside the stove, and the mousse whip dessert did little to dispel their questions. That 10% was a generous soul and extraordinary cook was not in dispute, however.

After the main course, they settled around the hissing Whisperlite stove (10% wanted hot chocolate before bed).

"Yep, that boil will kill whatever's hiding in the water…"

"Shhh," 10% motioned. "Listen."

A buzz of cicadas, chorus of frogs and melody of bats called back and forth from shadow to shadow. Nature's symphony, louder than a city, the full-blown song of a forest at night, building in numbers gradually like an approaching stampede. It is a curious paradox that calms the soul. Haunting. Beautiful. Natural. Entranced. They sat, an audience in the front rows of Bemis Symphony Hall. Applejack was starting to nod off when, like the oboe, 10% interrupted.

"So! I have something I want to tell you guys."

He's coming out, right here, around the stove.

"Secret's out – I'm a Quaker," he whispered. "Isn't that weird?"

Even the frogs and bats got quiet.

"Heck of a way to start a conversation, right? Then again, I've never been one for small talk. So, do you guys think that's weird?"

"No…not…really," Applejack said.

"It's honest. How can honesty be weird?" Futureman said and then realized how dreadfully wrong that was.

"Have you always been – a Quaker?" Applejack asked.

"My goodness no. I grew up in a regular old mainstream church."

"Why'd you switch?"

"I guess I started to feel like a worker in a factory."

"Factory-worker, huh? How do you mean?"

"When I got old enough to start thinking on my own, I realized that some of the stuff we did in my church had nothing to do with the things Jesus taught. In fact, some of it seemed downright opposite of what he said."

"Mm."

"I don't want to bore you guys."

"No, we're interested, seriously."

"We just got more focused on having the right stuff – technology, screens and sound systems and such. As many programs and activities and committees as possible – and I got in on all of 'em. It's like the whole point was to cram as many people inside the doors as we could. But the more people there were, the more alone I felt. Got to where I hardly knew anybody at all – just a bunch of folks standing around a conveyor belt singing watery songs about generic love and blessings." 10% shrugged and refilled his tin cup.

"Why do you think you felt like that?"

"I'm a people person. Surprise! Anyhoo, the goal became results, numbers – and to me, that's just impersonal and pointless. When that happens, we know we've lost our way. I think Jesus was a people person. He reached out to people with goodness and compassion. But he never promised that the way would be easy or that we'd make everybody happy and have big churches full of happy people. That wasn't why he came. There's my two cents worth." The tall man leaned back against his pack, his countenance hidden in the shadows as he stirred his hot chocolate.

"So how's your new church different? Why Quakerism?" Applejack asked.

10% moved forward, kind eyes and balding head reappearing in the light. "Love. I found love there. I see the love of Christ in the people. Oh sure, their ideas are a little quirky – but their faith is simple. Not simplistic, but simple. Simple enough to be real."

Applejack and Futureman watched him silently. The sensitive face revealed pain. "My whole life, people have been – unkind. They've judged me for the way I am or what I appear to be. And many of them claimed to be quote – unquote Christians. Oh, I know, I'm an easy target." 10% poured out his cup and wiped it clean. "All along-in all the wrong places – I was looking for that one thing. But, you see, there is only one who can give it." His smile was pure and clear like the Maine air. "His love is always true."

At once shamed by their own petty suspicions and inspired by the power of this man's raw honesty, Applejack and Futureman waited quietly in the settling dusk.

At last, 10% broke through. "So, what brought you two unsavory characters out here?"

"That's easy for me," Applejack laughed. "I've wanted to do the AT my whole life. But I'm not even sure I know why this guy is out here." He pointed at Futureman.

"I guess that is a little complicated." Futureman looked up through the trees. "I follow Jesus, too – both of us are believers – but like you said, the way is hard. I've been very confused about things for a while myself and it's not easy to sort them out, with all the distractions. We can get pretty busy, know what I mean?"

"Yes."

"I guess I was looking for the solitude to figure out what the faith really means. What prayer is. I want peace. I want to know who God is."

"When did you decide you could find that out here?"

"Pretty stupid really – one night a few months ago, Applejack and I got bored and decided to paddle around a drainage pond."

"A drainage pond?" 10% interrupted. "Like a doo-doo ditch?"

"Actually, it did stink a bit."

10% pinched his nose.

"While we were on the pond, Applejack asked me if I wanted to come with him on the Trail and –"

"Wait a second." A wry grin appeared on Applejack's face. "I never asked you. You invited yourself."

"Whatever. Anyway, I decided the wilderness would be a good place to pray for answers to those questions. So I came."

10% nodded. "I think Jesus felt the same way about the wilderness. I hope you find what you're searching for." He rose to his feet. "Well friends, I need my beauty rest. You'll probably be gone when I wake up – I'm a late sleeper – but I wish you well on your journey. Night-night." He turned toward his tent and was gone.

Applejack and Futureman lingered, unwilling to release the final strains of night's symphony. *Other worlds,* Futureman thought, curling his bare toes against the ground. *Right here in the soil, creatures below, untold giants crawling, moving, spinning outward from the center of the earth – come and get me.*

"Hey, Applejack. I almost forgot. Tomorrow's your birthday, isn't it?" he asked, breaking apart the embers with his one good trekking pole.

"By Jove, you're right, it is. You start to lose track of things out here."

"What do you want?"

"What do I want?"

"Yeah."

"I want what everybody wants. World peace. And a Winnebago."

"I'm not sure I can get those things by tomorrow, Applejack, but we'll head into Andover in the morning and see what happens."

They poured what was left of their snakewater onto the coals and crawled into warm bags.

10% was still snoring in his tent the next morning as they set out through the oldest forest in Maine.

Between Elephant Mountain and Old Blue, a corridor of old growth red spruces has been browing for centuries, untouched. Thunder protested along the east side of the ridge as they passed through the evergreen hallways. Pinned under an organism so dense and resilient that nearly all sunlight was blotted out (deftly absorbed by the ancient trees themselves), Applejack and Futureman – dull-witted as they were – began to clue into what was going on around them.

Things seemed amiss. The clouds carried an ill color, jaundiced along their edges. The wind was sporadic and harsh. Something was poisoning the forest.

Finally, they spotted the culprit.

Coming down the Trail toward them was a dark figure. As soon as he caught sight of them, the scrawny man curled his nose and licked it with the tip of his tongue. *A Rat of Nihm?* Futureman wondered.

 He began his filthy monologue before they even reached him. "My name is Slowfoot. I'm from Boston," he said. "I'm a repeat thruhiker," he said. "I hiked the entire Trail naked," he said. "I got arrested in Virginia for being naked," he said. "I had a boner most of the way," he said. "Sometimes I masturbate while I hike," he said. "I've met all kinds of people on the Trail who also like to hike naked," he said. He described them in great detail – everything about them – in great detail. "Swollen breasts!" "Raw nipples!" "Chafed testicles!" "Red, icy balls!" "Zitty butts!" "Runny farts!"

A particularly raunchy version of *The House of the Rising Sun* droned inside Applejack's head.

"You guys ever hiked naked before?" Slowfoot asked. "Wanna give it a try?"

At last, Applejack had had enough. "Today is my birthday, Slowfoot. Thank you for sharing your thoughts and experiences with us, but perhaps you should keep them to yourself from now on. It is my birthday, and I want to go now."

Slowfoot's residue had slimed the noble, timeworn forests between Elephant Mtn. and Old Blue. As they walked, they could smell which trees he had marked with his urine. They could hear the mountains gagging round the imprints of his feet. Apology was needed.

XIII

Applejack lurched forward through the trees, three miles above South Arm

Road. Every corner turned into one more. Andover's gotta be around the next one, the next one, maybe the next one. Finally, through the leafy lattice, he made out a big red truck and a smiling man standing beside it. The man seemed to be waiting for someone.

"I'm Earle Towne," he said as Applejack approached. "But some folks call me Bear. Beautiful day isn't it?"

"Yes sir, sure is. My name is Appl…"

"I know who you are, son." Bear clapped his hands together. "When will Futureman be along?" His foamy tangle of salt-and-pepper beard bounced as he spoke.

Huh? *Who is this guy? How does he know our names?*

"It's OK, my lad. I think I see him coming now."

Applejack turned. The spruces seemed to be bending toward the wind. He couldn't even hear Futureman, much less see him.

"Let's get your things into the back of Big Red here. Yep, yep. You two are coming with us. It won't be long before my wife, Honey, will be stuffing your insides with a good meal. In you go, now." Applejack climbed in, as Futureman emerged from the woods.

Anywhere else, this sort of amiable coercion would indeed arouse suspicion but something was different with this Bear fellow. His melodic voice held a certain irresistible quality. His arms revolved through the air with the best of intentions.

A blanket of pebbles lay over South Arm Road, popping onto the mud flaps and the undersides of the truck. Sunlit bugs swam in the air. Bear was content as he drove through the dust toward the tiny town, saying little. Perhaps it was his custom to allow things to speak for themselves. The people of Andover smiled and waved at the sight of Big Red.

"How about we take a trip to the Andover Mall. Would you like that?" Bear raised his bushy white eyebrows. "I expect you need to pick up some things, eh?"

"Sure, sir, if that's what –" *A mall? Is this guy serious? We're in rural Maine. There are barely roads and telephones. There can't be any malls.*

"You two will enjoy a trip there, I expect. Just the thing to lift your spirits." He winked and turned Big Red toward the outskirts of town.

Maine's good roads are bad enough, ravaged by the brutality of long winters. Things certainly weren't getting better as they moved further into the countryside. Pebbles became mailbox-sized rocks. Bumps turned into knee-deep trenches, brimming with high-mountain run-off. Town dirt became country mud. Big Red rolled on.

"Um. Mr. Towne, you did say that we were going to a mall," Futureman said.

"Mister is for men in suits, my boy. You call me Earle or Bear."

"But Earle, this place really doesn't look…"

Bear smiled and breathed pine through his beard. "Almost there, my boy."

Passing quickly between the chunky hills, Applejack and Futureman settled into their seats. Here and there, wildflowers sprang up between the rocks. Unused to the speed of a vehicle, the low country passed in front of their eyes like a midnight schoolbook. The hum of the road reminded them of their exhaustion.

"Ah, here she is. The Andover Mall." Bear spun the truck left onto a gravel road through a chain link gate and down a path into the epicenter of a junkyard. "Need anything?" His eyes sparked.

Bear lived on the edge of town in a large log cabin. The quiet pride on his face suggested that he had built it with his own hands. A twelve-foot tall leather tepee framed the driveway.

"Home is where I live, and this is home. You can stay inside if you like, sleep under the stars if you choose, or build a fire in the tepee and howl at the moon. It's up to you. You tell me. There will be quite a group – fine folks joining us tonight for the feast." Earle trotted up the stairs through the open door.

Before entering, Applejack and Futureman unloaded an old chair they had picked up at the mall and rested it beside the cabin. Futureman was gathering a sense about this place, a crackle at the tips of his ears, felt like home. *Broken things are mended here.*

Inside, work was being done, people filling glasses with ice and carrying heaping bowls into a long dining room. Hikers, vagrants and world travelers had collected for supper. Some were staying the night. Some had been here for a month. Blackbeard and Colonel were among them.

"Good to see you again," Blackbeard said warmly, his brusque manner at bay for now.

"So Earle found you. I knew he would," Colonel smiled. He seemed pleased but the usual spark was missing somehow. He was hiding something.

Before there was a chance to investigate, a merry woman of grandmotherly years interrupted. *Honey* was stitched across her apron. "Not now, boys. Be plenty of time to catch up when the meal begins. Now, take these beans to the table," she said as she handed Applejack a dish of steamed broccoli and Futureman a basket of garlic bread. "And welcome to the family."

"That's my sweetie," Earle winked. "She's the light around here. Saves an awful lot on electricity."

Earle Towne had built the great hall for the sole purpose of hosting feasts. It was a simple room with a vaulted ceiling crisscrossed by reddish beams.

Stained glass shone from each end. Letters and photographs from grateful travelers adorned the walls. In the center of the banquet room stood a long oak slab with enough table space to seat fifteen comfortably. It was covered with golden chicken and blackened ribeyes, three-cheese casserole, olives, brie, grapes, snap peas, okra, beans, biscuits and berries, potatoes and wild rice, lemonade, tea and wine.

A table flowing with milk and honey.

Bear sat at the head, quietly admiring the spread. Here, everything seemed to come into the light. Faces, fears, worries, lies, hopes, all part of the event.

"Futureman, you're a man of faith," Bear said. "Would you mind saying a blessing?"

I don't remember telling him I was a..."I'd be honored to." It was easy to give thanks for a home so richly blessed.

Two English chaps, doing the North American tour, sat on the far end, salivating, heads swiveling. "Ya don' see 'is much 'n Englan."

"Unbelievable 'is is. Bes food we evuh seen er smelt."

"Excuse me, everyone. If I may say something, please," a woman named *Walking Prayer* said. She was a self-proclaimed Buddhist monkess. "Everyone, please. If I may."

The room grew silent. (For a number of reasons, when a Buddhist monkess is about to speak, you should listen).

Walking Prayer placed her hands in an ellipsis in front of her, roughly resembling the shape of her gray flattop. "While I was sitting here, preparing to enjoy this wonderful meal, an awareness grew within me – of PEACE and UNITY. I think we forget sometimes that what we truly feast on, more than food – is – PEACE and UNITY. Without these, we starve. Yes. It can. The soul can starve. But tonight we shall not starve. We. Are a prayer."

A brief. Eternal. Pause. The kind of benign moment of reflection Americans prefer before the rotation of bowls and baskets begins.

Here-here! True, so true! Souls can starve. Now pass the beans!

After dinner, Bear gave Applejack and Futureman the tour of hostel quarters – a basement bunkhouse, kitchen and a hiker den with couches. "These blankets and pillows have heard many conversations, many stories," Bear said. "Maybe the guitars will come out later. Who knows? Maybe some songs."

Behind the cabin a barn stood, dilapidated yet dignified. Here Bear did his woodworking – to keep the rust off his craft. "I needn't show you all the details. I'll leave it for you to explore. If you have an itch to carve or whittle or build, have at it. If you just want to dig through the fridge in the early morning, feel free. Now come, let me show you the field."

They passed corn and tomatoes and day lilies. Bear walked barefoot. He didn't wear shoes unless there was snow enough to freeze them. "Whenever you put shoes on your feet, you miss the ground beneath you," he explained.

Steady moonlight fell through dark layers of the soft landscape, again calling forth the silence they were coming to love. An awe emerged from the shadows, moving no more quickly than the slow arc of the crescent. Coyote calls found their way down into the valley. Or were they wolves?

The corners of Bear's mouth turned up. *They're back.*

"Earle, when you sit back at the table and watch everybody, you get this...this look," Futureman said.

Bear put his hand on Futureman's shoulder, "My boy, I'm afraid you're not able to understand that."

"Try me."

"No, no. It's mine. Not meant for you." Bear smiled.

"This is a good birthday," Applejack said to no one.

"A good day to be sure," Bear said. "Each day has enough worry and joy of its own. I've never seen much sense in keeping track of years."

"Thank you for picking us up and bringing us here," Applejack said.

"Thank you for finally deciding to drop by. And I want you to know that I expect you to stay a while, both of you. Maine has worn you out, I can see. You need to rest up for the Whites. Yes, yes, a little rest will do you fine."

"What are they like, the Whites?" Futureman asked.

Earl turned as if he could see them through the trees. "They're mountains. Your friend, Bombadil, claims it's where one goes to disappear." An eyebrow flickered.

"You know Bombadil?" Futureman said. "We've been wondering where he got off too. When did you last see him?"

"Oh, I see him now and then in the woods," Bear said. "Who knows where he is these days. I imagine he's somewhere on Old Speck but there's no telling. Seems unconcerned with the directions of north and south, that boy." The old man stroked his silvery chin. "He might be able to tell you more about those Whites. Seems his childhood is still lost somewhere in there. No, my place is here. The Mahoosucs are my mountains. I leave the rest for you to discover for yourselves." With that, Bear left them in the field, whistling softly down the road he had helped build.

Futureman's eyelids uncurled. Everyone was still sleeping, bunks filled, couches taken, floors covered. He opened the door to let in the day. Bugs flew in the golden air, trampolining off the light tubes. The screen door clanged behind him. Bear was in the garden on his hands and knees.

"I see the rest is helping already," Bear looked over his shoulder. "A few more days of Honey's cooking will finish the job."

"So what do normal people do around here, Bear?"

"Normal? Not sure I'm familiar with that breed but some folks enjoy a day hike. You boys can trot across Wyman Mountain and then come home for some more food and rest this evening."

Home. He called it home.

"Tomorrow, you'll go over big Baldpate. Then the Notch on the next day."

"The Mahoosuc Notch. People talk all kinds of things about the Notch." *Beware of the Notch! People lose their minds in there! Hikers have died in there!* Hearsay, rumors, exaggerations and legends. Funny, the evolution of fear.

"The Notch is where God keeps his favorite stones," is all Bear had to say about it.

Purist thru-hiking was like any other nonsense to Bear. His logic was rooted in the dangerous side of beauty, *where it gets a little weird, where things change.* Going by the book isn't what's important. *You don't have to carry a full pack to be a hiker. Leave your things here. Be free to run and roam. It's our playground.* The way of the slackpacker is an unthinkable faux pas to the purist, but in Bear's book, it's simply the smart way of doing things.

In the mornings he took Blackbeard, Colonel, Applejack and Futureman to the Trail. Late in the afternoon, he returned for them. For several days, through the mountains of Bear's grand kingdom, free from the old monkey-on-the-back, they leapt off roots and swung on branches like little children, losing track of time altogether. Tallying miles became to them as pointless as counting stars.

The Mahoosuc Notch is one of the true wonderlands of the earth. It was just as Bear had said. For one mile, in the fold of two magnificent peaks, God's favorite stones were piled everywhere, as big as houses. Water had been flowing there for millennia, fashioning a maze of sunlit tunnels and caves.

The four of them stretched the mile through the morning hours, laughing at themselves, how weak and whiny they had been. Now, they were so light they barely existed. They drank water from the subterranean river and climbed magnificent boulders like mountain goats. They were indeed boys at the playground, scooping ice from 30 degree caverns below, lounging on the sun-warmed rocks above. And at the end of it all, they went *home* for supper.

Finally, the Colonel had made his decision. He would be going back to Wincester, Virginia, where his family was. Some kind of bug had been ravaging his insides for two weeks now. He stopped often with bouts of diarrhea, his fluid levels depleting more and more with each passing day. Besides, a beautiful 17-year-old brunette was waiting at home. Over the phone, she had helped him see clearly the gravity of his plight, with her cuddling pheromone-laced whimpers. Once strong, the man-child warrior's desire to remain on the field of battle began to waver, ultimately relenting to his more gentle urges. He longed for a celestial Mormon lover.

Applejack tried as hard as he could. "If you go home, I will never forgive you."

"I just can't seem to get over this," Colonel replied.

"Maybe you should take some medicine. Maybe you shouldn't think about it all the time. Maybe you should wipe the drool off your face and break up with your teeny-bop girlfriend."

The Colonel bristled.

"All I'm saying is that I really want you to stay out here. Come on, give it a few more days." He slapped the Colonel on the back and went inside.

But the Colonel didn't give it a few more days. He caught a ride to Bangor that evening, got on a bus and went home to Virginia to kiss his girl and poop on his own pot.

He'd been a good friend to them. They would miss him. But in the end, a man has to follow his gut.

When he finally allowed Applejack, Futureman and Blackbeard to pack up and leave, Bear took them down a hidden road to a spot a few miles below the Mahoosuc Notch.

Earle Towne stood on the approach trail, belly poking out. "This is as far as I go. We part ways here." His look was stern yet tender. "I have no doubt about it. Yes, sir, I can see it on all of you. You're going to make it."

After a silence, Bear nodded. "My friends." And as men in the world, they did not wish to walk away from him in that place.

Bear watched them go. He had been there his whole life, standing there, watching, barefoot in that spot, in his red suspenders, each day his beard growing grayer, whiter. His children always growing up and leaving him. But he would hear others stirring the dust around the mountain bends on their way North and South, and his face would be the first thing they would see.

Don't you get sick of that road? Those same trees and same worthless, shiftless people that come through your cabin? The voices nag him, hanging in the hollow knots of the fallen wood, but Bear can't hear them anymore. Once they were important questions to him, but now they rot beside the stumps in the forest.

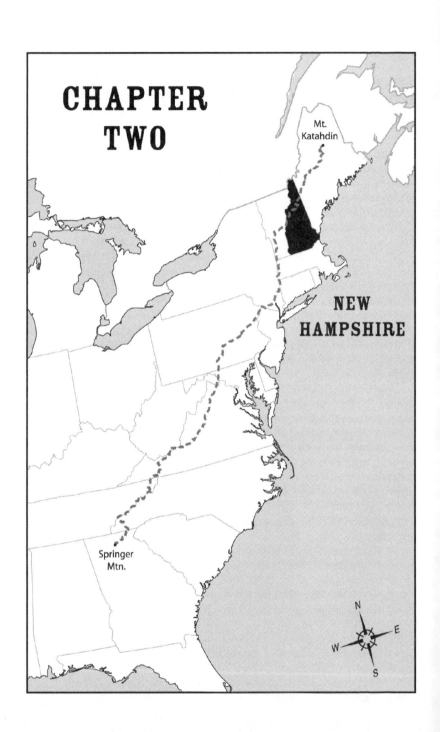

CHAPTER
TWO

Mt.
Katahdin

NEW
HAMPSHIRE

Springer
Mtn.

N
W   E
S

In the forest they found two small signs hidden among the oaks, one for Maine, one for New Hampshire. Some kind of boundary, at last. A month of sweat and spilt blood lay behind them. Their first state was defeated. But as they stood under the branches, breathing in, waiting for it – dignity of conquest, consummate pride – nothing came. Oak snored on. Rock and root dug still deeper. Feeling misunderstood and vaguely Sisyphusian, the men picked their feet up just high enough to clear the strange new realization. Tree was tree. Stone was stone and that was all. Lessons found in these mountains possessed no bookends. This was the world. Maine was New Hampshire.

I

Hemlock firs vibrated in the breeze, thick branches covered in witchbrooms. Dense hobblebush stayed the Trail. A white-throated sparrow flew through the forest singing *Old Sam Peabody, Peabody, Peabody.*

Blackbeard walked hard to Gentian Pond, making the lean-to by mid-afternoon. There he found a crude shelter overlooking a wide valley. Nearby, a pond of charcoal-fresh spring-fed water cast her echoes, suggestions that ricocheted off the mountains.

Time for a swim. No one's around.

When he returned from the pond, he found two men in the shelter. Their gear, strewn everywhere, consumed every square inch of useable space.

"Hey! Was that your stuff in here? Sorry, pal. We didn't know anybody was around," one of the men said. "Say buddy, me and my friend here got a large set up. Would you mind camping on the platforms out back?"

Blackbeard centered his head with a coal black gaze. "As a matter of fact I do."

Coming down the mountain, Applejack and Futureman had joined up with a tall Montana boy by the name of Big Blue. When they reached Gentian Pond, Blackbeard was retreating to the corner of the shelter, his pack and sparse equipment drawn around him like a moat. But he was holding his ground.

"Hey! Nelson here. Pleased to see ya!" Nelson held out a round hand. Sweat like a catfish lip stained his shirt. "You friends with Blackbeard the Pirate over there?" He laughed. A chin gullet shook back and forth. "He said you plan on going to Georgia, eh? I've heard of you people before. Never met one that made it, though. So good luck." He grabbed at the air like it was cotton candy. "We're hiking, too. Doing it the right way – short trip, full gear. Figured out years ago that's the best way. Been hiking since I was a boy. Bob over there's an Eagle Scout. He could teach you a thing or two."

Bob tipped his hat.

An array of hiking equipment spread before them: air mats, high tech stoves, colored Nalgene bottles, GPS, water treatment pumps, draped mosquito nets, short wave radio, thermometer, barometer, rain catcher, fold-up military shovel, storm matches, travel saw, a variety of Leatherman knife kits, heavy duty camp slippers, candle lantern, two tarps, two tents, tent pegs, several changes of clothes and a kitchen pantry worth of food.

"Eventually, you too will learn that preparedness is the most important thing," Nelson instructed. "A prepared hiker experiences no surprises. I'll bet you boys are starting to learn that, aren't ya boys?"

"I brought my collection of license plates. I have one from every state I've ever been to," Applejack said.

"I got struck by lightning on a tune-up hike before we came out here," Futureman said.

Nelson grew stern. "Boys, you have a lot to learn about hiking, and I sure hope you do it – before you meet a sad end."

Nelson continued his lecture, but the tall pines and needle-soft beds out back were calling them. Blackbeard was left to fend for himself.

Big Blue rose early, a farming habit from back home. Only a warm rectangular spot on the ground remained when Blackbeard came to the campsite at dawn, packed and ready, aggravation riddling his face.

"What's the matter?" Applejack asked.

"I didn't get any friggin sleep, that's what the matter," Blackbeard said.

"Bad dreams?"

"No, those two idiots yakked till twelve o'clock. Once they finally shut their mouths, they started rearranging all their gear, clawing and banging. Sounded like they were boarding up for a hurricane. Then, Bob proceeded to clear his sinuses for an hour, while Nelson snored at rock concert volume. Unbelievable."

"Why didn't you come camp with us?" Applejack asked.

"Because to hell with the yacht club, that's why. Let's get into town."

II

There it was below them, the shining city of Gorham, New Hampshire, grimly waiting for the barbarian hordes to descend. Beyond the peak of Mount Hayes, the Trail forked into two distinct paths. One, marked with blue blazes, led straight down into the heart of town. Years ago, this had been the old A.T. The other, the new A.T. route, was marked by fresh white blazes and led three miles around the edge of town.

In recent years, the Appalachian Trail Conference had been striving for a more consistent wilderness experience for hikers, re-directing the Trail away from civilization where possible. Such a strategy is understandable but to the tired and hungry hiker, indirect routes can be annoying. For southbounders, this split above Gorham is particularly vexing. Follow the old A.T. and you can be at the restaurants, stores and ice cream shops a full hour sooner (no hitching necessary) – an appealing prospect when you've just come from the long mountainous wilds of Maine. But to choose this path is to choose the way of the 'blue blazer,' an unthinkable compromise to the purist. In their view, this is the first step in a series of equivocations that will send the hiker along a downward spiral of shortcuts, taxi rides, raft floats, hot air balloon rides, and ultimately – failure. Perhaps they have a point.

For better or worse, Applejack, Futureman and Blackbeard chose the blue blaze.

The path wound down Leadmine Ledge through ripe blueberry patches – the biggest they had ever seen, the ripest they had ever tasted. Plump round berries fed on pure mountain water. Yet the sights and sounds of the city below distracted them.

Gorham, their first 'big city' on the Trail, was disconcerting even from a distance. Honking cars, burning rubber, exhaust, truck beds banging under heavy loads, traffic, red lights, storefront shoppers.

And the restaurants. Burger King. Wendy's. Pizza Hut. McDonald's! Those iconic arches – gold medallions in the sun. They could hardly catch their breath at the thought of – that crispy white bread. French fries bathed in vats of old grease, coated in salt. Ice cream formed into titillating ziggurat molds for America's children. Chicken globules – crispy, yet not. Filets of last month's catch drowned in a new ocean of tartar sauce. Apple pies wrapped in beach skin and, most importantly – Coca-Cola.

Blackbeard and Futureman dropped the natural berries that had come to them straight from the womb of a mineral-rich mother earth and trampled them underfoot, as they bounded toward McDonalds. Applejack, half-crippled from an ankle twist, limped slowly behind.

Leadmine spit out at the edge of the Androscoggin River. Directly on the other side was Gorham. Distorted waves of heat rose from the paved streets. Once again, they came upon two paths. In their rush, Blackbeard and Future-man failed to notice the huge bridge that crossed the river into town. They turned south instead, down an old dirt road that paralleled the city across the river.

They walked. And walked. And walked. Yellow arches always across the water.

"Where's the bridge?" Futureman asked.

"I don't know, but I want those fatty burgers," Blackbeard said.
"And fatty fries."
"And fatty pies."
"And fatty fudge sundaes."
"And fatty filets."
"And fatty nuggets."
On they walked.
Until at last they came to the restaurant. There it sat-across the river. It may as well have been a million miles.
"Should we swim?" Futureman's lip quivered.
"Current's strong. Plus it's too deep."
"I feel like Luke without a grappling hook."
"Indy without a whip." Blackbeard added.
"I wish we were in a movie right now."
"Yeah, that way we could win."

Applejack had seen the bridge. Applejack had walked into town. Applejack was eating a Big Mac.

"Should we turn around?" Blackbeard asked.
"Maybe. Yes. Fart! Caca! I don't know."

The town dwellers eyed them carefully as they ran down the road at last, insatiable cavemen, hands out, following a practically visible olfactory trail.

They found Applejack in a booth, mystery sauce in his beard, proud enough not to wipe it off. "You missed the bridge and walked down that river road, didn't you?"

III

Being the recluse he was, Blackbeard left them again to camp on the edge of town. Sore, stiff and full-bellied, Applejack and Futureman reluctantly set out to locate the post office. Expecting a food box from home – a pre-packaged cache of vittles bought in bulk to avoid the ravages of compulsive supermarket spending – they arrived not a moment too soon. Their box needed to be dealt with. It was being unruly.

Bobby, their good buddy from Tennessee, had enclosed a generous bag of garlic cloves, claiming it would 'renew energy levels and purify the body of toxins.' What it actually did was turn the box into a little monster. There it sat in the Gorham P.O. Alive. Living. A cranky, water-damaged rhombus, with eyes and a mouth, useless legs and tiny little arms, bothering all the other packages. Its odor had bled into the cramped office, quietly insinuating the idea of "going postal" to all the mailroom clerks. When Applejack and Futureman finally came to claim it, they were thanked profusely, a hint of unprofessional anger hidden within the gratitude.

An organizational genius, Bobby had agreed to the task because he really wanted to come with them, but after two months of deliberation, he'd settled instead for running base camp.

Bobby's job as a youth pastor was what kept him back in Knoxville. And he was perfect for it. He had the heart and the look. In his bureau could be found the nicest Patagonia base layer money could buy, alongside a thrift-store City Waste Management shirt (replete with reflective tapeline across the chest), white leather slippers (acquired at the estate sale of a mortician) and a $270 Arcteryx weather shell. Bobby was indeed a man of opposites, the kind of guy who hangs onto the top of a car doing forty-five down a dirt road, but is sure to be in bed by ten-thirty. He cared the world for people. And he was as reliable as garlic.

The package looked sad sitting in the bottom of the empty dumpster behind the U.S.P.O. It hadn't gotten a fair shake, hadn't had enough time in the world to reach its full potential. Brown tears started to swell in its eyes. Futureman explained, "Hey little buddy, this is the end of the line for you. Sometimes it's just your time to go, and that's that. Maybe it's not fair, but that's life. Besides, you're really disgusting. But don't worry little fella, cause soon there will be lots of trash in here for you to defile. Trust me." Applejack closed the lid. They heard it shifting around inside as they walked away.

"Here he comes again. Brace yourself," Applejack said, rocking back on the hot sidewalk.

Futureman grimaced. *He can't cross state lines. Surely, he's on probation.* But there he was, standing in the light, waiting for them. Reed. They steeled themselves for battle.

"Wow. I'm impressed," he said in earnest. An uncharacteristic gentleness had settled on his brown face.

"Huh?"

"I've gotta hand it to you, youse guys made it."

As Reed spoke, the transformation became clear to them. Words of compassion not insult. He reached forward and hugged them. Rough, but in earnest.

And that was all. There was no room for insults on this day. No whisky bottle brandishing. Just a giant mountain man expressing a rare brotherly affection. Sure, Reed would always think of Applejack and Futureman as 'dirty-rat ass-faces,' but he was proud (even fond) of them for walking through his neck of the country. They were kin now, and he would welcome them back anytime for some hard liquor and fudge squares. Anytime, anytime. Another little good-bye from Maine.

IV

Welcome to Hiker's Paradise, the hostel sign read. Bells clattered as the door swung open. Applejack and Futureman walked to the clerkless counter where a worn A.T. register lay open, ink drying on the last line. Maps of Poland and photographs of famous skiers crowded the walls. A swarthy man appeared from behind the line of beads separating the backroom. They smiled. He did not.

"Ess? My'elp'you?" Mouth clenched tight like the Berlin Wall.

"Yes, sir, we would like a room," Futureman said.

"Ostelle orr motil?"

"Excuse me?"

"Ostel…ORRR…mo-Tillll? Seffenteen dollar por ostel, forty por motil."

"Is there cable in the mo-til?"

"Wut doo oo sink? Eh veeninkeenah?"

"A veenin – what's a – you know what? Let's celebrate. We'll take the motel. Just finished our first state!" Air conditioning, cable TV, a private toilet and a *veenin keener* – appropriate spoils.

"Oak dokey. You sign hikerrr book. Dar's shuttle, iv oou vant. And iv oou vant rrride bike, out back, dey free. Yourrr key. Don vorget to zign book. Velcome to Paradise. Oak dokey."

There it was, the TV, standing in the corner like an intervenous tower, needles exposed, ready to drip the morphine, soothing, addictive, kaleidoscopic. A nootropic miracle.

After sharing a convenience store snack with the cast of *Law and Order*, they gathered their pile of biohazardous clothing and went next door to the Paradise Laundromat. Two women were seated outside on a bench waiting for their wash. Locals in flower print moo-moos.

One of the ladies, mid sixties, wiry hair and yellow teeth, greeted them. "Hullo there boys! I'm Sue. This is Ila!"

"Been hiking?" Ila asked. She was younger but plumper.

"Yes, we have."

"Bet you a million dollars we can guess where the two of you hiked from," Sue said.

"You're on."

"I bet you hiked here from outer space!" Ila screamed. Years of smoking roared in her throat.

Sue heaved. "Oop! There you go again, Ila, losing us another million!" They cackled.

"We're in the hole now! What? Eight, ten million?"

"More like twenty-eight!" Their husky laughter drowned out the rattle of the washing machines. It was contagious.

"Hey, wait a minute," Ila said. "What if they really did hike here from outer space?"

The women leaned in, intently.

"Ladies, we were hoping to keep it a secret, but I can see there's no fooling you. We did in fact come from outer space." Applejack pointed upwards.

Eruption. "Well hooty doo, Sue! Million dollar jackpot! Our debts are clearin up."

"Wait a second though." Sue whispered. "Where's you're space ship?"

Futureman thought about it. "We parked it on the roof."

"How'd you get it up there?"

"What do you mean? It's a space ship."

"You landed it there?"

"Yep. On the roof."

Ila reeled back.

"You boys are alright. Say, what's outer space like?" Sue asked.

"Cold." Applejack shrugged.

Laughter cleared the birds from a nearby tree.

"What's your ship made out of?" Ila asked.

"Dirty hiking clothes," Applejack said. "We had to disassemble to wash it."

The ladies careened and jolted until, at once, they spontaneously combusted. A vapor of laughter that rose into the sky. Alone, Applejack and Futureman soon became entranced by the hypnotic drone of the laundry machines.

V

"Chasing the naughty couples down the grassgreen
gooseberried double bed of the wood."
          -Dylan Thomas

It was nearly dark when they came out of the laundry room. The moon was up early. It didn't take long for the stars to follow. Applejack and Futureman found some quiet on the balcony steps. Futureman noticed in the shadows a woman walking briskly.

"Is that Little Moose?"

She walked by, failing to notice them.

"Little Moose!"

Little Moose turned. She spoke quickly, fragments spilling out. "Oh hey guys, so nice to see you, Paradise is something, huh, glad to be in Gorham, boy, finally out of Maine, wow, cool, hey, good to see you, good night, sweet dreams, love you, mmmwah." She blew a kiss.

"Where's she headed in such a hurry?" Futureman asked.

It didn't take long for Applejack to put the pieces together. *Some things in her hands-fresh towels, a bottle of wine, a bag of secret goodies. Hair wet from a shower. She hurries back to a private room where her clean smelling husband is probably pacing the floor.*

She knocked at the door. It opened immediately. She went in. It slammed shut.

"Mm-hmm, okay." Applejack glanced at Futureman. "An extravaganza of pent-up marital sex is about to ensue inside that room."

Futureman looked into the darkness, where night was coming into bloom.

"Applejack?"

"Hmm?"

"Do you think we'll ever find women to love?"

Applejack stared blankly ahead. "I hope so, Futureman. I really do."

They sat quietly. White nightingales gathered above, singing love songs over paradise.

VI

The zero was floating around in the room the next morning as they woke, clumsily bouncing off the walls and bumping into their foreheads.

"What do you want with us?" Futureman said.

"I want you to stay!" It said. "Relax. No need to hike. Take a nothing day. Don't go anywhere. You deserve it. Stay. Just stay."

"Enough! Leave us be. We will do as you say. Go bother the other hikers now."

Futureman opened the door to let the zero out, only now realizing what this promise would require: more gluttony and slothfulness.

Applejack caught a peculiar whiff as he entered the bunkhouse, a wooden smell, body odor infused with crisp, early morning moss. He knew who it was before he saw him.

"Friends!" Bombadil laughed and clapped his hands twice. "Nice. Nice."

"Where've you been? You have an odd talent of disappearing," Applejack said.

"Yeah, bros. I don't know, the weirdest thing happened to me yesterday." *Here we go again.*

"I was in the woods, and I heard this voice. It said, *Go to Gorham.* I said, *Gorham?* And it said, *Yeah, man, Gorham.* So I found a road and hitched to Gorham. This one guy picked me up and asked me if I wanted to come help him build a car that runs on water. Mainer's are awesome."

It was good to have him back. The journey always seemed a little less brilliant without him.

"Why don't you come grab some Subway with us. We can take the bikes out back."

"I could use some bread," Bombadil said.

Subway was on the other end of town. Bombadil rode his BMX junker as though it were new. Futureman could almost see the rusty spokes smiling, another chance in the world to make something of themselves.

A fluorescent bulb flittered in the Subway dining room. It had given Nametag April behind the counter a throbbing headache. And her most recent clientele weren't helping – a cluster of tenth-graders crammed into a corner booth talked about drag racing, backyard wrestling and genital piercing.

"HellowelcometoSubwayhowmayIhelpyou?" April recited.

Bombadil pointed at the six-foot party sub hanging above the sandwich line. "Is that thing real?"

"I don't know. Can I take your order, please?"

"I'll take that party sub," Bombadil said.

"Hah-hah."

"Seriously, is it real?"

"It's plastic."

"It looks real."

"Okay, it's real. What would you like to eat?"

"So it's not plastic?"

"Can I take your order please?"

"Who made it?"

"Does it matter?"

"Do they make a new one every day?"

"Can I fix you something?"

"Does anyone eat it, or do you throw it away?"

"One moment please." April went into the back room.

Debby – manager – came out, stretching latex gloves over her hands. "Sir, I'll have to ask you to place an order. There are other people waiting in line." Bombadil glanced at the other two people in line, Applejack and Futureman.

"Right, I'm sorry. Loaf of bread please."

"A loaf of bread?"

"Yes."

"Just bread?"

"Definitely."

"Sir, I can't do that."

"Why not?"

"You have to order something else."

"That's stupid."

"That's policy."

"Who made that policy up?"

"Are you going to get something or not?"

"All right, I guess I'll take a veggie sub."

Debby grabbed a loaf of bread and cut it. "What would you like on it?"

"Nothing."

"I have to put something on it."

"I'll take a veggie sub, hold the veggies."

"I have to put something on it, sir."

"I don't understand."

"I do. Something must go on this sandwich."

"Fine, cheese."

"What else?"

"Nothing."

The manager slapped some triangle Swiss on the bread and wrapped it. Bombadil paid her.

"Thank you, sir, and *(don't ever)* come back and see us."

Bombadil walked to the nearest trashcan and threw the cheese away.

Debby put April back on the line.

"HellowelcometoSubwayhowmayIhelpyou?"

Outside the restaurant, they could see the stone silhouettes of the Whites on the ebony horizon. Bombadil was in love with these mountains. He had grown up in nearby Connecticut. As Bear had said, maybe his childhood was still lost somewhere up on the peaks, along the stone stairs. Yet, he stood in awe still, on the tips of his toes, as if he were seeing them for the first time. He sang a song to himself:

On granite tops and tumble props
Through valley cuts and red stone ruts
We walk and talk and walk and weep
Over peaks on high and paths of sky
Under roof of tree and fallen debris
We walk and weep, think and keep
Grab the walls, clutch and cling
To free our feet, our souls we meet

In other worlds we sit up high
We sit and look, we laugh and sigh,
We sit and weep and laugh and stare
We climb and hit and pound the air
Never to mind, our troubles unwind
Never to find, we're walking blind
Yet climb up still, to find our will

On the way back to Paradise, Applejack rode ahead. Bombadil and Futureman played a boys' game behind, swerving back and forth on the broken sidewalk, trying to jump every little crack.

"Hey, what if you were Adam?" Bombadil asked.

"What do you mean?" Futureman said, crossing in front.

"First person on the planet, man. Don't you think it would be weird?"

"I don't know, I guess."

"What do you mean you guess? If you woke up in the middle of a world that was completely untouched, not a footprint anywhere. And not as a baby, but as a man. A thinking man." Bombadil jumped a curb.

"I think fascination and curiosity would overrule weirdness," Futureman said.

"You wake up and there's all these crazy creatures walking around that you've never seen before. You're totally alone."

"No. Not alone."

"I'm talking before Eve," Bombadil said. "You're the first person in the world!"

"God's in the Garden."

Bombadil hooked off through the flower bed in front of McDonald's. A man with a broom yelled at him. He swerved back to the street. "God is there, huh?"

He strummed the pedals and bit his lower lip. It was starting to crack into Bombadil's psyche. The pollen.

Days ago, somewhere in the woods, Tom had been sitting alone in a deep meditation. He had retreated into his spire, hundreds of feet from floor to ceiling. It was plain, nothing on the concrete walls. Corridors shot off in every direction. The air was crisp, like burnt wood. He was composing his music. It echoed off the walls and filed out into the woods.

Flower, flowers, drifting, sifting
Sitting mums and budding suns
Sing me a song of your own
Play me a tune, a rambling tone.

Pottle pittle, the flowers moan
Rest in wells, sleep felled and wake swelled
As morning comes to take your shells

A man, walking in the woods, interrupted the song, calling to him from the ground below. It was Bear.

"Hello there, my friend!"

Bombadil jumped up, "Old man!"

"Older than many and younger than some. May I help you?"

"How did you get here?" Bombadil asked, surprised.

Bear held his arms out, "Am I not welcome?"

"Well...it's just that..."

"Where do you think you are?" Bear asked.

"In my meditation."

"Regardless, you're still in the forest, in my back yard."

Bombadil lifted an eyebrow.

"No matter, friend. It's neither here nor there. I came because I heard your song. It's not bad, not bad at all, but if I may make a suggestion..."

Bombadil noticed Bear's feet. "You're not wearing any shoes, old man."

"That's right. Can't feel the ground beneath you if you do," Bear said.

Bombadil smiled. "I like that. Make your suggestion."

"Your song is missing something."

"What's that?"

"Pollen."

"Pollen? So how do you suggest that I –"

"Hey. It's your song. You tell me."

Bear continued on his way, letting Bombadil return to his spire, but a voice and a question were distracting him. They were in his head. The question, his own: what is pollen? The voice, a whisper: *Gorham*.

Applejack retired for the night. Futureman and Bombadil found a seat on the porch to continue their discussion about Adam and Creation.

The ancient civilizations composed some interesting theories about human origins. The Mesopotamians held humans to be the byproduct of heavenly wars and feuds between the gods, created as slaves to finish certain building projects given to the lesser gods. Egyptian origins were based on various ancient myths, nature worship, and many deities. It was common among Egyptian kings, considered to be gods themselves, to construct new theologies of origin in order to legitimate their rule and secure the dynasty. For this reason, theologies differed from one to the next but they all centered around the Nile, the source of life. From the water, a god rises and from his seed, humanity.

The creation account of the ancient Israelites was not centered around epic battles between gods, nor was it constructed to legitimate a human kingship. There was only one God – Yahweh – and he was king over all. Out of his perfection, he spoke perfection into being and pronounced it good. Because of this, the Israelites viewed humanity not as a side project of divine fancy, but as the centerpiece of all creation on earth. Human beings had been brought to life by the very breath of God himself and were created to worship their Creator and work in harmony on his earth. Even the king of Israel himself was subordinate to the Law of Yahweh.

"So humans were created as perfect beings," Bombadil commented.

"A perfection that we lost," Futureman said.

"How? Why?"

"I'm not entirely sure. Some say God gave us a will, a choice to worship Him – would it be true worship if we didn't desire it? Others say He allowed humans to worship themselves so that they might, in the end, see His glory displayed. I think they're both true. In any case, He permitted a tempter to enter the picture."

"Satan," Bombadil said.

"One of the names by which he is known, yes."

"The Great Liar."

"And the great lie is to convince us that God is not who He says He is, and that we can be like Him, knowing all things. Adam and Eve accepted this lie. By choosing to eat from the Tree of the Knowledge of Good and Evil, they were choosing to believe the lie that they could be like God. Thus, we have *the fall*, whereby sin, death, decay, pain and separation came into the world."

"Humanity was kicked out of the Garden."

"And we've been trying to get back into Eden ever since," Futureman said.

"How do we do that?" Bombadil asked.

"Maybe we can't do it."

Bombadil remembered all of a sudden. It was at Rainbow Stream Lean-to back in the Wilderness, with Ringleader, Krom and Lollygag, when Ringleader had leaned forward to inquire, "What exactly is the Good?"

Krom shook his head. "Good is arbitrary."

Ringleader didn't agree. "No, it's not. It can't be."

"Why not?" Krom asked.

"Because doing good things is not arbitrary. It makes the world a better place, and that's the point," Ringleader said.

"Okay. True," Krom admitted. "But how do you interact with it?"

"The way you interact with your cat or your brother," Ringleader said.

"What the hell does that mean?" Krom asked.

"It means something, and something never means nothing." Ringleader rubbed his head front to back.

"What?"

"It means it's just a part of you," Ringleader restated, "Like everything else. I don't know."

"Alright," Bombadil broke in. "But where does *it* come from?"

"Who knows where? From everywhere," Ringleader said.

"But is there some basis for it? Something that tells us what *is* Good?" Bombadil asked. This was not like him, to want to distinguish, differentiate, identify.

Ringleader waved his hands in circles. "We can't really understand it. It's just there. It's everywhere."

"How about a designer? Someone who initiates the Good." Applejack asked.

His voice startled them. He had been listening quietly in the background.

Ringleader came back. "Like a designer that operates out of The Good? Yeah, I've thought about that. A higher power."

"More like – a designer who *is* the Good?" Applejack asked.

"How so?"

"If the designer operated out of The Good, then it would mean that he was himself subordinate to The Good, a design himself."

"You've got it all wrong. The Good is an idea, not a being," Krom said.

"Why separate the two? It seems the right question to ask – not how can we know *The Good*, but how can we know *The One* who is good?"

"That doesn't make any sense," Ringleader said.

Bombadil crossed his legs. "Hm. You're talking about Jesus aren't you?"

"Yes," Applejack answered.

"What about Jesus?" Krom asked.

"Everyone agrees he was a good person, right?" Applejack said.

"Of course. His way was love. Love is good," Krom said.

"Jesus said that there is only one who is good, meaning God, but he also claimed that he was God. A serious claim. So if we say that he was a good person, should we not consider the possibility that he is more than that?" Applejack asked.

"Wait. Wait. But Jesus was a man," Ringleader said.

"Yeah, a man – who also claimed to be the Son of God," Bombadil said. "That means a part of God, it means he is God, right?"

"He was killed for saying this."

"Listen, there's no way of knowing if he really is or isn't. So I don't see how it matters," Ringleader said.

"There is no knowing in the sense that you mean it – some kind of conceptual thing. Knowing it can come only by faith. By an encounter through believing," Applejack said. "If Jesus isn't the one who is good, then he's either crazy or a liar. But if he's telling the truth…well, that changes things, doesn't it…"

"Well, maybe," Ringleader said, "but we'll never be able to prove it."

"We can't really *prove* anything. Everything leads ultimately to the doorstep of faith."

From there, the conversation trailed off into a distorted collage of meditation and metaphysics and the specifics were soon lost. But it left some pollen on Bombadil.

Now, on the steps of Hiker's Paradise, a question. "Does restoration come through Jesus Christ?"

"That's the question," Futureman said.

"The Fall broke our perfection and worship of God." Bombadil's eyes were bending, trying to put together pieces of a puzzle he had long been working on. "And Jesus…fixes…the Fall."

"Yes," Futureman said.

"He is the doorway. Our return to Eden."

"And beyond."

Faith was descending on Paradise. A dense smog came in underneath to thwart its settling. Bombadil had not considered closing his realm of open-ended possibilities until now. To him, all spiritualities led to the same place, many paths, many truths, whatever you feel. It was a convenient plan whereby he could retain control of his life, remain the master of his spire. 'Oh, to be like God…' the serpent whispers. *But if these revelations about Jesus are true… then the search is over. He would be the fulcrum. The way, the truth…*

And the life.

As Bombadil considered the narrow way, his mind and body experienced a strange anxiety that ricocheted off the black water mist. "To die to oneself? To worship another?" He was suffocating.

"So truth is a man…a man who is God…a God we were made to worship."

"I believe so, Tom. That is where our life is hidden."

"Hidden? So now what?"

The revelry of darkness jeered at them. It picked them up and carried them in a parade of broken tambourine and crude lyre to the edge of the city, where the useless things of the world are left to return to dust, and there threw them into a pit of quicksand.

As he sank, watching all things go, Bombadil decided he would sing a song – one last salvo for the world he knew:

Genesis, the beginning of all things
Has brought us here with the end it brings
Blanket of black, tar pit tack
To do what we must, back to dust
So questions, man your battle stations
Shoot your bows and arrows
Fire them straight and narrow
Into the fog where there is no aim
Into the midst of quandary's game
Lift your wanderings and deeply peer
Into the black smog where echoes die
Into the dark vapor where truth is a lie
There is nothing there, nothing anywhere
There is no more bloom, no white flower June
No trees in rain, no sweet Mary Jane
Nothing at all, it's all built a wall
Sinking deep and thinking steep
The Mountain heights are gone

The last tuft of Bombadil's long chestnut hair disappeared under the surface. Total darkness settled over the pit. Futureman's chin was tilted back, descending beside his lost friend. He had one eye above the wet sand to see it. A single spore in the dark. Somehow finding a path through the black blanket, it fell onto the surface of the quicksand and began to sink, glowing dimly in the mud. Reaching Bombadil's mouth, it became a fire on his tongue.

I breathe my last breath
Take sip of this dark depth
Here at the end, at Genesis, I begin
Take heed of the man Jesus
God in man, come to meet us
Open my heart in this rotting mort
The eternal calm of death's balm
Where men and women die
And live again

Bombadil opened his eyes from his meditation. The mist was gone. *Pollen!* He began to laugh. It was two in the morning.
Hikers stirred in their bunks. "Shut up! Go to bed, you potheads!"

Bombadil ran inside. "Applejack…Applejack…"

"What?"

"There is only One who is Good."

It was on Tom's face, deep in his eyes. Windows to the soul. Applejack arose from his slumber and embraced Bombadil. The two men hugging, there in Paradise.

Tom Bombadil left for good the following morning. He had called his brothers in Connecticut to come and play in the mountains for a while, to get lost again, revisit their childhood. He had some new discoveries to make in the world. To share with them. They were on their way.

There, in the sunlight, he said goodbye to Applejack and Futureman. Brothers. They would never see him again on the Trail. On the Appalachian Trail.

VII

A mule of a weather system was on Tom Bombadil's mountains. They watched from the safety of Gorham as clouds like city blocks rolled across the granite towers. *Disappearing into the Whites*, he called it.

They won't permit neutrality, mountains that is. Like the thunder, they confront us, always demanding something – whether it be awe, respect or just plain fear. Yet as Applejack and Futureman stood there – heels rocked back, pupils wavering, struggling to absorb the magnitude of these stark-naked-in-the-sky giants – they weren't sure what they felt. *What are the butterflies saying? What is it? Oh, yeah. Got it. Vulnerable, like a child.*

Neither one of them had ever seen anything like these White Mountains. Not the Bitteroots, or the Tetons. Not the Bighorn Range. Not even Kilimanjaro, the icy prince of the Serengeti, had rattled Futureman like this sight. *It's the storms. Once I get up there, I'll be driftwood on the ocean. There's nowhere to hide.*

"We should slack a twenty-two over Carter Dome and Wildcat tomorrow and stay in town again. Let the weather calm down a little before we push on," Applejack suggested.

Futureman watched as a thunderhead ate the top of Mount Madison. "That sounds just fine. I'll arrange the shuttle." *We'll see what we can do soon enough.*

Applejack took one last look before he closed the door behind him.

It was 5 AM when they started walking. The storm still hovered over the range, stalled out. Dense fog clung to the krummholz forests of balsam fir and black spruce. Sunrise couldn't break the cloud cover down. No birdsong.

About six o'clock Blackbeard appeared out of the mist, stepping down the boulder staircase that masquerades as trail. He smiled wide, pleased to see his two pals.

"Haven't seen you guys since the Golden Arches. Why are you goin' north?"

"We took the easy way out. We decided to stay in town another night," Applejack said.

"Maybe, you guys can catch me over on the back side of the Presidentials. I'll probably have to hole up somewhere. It could get ugly."

"Can't be worse than Maine."

"Who knows?" Blackbeard picked at a stone with his stick. "So it's been good, right? Hiking together and everything?"

"Of course."

"Absolutely."

He shifted his weight to the other leg. Stood silent, in the whistling wind.

"Well, we should probably get movin," Applejack said. "We got seventeen more miles to do before this storm revs up."

"Yep." Blackbeard knew it was time to go yet he paused for another moment, unsure of his next step. "Alright then, I'll see you guys soon. The three of us still have some hell to raise in New Hampshire." He lurched forward and gripped the two of them with his hairy arms, then with a nod, he plunged past and down the staircase.

A hundred yards up the stone face, Applejack got it – the meaning of Blackbeard's odd behavior. He had been telling them, in his stoic, macho New York way, that it was time to part. That the journey ahead would be his own. Applejack turned to call back to his friend, to look him in the eye, to let him know. But it was too late. He had disappeared into the white mist. Another thorny lesson of the Trail. At any given moment, on any old mountainside, you might lose your friend, a casualty of fate. And there's not a damned thing you can do about it.

VIII

Mt. Madison is the first peak of the famed Presidential Range. It sits along the eastern end of a horseshoe valley across from Mount Washington. A simple, wooden sign -weathered and barely legible – is lodged in the rocks on top. Wind scours it almost constantly.

They found a pack scale at the visitor center at the base of Madison.

"How much do you think they weigh now?" Futureman asked.

"Let's see, mine's reading at...forty-one," Applejack said.

"Mine's forty-three. Nico said thirteen? Impossible. Is it possible?"

A gray-haired park ranger came into the lodge. "Boys, if you were thinking about heading up Madison, conditions are deteriorating pretty quick, zero visibility. I'd think about reconsidering." She spoke sternly.

"We're used to it. We're thru-hiking," Applejack said with bravado – the male recourse against fear.

"I know that, sonny. I can smell you from over here. But hiking the Whites is a different story. Weather can be treacherous. Not a year goes by that something bad doesn't happen to somebody up there. But hey, I only hiked the Trail three times myself and lived in these mountains my whole life. What do I know? If you Sobos think you've got the stuff, be my guest." She went into the office.

"Geez, what a pessimistic lady," Futureman said. "It's just a little weather."

At tree line, they paused in a cradle of alpine azalea. Just above, it seemed as if the wind were moving the very stones. Pushing ahead into the bank of white, cold fog ripped over them, unrelenting as a blizzard. Poles useless on the slick stone, they compressed them and strapped them to their packs. Futureman bent low using all fours like a three-toed sloth, pushing and pulling his way up the craggy spine. Within moments he was no longer visible to his friend.

Applejack could barely see the hand in front of his face. Wind blew south then north, belting him with bursts of rain. Slapping him around, the unfortunate son. The gusts pushed him down onto his hands and knees. He crawled upward. Every foothold and handhold seemed crucial. *Where am I – in the goldarn Himalayas?* Using a boulder for support, he stood up and leaned into the gale-force winds. The skin on his face pulled back. One of his contacts slipped out of his desert-dry eyeball and blew away like a speck of dust on the breath of Aeolus. No matter. He couldn't see anyway.

Any real trail had ceased to be a mile back. Only occasionally could he find a blazed cairn. Up was the only way. Winds grated the rocks like sandpaper. Thoughts scattered, disoriented. *How far down? Would anyone even know?*

Through the mist, he saw forms hobbling, coming down – toward him, mummified in the white enveloping stew. Their steps were choppy. They were stumbling, centrifuging. A man and a woman. She was borderline hysterical. One cruel catastrophe after another playing out behind her eyes. *The book said dozens of people have died on these mountains. It happens to somebody every year. Maybe, this year...* she thought.

"You guys need anything?!" Applejack shouted into the man's ear.

"Whaaat?!"

"Do! You! Need! Anything?!"

"You're crazy to go up. Wind's close to a hundred on top!"

"How far is it now?!"

They didn't stop. The man gripped the woman: "You can do it!" Then, they were gone.

After crossing four false peaks, Applejack began to wonder if he had somehow gotten onto the wrong mountain. He shouted into the din for Futureman, but no response came. *Guess I'm completely alone now. But this is why I'm out here. To feel. Alive. And scared stupid.*

Alone, Futureman found a cleft between two of the bigger rocks, a place to rest. He collapsed his body between them. The howl grated against the edges of the opening. He felt warm inside his makeshift cave, imagining hollow quiet and water dripping from the ceiling, straight down. He gazed out of the hole into the white fury. *A new perspective on peace. Maybe I could go to sleep.*

The prospect of reentering the storm seemed preposterous. He saw himself being carried off the mountain, winnowed like chaff. Then, suddenly, the wind died away and the sun shone on the wet rocks. *Odd. I must have found a portal.* He poked his head out of the womb. The storm was cycloning around the summit, a narrow core of light, sky above blue and clear. *The eye of the storm.*

Applejack had nearly given up on reaching the summit when it finally appeared. There was barely anything left of the ravaged sign. He gripped it, rubbing his thumb over the yellow chipped wood to see the elevation mark. *25,363 ft? Not very high, really.* Directly above his handkerchiefed head, the sky started to break apart. He looked up. *An opening. There.*

A shout found his ear through the torrent. He turned and found his friend nestled beside the rocks 30 yards below. *How did I get in front of him?* They raised hands at one another and then it was gone. The eye had imploded. Consumed, just as they were, once again in the squall. White froth spun to gray, rain hurtling down through the sky. The heavy tears of a lover.

Big Blue was sitting at a table inside Madison Hut, dry, safe from the weather, engrossed in a book he had found in Gorham: *Emerald Child of the Dawn*. The paper jacket pictured a half-naked witch-princess rising like a phoenix from a fountain of green flames. Applejack joined him, dripping water onto the varnished, wooden bench.

"Good book, Blue?"

Big Blue didn't look up. "It's really interesting. Don't let the picture fool you."

"Or the title?"

Futureman barreled through the doors, sopping, exhilarated. "I can't tell if I'm on a mountain or lost at sea."

A dozen long tables lined the main room. In the back, there were two bunkhouse wings, enough room to sleep thirty. The hut had an indoor toilet and running water.

"Hey fellas, I'm Katy." She was in her twenties, curly hair, one of four crewmembers. "You guys lookin' for work and a place to sleep?"

"If you got it."

"We do. Hard work, too. About twenty minutes of dishwashing. You think you can handle that? Great. Now relax and I'll get you some hot soup. You look like you could use it. It's getting crazy out there. Then again, it's just another day in the Whites."

The White Mountain hut system is impressive. Seven huts spread out strategically over the range. Visited by thousands each year, they provide a place to experience the wild Whites in relative comfort and safety but reservations are expensive by thruhiker standards. Without the good fortune of landing a work-for-stay spot, thruhikers are left to fend for themselves. Open camping is considered illegal and sanctioned camping sites are scarce and well off the Trail. Consequently, there aren't many options. What should be one of the most savored stretches of Appalachian Trail can become a mad dash to find cover, sometimes legal, much of the time not.

On this particular stormy night, Madison Hut was booked solid. The only beds available were the tops of three dining room tables. Applejack, Futureman and Big Blue took them gladly. After gratefully ingesting the house leftovers, they moved the salt and peppershakers aside and crawled into their bags. Wailing wind lulled them to deep sleep.

Applejack poked his head out. It was early. The wind had finished her complaint. It looked like a clear day was coming. Big Blue hummed quietly, strapping his pack on, about to head out the door. He spoke softly.

"I'm going to make for Washington while I can. See you on down the Trail. Maybe." Another goodbye.

After breakfast, Applejack and Futureman set out by way of Jefferson and Thunderstorm Junction.

"Today we climb Mount Washington, Futureman. I have been looking forward to this day since I was a boy reading Ranger Rick."

"Is it strange to know that it's here?" Futureman asked.

"I don't know. Like everything else now, it just is what it is."

The Presidential Range is the centerpiece of the Whites. The peaks were named for our nation's finest. Mt. Washington, standing at 6,288 feet, is at the epicenter of the range, famous for its staggering beauty and atrocious weather. Distant fronts – nor'easters, counter winds from the Atlantic, jet streams down from Canada, spitfire storms from Lake Champlain – pull into the valley and slingshot up the slopes, converging at Washington in unparalleled ways. In fact, the highest surface wind speed ever recorded on the planet was documented on April 12, 1934 by meteorologist Salvatore Pagliuca at the Mount Washington weather observatory. Salvatore survived the 231 mph wind by anchoring himself to a rope, a human weather-sock. Nevertheless, when the sky isn't unhappy, the view from Washington unveils an extraordinary span of earth. Some even say that on a clear day one can see Canada to the west and the Atlantic to the west.

Applejack stopped to relieve himself on Thunderstorm Junction with 45 mph winds gusting against his back. *I've got quite a bathroom, here on top of the world,* he thought.

Seconds later, Futureman turned and shrieked. "Oh my gosh, dude. What are you doing?

"Nothing…Shut up…I'm trying to get this situation in hand." Applejack's legs were serving as a funnel for the wind, and, impossibly, missiles of urine shot up onto his contorted face.

"Why are you peeing all over yourself?"

Applejack was dancing bowlegged. "I'm not, you fool. It's the wind! The wind!"

"Aim it down."

"I can't. It's – it's beyond my control!"

Applejack's face was dripping. Futureman was curled up on the ground in a dry-heave, struggling to catch his breath. "That's the funniest damn thing I have ever seen. Ever."

Applejack stepped over him, wiping his forehead with the sleeve of his shirt. "Get off the ground you imbecile. Don't be an animal."

A giant horseshoe of ashen rock stretched across the gulf before them, casting a long shadow of several miles over the pine valley. Dread and peace cohabitate on their naked forms. The Imprimatur rests on every crop of rock and in every mound of chalky-white earth. Across the chasm, a great but indiscernible distance stood between them and Washington, yet Futureman felt as if he could reach out and touch it.

Wedged between blue sky and gray stone, they crossed the ridgeline. Applejack wept. Too much beauty. Too much, too much. He hid the tears from his friend.

The grandfather cone of Washington sat upright against the backdrop of sky. Train tracks cut around the mountain like a barbwire necklace, a quaint (hideous) anachronistic subtlety. The Park built the tracks years ago with the generous entrepreneurial dream of hauling anybody and everybody up to the tourist center – a clumsy, multi-stored crate of concrete, replete with snack bars (they'll be famished!), gift shops, pay-per-view telescopes (Look! Two people making out in Gorham!) and parking lots. A nicely paved road, another convenient alternative to exercise, was carved into the mountainside, making the quick trip up from civilization *more quicker*. What had been a quiet, magnificent mountain for millennia was now a circus of exploding stars and gigantic sundaes. [Note: bumper stickers can be purchased in the gift shop, "This Car Climbed Mount Washington" or "Honk If You Love The Whites!"].

"I can't believe they put a train here," Applejack said.

"We should definitely moon it if we see it," Futureman responded.

Out of touch hiking enthusiasts and old-fashioned nature lovers have done what they can through the years to preserve the serenity of the peak but true progress does not wait for anyone. Somewhere along the line, perhaps after too many failures, New England's tree huggers ran out of ideas. Frustration got the best of them. They resorted to childish behavior, forming an organization called the new AMC (Appalachian Mooning Club). In short, members pull their britches down at all vehicular visitors. Middleschoolers, shameless and pissed. Naughty children with master's degrees.

"What do you think? Should we join up?"

"If one comes by," Applejack said.

They saw the smoke rise from below. They heard the chugging of the vacation train lumbering up the mountain, defying gravity and common sense, on an unnatural and ungodly collision course with the Appalachian Trail. Tourists hung their camcorders (heads?) out of the locomotive's open windows. Greedy for a scenic view, a breath-taking sight. Well – they got it.

Applejack positioned himself. "Get that disposable out, buddy. We're going to need photographic proof of this."

Some of them catcalled, some winced, some covered their children's eyes and others whistled. The conductor grabbed a piece of coal. They were well out of range, but he threw it in their general direction anyway. Applejack slapped his fanny for them. Futureman did the twist.

The steam engine hooked out of sight.

"They asked for it."

"They sure did. Whoever they are."

The view "from Canada to the Atlantic" they were hoping for was stolen from them by a cement-dense cloud that blew in minutes before they reached the top. Light shone forth from within it, nonetheless. Flash bulbs exploded as tourists lined up to make a memory with the Mt. Washington sign. People

and cars were everywhere. Japanese fans of American baseball snapped pictures of each other. Crown Victorias and Mark Vs edged through the mob.
Tour buses from Jersey and Delaware unloaded, spilling fanny-packed Chee-
to-eaters out onto the lot. There was more action than the red carpet at Man-
n's Chinese Theater.

"It's so windy up here."

"Darn, I think I left my tripod back at the hotel."

"We gotta get one of them bumper stickers."

"Honey, would you get the children down off those rocks?"

"I shoulda brought my rain parka."

"Who are those mountain people?"

"No way! You guys walked up here?"

"Mommy, I saw that hairy man's bottom."

Conspicuous signs with arrows were posted just inside the door, directing
"all thruhikers" to go visit the "special room" set aside "just for them." The
arrows led Applejack and Futureman deep down into a concrete storage closet in the basement, a dimly lit holding tank for cleaning buckets and un-used
trashcans…and thruhikers.

Futureman set his pack down in a puddle of sooty condensation. "This is
cozy."

"Are we allowed upstairs, or do they bring the buffet down to us?" Applejack said, leaning his head back on one of the rubber cans.

A man in the corner cleared his voice.

"Oh, we're not alone. Hello there," Futureman offered.

The stranger closed his yellowed copy of *The Grapes of Wrath*. "Nice day
up here on Mount Washington, isn't it?" He had a soothing Carolina voice,
the kind that lulls you to sleep.

"How long have you been here?" Applejack asked.

"Well, I got to the top last night at two in the morning and slept out on the
sidewalk."

"In that screaming wind?"

"Yep. Pretty strong wind, wasn't it? I'm Cool Breeze by the way. Pleased
to meet the both of you."

"You too. Quite a circus up here, huh?"

"Indeed."

"So you started up in Maine?" Applejack asked.

"I did. I miss Maine. I miss the people up there. They were down home."

"Yep."

"They know how to treat a fella up there." A pleasant memory flickered
over Cool Breeze's face, like the shade tree at Grandma's house.

"What do you think of New Hampshire so far?"

"What do I think about New Hampshire so far?" The memory snuffed out. His demeanor hardened. He leaned forward. "Fuck New Hampshire! That's what I think. Sure, Mainers are a little rough around the edges, not sophisticated like these stuff-shirts. But at least they're well-mannered, decent folk. They look at you in the eye when they speak to you. They listen to what you have to say. Not New Hampshire people. F#&%ing New Hampshire people don't f#$%@ing look at you in the f#@$ing eye when they're talking at you. They don't f#&%ing listen to a f#%@ing word you have to say, self-serving cowards, prickly sons of bitches. Well, they can all eat my shit."

Oh my.

"What do you all think about it?" His voice echoed through the dingy cell.

The eyes. The eyes. Look him in the eyes.

"Uh, well –"

"And that's cool if that's the game they want to play, f#@%ing preppies. I'll play the "F%#@ You!" game long as I know that's where we stand. I'll play it all day long. What's that BS motto they've got on their preppy little license plates? *Live free or die?* Yeah, I get it, New Hampshire. Well, I'll take the former and they can take the latter-and we'll call it f#@%ing even."

Anger management.

Zen meditation.

Penance.

Lithium.

Exorcism.

Something.

"So, there's my piece, boys. Sorry 'bout goin on like that. I can get a little worked up from time to time." He eased back in his seat. "But you see my point don't you?"

Futureman stood. "You know what? It's been a while since I called my mother. I should probably go call her. It's been nice talking to you though, Cool Breeze."

"Hey, that's a good idea," Cool Breeze said. "Real stand up of you. Let her know you're okay. She's probably worried sick about you. You know how mother's can get, God bless 'em."

Alone with the man, Applejack wished to avoid any topic that would induce another bipolar tirade. He chose one carefully.

"So. How is the snack shop upstairs?"

"Oh, you want to talk about the f%#@ing snack bar, eh?"

Oh no.

"Which part? The overpriced microwaved pies or the girl at the f#@%ing check out who won't f%#@ing look at you in the f%@#ing eye? But she sure didn't have a problem looking at my f#@%ing candy bar in the eye.

Now explain that."
Mommy?

Effective tourism is like a good contortionist act. Squeeze two hundred people into a souvenir shop no bigger than the average household kitchen and you've got yourself a real moneymaker. Applejack and Futureman wiggled their way through the building and out into the fresh air.

On the other side of the mountain, the crowds were thin.

They walked the ridgeline for miles, a pristine stretch long enough to assuage the disappointment of Mount Washington. The sun was overhead, high noon, a white-woven net of clear sky. Mizpah Hut was just ahead, a good place for shade and water, maybe some leftovers for lunch. Ah, the beggar's life – when you got nothing to gain, you got nothing to lose. Inside the hut, they met Rabbit, a thruhiker. He was sitting quietly, dipping pieces of bread into some lukewarm lentil soup.

IX

Rabbit was a satanic priest who worked with children. At least that's what he said. He wore black shorts and a cut-off-belly tank top. He had big eyes and buzzed hair like a marionette doll. He didn't look like a Satanist, but then again, what do Satanists look like? Like you or I, right?

"Uh, are you serious?" Futureman asked.

"No, I'm really a physical therapist. That was a joke." He produced a dry, indecipherable grin and jerked his chin slightly but distinctly to the left.

Rabbit wasn't really a devil-worshiper. His approach was much more direct. A fascination with the human body and an addiction to precision praxis had led him into the field of therapy. Before beginning the Trail, he had carefully compared and finally purchased the appropriate equipment – no more, no less – and completed all the recommended pre-hiking. He took the proper dosages of ibuprofen at the proper times. He even gave himself altitude rewards for positive reinforcement (one Jolly Rancher every thousand feet of elevation) and painstakingly recorded his progress. For Rabbit, life was an exact science. Even the girlfriend was scheduled in.

After 336.9 miles of hiking, Rabbit had effectively reduced his Trail life to an equation (X miles, Y variables). What he did not know was that he was about to enter the erratic, free-flowing flub of Applejack and Futureman – as manageable as a fart on the Oklahoma wind. It would be a mutually beneficial arrangement. Obviously, they needed some structure.

"Let's go." Rabbit pointed his nose southwest.

Mid-afternoon, they came across two middle-aged men heading toward Mizpah Hut. One of them was moving funny, arm clutched, teeth clenched.

Rabbit noticed. "What is the problem here?"

"I fell and I'm pretty sure my shoulder is dislocated," the man said. "I don't suppose you know if there's a doctor or somebody like that nearby?"

"Well, you're in luck. I am a physical therapist," Rabbit said.

Relief flooded the man. "Thank heavens!"

His partner relaxed.

"Let's have a look at it, sir." Rabbit inspected carefully. "Yep, it's dislocated all right. Pretty bad. You'll need to get some help right away."

The man giggled nervously through his pain.

Rabbit's expression didn't change.

He's not joking. He's serious.

"Well…can you pop it back in, please?" the man said.

"I'm afraid I can't do that. It's against procedure," Rabbit said.

"Procedure?"

"You are not one of my patients. I could be held liable."

"Liable? We're on a damn mountain! My arm is hanging in a sack of loose skin! I'm not gonna sue you. Please. I won't even ask your name."

"Sir, there is a hut a few miles ahead. They will get you the help you need. I suggest you head there immediately. Good luck." Rabbit continued on his way.

Applejack and Futureman shrugged sheepishly at the two men.

"Rabbit, why didn't you help that guy?" Futureman asked, catching up to him.

"I don't take chances when my job is on the line."

"Your job? But –"

Applejack punched Futureman and shook his head. *Let it go.*

Rabbit moved ahead with no regrets. They struggled to keep up.

It was late by the time they made it to Webster Cliffs. They hid their tents in a tuft of trees, just in time to see day and night waltz together beyond the granite walls of Zealand Ridge.

They rose before dawn and scissored their way down the cliffs, beginning yet another day's climb, back into the high mountains and hot sun. Another hut was perched beside the famous spill of Zealand Falls. Long and tiered, the falls decanter down several hundred yards of smooth rock, filling wide basins. Folks were scattered along the water's edge, splashing in the pools, picnicking in the sun.

The three of them climbed to the top to enjoy the natural springs and alpine spring-melt. They had the area to themselves.

"I could die happy right here, right now," Applejack said, resting his head on a rock.

"Yep," Futureman agreed.

Light wind. Contented silence.

"Tolstoy said: *If you want to be happy, then just be*," Rabbit offered.

Stale breath. Voice.

"Hm," Applejack said.

"Huh," Futureman said.

"Robert Louis Stevenson said: *There is no duty we so much underrate as the duty of being happy.*"

Polluted clouds. Acid rain.

"Mmmm…"

Third attempt: "*If you have to ask yourself if you're happy, then you cease to be so.* Anonymous, I think."

"Rabbit!" Applejack stood.

"Where – why are you leaving?" Rabbit asked.

"I had to *ask* myself," Applejack said. Shoving his feet into his boots, he stalked off down the Trail.

Rabbit called after him. "I was merely trying to point out –"

Futureman shot him a look. *Let it go.*

Rabbit was ready to get a move on. "To stay on schedule, we need to cross Lafayette by late afternoon," he informed the group. It was morning, sun barely visible. "At the base we will hitch into North Woodstock for a re-supply. Up and at 'em."

"What do you mean by *we*?" Applejack rubbed his eyes.

Futureman was still snoring.

Rabbit pulled them onto the trail with a promise to relax once they got to town.

On this southern side of the White Mountain chain, along the gnarled peaks of Little Haystack, Liberty and Lincoln, peace and solitude found room to breathe. Distant and difficult, these hills remained uninteresting to the crowds. Natural stone stairs stepped up the old granite toward the spiny crests. Large fields of lichen, fern tail and sedge covered the range, the soil rich with organic matter enough to support the larger root systems that were sustaining red maple and white pine. It was here that Futureman began to understand Bombadil's love for the Whites. *In these discarded peaks – unpublicized, unspoken of – this is where Bombadil got lost. His laughter is in the tops of the trees.*

There stood Mount Lafayette, lonely stepdaughter of the Whites. It falls short of Washington by a mere 114 feet but what it lacks in height, it makes up for in austerity. As the AT walks along this Franconia Range for several miles, black pitch crags and burn spots mark the frequency with which the mountains are struck by lightning.

They left Lafayette in the twilight, a blank canvas sky spread for sunset to paint. Over his shoulder, Futureman watched as the colors dripped down from the dusty firmament. Pink # 3. Red #7. Purple #4.

Before long, a beat-up Plymouth Reliant pulled over on the shoulder of the highway. When they rolled into North Woodstock, they found that a Christian music festival had taken over the town, packing the streets with an unusually high concentration of *Lord's Gym* T-shirt-wearers. Vendors lined the avenues, selling tools of the new evangelism trade: tie-dye Bibles, God-wear, *agape* bracelets, Testamints (sugar-coated scripture, get it? Testamints. Get it?), and signed posters of Christian rock stars.

They drove around for an hour looking for a vacancy. Their final stop was the *Last Resort Motel*. It wasn't clear whether the "No Vacancy" sign was off or just broken.

"In for the festival?" a smoky, over-fragranced woman asked, as Future-man came through the door.

"No, just need a room," Futureman said.

"Gotcha. It's ten an hour. How long you need it for?"

"No, you don't understand. Me and two friends are going to be staying for the night."

"Two friends? How exciting."

"No, we're hikers, just need a place to rest up."

"I'll give you a deal, sonny, this bein' your lucky day and all. One bed. Twenty bucks."

"No. Two beds. My friends are guys. I'm hiking with them."

"Your secret's safe with me, youngun."

"Can I have my key, please?"

She slapped the key on the counter. "Have fun. You need anything, you know where to find me."

"What's with the one bed?" Applejack asked, as the door swung open.

"Don't worry about it. I'll sleep on the floor."

Rabbit suggested a local seafood joint he'd seen a half-mile back. He had an itching for a cod sandwich. As usual, Applejack and Futureman made for the golden arches, three blocks down from the Last Resort.

"You can't go there," Rabbit objected.

"Why not?" Futureman asked.

"Because it's fast food."

"So."

"Fast food is the enemy," Rabbit said.

"No one's denying that," Futureman said.

"You guys aren't concerned about it?"

"There are a lot of things to be concerned about," Applejack said.

"Fast food buys bad meat from slaughterhouses who abuse immigrant workers."

"Welcome to capitalism."

"Fast food restaurants sell meat that has E. Coli in it."

"Accidents happen."

"They brainwash children with clowns and cute commercials."

"TV equals brainwashing, Rabbit."

"But it's making us fat and unhealthy. Obesity is a serious problem."

"True, but so is lack of exercise."

"Fast food stands for everything that is evil and corrupt. It stands for everything we should be against. You're hiking the Appalachian Trail for crying out loud!"

"So…does this mean you're not coming with us to McDonald's?"

Rabbit cocked his jaw and mumbled something about *freethinking* and *sacrifice* as he walked up the street to the local seafood chain, where he consumed a cod sandwich freshly unloaded off the same diesel truck that had been at the freight door of McDonald's a half hour earlier.

Later that night, leaned back against a studded leather headboard, Applejack watched reruns of *M.A.S.H.* The sky outside: dark and starless. The forecast: rain. During a commercial break, Applejack suggested a zero for the following day.

"No, I can't. I won't. Too much reward is a debilitating thing," said Rabbit.

"Too much routine is a debilitating thing."

"It's not on my calendar."

"I've got an eraser."

"The body will re-energize itself."

"Mine won't."

"We'll just sit and watch TV."

"We'll watch Discovery and National Geographic. And maybe a little VH1."

"You two will be the death of me."

X
"Call it not waste, that barren cone, above floral zone, where forests starve."
                    -Thoreau, describing Mount Moosilauke

A couple nights later the lightning finally came in. Not as cannons, but as a constant string of ladyfingers, painting their tents blue, a soothing crackle that hushed them to sleep.

Futureman woke in the early light to the sound of Rabbit scratching on the side of their tent. It was still raining. Rabbit unzipped the opening and poked his head through, soaking wet, dressed and ready to go.

"What, Rabb…" Futureman rolled over.

"Howp!" It was more a sound than a word.

"Huh?"

"Hawp!"

"What do you want?"

"Up and at 'em!"

"It's not even six yet. It's raining. We're sleeping."

"Got to get up now. Got to get hiking."

"Relax. There's plenty of time to get to Georgia," Futureman said.

"We're not going to Georgia today. We're going twenty miles past Glencliff, like we planned back in Woodstock to make up for the time we missed because of that zero."

"We're not on a plan, Rabbit. You know that."

He bounced on his calves. Thinking. "Okay. I'll meet you there tonight. If not, I had fun hiking with you guys. Goodbye." He zipped up the tent.

"Well, we ran off another one, Applejack."

Sleepy nonsense arose from Applejack's bag.

Futureman smiled. *I liked that guy.*

Countless northbounders had said to them, *The Trail is cake after Mt. Moosilauke. You'll be able to fly after you get out of the Whites.* But Applejack and Futureman were in no rush to leave the mountains. For those southbounders bent on finishing the Trail as fast as possible, Maine and New Hampshire had slowed their goals of 20 or 25 miles a day to 12, 15, maybe 17. To Applejack and Futureman, Moosilauke meant the end of one journey and the beginning of another. It was a final goodbye to the great northern woods. The last spire of lightning white earth.

At the base of the mountain, they ran into an old man hobbling along the path. He carried a carved walking stick.

"Looks like you boys are in a hurry," he said.

"We are," Futureman said.

"And we aren't." Applejack said.

"We're going over Moosilauke."

"Pretty excited about it."

"But we love the Whites."

"So we're also sad to leave."

"It's pretty fantastic."

The man smiled at the excitable young men finishing each other's sentences. "Yep, these peaks and trails...they got a way about them, don't they?" He dug his stick into the dirt. "Takes a good long while to figure 'em out. I been trying for years now. S'pose I never will. And that's okay, I guess." He walked on.

The north end of Moosilauke winds up a vertical path beside a waterfall. Applejack and Futureman peered up the natural ladder. A massive black cloud was coming together, piece by piece, above the barren cone.

Applejack pointed a pole at the peak like the Babe calling his shot. "This is it, Futureman, our last big mountain. For a long time, at least."

"To Moosilauke."

Applejack had been wishing for a clear day to cross it, to look out over the path behind, but somehow good weather just wouldn't have felt right.

The wind had already scattered Rabbit's tracks. Curious old foundations of stone ruins lay shattered in spots. Maybe old homesteads or fortresses. A vast field of wind blown grasses, sharp bladed and resilient, covered the dome. Dollops of rain fell horizontal in the wind, like marbles on their foreheads and knuckles.

They sat for a while between the rock walls. She seemed to have a gracious way about her, the mountain, in spite of the bleak goodbye coming down, bidding them to unburden themselves. Confess.

Applejack and Futureman shouted at the tops of their lungs into the deafening wind, words they wished not to carry with them anymore.

"I don't know as much as I let on!"

"I have secrets!"

"I'm a hypocrite!"

"I like to lie about things to make myself look better!"

"I doubt my faith!"

"I'm insecure. I pretend."

"I like REO Speedwagon!"

Descended over Moosilauke, they walked out of forest into a pastureland of rolling green hills, where the sky was clear blue and cattle were chewing their grasses in the sun. The bovines looked up at Applejack and Futureman, still soaked from the rain, shirts beginning to steam.

"Applejack, weren't we in the middle of a gigantic storm, like, ten minutes ago?"

"I think so."

The rhythm felt strange all of a sudden, timing off, one foot steady, the other hesitant. It was a new stride, one unwieldy and awkward. As though brand new.

XI

They came upon a country road, old and overgrown. A car probably hadn't come by since the Reagan era. Tall sugar maples lined the road. Poor-man's pepper and wild buckwheat grew on the banks and in the cracks of old concrete. A warbler was sifting through the trees. He sang a song about eating insects.

A sign staked into the ground said, *Hiker's Welcome Hostel. One-mile.*

"Should we?"

"Seems like a friendly road."

Hiker's Welcome was Pack Rat's place. He had fallen in love with all trails walkable years back. Inheriting the hostel from another hiker, he was glad to keep it in good use.

It was a barn, more or less. There was a huge fire pit in the back yard. Dozens of man-made tents created by the proprietor himself were pitched everywhere, tied to trees and strung between hiking poles. Bizarre designs built with ultra-light technology in mind – thinly woven fabric, no poles, no heavy-duty lining or fat zippers or pouches. A single element had directed the designer: keep it light. Rat had caught the fever of lightweight hiking back when he did the Pacific Crest Trail from Canada to Mexico.

Trade weight for wings.

Inside the barn, hiking equipment and all kinds of gadgets decorated the walls, personal designs and light gear prototypes collected from edgy Oregon companies, gear geeks and hiking exhibitions. Backpacks that turned into sleeping mats, biodegradable rain jackets – the future of the hiking world. Barely-there objects made innuendos, as Applejack and Futureman looked over them in wonder.

Whispers. "Take us." "We are light." "Lay your burdens down."

Maybe they're right, Applejack thought. *Maybe the world is too heavy, the burden too great. It doesn't have to be that way.*

Futureman stood in the afterglow of revelation. Always plagued by Nico's preposterous claims, he searched still for the infamous thirteen pounder. Perhaps here he had found opportunity, driven as Captain Ahab to his whale. *It is possible.*

"Take care of the ounces, and the pounds will take care of themselves."

"Why in the world am I carrying a candle lantern?"

"Bobby."

"We've got to get rid of everything we don't really need."

"Extra socks, knives, cooking utensils, bandage rolls."

"If we don't use it every day, then it goes."

"Pill bottles must be consolidated into one."

"Heavy plastic and anything glass has got to go."

"One pair of clothes to hike in, one to sleep in. No need for more."

"Make the switch."

"Save a pound, pitch the Nalgenes, use Gatorade bottles instead."

"Reggae was right."

"I don't need Listerine out here."

"I'm sending my sleeping bag home. It won't get cold this summer. I can carry a fleece liner." (Wrong)

"I'm cutting the handle off my toothbrush, a few more ounces. I don't use that part to clean my teeth anyway." (Right)

It took an hour to reduce their pack weight from forty pounds to twenty-seven.

Twenty-seven's still heavy. What else can I do without? Applejack wondered. Then it hit him. *It's in the pack itself.*

"What do I need with a frame anyway? That's why God gave me a spine. There's four less pounds, right there. But where can I find this gossamer creature? Durable yet light as a feather."

The answer called from the bunkroom wall. A small pack hung from a nail, the words *Wild Things* stitched on its shell.

Applejack lifted it off the nail. The unbearable lightness of being. Pack Rat had used it through the entire PCT. Frameless, designed for ice climbing, Wild Things weighed less than two pounds.

"I'm ordering a GoLite," Futureman said. "No frame. One pocket. Padless hip straps. It weighs under a pound. I read about it."

"It'll be *weighting* for you in Rutland, Vermont. Welcome to the future of hiking," The GoLite sales rep said on the phone.

"My little Moby, my Great Light Whale."

Shedding more of their worldly possessions, Applejack and Futureman were seized with liberation. Tomorrow they would pursue their first 20-mile day.

Futureman bounded ahead, light, fast, imagination in overdrive. Applejack followed at a distance, in step with reality, becoming acquainted with his lighter burden and the quicker pace that came with it. A benign wind blew through the trees. The path was rolling and soft. He noticed the easy sway of the paper birch, the stark aroma of the bergamot. A perfect wood. The birds had come out to sing.

"Jay! Jay!" A blue.

"Swall. Swill." An eastern gray.

"Twirp, tweep, tweep." A chickadee.

"Squeak. Squeak-a. Squeaka…squeaka…squeaka."

That's no bird. A lurching squeal echoed in his ear. He stopped. No sound. He started again. There it was again.

Squeaka…squeaka…squeaka.

"You gotta be kidding me. Dadgummit! It's this new pack."

Futureman walked effortlessly. Trillium debris and hemlock seeds had been stirred by the wind and were floating like plankton schools in the understory. *I'm hiking on a coral reef in the highest ocean in the world. Is there anything better than this?* Neutrally buoyant, Futureman drifted along. The weightlessness was nice, oh so nice.

Applejack pounded against the path, fighting hard to boot the squeak out of his psyche. It grew louder with every step. By the time he caught up with Futureman, a gargoyle had perched itself on his shoulders.

"Futureman, I'm about to go insane!"

"Why? It's like a dream out here."

"Wild Things is squeaking, and I can't take it anymore!"

"Wild things? What are you talking – ah, the pack. Squeaking?"

"In my ear!"

"Rubbing a little? C'mon, all packs do that."

"No, it's like there's a wet swamp lemur giving birth right inside my ear. I've tried everything. It won't stop."

"Did you try –?"

"I tried everything! It's so bad that a mile back I even thought about…"

"Dude…you didn't."

Quitting is the word you never say. You can complain and cry and moan. You can curse the woods, pout and stomp through the forest, denigrate esteemed Trail personages, shout profanities at the sky, eat your own arm, but never are you ever to mention the word Q-U-I-T.

"Put it on! See for yourself."

Futureman tried it out. *Mm, this is comfortable, yeah I hear something, a little squeak, not so bad, just a…oh gosh.* An off-key dissonant retch of a sound, the noise of wet Styrofoam rubbing together, begged the hairs on the back of his neck to opt for suicide.

"You're right. It's bad."

"Can't you do something about it?" Applejack whined.

Futureman wedged a scrap of cloth around the foam. "There. All better."

Applejack started walking. It had worked. Wild Things was satisfied. Applejack could hear the birds again.

Their first twenty ended on Smarts Mountain. There, a fire tower climbed high above the canopy. The perfect spot to watch the sun set the red pine forest on fire. That night, a cold nor'easter blew through the valley. The thimbleberry pulled inward while the jack pines opened parcels to collect the cold.

Applejack shook inside his thin fleece liner, a warning from the past rattling in between his teeth. *You just never know about the Appalachians. Winter can sneak up on even the hottest summer day.* His gamble was already proving to be costly. Cold and shivering, he dreamed of walking on that long golden trail back to Zealand Falls to sit in streams still glistening in the sun. Those pools would do just fine to keep him warm. If only he could sleep long enough to get there.

XII

Applejack sat up in the thin light, still shivering, muttering about nature's cruel love affair with punishment and humiliation.

"So, today we go to Hanover," Futureman said.

Applejack brightened. "There will be warm water in Hanover."

From Velvet Rocks, they peered down on the bustling town. Cute cafes and wooden shops lined the pristine streets. Dartmouth University sat at the center of town, a palace. First things first, they went to the post office to pick up Bobby's latest garlic-infested care package.

Back in Glencliff, Applejack and Futureman had informed Bobby that they wanted to replace Futureman's tent with individual bivy sacks. Bobby rejected the idea outright. "You guys are making a foolish decision. What difference is one pound going to make?"

"All the difference!"

Bobby reluctantly engaged in some research and found what he claimed to be the best bivy sack he had ever seen. He sent two of them and a new pair of Garmont trekking shoes to Hanover. Applejack's Montrail boots had blown a gasket under the strain of the first five hundred miles. He opted for lighter trail shoes this time. *Weight on your feet is still weight.*

Outside the P.O, they met an interesting little family. They were thruhikers, all of them: father, mother, a little boy and a little girl. They'd come all the way from Georgia, home schooling the children along the way.

Applejack was in disbelief. *What sort of nuclear unit is this?*

Futureman bent down to talk with the children. *Cascade* was almost eight. *Speedracer* was ten.

"Why is your name Futureman?" Cascade asked him.

"Because I'm from the future."

"Nuh-uh, not really."

"So what's in the future, Mister Futureman?" Speedracer demanded.

"That's a good question. Let's see. For starters everything floats. Cars, restaurants, people, pets."

"That's not true," Speedracer said.

"I tell you, it is."

"What else? What else is in the future?" Cascade danced up and down.

"Dinosaurs," Futureman said.

"Dinosaurs?" Cascade crinkled her little eyebrows.

"How in the world are there dinosaurs?" Speedracer asked.

"That too is a good question. See what happened is – millions of years ago when dinosaurs roamed the earth, there were also mosquitoes. Some of the mosquitoes bit the dinosaurs and then some of those landed on trees and got caught in the sap." The kids stared blankly at Futureman. "The sap preserved them. Future scientists found some of those mosquitoes and extracted their blood and...BINGO! Dino DNA."

Cascade and Speedracer giggled.

"You don't believe me?"

"That's from *Jurassic Park*, silly," Speedracer said.

"But it was a good story. You're funny." Cascade patted him on the shoulder. The fuzzy man melted. They waved goodbye.

There is hope for the family yet.

It didn't take long to sniff out free lodging. Nearly every hiker in town had collected at the only Dartmouth fraternity house still hospitable to hikers. During an earlier, more open-minded age, many fraternities opened their doors to the voluntarily homeless, but legend held that one careless hiker had ruined it for everyone by starting a fire. Now all frat houses were closed, but for one. The Panarchy.

A number of flower power types were gathered on the lawn, lounging under the spruces. Hikers napping in the sun and throwing frisbee with their sheep dogs. Hikers jumping on the trampoline in their underwear. Hikers playing guitars and banging tribal drums. Applejack and Futureman dumped their new equipment onto the grass, excited about trying out their newest lightweight innovations.

Applejack stepped into his Garmont shoes. They were too small.

"Awesome."

Futureman climbed into the best bivy sack Bobby had ever seen and within minutes was suffocating inside a smothering cocoon of black plastic.

"Fantastic."

They were glum, Applejack shoeless, both tentless. They considered the consequences, the miserable nights and days they would be spending in the near future, and they had to laugh. Applejack threw his shoe and dove into his asphyxiation sac. Together they rolled around on the lawn like birthing larvae, unable to resist the heathen revelry of the flower children.

XIII

Pizza gets on the brain sometimes.

A table of northbound thruhikers had collected in the corner of a local pizza joint when Applejack and Futureman walked in. One of them motioned an invitation. He was wearing a "mountain kilt," a clever term devised by Marmot, Mountain Hardware and a handful of other gear companies forward-thinking enough to market the garment to a sexually confused generation. Masculine yet sensitive, the mountain kilt connotes Anglo freedom and daring self-expression for the gender-bending hiker, the perfect compromise for the metro sexual outdoorsman.

The wearer introduced himself as *Valley Girl*. He grinned beneath a yellow Shirley Temple haystack of macaroni hair and pulled up two chairs to make the count nine.

"You guys are Sobos, aren't you?"

"Yep. Y'all heading north?"

"You know it. Ka.Tah.Din." He karate chopped each syllable as though it were a Swahili word.

Valley Girl was the spokesman. The other Nobos were happy to let him do the talking. A tight bunch. They had done a lot of grinding together. Fast approaching the two thousand mile mark, they were inherently leery of Southbounders. A few hundred miles didn't necessarily demand respect. But Applejack and Futureman hadn't met a Northbounder yet who wasn't at least a little anxious about the ranges of New Hampshire and Maine.

They introduced themselves. *Zen Master. 7 Layer Burrito. Biphph. Rich Man/Poor Man. The Real McCoy.*

"What's your name?" Futureman nodded at the stringy surly one who wasn't talking.

"Uh, he's the *Big Lebowski*." Valley Girl jumped back in before the silence got too loud. "So, what do you think so far?" He uncrossed his legs and leaned up to the table.

"Seems like a nice place but I haven't tried the menu yet," Futureman said.

Nobody laughed.

"It's been good. You guys are going to love it." Applejack compensated.

"But it's real, real hard. Hopefully, some of you might make it." Joke number two. Nothing. "Boy. You guys are serious."

"Not really," Real McCoy said.

"You're just not funny." Lebowski lit a cigarette.

Futureman placed an order for a large supreme.

"Hey, have you guys run into Baltimore Jack anywhere?" Applejack asked. Baltimore Jack was legendary on the Trail, known for his penchant for perennial thru-hikes. His fabled deeds moved up and down the Trail like poison ivy, stories of beer and brothels, beggars and bears – the sort of tales that grow in gossip until they become immortal. Applejack wanted to know if any of them were true. Rumor had it, Jack lived in Hanover.

"Sure did. Some of us hiked with him. He's a cool guy, that Jack," Biphph.

"He's a wild man. I liked him but wouldn't want to hang with him for long."

"He lives here, right?"

"Does he?"

"Yeah, I think so. Does some kind of work commune in the winter and then goes back out on the Trail in the spring."

"Hasn't he done the Trail like twelve straight times or something?"

"It's not that many."

"Still, I gotta hand it to him. That is amazing." Zen Master said.

"I don't see what's so amazing about it," Futureman said, cheese in his beard.

Everyone looked at him.

"I mean, in all the world – among everything else there is to do – why repeat this one thing over and over. Seems a little boring, that's all."

Lebowski shot him a look: *You haven't done it once yet, you rookie.*

"Doesn't Bryson live here too?" Applejack asked. The Nobos shifted uneasily, staring down at shoe tops. Lebowski perked up.

Valley Girl tried to head him off. "So where are you guys –" It was too late.

"Did you say Bryson? Bill *Shithead* Bryson?" Lebowski asked, anger rising.

"He a friend of yours?" Applejack asked.

"He's no friend of any thruhiker." There were levels here. Applejack had pushed a button. "Bill Bryson doesn't know a thing about this Trail."

"Do we have to get into this again?" Valley Girl whined, wishing always for happy-go-lucky. Heavy debating hurt his sunshine soul.

"No, we don't. It's just that the very sound of his name disgusts me. I'm sick of hearing about that piece-of-crap book that he sold to the whole country. How that clown could ever think that he had anything to say about the AT is an absolute freaking mystery." The book in question was the runaway national bestseller *A Walk In The Woods.*

"Simmer down, Lebowski. Be the Dude that you are," Valley Girl said.

"No really. It's alright. I want to hear this." Applejack was intrigued.

The Nobos rolled their eyes. They had heard Lebowski's speech fifty too many times.

"He hates Bryson because he only hiked a third of the Trail and then wrote a bestseller about it," Biphph said. "I personally don't think it's a big deal."

"It's a big deal because he didn't tell the truth about it," Lebowski said.

"What do you mean by that? I thought he made it pretty plain about what he hiked and didn't hike. He never claimed to be a thruhiker," Applejack said.

"It's not just that. He made it sound so dangerous and alluring like ferocious bears are running around everywhere, people always needing to be rescued from the bloodthirsty wilderness. It's not a trip through the Congo. It's just a Trail. When was the last time that you were miles and miles away from civilization out here?" Lebowski jammed his cigarette into the ashtray and lit another.

"Maine." Applejack nodded slowly. "Honestly, there will be times when you don't see a road or hear a plane for days. It's a lot more remote than anywhere else on the eastern seaboard. It's not like the south."

Lebowski didn't like that answer. He glared, waiting for more.

"Besides, what's so bad about overdoing a story a little bit? Doesn't every good storyteller? Hemingway did it. Jack London did it. I'm not saying that Bryson is in the same league as those guys, but I thought the book was pretty good."

Lebowski pressed his hand onto the table, slowly turning his knuckles white. "What's so bad about it is that now this Trail is swamped because of that guy. Sure he might be able to spin a good yarn but who's not going to wanna rush out and conquer the world after reading that kind of crap? You should have been down south with us when a couple thousand other heroes were leaving from Springer. The whole approach trail is covered with trash and gear that those starry-eyed losers were too lazy and wasted to pack out. We didn't have a shelter to ourselves until we got halfway through Virginia. But you wouldn't know anything about that. It's like that freaking kids crusade in the Middle Ages."

"Man, all that's behind us now." Zen Master was tired of the rhetoric.

"And another thing. Did you ever look at that sentence on the front of his cover? Some clueless critic from the *New York Times* wrote it. Did you ever read it?"

"I don't think I've noticed it, no."

"Prepare to have your mind blown. Hang on. I've got it here. Just – a second." He pulled out his plastic wallet. He had clipped the quote and carried it around for fodder.

"As you can see, Lebowski feels quite strongly about this," Biphph said.

"I'm not the only one. Here it is. Get this. 'The best way of escaping into nature is to read a book like *A Walk in the Woods*' says Christopher Lehmann-Haupt of the New York Times. Can you even – I'm stupefied. It leaves me utterly speechless every time. There are so many things wrong with that statement. It's ridiculous in every conceivable way." Lebowski's discourse was beginning to attract attention from the other tables. "That just says it all, doesn't it? I mean do I even have to go on?"

"Let me see that." Applejack took the scrap of paper. It appeared to be a photocopy right off the cover of the book. "Hmm."

"Let that sink in, buddy. Let it fill your innermost being with the crushing weight of its meaninglessness. The best way of escaping into nature – is to read a book. Did everybody get that? Don't chase mountaintops. Don't dive the giant coral reefs of the world. Don't even bother going for a weekend camping trip in the family pop-up. Read *A Walk in the* effing *Woods!*"

"Well then!" Valley Girl said. "Everyone done with their pizza? What do you say we go find us some crazy Dartmouth party action?"

Lebowski retired to the Panarchy with his worn copy of Rousseau's *Social Contract*, leaving the eight of them to survey the palace streets. The town was in the wind-up stage before fall semester. The Greek houses were largely empty, waiting for the collegiate sustenance of clamor and bombast and beer to fill it. But signs of life were signaling from two houses at the end of the street.

"Stay here. I'll get us in." Valley Girl tapped each fence post softly as he sauntered up to the door and slipped inside. Two minutes later three gentlemen in suit coats escorted him back out.

"I know when I'm not wanted," Valley Girl lilted. He crossed the street toward the Pike house. Light was coming from the basement.

"Anyone who wants to go to a keg party, follow me."

They walked into the Neo-classical foyer, down the grand staircase and into the basement where the light was coming from. They paused in the hall. There was no party, no music, no noise at all except the monotonous journey of a ping-pong ball. Valley Girl, who by this point had taken off his shirt, peered around the corner to see who was playing.

Two guys were hitting the ball back and forth. Each one had an open can of Natural Ice sitting on his side of the table. They weren't really playing. They weren't even talking, just standing there getting slowly, quietly loaded, minding their own business, hitting the ball back and forth, frayed Pike hats cocked back on their heads. They were probably sophomores. Old enough to be there, young enough to think they could get the best rooms if they were the first ones back. Valley Girl glided into the room in his skirt.

"Hello there, gentlemen. Having a back-to-school party I see."

"What do you think you're doing? Who are you?" This one had some weight on him and a strong sense of entitlement.

"Oh, I just smelled some party action down here, and I wanted to get in on it." The beefy frat boys were more than a little uncomfortable with his tone as he strutted around the table, his fingertips lightly grazing the net. "I guess I should say *WE* wanted to get in on it." Everyone else streamed into the room.

"Where's the beer?" Rich Man said.

"Get me one," said Val.

"Let's get some music going in here. This is boring," Biphph said, plopping down in somebody's Lazy Boy.

"I got winner." 7 Layer Burrito grabbed a paddle off the floor. The frat guys reacted strongly to her. She was by far the most perversely unclean female they had ever seen, dirty even by thruhiker standards. That was her gimmick.

The fratters retreated to an out of the way place by the wall. What else could they do but ignore what was going on? Sometimes that's the only way to deal with nuisance. Wait and hope. What they didn't know is that their problem wasn't going away anytime soon. Almost without exception, thruhikers exhibit two distinct characteristics in varying degrees of concentration: narcissism and perseverance. Both qualities tend to be manifested in the extreme. First of all, someone who would put all of his relationships on hold, suspend all obligations, temporarily (or permanently) forsake responsibility of every kind and make his or her mother cry is not going to care if others deem his course of action to be inappropriate, rude or otherwise. Secondly, someone who would walk two thousand miles for the yell of it is not going to be out-lasted or out-waited by a fraternity boy. Fifth-grade bullies might go away when ignored, but Zen Masters and Burritos never do.

"Do they have any Foreigner or Journey or anything like that?"

"Nope."

"What about Melvins or Pantera? Something along those lines."

"Uh-uh."

"Tony Bennet?"

"Yeah, right."

"Spyro Gyra?"

"I'm looking but I don't really see anything worth listening to. They've got a boat-load of Dave Matthews and ska." The Real McCoy was taking CD's out of the rack, opening them, tossing them onto the couch.

"This is piss-beer. Agck." Valley Girl set down his fresh can of Natural Ice onto a dusty pile of *Maxim* and *Stuff* magazines.

Applejack and Futureman were standing by the back stairwell. Applejack, with moderate levels of both perseverance and narcissism, tended toward quieter settings where he could reflect inwardly for long periods of time. Futureman was the anomaly. His narcissism reading barely bumped the needle and perseverance, in his case, was intensely case-specific. At that moment he had no interest in bothering anyone.

"Us southbounders don't normally go for this sort of thing," Futureman said.

"No. We're too pensive and sullen," Applejack replied.

"Let's go back to the Panarchy House and read some poetry."

"Let's go back and write some poetry."

They slipped out the door and into the confusing, New Hampshire night air.

XIV

It was pitch black in the tiny concrete Panarchy basement, where thruhikers slept. Applejack's bladder was about to burst. The exit sign cast an eerie red glow over the windowless room. Contorted, heavy-breathing bodies filled every vacant inch of mattress, cot and floor.

The August sun was pitched at mid morning. The noises of the busy town bombarded his ears. Barely concealing himself behind an elephant plant, he evacuated his kidneys and mumbled a tentative itinerary for the day. "Eat large breakfast. Get to outfitter. Eat lunch. See movie. Eat first supper. Take nap on trampoline. Eat second supper. Plot communist insurrection. Go to bed early."

"What was that about communism?" A familiar voice sounded behind him. "Nico! Hey, man. You made it out of Maine. Good to see you."

"You a commie or somethin?"

"Naw, I'm not a commie. Just beef-witting to myself in the morning, you know."

"I was just yankin ya chain. Ya into that shit, right?" Nico punched Applejack on the shoulder. A good joke to use on homosexuals. He'd been waiting to use it. He still thought Applejack and Futureman were lovers.

"Where did you stay last night?" Applejack asked.

"I just got heah."

"What do you mean? It's like nine in the morning." Applejack pulled a tangle out of his beard.

"Well, I was sittin' in this bar in Littleton round midnight, drinkin' and –"

"Wait. What do you mean you were in a bar in Littleton? Littleton is nowhere near here."

"Hey, what's with all the questions? Youse is a little testy. You and Futureman have a fight or somethin? I hitched to Littleton from Webster, and –"

"Nico. Webster Cliffs? Littleton? Dude, you're a hard-core purist. You skipped tons of Trail."

"I got lost comin offa Webstuh Cliffs, okay. I took a wrong turn and came out in the middle of nowhere. I was devastated. I sat down on the road and started cryin, you believe that? Me – Mr. Army – cryin. Then this dude comes by in his pick-up and gives me a ride to Littleton. So, I'm in the bar beside this chick and she's smokin and blabbin, and all of a sudden she starts quotin all this eastern meditation monk philosophy shit, all night she's talkin this stuff, and I don't know, bro, somethin happened. Like nirvana and one-ness and shit. I got this new perspective. I'm seein it all different now."

"Let me get this straight. You're saying that you've been cured from purist hiking by eastern philosophy that you learned from a girl who picked you up in a bar in Littleton?"

"Somethin like that. Anyway, youse is lookin at the new Nico. I'm not a thruhiker no more. I'm a journeyman now. No boundaries. Just open road."

Applejack ran his hair back. "Alright, man. That's your call."

Hanover was blooming. Capitalism flowered in every direction. Members of the upper crust towered above them: businesswomen, doctors of paleontology, cardiologists on vacation, brokers out for lunch. They stood high – twenty-eight, twenty-two, twenty-four feet tall. Applejack and Futureman scurried between the gigantic shoes, trying not to get squashed, listening to the fray of voices.

"Buy." "Sell." "Your future is now." "Welcome." "Welcome." "Why I'm the President of Dartmouth!" "Of course." "Of course." "It makes perfect sense." "Classes are not cheap." "You have to buy them." "Education isn't free, you know." "You'll want to sell them as soon as you can." "Buy." "Sell." "Your future is waiting." "Have you given any thought to what your epitaph will say?" "What's wrong?" "Well, let me check my schedule." "I'm filled up for the next indefinite time period." "My money is cheap, but my time isn't." "That was a joke." "Hum, hum, hum." "Uh huh." "That's too many days for you to count." "Yes." "Yes." "You need an education." "It isn't free, you know." "You have got to try those boysenberry muffins at the kitschy café across the street." "They will just kill you." "You will die." "Seriously, have you given any thought to what your epitaph will say?" "It is important for your future." "Buy." "Sell." "We're counting on you."

Futureman felt dizzy. *I'm going crazy. Am I going crazy? What am I not understanding? Are they crazy? Who's crazy here?*

"It's Sunday morning," Applejack said.

"Huh? Cool, let's do it."

"Do what? What are you talking about?"

"But first I need to buy something."

"Are you okay?" Applejack asked, a little concerned.

"All this commerce is making me crazy. I don't know. I have to buy something. Cotton! You miss cotton? I miss cotton. I'm gonna buy me some cotton underwear."

"What in the world, Futureman?"

"From the GAP, yes, from the GAP."

Applejack stepped aside. "By all means."

Futureman brought a stink cloud with him into the GAP. As the clerk approached him her sales enthusiasm shifted to caution.

"May I help you?"

"Underwear," Futureman grunted.

The saleslady snorted, trying to conceal it. Her eyes began to water. "Follow me please. Our collection is this way."

Bananas. Hot chilies. Green. Yellow. Stars. Stop Signs. Martinis. Black. White. Bikini. Boxer brief. Tight. Loose.

$19.99. $14.99. $9.99.

"I just need one pair of cheap cotton underwear."

"Well, we have a pack of three-in-one on special for $8.99. An excellent deal. Our cheapest single pair is $9.99, I'm afraid."

"I'm not afraid. One pair will do."

Jenny was blowing bubbles at the cash register, playing with her belly button jewel, when Futureman materialized in front of her like a burp. She wore a breast enhancer flower blouse and low cut jeans that accentuated her tanned potbelly.

Stunned, "Oh my gosh. Uh, thank you/for the GAP. Will that/find/you all?"

"I'm reckon so, darlin. I wouldn't have to buy this pair, but my underwear goes through a lot of wear and tear, you know what I mean?"

Jenny folded her mouth in. Her bottom lip reached for her nose, "That'll be/um/ten six-ixty. Ten sixty-two, please."

Futureman laid two fives and a one on the countertop. "Sorry. Money's still a little wet from the last few days. Plastic bag doesn't keep all the water out. You can keep the change."

"Th/aaaaa/nks?"

"Say, you got a changin' room I could use so as to get into these new skivvies?"

"Cert/sir/Sure," she said.

Applejack watched through the window, laughing.

"You know you're gonna have to throw those away once we hike out of here. They're useless out in the woods," Applejack said as Futureman exited.

"Yes. But I'm wearin 'em now, and as far as we know, now's all there is."

XV

The sign promised that the bus came at 12:55. It was 12:50.

Fifteen minutes passed, but no buses did.

They were sitting on the bench under the Public Transit sign. They need-ed to get to the Eastern Mountain Sports store in West Lebanon to rectify their poor equipment decisions. New bivvies. A lightweight, summer bag. New shoes.

"Bus should've been here by now," Applejack said.

Futureman read back over the sign with a defeated smile. "It doesn't come on the weekends."

"I guess we'll have to find another way to the outfitter."

"We can walk. It can't be that far."

"I think it's about ten miles. This is our day off. I'm not really in the mood."

"How do you suggest we get there, then? These yuppie wagons aren't going to pull over for us," Futureman said.

At just that moment, a silver Baxter Porsche convertible pulled up beside them. The driver slid his sunglasses down and said, "Name's Mark. You guys look like you need a ride to the EMS."

Futureman stared at his reflection on the hood.

Applejack went to the curb. "Are you serious?"

He pointed at the leather passenger seat. "Hope you don't mind the seat-ing arrangement – these damn convertibles. You guys will have to squeeze in."

Applejack smiled weakly at Futureman. "Shotgun."

The Porsche purred over the asphalt. The wind rushed. Futureman sat pressed against the door, mouth open, head above the windshield. His resem-blance to a slobbering golden retriever was uncanny.

The generosity just kept coming for Applejack and Futureman. That evening Mark offered to treat the always-hungry men to dinner at the five-star Hanover Inn.

Waiting for a table in the lounge, he called the bartender over. "You see these two guys? They're thruhikers. Walked over five hundred miles from northern Maine to get here – and now they're going for Georgia, another fif-teen hundred miles!"

The barman rubbed down a glass. "Why would they do something like that?"

"To strike out for new territory. To be free." Mark said, getting worked up. "To leave behind the worries of fast-paced life."

"If you're so excited about it, why don't you go do it?" he said stoically.

Outside on the patio, "Bottle of shiraz. Calamari. Crab cakes and some smoked salmon for starters. We will be taking our time, tonight. Thank you." Mark had done this before. Plenty.

"Maybe that guy is right, Mark. Why *don't* you hike the Trail?" Futureman asked.

"I tried. Have a trail name and everything. *Serendipity.* I'm one of those who left from Springer last March and didn't get very far."

"Why not?"

"I've been trying to figure that out," Mark said.

The wine arrived. Mark sipped and nodded. The waiter disappeared again.

"Enough about me. I want to know what the Trail means to you."

"A lot of things, Mark." Applejack said. "It's been a dream of mine ever since I was a kid. Adventure and all. After college, I began to wonder if it wouldn't be selfish to take six months out of my life and walk away from everything. Then I started to feel this need for solitude and silence. Time to get to know God better. So that's why I'm out here on the Trail, I guess. At least that's the ideal. The childhood dreams never really go away. Plus, I love the woods. Time to write, to sit by streams, meet interesting people, get a feel for New England. I could go on."

"Interesting. So, what god are you referring to? There's so many these days," Mark said.

"The God of Scripture, the Bible. The New Testament speaks of his son, Jesus, as the same God," Applejack held his glass up to the light. *Truth Serum.*

"Ah. And you, Futureman, how did you get here?"

"Complete whimsy, if we're being honest. Guess I'm piggybacking on Applejack's dream but I've wanted simplicity in my life for a while, too. Connectedness with creation, serious prayer. The Trail seemed like a good place for those things."

"So have you learned about *prayer* by being in creation?"

"Beginning to. It's a slow process, though. Didn't Einstein say something like, *Look deep into nature and you understand everything better?* I think he's right. There's this rhythm to the woods, a complex sort of order. When I'm in it, I begin to see how my own existence fits into that bigger design and prayer starts to seep in naturally. Sometimes, I just find myself praying – without even really meaning to. The hard part is coming back into the so-called real world. I start to lose the sense that things are woven together. Maybe, the noise drowns it out."

The attentive young waiter was back. Mark waved him away.

"I've spent my entire life in that so-called real world," Mark said, "working and posturing and plotting my way to the top. And I have had some considerable victories in that world. I even owned a successful graphics design company in New York. But giving some thought to my place in the grander scheme of things, I became tired – even apathetic towards it. I do believe in a creator, I think. Supreme design. But I've never had reason to believe that it is close or that it – he – wants to have anything to do with me."

"So why are you here in Hanover, picking up dirty hikers and taking them out to dinner?" Applejack asked.

"I read about it one day and decided to sell my company – no regrets. I left the big city and headed to Georgia. Then, next thing I know – three weeks in – I'm calling it quits." Mark looked around, up into the hazy night sky. "Hell. I don't have anything to lose. No wife. Fell in love once, long ago. Don't have any children. But I've got time and money. So, since I quit the Trail down south, I've spent the last few weeks driving her up and down. And I keep my hiking things close." Mark hailed the waiter and ordered for all three of them off the French menu.

Applejack looked at the man across the table from him. He was polished, accomplished but no more content than anyone else – this was the side of Mark he could understand. "Mark, I've found that it takes some time out here to be de-programmed, you know. But after you settle in and start to really seek God, your place in this world sort of comes into a fuller focus. See, I think God does want to interact with people. Scripture is full of such stories. That's what God does. He calls out to them."

"Well, I don't know that I'm any more sure of things than I was, but I don't think it's coincidence that I ran into you guys." He smiled and held up his glass.

After watching Applejack and Futureman ingest several courses of salad and filet mignon and swordfish and alfredo and French bread and silk pie, Mark said:

"Is there anything else I can do for you guys?"

"You've done enough," Futureman said, mouth full of chocolate mush.

"Actually, Mark," Applejack put down his fork. "There is."

"What?" Mark said eagerly. "You name it."

"Why don't you pack up your gear and hike out with us tomorrow morning."

Mark leaned back in his chair, began turning a bread knife over in his hand.

Nico was standing in the yard when they waddled onto the Panarchy lawn.

"Yo. Heard about your luck. Got yourselves a sugar daddy, huh?" Word travels fast on the Trail. "Silver Porsche, five-star dinner. Musta been a good time."

"What are you saying, Nico?"

"I'm sayin' that if I was like you, I'd be into it too. That's all."

"Nico, we're not gay," Applejack said, in no mood for games.

"Hey, I said it was cool with me. I don't care. I'm a journeyman. I know every man has his own path –"

"Futureman and I are good friends. We go way back, Nico. You're assuming we're gay because we respect women and don't try to hump everything like the animals do."

The tough New Yorker feigned offense. "Why ya gotta cut it like that, bro?"

"Nico, Mark didn't come on to us. In fact, he didn't say a word about sex. He may be gay. He may not. I have no idea because it didn't come up. He's a good man and he needed someone to talk to. And that's all."

His mouth hung open, this time truly hurt. "Yeah. You're right. Sorry. Sorry that –"

"Nico, It's OK. Too much wine, maybe. Good night."

Mark was out on the street early. The digital thermometer on the Hanover Bank marquis already read ninety degrees. It was eight fifteen AM.

"I didn't hardly sleep at all last night," he chuckled. "Guess I'm kinda nervous."

"That's alright," Applejack said. "I'm always a little nervous when I leave the city. Never know what's gonna happen."

Mark fell in with their pace. Futureman noticed that his gear had some wear on it. They were determined not to insult him by coddling through miles but it wasn't going to be an easy day. There was a long road walk to the trailhead. Heat rose in waves off the black tar surface.

"This is a pretty big day for you two," Mark said.

"Why do you say that?"

"You're passing into your third state."

They hadn't realized it. "Wow, you're right."

"Two down and twelve to go," Mark said as they crossed the historic bridge over the Connecticut River.

It was over one hundred degrees outside. Applejack and Futureman staggered up to a country deli on the side of the road. They had come ten miles through the easternmost forest on the Vermont trail and were now on the outskirts of the tiny town of South Pomfret. The store had appeared just in time. Even underneath the forest-blanket it was virtually unbearable. No wind penetrated the trees. Even the animals had disappeared, searching for mercy.

Applejack drenched himself with the garden hose on the side of the building. Futureman pushed the door open. A cowbell rang above him.

"Quite a day out there," the deli owner said, standing in front of an old metal fan.

Futureman slopped down onto one of the spinning stools that lined the sandwich counter. "Yessir. A real inferno."

"You better get used to it. It's supposed to stay around a hundred for the next week. And dry as a desert, too." The man poured Futureman a tall glass of water.

"Thanks."

Applejack came in, leaving a network of channels and lakes on the floor behind him. The heat had driven away his hunger. He drained three large orange drinks one after the other. Perhaps, more was going on inside him than simple dehydration.

"I hope Mark's OK. I'm starting to feel like we shouldn't have left him," Futureman said.

"He's a big boy. He'll be along soon."

Two hours. The cowbell rattled again. He wouldn't have looked any better if he had gone fifteen rounds with Joe Frazier. Mark dragged his body over and collapsed on a stool.

"I'm done. No more. No more. I'm done." He dropped his arms to his sides and dive-bombed a thousand pounds of throbbing head onto the counter.

"You alright, buddy?"

Mark was barely lucid. "Give me a few minutes," he said to the counter.

An hour later, the exhausted man came to. "I really had a fun time today." He took a slow breath. "But I think I need to go back to the Inn. I'm going to call a taxi and go back to the Inn...I need to go back to the Inn." Again, he lowered his head.

"That's probably the best thing." At least that's what Applejack said aloud, but as the yellow cab pulled away, he was grieved, feeling in some perverse way that he had failed himself. There was a part of him that identified with this desperate man – or wanted to. Mark had reached a place in his life where he was impoverished. Not outwardly, but in his spirit. He was hungry for something and he knew it.

Mark was honest about who he was and was not. Applejack envied that.

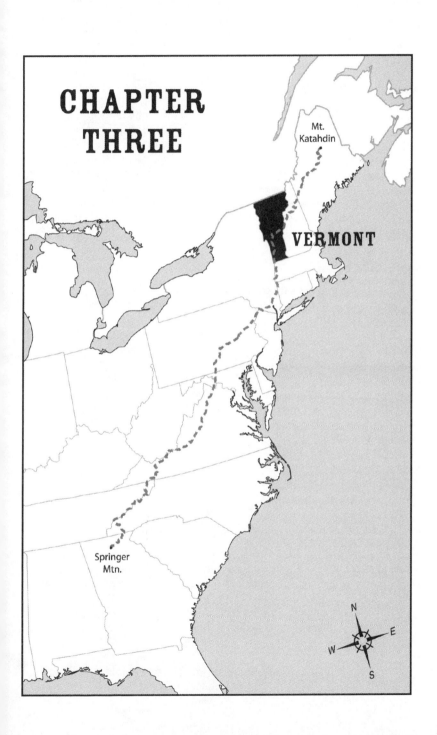

CHAPTER
THREE

Mt.
Katahdin

VERMONT

Springer
Mtn.

N
E
W
S

Hell just posted the ten day forecast. No relief in sight. Only a train of end-less days, soldered together like Aztecan chains and stretching before them across the rolling Vermont countryside. An anachronism? A dangling modi-fier? Somehow, it had slipped in, between the shallow breaths of their latest fallen compatriot. Now, in this new moment of weakness, they were being shadowed by a new companion, this one cunning and insidious as a virus. The system was compromised...but there was a counteragent. In ignorance they blundered ahead, unaware that crosses were falling out of the pale Ver-mont sky.

I

"We might as well suck it up. The sun's gonna be after us for a long time."

"It's too hot for this stuff, too hot out here. Something's wrong. I can feel it," Applejack said.

For a mile or so, the trail borrowed another country road beside a river before crossing a bridge. A rope hung from its underbelly. Carefree Vermont children were swinging on it.

"Last one there's a stupidhead," Futureman said, already shirtless.

"I'm fine with stupidhead. I just wanna sit," Applejack said.

The children celebrated as they heard the sound of Futureman's pasty angloid skin smacking against the water. They laughed when he emerged beet red and groaning.

"Come on down, buddy. Water's nice and cool. Might wash away your sins," Futureman grinned. Washing of sins was pushing it a bit. Applejack would settle for a cool-down.

Eventually the kids got bored with the rope. They wanted more.

"You want me to jump off the bridge? You kidding? From way up there? Not a chance. No way." Applejack said.

His toes gripped the rough lip of the rickety bridge. Everything was going fine until a horn from a passing car rattled his eardrum. Applejack's back-side hit the water first. The rest folded like a chair. Futureman dove in after him.

Our heroes! The children shouted playfully and followed them in, one after the other, flipping and cannon-balling on the way down. They'd pulled this trick before.

When the last child had gone home for lunch, the two grown men were left under the bridge, watching the green water swell and flow by.

"What're you thinking about?" Applejack asked.

"Just remembering."

"Remembering what?"

"Uh, childhood."

"Childhood is a big world. I guess the kids reminded you of being young, eh?"

"Yep." Futureman leaned back against the bank and closed his eyes.

"So, which part of your childhood were you thinking of? There's the toddler years, then elementary school, then middle –"

"None of it. All of it. Who cares?"

"You think about the past a lot don't you, Futureman?"

"I guess."

"Why do you think that is?"

"Don't really know."

"Maybe –"

"Could you just shut up with your questions, Applejack? I'm thinking about when I was a boy – I can never go back to that. There! Are you happy?"

"Sorry to be annoying. I just wanted –"

"Just wanted to – what? Psychoanalyze? Evaluate my level of maturity?"

"No, not at all. Just talking. That's all, man. Sorr –"

"Actually, no, you weren't just talking. You're rarely just talking, Applejack. You're almost always trying to analyze things and get inside somebody's head. Has anyone ever told you that you think you know everything?"

"Uh –"

"Has anyone ever told you that you always have to be right about everything? Guess what-you don't and you're not. People aren't just case studies."

They sat in silence, a swath of guppies spinning carelessly about their ankles and toes. At last Futureman stood up.

"So. Let's hike."

The terrain of eastern Vermont is lovely. Rolling hills. Chessboards of green and yellow farmland. Abundant stands of northern hardwood. Here, the yellow birch disperses a million seeds an acre. Vermont's famous maple syrup is made from these sugar maples. And the golden crowned kinglet makes his home among the eastern hemlock, an old tree capable of producing cones for up to 450 years.

Clinging to the memories of his boyhood, Futureman ambled through the patchwork of farm and forest searching the shadows for the forts and treehouses of his youth. Perhaps they had found their way north with him, bringing relics of his past, buried in lunchboxes and wrapped in tree bark. Plastic soldiers, matchbox cars and rolled-up treasure maps from his days as a pirate.

Applejack plodded along slowly through the hottest part of the day. The relief of the cool water had long since faded. The hills seemed strange, arduous, caving in on top, pounding down loosely as if he had no balance. He'd already drained both drinks from the store, yet no sweat came from his pores. He came upon a dozing Futureman, reclined under a granddaddy oak, sweat-drenched dirt beneath him.

Applejack took a knee. "Gennin' some rest. Thaz good," he slurred, pencil-shavings sticking to his tongue.

"Hey man, I don't know why I jumped on you back there," Futureman said. "I just –"

"Naw. Dizzerved."

"Sorry."

"Me too." Applejack braced himself against the tree. Short, shallow breaths. "I'm real not feeeng too well." His eyes were laced with purple. His tan face had grown chalky.

"You're just adjusting to the heat. Couple of days, your body'll be okay. Just keep drinking water."

"Don't know. Man said streamz dryinggup. Worrz me a lil. I have problemz with heat sometimez. I got real hot once when I was boy. Ended up havin to go to the –"

"Aw, we'll be fine. Just gotta keep walking. We'll find water."

Man was right. The sun was drying up all the streams. And after it finished that task, it started in on the springs. Applejack's usual pace of three plus miles an hour turned to little more than one. Three hours gone, and he was barely four miles above the river. It was as if he had never hiked before. *Something about the dirt here. Seems different. Like sand.* Applejack stared at the tops of his shoes. *Boys, I need you now. Don't let me down. Not yet.* He clutched the side of the tree and sucked in thinly. One mouthful of tepid water remained in his bottle. *Got to save it. Couple more miles to go.*

Futureman had gone ahead, occupying himself with the search for water. For two more hours Applejack labored on, hoping for the best – hoping that this was just an anomaly, a hitch, and a good night's rest would set him right. So to distract himself from his fears, he counted the chipmunks, squirrels, and occasional deer mice that scampered among the seeds of sunlight planted along the path until – an awkward spasm caught his eye. A flailing bug against his forehead. A kamikaze, whirring, tailspinning in the sun. It disappeared. *Crazy blind moths.*

He shuffled on, looking along the ground. Again, a splinter of light in his peripheral vision. He flinched, and before he could raise a hand, the spastic flutter of beige corkscrewed through the air and drove itself deep into his ear. A providential fluke. Applejack convulsed. His poles fell to the ground.

"Hawl! C'mon. What the –" He slapped at his head. "Whore of Babylon!"

Futureman perked up. Is that Applejack?

"Fuhrorhman!"

Futureman found him half bent, swatting at the air.

"What's happening here?"

"Ihaveamothinmyear?"

"What?"

"I. Have. A. Moth. In. My. Ear."

"Are you kidding me?"

"No."

"Well, pull it out."

"I can't pull it out, you numbskull. It's practically in my sinuses."

"What do you want me to do?"

The moth beat its wings furiously beside Applejack's eardrum. RRRVVDRRRVVVRRRDDDRRRRRVVVVVVVVVVRRRRRRRD-DDDDD. A hemorrhaging hummingbird. A caged metronome. A panicked window fan.

"Aaaah. It won't get the HELLOUTTAMYHEAD."

"What do we do?"

"Get out your headlamp."

"Okay."

"Hold it up to my ear."

"Ah! The light will draw it out. That's clever," Futureman said.

"It worked the last time."

"Last time? This has happened before?"

"But it was a roach. Now do it."

RRRVVDRRRVVDERRRVVDERRRVVDEEDEERRVVRRRRRRR.

"Ahh!"

"What's going on in there?"

"What do you think? A freakin' moth is going freakin' crazy inside my freakin' head!"

Futureman held the light up for several minutes. No change.

"Partner, we got either a real dumb or real blind moth on our hands here."

"Gyaah."

"What can I do?"

"Nothing. Let's get to the shelter, so I can find a rafter beam to hang myself on."

Valley Girl and 7-Layer Burrito were sprawled out on the dirty boards, post-dinner.

"Hey y'all! What…is…up?" Valley Girl shrieked as they came into view.

Applejack's eye sockets were hollowed out, his forehead in a permanent wrinkle.

"Oh, the usual. Walking. Pissing. Wondering how in the samhill I got a moth stuck in my ear."

"What? Oh my gawll, dude. No way. For real, you have a moth in your ear? Hey Burrito, Applejacks has a moth in his ear!"

"No way, that's awesome," Burrito said. "I mean – no way. That sucks. Does it hurt?"

"Well, sort of. Mostly just…nauseated. I need to lie down now." Applejack said.

"What are you guys doin' here, anyway?" Futureman asked. "Aren't you going in the wrong direction?"

"Oh, yeah. I don't know, so like me and Burrito were so stoked about going into Hanover on Friday night that we hitched in from V-12." Valley girl inched toward Applejack's moth. "An hour later we were, you know, chillin' at the pizza buffet. That's when we saw you guys – hey dude! I've got it! I'll make you, like, a Q-tip or something. So you can smoosh it."

"Thank you. But I think I'll just rest here for a while." Applejack pressed his face on the wood.

Valley Girl wrapped some pocket lint around a twig and hovered over Applejack.

"Thanks, Valleygirl. But I'm just gonna –"

"Here dude. Kill it. For real, dude."

"No, really Val, this is what I –"

"Applejacks. You need to kill it, dude. For real. Put this in there and smoosh it. Applejacks. Here. C'mon. Applejacks. Kill it. Applejacks."

"Applejacks."

"Applejacks."

Heat loitered in the static sky throughout the night, clouds trapping it under heavy hands. With morning, it re-ignited. Applejack lifted his head off the shelter slab, disoriented. Queasy. With the aid of a precious quart of water, Valley's homespun Q-tip had indeed destroyed the evil intruder, but it could not extract the remains and a flaky corpse was left there to quiver lightly against Applejack's eardrum. Dead weight on the equilibrium.

Futureman was dressed and packed, impatiently stirring a pot of oatmeal, a stern look on his face. The warm night had addled him. He was ready to do some hiking – spider-bite-special-ops kind of hiking.

"Morning. You feeling any better?"

"I don't know," Applejack said.

"Let's eat and get some energy in us. We've got a twenty-two today to Stony Brook."

"I don't know if I'm up for that. It's gonna be so hot."

"You'll be fine. Get up."

Applejack lagged behind, dragging vines and tree stumps and concrete blocks across the dusty ground. His head felt like a cracked gourd. They found only empty creek beds and dustpan springs. Yet Futureman spurred his friend on with the promise of water.

The incinerator burned overhead, pouring out her molten joy, vaporizing 10,000 centuries of dihydrogen oxide, gaining strength from weakness. By lunchtime, the temperature had spilled into the hundreds.

At the bottom of Thistle Hill, Applejack peeled his drenched shirt off and collapsed under a withered poplar. He forced down a handful of peanuts and jerky. There was no water.

"No more today...stay here."

"We have nine miles left," Futureman insisted.

"Can't..."

"Yes, you can." *Stop being a baby.* "You're a thruhiker." *Suck it up.* "Here, have my water. Rest for an hour but then we head out. It's just nine miles."

Sundown caught them two miles from Stony Brook shelter.

"Pleazssstop. Camheer pleazz, you hav the tendt buddd. Pud idup, pleazzz, cambright hea –"

"Almost there. Two more miles." Futureman pushed. A test of mettle held itself out before him – this longest hike on the hottest day. He could find no pity inside himself for achievement demands sacrifice. "Not far," he said mechanically. "Not far. We go on." The bone-dry words rang like a death sentence in the sepulchered-ears of his wasted friend, Applejack.

In the morning, Applejack woke facedown in the dirt near the ash of a fire ring – couldn't remember how he got there. His empty water bottle lay sideways, beside him on the ground.

"...and far as we can tell it's still in there," Futureman explained with a laugh. A half-dozen Northbounders rolled and slapped their knees.

"Hey! He's awake," they called.

Everyone waved.

"We got to get that little fella outta there!"

"Don't want to go into town with an insect in your ear!" Cackles, more knee-slapping.

Futureman walked over and offered a cup of rice. "Here. Eat something."

"Can't. Not without water." Applejack licked his cracked lips.

"Well, take your time. I'll meet you down at that road for lunch later on," Futureman said. "Don't worry. We'll find water today. I promise."

The rare bit of early-morning humor had cheered the Northbounders up. They waved and chanted, as they set out.

"Here we come, Ma-aine. Here we come. OOH. OOH."

"Here we come, Ma-aine. Here we come. OOH. OOH."

To Applejack, their marine corps charge sounded hollow and unconvincing, smothered under the trees by a worn blanket of heat.

Futureman followed his nose into a small gully and found the day's first glimmer of hope – a sliver of clean water. He filled his bottles, returned to the Trail, made an arrow in the dirt and continued on, pretending Applejack would see it. At mid-morning, he stopped for a snack where he was met by a trio of nobos.

"Hey, there is a man on up the way," Futureman informed them, a flicker of worry and guilt beginning to surface in his mind. "Would you check on him, make sure he has some water?"

They agreed.

The first hill out of camp had slaughtered him. One mile by ten o'clock. The second one. Vertigo. In a ditch by eleven. Writhing. Vomiting. *I can't make it. Can't. Me? On my own? Barely an amoeba slithering through these endless woods? Molehills compared to the mountains of Maine, yet every one takes me to the very end. Keep walking. God, I'm ready. If it's time to go. Don't stop. Get up. Getupgetup! Legs, keep walking. God. I can't make it. I know you. Remember? I have to-You have to carry me.*

Somehow. Somehow. 103 degrees is fire. Dive-bomb. Shell-shock. Dry as dust, dry as bones, homeword bound, lost boy, not found down and doubt, shelter hell-her fall-out skeller-skelter, she-got-none-soul, lay-me-down to let-me-be, nevermind those littlebity thingz, too late now, cannot wait to see that gate of glory-be to father, the good bestman, need it, though – water, living water for my – deep well, deep, blue crystal lily-sweet well, not a mouth of damning shitting – ifting sand, grit, flaming looming brand – it'll be ecstacy then, don'come easy or free, like-the-bez thingzz, long haul mother-mauling trip, on paper, like the last time – worse even, snake-skin lip, tar-pit tack-dead, leaves eating-bugs, eating and drink-ing the dusty-mustery road, wish-it-was-mud-instead, drink-shit kerouac, out-of-whack mind-control, my electrolytes, I tend to lose my legtrolytes, you know, on a acid-bitter day, a gall day like today, hate, fear, futurehate, why now future, what's left now man, past, there he is God, again, I see him, he's back for me – that old Scorpion – it's stinging-time for me, God, crippled lame dead duck, on a wire, on a string, on a hill. I know it now. My teeth are on fire, one alone. All alone. I'm alone, onahill.

Around noon, completely and entirely away from the Trail by an over-grown southwest half-mile, Applejack, out of the corner crack of his tear-dried desert-drug eye, saw a man whose shiny bald head and kind brown pin-prick eyes looked like the shiny bald head and kind brown pin-prick eyes of his late barbering grandfather – Jack. He felt, instead of the mean, surly sun – the grip of a steady barbering hand upon his sunken, ground-grown shoulder. Applejack's voice went quiet and his blue eyes went to black. On a hill. On a hill.

It was a hundred in the shade. Waiting. After three hours, it dawned on him. *Applejack's in trouble. He's really in trouble. Oh God, forgive me. I've been an asshole. All this time. I drove my friend into the ground. What have I done?*
    Futureman raced frantic, retracing his way. Guilt gripped him. Fear-of-the-worst propelled him. *This is not good, not going to be good at all, if I don't get there soon.* Jumping over a knot of roots, he crossed around an oak and out into a blinding, Redwood-wide hydrant of angel-white sun-shine. Applejack crashed through the scrub and tumbled onto the road beside him, one foot sliding over the other, eyes glazed then closed, his face colorless and glossed. He was smiling.
    "Applejack! Brother! Oh, thank God. Sit down here." Applejack fell limp in his arms. "Alright, take it easy. You're gonna be okay. You're gonna be alright. We're gonna get you some help, get you out of here."
    "Seemso…nice…map sayten more then home. We'll get to last place, tonight, somehow. Somehow."
    "Alright. Drink some of this. Just rest now. Hang on."
    Futureman was overcome. *What? What do I do?* No one had come down the way since the nobos. He could walk out to get help, but Applejack would have to stay here alone for a long time. Somehow he would have to get him back on his feet and lead him to the highway, nearly three miles away.
    God, forgive my arrogance, my selfishness. God, for my friend. "Apple-jack, I'm so sorry." He slid Applejack's arms around his shoulders and

headed up the forest path toward Vt. 100.
    Somehow. Somehow.

II
"All the believers were together and had everything in common.
Selling their possessions and goods, they gave to anyone as he had need."
                              -Acts 2:44-45

Futureman collapsed onto the shoulder of the highway, Applejack attached.
He was lucid, but barely.
    "Hang on buddy, I'm gonna get us a hitch into town."
    A half hour passed. Thumb out, arm up, waving. "Somebody help me!"
    The costly automobiles sped by, effortlessly. The vole-mice looked on,
curious. *Strange human, seems lost. Looks like the other's gonna be crow
meat soon.*
    "C'mon! What's wrong with you people?"
    Across the road a painter's van pulled to a stop. The man inside bent
over a crinkled map.
    "Hey. Hi. Listen, I need some help. I gotta get my friend here to Rut-
land, pronto."
    "Brother, that's like fifteen miles back the other way," the driver said.
    "Yeah, I know that. And I'm sorry for the inconvenience but –"
    "I'm late for an appointment as it is, brother. Paintin these yuppy man-
sions out here. You know how these people can get. Sorry, brother."
    "Listen, it's an emergency. I really need to –"
    "Bro, I just can't help you. There's a ranger station about a mile down."
He pointed. Futureman turned.
    Tires spun and dust filled the air. "What's wrong with you?" he shouted,
coughing. "And don't call me brother!"

Futureman reattached Applejack and hobbled to the ranger station, stretching him out on the lawn under a balsam.
    Behind a screened-in window, a young woman in her twenties – black-
rimmed glasses, rosy cheekbones – twirled a pigtail and talked on the
phone.
    "Yes sir, I understand …uh, huh…yes, I understand that you camp here
a lot, and believe me when I say that we appre…yes, sir, okay, okay, I'll see
what I can do." She hung up the phone. "Oh my good grief, my goodness,
folks! Wipe your own behind!"
    "Some people," Futureman said.
    It startled her. "Oh my, gosh, I'm sorry you heard that." She scrunched

her eyes. Little canary laughter vibrated the edges of her mouth. "I'm Jesse, your friendly potty-mouthed park ranger. What can I do for you, Mr. Hiker?"

"Jesse, I'm Futureman."

"Oh. Well, what can I do for you mister-future-hiker-man?"

"Jesse, my friend Applejack is laid out on your lawn over there."

Jesse peered out the window. "Right. And you want me to dispose of the body."

"Umm –"

Jesse ate her hands. "Oh my god, he's really hurt, isn't he? I'm so sorry, I'm so stupid."

"No, he's not gonna die. He nearly had a heat stroke a couple hours ago. But I need to get him a bed, some food and water. I was trying to get a hitch into town, but none of the locals would –"

"Oh, phphssss. This is a resort town. There's a big sign down the road that says *rich pricks stop here*." Jesse covered her mouth. "I'm not really supposed to use swear words on the job."

"It's okay, Jesse. Do you know the number of a cab service?"

"Yeah, but it'll be expensive. If your friend can wait and just rest, I get off soon. You can go into town with me. What does he need for now?"

"I think with some juice and shade he'll hold up."

"Well, it just so happens that I have juice and a big piece of banana nut bread in the back. How's that for park service?"

Applejack came to just in time to see Jesse's inquisitive eyes and kid-tongue poking into view.

"There you go. So you're pretty sick, huh?"

"Not really. I just pass out sometimes," Applejack muttered.

Jesse sighed. "Yeah, me too. Too much acid during the nineties."

"We all have dirty files," Applejack said.

"Wow, you're cool too. Two cool boys, stranded on my lawn. What ever shall I do?" Adorable.

"I have some friends in Rutland that might take you in for free."

"Who are your friends?" Futureman asked.

"They live on a..sort of a…commune. They're really nice and they love guests."

"A commune? Yeah, we'll stay." *Of course we'll stay.*

"Oh, you'll love them. They're super nice. I'll call them."

Ten minutes later, Jesse had a reservation (if that's what you call four days on a commune). "Applejack, I told them about you, and they said you'll be feeling better in no time. They're very health conscious. Herbs and things. Oh – are you guys – religious?"

"Why?"

"Well, these people are – I don't know how to explain it – they're a mix between Judaism and Christianity."

"Interesting. We're kind of into hybrid Christianity ourselves."

"You'll be delighted, then."

Jesse drove like she didn't have hands. She tapped on the accelerator randomly as though it were optional and checked the rear view every three seconds. When a car was braking thirty yards ahead, she'd jerk the wheel, prepping for the inevitable collision. Applejack managed a smile. *No distance perception, whatsoever. How the world's colors must be whirring about her.* But all the years of hallucinogens had not been able to touch Jesse's spirit and wild, wild love.

On the way to wherever it was they were going, Jesse made a stop at her house to take the terrier out for a quick walk. Applejack rested on a neighborhood picnic table while she bared her soul. Jesse was lonely. In less than an hour, she told them about her druggie past, her strained but growing relationship with her parents, her frustrations with the Park District, why she had become a vegan, her struggle with manic depression, her short stint with lesbianism, her obsession with the icons of the Eastern Orthodox Church and her current addiction to free coffee at a local Episcopal Sunday morning gathering.

This kind of honesty is rare.

Jesse's car jolted to a stop in downtown Rutland. A man with a beard was waiting on the sidewalk in front of an exquisite set of red mahogany doors. Above him, a sign read, *Back Home Again Café*. He wore a white linen shirt draped over dark brown sus pants. His hair was pulled back into a short, tidy ponytail. He smiled, arms unassumingly at his sides.

"Hello, Jesse. Good to see you again."

"You look nice today, Jeush."

"I wear the same thing everyday," Jeush said.

"What can I say? I really think you chose a winning outfit all those years ago."

Jeush grinned. "Applejack, Futureman. We've been eagerly awaiting your arrival. Please. Are you coming in, Jesse?"

"No, I have some stuff to do."

"Will we see you again, Jesse?" Futureman asked.

"You'd better." She scribbled her number on a gum wrapper. "Call me before you leave town. Jeush, give everyone my love."

"You know you're welcome here, Jesse. Anytime." Jeush said, intensity registering in his eyes.

"Yeah, I know."

The walls of the café looked like they would bleed if cut. Tables and chairs were hand-carved, crafted with red hickory, gnarled ash and stretched leather, each piece unique from the other. The bar in back, in lieu of whiskey sours or dirty martinis, served yerba maté and wheatgrass shakes.

Jeush explained that community members did not have other jobs. Running the café was their vocation. They worked together. Even the kids helped out. A teenaged boy passed beside Futureman, smiling, a pile of dishes in his hands. A little girl skipped along, broom and dust pan in tow. *Robot children. Normal kids don't work like this, and if they do, they are not happy about it.*

Applejack and Futureman were honored guests, treated with an unearned reverence. Every person in the community – men, women and children alike – seemed to already know about them. Jeush led them to a table prepared for them in the back corner next to a sunlit window. There, they found sparkling water, bowls of salad, fruit, wheatgrass frappes, mugs of maté and freshly baked bread.

Applejack and Futureman set their packs down. "We don't know what to say."

"It's our pleasure," a woman said. "I am Shishana." Her soft gray hair was pulled back, hanging down to her waist. She wore a simple homemade dress.

Another man stood beside her. "I'm Timnah. Hello."

They said their names with emphasis. Pride.

"Your names sound like – Hebrew," Futureman said.

"Very good. They are. When someone joins the community, they take a new name – as a sign of the new life."

Jeush explained, "We are a community committed to the teachings of our Master, Yahshua. Some call him Jesus."

"We're followers of Jesus ourselves," Applejack said.

"That's wonderful. It's nice to meet people who believe in his ways," Shishana said.

"We've never seen anything quite like this, though," Futureman said.

"We are the 12 Tribes. It probably sounds a little weird to you, but that's okay. We are the restored family of Jacob, the new commonwealth of the ancient Israelites. God's people, made up of Jews and Gentiles. We have all surrendered to the call of Master Yahshua and have forsaken everything to follow him."

"I didn't know this existed," Futureman said.

"Now you do," Shishana said. Her words were few and gentle, but her soft eyes beckoned. *Proselytized. Join us, right now. Your possessions, your worries, your burdens, your fears, leave them behind, and join the family of God.* "There will be plenty of time for talking later. Now you should rest and eat. Especially you, Applejack."

"We'll bring you some more food. Whatever you like. It's our pleasure," Timnah said, returning to the counter.

Applejack chewed his salad slowly. "Futureman, this is more than a commune."

"Yeah, no kidding. We just stepped into another world. I have to pee."

"Alright. Did I miss a segue there or..." Applejack said to himself as Futureman left abruptly. "What a weirdo."

Even the bathroom was beautiful, with trim so ornate that Futureman felt guilty for soiling the commode. Beside the toilet, a framed cartoon hung on the wall. In it, a 12 Tribes family stood on a crowded street. People shouted and jeered at them: "Narrow-minded fools!" "Cult followers!" "Freaks!" The normal people had television sets for heads.

When Futureman returned to the table, another man was sitting with Applejack. Frizzy hair shot out of his ponytail. He wore circular glasses barely larger than his eyes.

"Futureman, I'm Sharesh. Hello." He spoke pointedly. "Applejack tells me you went to Wheaton College."

"I did."

"So did I!"

"Really? Small world."

"Yeah, and he tells me you guys are from Knoxville."

"That's right."

"My wife is from Knoxville!"

"No kidding."

"So, here's the plan. We've decided to take you to Cambridge, to the Common Sense Farm. We're going to leave in five minutes."

"Wait. What?"

Applejack shrugged his shoulders, too tired to care.

"It's beautiful out there. Just the place for Applejack to rest and recuperate and for you both to see what we're about."

Futureman paused. The Back Home Again Café might have been a perfect front for luring naïve nobodies into a sinister coven of human heart-eaters but somehow these people didn't seem the type. Besides, there was free food.

In the back of the car, Applejack collapsed again, the sound of lines on tires drumming him to sleep. Futureman sat in the passenger seat beside Sharesh.

"Can I ask you something?" Sharesh said. "At home do you attend a church?"

"Yes. Why?"

"Do you find that your church follows the way of Christ?"

"What way do you mean exactly?" Futureman asked.

"Are they intimately connected to loving God and each other?"

"Well, that's the big problem, isn't it? That's what Christians are trying to solve."

Sharesh took his eyes off the road for a second. "So, in your experience with your church, is it being solved?"

"Huh, let's just say that more time is spent on the technology budget than on the real needs of real people." More than youthful impetuosity came through Futureman's cynicism, the resignation of one whose childhood home had burned to the ground.

"It bothers you, doesn't it?" Sharesh asked.

"No, not at all. I think it's great."

Sharesh chuckled. "Have you ever thought that this organization you attend might not be the real church?"

Too direct. It caught his breath. "That's a scary question, Sharesh."

Sharesh gripped the steering wheel. As they drove down the highway, Futureman noticed a sadness in the strange man's eyes, as though he were watching the sun turn to blood. In Hebrew, Sharesh means *zealous*. "But let's consider: if you follow Jesus, it's because you love him, right?"

"Right."

"So then why are Christians so connected to possessions when Jesus so clearly warns us of their dangers? Why do churches worry about youth centers and worship screens, as you say, and spend so much energy on stadium crusades and quick converts – while their brothers and sisters *in* the church are broken, hurting, needy and floundering in isolation? Does it make any gospel sense?" Sharesh had realized long ago that easing people into an ideology was not his style. He spoke strongly, a lifetime of contemplation flooding out.

"I don't know. Maybe not," Futureman said.

"Then why is it accepted as Jesus' Church?"

Futureman felt cornered. He didn't know what to say.

Sharesh forged on. "Does Paul not write in Romans 12 that we are not to be conformed to the pattern of this world, but are to be transformed by the renewing of our minds?"

"Yes, he does. I know what you're saying. I think about these things, too," Futureman said.

"And what are you doing about your thoughts?"

"Well, heck, what are you doing about it, Sharesh?" Futureman asked. "We're here because we want to hear what you guys have to say – well that and Applejack's near death experience back there."

"Let me ask you this? What was the early church like?"

"I assume you're referring to Acts 2."

"Yes."

"They were communal, I guess," Futureman said.

"Exactly. Devoted to one another. They sold their possessions and laid the money at the disciples' feet so that it could be distributed equally. Jesus' teachings thrive in this context. 'If you do not love your brother and sister, then you do not love me.' Is that not what he said? Don't you think it's a little too easy to hide in the pews on Sunday and then retreat behind our own private walls every other day of the week?"

"Well, I don't know…"

"You remember the rich young ruler in chapter ten of Mark, verses 17-31?" Sharesh knew his Bible.

"Yeah."

"What was the question he asked Jesus?"

"He asked him what he had to do to be saved?"

"Very good! And what did Jesus say?"

"He told him to sell his possessions and give them to the poor."

"Actually, before that, he listed the last six of the Ten Commandments, don't murder, steal, lie, defraud, commit adultery, and honor your father and mother, to which the man responded, *Teacher, I have kept all of these since I was a boy.* That's when Jesus said, *One thing you lack: go, sell everything you have, and give it to the poor.* He was saying to the man – a man who thought he was keeping the commandments – that he really was not. You see, even though he knew the Law mentally and culturally, he had never truly given his life to God, and thus had failed to understand the heart of the Law: the love of God and the love of neighbor."

"So you're saying that you literally have to sell your possessions in order to follow Jesus and be saved?"

"I'm saying you cannot love God and neighbor and hold on to your life at the same time."

"And having possessions is holding on to your life?" Futureman was defensive, moved by Sharesh's fervor, yet clinging to the life he knew.

"Why should we not take Jesus literally on the point of his teachings?"

"Well, you know, his teachings are somewhat hard to understand. He uses parables that are kinda cryptic and…"

"No! That's a misunderstanding. They are not meant to be cryptic. They are practical ways to live out the Law of God. Jesus spoke the truths of heaven in terms we can understand. Very simple. Modern theology has built such a complex of categorization and terminology that the really practical teachings of Jesus are hidden from people – made into unattainable ideals and saved for fancy sermons. No, Jesus was talking to ordinary average people. He intended that they interpret what he was saying in an ordinary, accessible way. Personally, I think that most Christians prefer the confusion and complexity because it puts us in the clear. *If we aren't meant to understand, then we aren't accountable. No sacrifice necessary. If it's too hard to really grasp, then I can go on living the way I always have. I don't really have to lose my life to find it. I just have to be willing to.* Repentance becomes unnecessary, transformation is lost, and the body of Christ remains a distant, beautiful concept but never a reality that impacts people personally. Never the living breathing body of Jesus that he himself was talking about."

Futureman shifted in the seat. *This is not just rhetoric. This guy is living this.* He was reeling on the inside. Trying to hold on, wondering if he had been lied to his whole life. As his mind cast about for the familiar, thoughts of his struggling church back home did not bring comfort.

"I can see that you're taking this hard. It's okay. Truth takes time."

"No, it's not okay, Sharesh. I don't really know what –"

"We in the 12 Tribes have sold all our possessions. We live for the sake of Yahshua and his body of believers, not for the sake of self. We have become the Commonwealth of Israel, the new 12 Tribes of Yahweh's people, made up of both Jews and Gentiles – a kingdom of priests."

Up to this point, Sharesh had been using regular language for the most part, speaking plainly in a way that Futureman could understand. But now, he seemed to have slipped back into some kind of stilted lingo.

"These are the teachings of our Master Yahshua and they are the teachings of the whole of the Bible," Sharesh said, eyes on the road.

Futureman's whole being had been strangely stirred – by the zeal, by the total commitment of these people, the radical lifestyle, the simplicity of their trust, even by Sharesh's seeming command of scripture. And yet something was a little off, too soon to tell quite what it was.

Applejack's face appeared between the seats. "Sharesh, can we pull over? I gotta find a bathroom."

"Hey, that's a good sign. I have to go myself," Sharesh smiled in the rearview.

On his way out of the convenience store, Applejack grabbed a bag of Doritos and some lemonade and dropped them at the register.

"You're gonna put that poison in your body?" Sharesh said.

"Poison?"

"That stuff will rot your insides. It's no good."

The clerk rolled her eyes. "You gonna buy 'em or not?"

"Guess…not."

"You'll be eating organic food from the farm soon. That's what you need right now, not MSG-flavored chips."

Sharesh drove them to the outskirts of Cambridge, New York. Forgotten, almost hidden within the lush hinterland of that beautiful state, the Common Sense Farm waited patiently for them. From a distance they could see the huge manor house, a well-kept old mansion propped up by columns and guarded in the rear by a quaint cottage. Everyone in the community shared these two homes.

The Common Sense barn sat across the field. There were no cattle or horses or sheep inside. In their stead, a network of immaculate industrial machines were producing hundreds of gallons of shampoo and hand soap each week. The 12 Tribes contracted with chain stores and international businesses for a number of products and the Common Sense Farm had its own niche. Yet, according to Sharesh, the community's concern for capital gain was peripheral. All profit provided for the basic needs of this commune and others; and any surplus went to outreach projects and other 12 Tribes needs around the world. In addition to soap making, the Common Sense families grew enough organic food to largely feed themselves and several other surrounding communities.

As the sun was setting, the car pulled into the circle drive of the old manse, where several folks were already waiting to greet them. After an evening of homegrown dinner and lively conversation on the porch, Applejack and Futureman retired to a room in the grandmother cottage where they found their beds already turned down and baskets of ripe fresh fruit beside each one. Applejack fell asleep marveling over the lovely get-well card some of the little children had painted for him. Futureman could not sleep but he closed his eyes anyway – eyes full of wonder and bewildering beauty, eyes pressed by tears. Greed and envy seemed a remote worry for these simple people. Any notion of private ownership had been eradicated from their lives. Applejack and Futureman had been treated with generosity and grace, joyfully welcomed into this tight circle of life. These people were unique. They were willing servants.

In the morning, they ate natural oatmeal and yogurt, fresh strawberries and homemade whole grain bread. After breakfast, everyone gathered for the daily worship service, a time filled with earnest prayer, dance and song. Futureman joined in eagerly, the children smiling as he clumsily attempted the steps. Applejack – sore, weak and ever watchful – observed in quiet.

After the strange, intoxicating service, he went back to the room to sleep. An open window pulled the light in. An amber patch of early morning reached across the floor. Handmade drapes swayed, blown from the light wind of a nearby garden, the cool scent of herbs drifting from the soap barn on the hill. His broken body churned inside, battling evil, fighting to bend itself back to health. Sinews and tendons re-fortified, the liquids of nature replenishing his dismal electrolyte count, restoring the weak membranes of his cells, of his soul.

Meanwhile, Futureman set out to explore the farm, hope and wonder in his eyes. He watched the people as they went about their day. Invigorated, perplexed and hungry, he shook hands, picked vegetables and traded stories with them, studying their curious words and unworried faces, their labor and treatment of one another. He felt as though his heart was turning to liquid and running down around his ankles – melted by this unexpected convergence of word and deed. *This is a new world. Isn't it?* He wondered aloud to no one, walking barefoot through the prickly grass – dying to believe, to understand this place forgotten by the world abroad.

Religious communities have always existed along the fringes of society. By nature, they blur the line between acceptable faith and that which is considered extreme or even dangerous. Here we find an interesting tension because any religion sets its adherents apart, necessarily, yet we as humans are wary of alienation and normally protect ourselves from anything that would require it in the extreme. But sometimes we find that the call is too strong or the rewards are worth the sacrifice. We can step into a shadowy region that requires a marked departure from the normal course of humanity. From the mainstream, it is evident that the line has been crossed. But how, why and who has authority to make such determinations? How far is too far? How much too much?

Futureman sat on a fencepost, watching the life of the Common Sense Farm unfold. Some of the wives worked in the hot sun, tilling, hoeing. Inside the manor house, several men were discussing a business proposal from a client.

It was clear that a patriarchal sort of mechanism was at work. The children were indeed well behaved and hard working. Raised without a sense of entitlement, they fought very little when they played and possessed an innocence of spirit, a curiosity that made them – unsophisticated. Obedience was the immediate response to the commands of their parents. Whining was not. They were educated by the community, could read, write and speak very well. In addition to this, they learned trades and skills specific to the needs of the community. They would grow up without high school diplomas and university training but with unshakeable job security.

That afternoon in the soap factory, Futureman asked Jonas, one of the single young men, about higher schooling. He responded, "Why go to a secular university when you can go to the University of Yahshua?"

Pieces of a puzzle lay scattered around Futureman's addled mind. *Is this what Jesus meant? Do the women and children want this kind of lifestyle? Are they allowed to want another? I wonder how many kids have been born here. Is this what children are like when they don't eat candy? This kind of isolation can't be healthy, but are they really isolated? And if so, isolated from what? From isolation? The world isn't healthy. Every heart is dark, so what are they not telling me? Do the kids ever spy on the adults having sex? Do the adults ever covet each other's spouses? What is discipline like around here? They do not spare the rod; are the father's too tough on the children? Why do they embrace Hebrew customs if they say they are Gentile believers? What is the difference between being pure and being brainwashed? Where did the 12 Tribes come from? What is true freedom? What is true worship? Why does this place seem so beautiful? And something is making me feel uneasy – is it just me, or is it God saving me?*

Futureman called home that evening to give his parents an update. His sweet, koala-bear mother answered.

"Mama."

"Sweetheart! How is my favorite son doing?"

"Your *only* son is doing pretty good, but he's not hiking right now."

"What is he doing? And why are we talking about you in the third person?"

"He's well. I don't know why I'm talking in the third person. I'm on a commune."

"A commune?"

"Yeah, Applejack almost had a heat stroke on the trail, so we got off in Rutland, Vermont to rest, where we met this girl there who had these friends, turns out who live on this quasi-Christian commune called the 12 Tribes in town and there we ran into this guy who brought us to their farm in Cambridge, New York, and so that's where we are right now. Applejack's in bed recuperating while I'm roaming around this place – we're like a hundred miles away from the Trail, it's crazy."

A profound silence filled the phone line.

"Mom? You there?"

"Yeah sweety, I'm here," she said, still trying to understand what sounded like: *Applejack almost died, but he didn't and they visited a cult where they were kidnapped by a man who is holding them hostage on a commune... and tribes of some kind are involved...somewhere in New York.*

"And you chose this?"

"Well yeah. How often do you get to stay on a commune?"

"Ah."

"It's really baffling, very beautiful, but then there's – I don't know, somehow, something's just not – adding up all the way. I can't figure it out. Don't know how long I'll be here, but I'll call you when I leave."

"Honey, are they hurting you?"

"Oh, no, it's not like that. I'm fine. I can leave whenever I want."

"Are they listening?"

"What? No. OK – I know how it sounds, but everything's okay. Really. And I'm calling on their phone long distance, so I have to go. Talk to you soon. Love you."

"I love you too, honey."

"Bye Bye."

For a solid hour, Mama sat by the phone, with only her fingernails to keep her company.

"Alvah, all of you wear the same clothes and look very similar to each other," Futureman said, sitting on a bucket outside the soap factory. Alvah was in his early twenties, hard working, unmarried, honest, hopeful.

"Yes, we do," Alvah said.

"Can you explain the ponytail?"

"Yes. Hebrew priests used to wear their hair like this, as a sign of separation for the purpose of God's work. We do it as a sign of our own separation to do the work of the Kingdom of Yahshua."

"Do you have to wear your hair like that?"

"No."

"But everyone does."

"Yes."

"Why?"

"We all choose to."

"Can you choose not to wear your hair in a ponytail?"

"No one would choose that."

"Would the community deal harshly with you if you cut it off?"

"No, I don't think so. It's not required that we wear it. We choose to."

"What if someone didn't choose to?"

"You have to understand that individuality is a lesser concern here."

"So how is individuality expressed here?"

"The focus is on how we can best be used. We're happy to give our talents for the sake of others. We strive to be equal. We are dead to ourselves, and we live for the sake of the community. I don't ask to do what I want before filtering my considerations through what would be best for the community."

"And ponytails are best for the community?"

"As I said, it is a sign that we are priests, set aside for the work of our master, Yahshua."

Applejack ate a peach from his basket of fruit as he sat at the window of the old house, looking out over the farm. A woman picking tomatoes in the garden. A string of children walking together, chewing on hay. A solitary man tying his ponytail in. He stopped and looked up at the window. Waved. A smile carried across the gap.

The message from the community was clear.

Come and stay for a day. Or come and stay.

Over the past two days, as he rested, he'd watched his friend pace the grounds, play, sing and dance, had listened to him mutter fragmented questions and half-truths, desperately trying to put things together. Now that Applejack's body was growing strong again, poisons rubbed out and resolve reanimated, he was able to sense a different area of weakness. Somehow in the last three days his soul had been frayed, as well.

"So what's this 12 Tribes stuff all about? The whole Commonwealth of Israel thing? The bizarre insistence on Hebrew customs and the name Yahshua. And then there's the folk dancing, priestly ponytails?" He said to Futureman.

"I know! I don't know."

"But then I look at the beauty of it, the fruit of it? The healthy children, the unity, the hard work and contentment? What does it all mean?"

"That's what I've been trying to figure out!" Futureman was glad to see that Applejack's Sherlock complex was up and running. "Sometimes I think Acts 2 is alive here, and it makes me want to drop everything and join, and then at other times I get this feeling that we're in the middle of some sinister cult."

"We need to talk to Sharesh."

They found him on the back porch of the main house, sitting beneath the columns, reading.

"Gentleman! Good to see you. Applejack, wow, you're looking much better."

"Yeah, I guess you knew what you were talking about."

Sharesh could tell there was more than small talk on their faces. "So tell me, what's on your minds?"

"Alright, we've been going over things the past few days, and…"

"You want an answer."

"Yes, to a specific question."

"What's the question?"

"Sharesh, I know you don't use the word Christian, but I see you clearly as a follower of Christ. A brother. So what, then, are we to you – brothers, or something else?"

Sharesh closed the book and smiled, a glimmer of light in his eyes. He spoke carefully. "You are searchers. Looking for the truth, and I believe that God has brought you here for a reason."

"Searchers, OK. Then, do you believe we have to join the 12 Tribes in order to be saved?"

"It goes back to what we were talking about earlier. You have to forsake all possessions. Galatians 2:20. The old man must die and the new man given a chance to live and grow."

"What if I sold everything and lived completely for the gospel, but did not join the 12 Tribes, like Mother Theresa? What then?"

"Why would you not join the nation that God is building? God's will is being worked out through the 12 Tribes. Not because of who we are individually, or our name, but simply because we are His people. Why would you want to be outside of God's people?"

"So how can you say that the 12 Tribes is THE family of God?"

"Because it is the only church living in the way of love. It is obvious that God's Spirit has come back to the church in the 12 Tribes."

"Are you saying that for the last two millennia God's Spirit has not been in the Church?"

"If God waited several thousand years after his promise to Abraham for the right time to redeem humanity in Jesus, why wouldn't He wait 2,000 more for the right time to restore his church?"

"But how did the 12 Tribes come to be the pure church?"

"Revelation speaks of the church in Ephesus. Many good deeds, including the expose' of false apostles. But they had forgotten the most important thing, to love the Savior with an undying, incorruptible love. John says, 'I hold this against you: You have forsaken your first love. Repent and do the things you did at first. If you do not repent I will come to you and will remove your lamp stand from its place.' The church did not repent, and their lamp stand was removed. One by one churches started to fall, forgetting their first love. As the sincere died off gradually, none were left who had the Holy Spirit inside of them, until there was nowhere on earth for the Spirit to work, and so He returned to where He came from. Until thirty years ago, when there was one who received the Spirit and returned to the first love. Our founder."

"One man?"

"Yes, who received the Holy Spirit."

"And you guys believe there has been no other in all that time, almost two thousand years?"

"Consider the doctrinal quarrels of the second and third centuries, the politically forced 'unity' of the fourth century, and the resulting persecution of dissenters in all the centuries to follow. What about the unrestrained butchering and rape of the Crusades and the inhumane tortures of the Inquisition? What about the gross immoralities and political intrigues of the popes and bishops?" *Zealous.* "The religious wars resulting from the Reformation? The continued persecution of dissenters by both Catholics and Protestants until modern societies stopped burning, drowning and beheading people? What about the multiplied quarrels and denominational splits that have happened in the last few centuries, once coercion was removed? Are these things not defined as ways of the flesh in Galatians 5:19-20? Can those who do such things inherit the Kingdom of God?"

"You make a good point. Much of Christian history isn't exactly a picture of love and harmony, but…"

"Thirty years ago, our founder, a man who said in his heart – *All I want to do is love* – was entrusted with the Holy Spirit. He was the pure spiritual seed that had been preserved for just the moment that our master Yahshua deemed worthy. That man went out and found others who wanted to do the same thing. Together they followed Yahshua and soon found themselves living in the community. The result of this work is working communities all over the world, Russia, Romania, Australia, Brazil. All like the one you now see before you, as the early Christians saw before them. This is the answer."

After a moment, the ardor evaporated from Sharesh's face. He looked at the care-worn travelers with affection, and the grizzled benevolence returned. "You have found peace, friends. End your long search. Right here, with us."

They had no further questions. They ate their last breakfast on the farm. The earnest, compassionate people continued to smile and serve. A silent tear slipped down Futureman's nose. An unseen burden rested on Applejack's back.

Come and stay a day. Or come and stay.

It was hard to leave. To rejoin the restless wandering that had brought them there in the first place.

And so, they sat in a motel room in Rutland and ate ice cream for two days. Saying little, suffering more from confusion than depression. Jesse was on stand by, just in case.

"What is it?" she asked.

"Your friends, Jesse. They have the power to ruin people."

"Oh, I know. They are so lovely, aren't they?"

"Yes…they are."

"Well?"

"Show us your collection of Eastern Orthodox icons again, would you?"

"Oh," Jesse said, batting her eyes. "I'd be delighted to!"

II

Jesse plopped them back on the Trail. They didn't know where they were, what they were doing. It took a mile to soften their memory. Two to break their rhythm of rampant contemplation. Three to find their feet and legs. Four to free them.

The day was light and 78° cool, adding to Applejack's resolve. By sundown he and Futureman were on a hill overlooking Governor Clement Shelter. They paused to listen and look. There was evidence of some recent activity, but all was quiet for the moment. They saw the place as it had been described to them, sitting lonely on the bend of a dirt road.

Dark legend shrouded this shelter. The Hiker's Companion discouraged overnight stays at Governor Clement Shelter, noting that several "incidents involving rowdy visitors" have occurred there. Stories of bizarre violence and redneck torture had filtered down through the hiker circles in that hushed way that real urban legends travel. There had even been mention of rituals, strange stacks of rocks scattered around the fire pit and the odd bit animal bone here and there.

Most hikers stopped in to test out the mythology over a sunny lunch break, before moving on for the evening. Applejack and Futureman, however, had every intention of staying.

There was something irresistible to them about the mysterious nature of the redneck. His existence is a conundrum. Too many inspiring tales of redneck debauchery and derring-do had seasoned their Tennessee upbringings to drive the two of them away. In their memories, there was the austere beauty of the redneck swan dive gone awry on The Sinks. There was the ribald splendor flowing from the mouth of the redneck poet as he pronounces his free-spirited declaration to the world – "Cain't be stopt!" There was the drunken redneck who famously strapped a jet engine to the rooftop of his car, onlookers on hand to witness his last words, "Hey, watchiss." They decided to stay just in case.

A mix of artifacts littered the ground: crushed PBR cans, frayed rope-like sutures, one half of a sprung handcuff clamped on a rock like a talon. As they approached the stone cropping of the shelter, they saw that most unmistakable sign of human presence. Smoke, rising over the top of the shack in small clumps.

A normal-looking man was seated in the dirt smoking. He was thirtyish, not quite six feet tall, three days of red Irish growth on his jaw. He was turning through the most recent edition (but aren't they all timeless, really?) of the *Weekly World News*.

"They found Satan's face again," the man said.

"That right?" Applejack asked.

"Yeah, last week, billowing out of a nuclear power plant...again. Got a picture of it and everything."

"So the Devil *is* behind nuclear power," Futureman said.

"Yeah, I guess. One would think Satan's presence couldn't be captured on film. This here picture diminishes his mystique." The man tongued his cigarette to the corner of his mouth. He folded the paper and held out his hand.

"I'm Jester. Nice to meet you."

"You staying here tonight?" Applejack asked.

"Yeah, you?" Jester said.

"Wouldn't miss it."

"Wouldn't miss it? Why's that?"

"Just wouldn't."

"Fair enough," Jester said.

"You hiking the Trail?"

"Yeah, but not the A.T. Did it two years ago. Now, I'm hiking the Long Trail. Runs from Vermont to Canada, shares this section of the A.T. Told myself I'd come back and do it one day. Today's *one day*."

Futureman gathered wood. Applejack worked on the fire. Jester cooked his rice and puffed on some more Camels. Tension remained the fourth party throughout dinner.   Generally hikers are very open with one another. There is an immediate, peculiar trust that doesn't have to be earned. Most people wouldn't think of spending a night in a room with someone they had never met. Thruhikers do it all the time. But on this night, an edge of caution was needling the three of them as they sat there on the ground, waiting.

"So, Jester. Let's hear some more of those headlines."

"Alright."

NASA Finds Oil on the Moon. Gas prices fall to 10 cents a gallon as Arab oil becomes obsolete.

"I don't know which is more unlikely."

Angel Shot By Duck Hunter Reappears Over Lake. Searches for Shooter.

"Hell hath no fury like an angel scorned."

"Nice. Here's a good one."

Mangator found in the Louisiana Bayou.

"Mangator?"

"Half alligator, half man. Mangator."

"Which half is which?"

"There's a picture of it here. Man uppers. Gator lowers. Now there's a harmless creature."

As they spoke, the fire flickered against the trees. It seemed as if the edge of the wood was concealing something. Night birds had collected on the oak branches and were peering through the dark.

"Jester, when you hiked the Trail, did you stay at this shelter?"

"Nope. Nobody I was hiking with would stick around. We heard some bad things about this place. I wanted to see for myself."

"What have you heard?"

"Nothin' I expect to be true. But you know how legends grow out here."

Unlike most shelters along the Trail – either lost in rhododendron mazes or tucked away in the hollows of hills – the Governor Clement was out in an open field, vulnerable, near a dirt road, making it easily accessible from a nearby highway. It had been built in 1929 by the Governor of Vermont himself, a sturdy structure, exceptional in quality and design. Constructed out of rough stones, it had the appearance of an old abandoned homestead. There was even an indoor hearth and fireplace. Yet, despite the quaint touches, the shelter had to it that peculiar feel that says *somebody was just here*.

It was *dark* dark. The fire was waning. After Jester had burned down his last cigarette, he stood up and cast his ear one last time toward the black. Nothing but forest.

"I don't think anything is going down here tonight fellas. I hope you're not too disappointed. I'm gonna hit the sack." He stretched upwards. His chest rattled like a dashboard.

"Nothing's going to happen," Applejack said. "We got worked up for nothing. Besides, those types are picky. They're looking for Boy Scouts and runaway teenagers – not three rugged, dangerous men like us." Applejack closed his book and disappeared into the stone shelter.

Futureman looked up at the quarter moon, it's faint glow settling upon the roosting oaks. He walked to the edge of the road, looking for some assurance that Jester and Applejack were right. He stood with his hands on his hips, prying into the shadows with his retinas. When unleashed, Futureman's imagination had a way of getting the upper hand on reality, but there were times when it could be trusted, managing to capture that predilection hanging in the air. A sixth sense. *They're coming.*

Though asleep, their brains never shut down, filling their dreams with those twice-lived images of reality littered with nonsense.

At midnight, Futureman opened his eyes. He craned his neck toward the mouth of the shelter and sat up. In the dark. A distant noise.

Applejack and Jester stirred in their bags.

The sound grew louder, clawing up the hills. It woke the other two.

No one spoke, unable to force out words.

Do we have time to get away before they come?

Is there anywhere to hide?

Where's my knife?

They had waited too long. The boards underneath them shook. F-150s, Rams and Silverados, 450's and 455's chewing the mountains down. Applejack and Jester tried desperately to muster something resembling bravery, even calm, but they were frozen in their beds. Futureman stood. His bag slid down. He watched, bare-chested in his underwear, as the trucks wheeled and spun around the fire. The strange shrieking of men and women ricocheted inside the open shelter.

One by one the caravan of trucks hemmed the shelter in. Four. Six. Ten of them, facing the three terrified men, their sweaty eyes dancing in the blinding radiation of KC floodlights. Several revolutions of the moon, trans-continental bird migrations, ocean cycles passed before anyone stepped forward to speak.

"What are you filthy dogs doing here? This place is ours."

Futureman walked out in front of his friends. His body silhouetted in the lights.

"We're just hikers. We never –"

"Who told you little bitches about this place?" Another voice barked.

"Don't suppose anyone knows you're here?" Two and three doors opened. Dark forms stepped to the ground.

"Where are your packs?" The voices closed in.

"They're in –"

"Why are you afraid? Don't be afraid," another one trilled lowly.

Their voices crowded the shelter. "Don't worry." "We won't hurt you." "Show us where your packs are." "You don't have friends camping nearby, do you?" "Why are you worried?" "This is not your place." "What's you're hurry? Stay awhile."

"No. Please. Wait just a – we're just…" Futureman held up his arms, ready to deflect blows. A veil of dust swirled about him. "We don't want any trouble. Whatever it is you want. Just."

A burly figure stormed forward, across the wall of light from the left. Futureman shrank back. Then, in the blinding light Futureman narrowed his eyes and detected a smile. The burly man patted Futureman on the shoulder. "Naw, dude! It's OK, man. Everything's OK. We're just playing with you guys. Naw man. Everything's fine."

"What? Are – are you serious?" Futureman stammered.

"We's just crappin with ya. We knew you guys is hikers." The big man looked into the shelter and tipped his hat. "We just come out here to party sometimes." He turned and moved back toward his purring Scout.

"Yep. If we'd known you guys was in here sleepin, we'd have just gone on down 'cross the creek to the beach. Sorry to bother you."

"You guys is more'n welcome to get it on with us," another said. "We got eight or ten cases a'beer. It's on us. You deserve it, hikin' all that way and all. Purdy awesome."

"N-no. Go ahead. We'll just stay in here and get some rest, big day tomorrow and all." Futureman slumped down on the boards as they drove away.

They heard the party going all night long. Hollers, revs, whistles and yelps. When daylight finally crept through the trees, they weren't sure they'd slept at all.

III

Jester's pace pushed them deep into the hills, on the claim that a couple of young ladies would be waiting for them mid-afternoon with some Trail Magic at the foot of Killington Mountain.

It is not uncommon for thruhikers to run into these bearers of kindnesses both big and small, known as Trail Angels. Commonly, Trail Magic will consist of a cooler full of cold drinks and fresh fruit. Without the novelty of refrigeration and with little space in their packs, these things are like gold to hikers. Some angels bring grills and cook steaks, hamburgers and hot dogs right on the trail (the smell beckons, magic ahead!). Often, local angels will keep a cooler at a Trail intersection, stocking it daily. Others provide basic supplies: batteries, new socks, a good book. Not infrequently, an angel will wait at an intersection and take a hiker to a nearby restaurant for an all-you-can-eat night on them.

That morning, the lighter air made for easy work. Applejack needed to see this kind of sky for a while if he wanted to make it through the summer. Right on schedule, they walked out of the timber into a gravel parking lot to find two pretty girls, *Beanpie* and *Alleycat*, sitting on lawn chairs, ice cold drinks in hand.

Jester nodded. "I told you it would be worth it if you hung with me."

Beanpie and Alleycat were both experienced hikers, having logged over 5,000 miles between them. Beanpie had done the entire Pacific Crest Trail from Mexico to Canada and both of them had done most of the AT. They spoke without pretension. The more miles you have under your feet, the more you understand it is from the dust you have come.

"Oh, before I forget," Alleycat said. "There's a guy sitting up on Killington. I believe he's waiting for you two. He said his name was Captain or

General or something like that." She pointed south.

"The Colonel!"

He was waiting for them a few hundred yards up the Trail, sitting cross-legged on a rock. He looked the same as the day they'd met him in the Hundred-Mile Wilderness. The same as the day he'd left them with Bear to return home to Virginia. Smiling. Golden.

"I couldn't do it. I couldn't stay away," Colonel said.

Sitting at home, trying, failing to recover from his strange stomach illness, he'd had little else to do but worry. Worry that he'd never be well again. Worry that he'd never get back on the Trail again. Worry that he had made the wrong decision by staying out of college for a year. Worry that although his girl was glad he came home, she would secretly think him a coward – a man who could not keep his word. Worry that Applejack and Futureman thought less of him.

The Colonel looked up at them with deference. "You guys mind if I hike with you into Massachusetts?"

"What kind of question is that?" Applejack reached down and pulled the Colonel to his feet.

They did twelve more miles by nightfall.

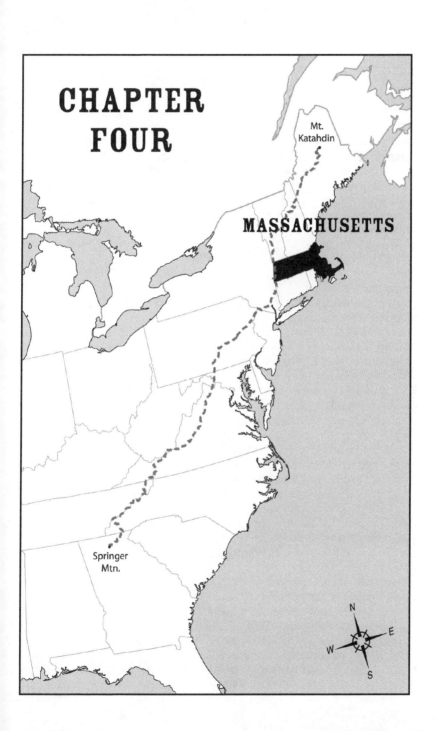

CHAPTER FOUR

MASSACHUSETTS

Mt. Katahdin

Springer Mtn.

N
E
W
S

As they stood on the edge of the forest looking back into Vermont, they wondered what new fears would stride forth from the darkness to greet them with beer and jokes. The world is full of foes, is it not? Some real, many imagined. The sun had come to claim Applejack. The shadows had come for Futureman. All things the Master's, what can this mean? What kind of companions exist in this world and the next, there in the nexus of two worlds as they collide? Small towns and patchwork farms lay ahead. Other vague realities lay behind. The three men turned south. A fresh start. Another new day.

I

Tom is a butcher. He is in his fifties. He's single. He's bald. He cuts cow thighs and rumps and sprays the leftover blood off the metal slab at the local grocery store. For dinner, he brings home flanks, prime cuts, kielbasa, ribs and, of course, the bacon.

His house is but a few feet away from the AT in the town of Dalton, Massachusetts. It is a quaint home with yellow shudders and a screen door to let the breeze in on those nice days.

Tom lives with a cat, which has the run of the place, a bed in each room, a mound of fur balls in the corner of the den. That coated-turd litterbox aroma has acquainted itself with every fiber of every room. Tom can't smell it anymore. Tom's visitors can.

Tom's porch wraps around the front of his house. It has a magnetic force like the American embassy in Khartoum. Safe and welcoming. It is wooden, but the instant a hiker beds down on it, it transforms into a soft foam pit – inescapable and cute as the Bastille. That's what they'd heard.

Tom stood on his famous porch that afternoon. He looked down the street toward the north to spy any oncomers, knowing if any came they would be gone just as suddenly. But Tom is a meek soul and expects no return for his kindness. Cheers to Tom.

Applejack and Futureman had heard about him and his porch from several Northbounders, but between the throes of Applejack's heat blight and their foray into the world of Common Sense, they had forgotten.

They got wind of it once again 5 miles out from Dalton, on the shores of Gore Pond below Crystal Mountain. A small pack of wild humans were lapping up water from the reservoir. Two of them, *Frodo* and *Pug*, were funny- shaped, short, stubby, crumpled hair, matted with what looked like molasses. The other one-tall and hooked, leering, browned with soil, burned by sun, rotten-breathed-towered above them. This one went by the name of *Yukon Rasputin*.

It was obvious he had been telling dirty tales to his underlings. They were sucking breaths. Frodo was missing a front tooth. The other one, as he listened, sorted through a clump of cotton froth that had collected on his bottom lip.

"Where you two goin?" Rasputin snarled as Futureman and Applejack neared.

"Down the Trail. You?"

"Me? Oh, wherever there's a good sheep farm, I guess," Rasputin said lustily. He turned his lips out and moaned, "B-a-a-a. B-a-a-a." Old beer on his breath.

Frodo rattled beneath him. Pug snorted.

"Yep. Enjoy." Applejack moved ahead, ignoring him.

Rasputin stepped across the trail. "You got somethin against sheep?"

"Nope. Every good farm needs –"

"B-a-a-a. B-a-a-a." Rasputin moaned again. Frodo and Pug sniggered.

"Well, it was a pleasure. May we?" Applejack stepped around him. Futureman followed suit.

Rasputin called after them, "Hey, if you go into Dalton, be sure to stop at Faggot Tom's."

"Who? Excuse me?" Applejack turned.

"Tom the faggot. Faggot Tom. And when you get there, tell that Faggot Tom that Rasputin, Frodo and Pug all said hi. We think he's swell, don't we boys?" Rasputin swatted Frodo across the back of the head and slapped Pug in the mouth.

Applejack halted on the street, in front of a house.

"What?" Futureman asked.

"That's got to be Tom's," Applejack said. "Look at the sign in the yard."

614 miles ← Katahdin / Springer → 1546 miles

"Man, we've come a long way."

Colonel was lagging behind. The initial adrenaline rush from his reunion with the Trail had worn off, and it was becoming apparent that time off had not solved his old diarrhea mystery. He finally caught up, aggravated and testy.

"Guys, back there at Gore Pond, did you run into –"

"Yeah."

"Did he –"

"Yep."

"Is this –"

"We think so."

Tom was standing behind the screen, cat at his feet. "What d'ya think, old fella?"

Cat meowed.

"Yeah, they look alright. Let's fix 'em some sundaes." Tom had already moved past Rasputin, ready to try again. Yesterday was yesterday. Kindness is kindness.

"You boys just enjoy the shade. Put your things on my porch and have a seat on that picnic table under the tall oak there. I'll be out shortly with some ice cream sundaes for you."

Tom brought the sundaes out in silver bowls, three scoops deep with real whip cream and chocolate-coated wafers. "Enjoy. My yard is good for camping. Porch is quite comfortable, too. Stay as long as you like. Jerry comes in and out of the house. He's a nice cat and loves company."

"We appreciate it, Tom, but we've got to get on down the trail after we finish this ice cream," Applejack said. "We're trying to make up some miles in the next few days."

We are? Futureman thought.

"I don't mind either way. I'm happy to have you at all." Tom went back inside.

Jerry was still sitting at the door.

"What d'ya think old fella?" Tom said.

Jerry meowed.

"You're right. I better put some mattresses out."

Oak stretched and groaned in the sun the next morning, as did the Colonel. His worries were growing. He hadn't expected the diarrhea to pick up exactly where it had left off in Maine. Now he knew he wouldn't be able to keep up. He wasn't about to ask them to slow down on account of his mud pies, but it wouldn't be long before he fell off the back end. And being alone was something he could not contend with, not in this condition. That's when he heard barking next door, and that's when it hit him.

A dog. It's perfect. I'm gonna buy a dog.

Applejack rubbed his eyes and asked again why exactly were they sleeping on a porch instead of in the woods.

"I'm gonna get a dog. So, what do you think?" Colonel asked.

[Applejack's mind flashed back: a tiny dog, barely canine – one of those drop-kick dogs – somewhere in the fragmented Wilderness, halfway through a black bog, stupefied. There was a woman – a beautiful woman – northbound, legs toned, golden. She came around the corner, locked into an Olympian pace, passed without a word, plowing through the muck. From behind, a little Pekingese yapped incessantly, plunged after her into the bog and began to sink, its little eyes needling back and forth like a seismograph. The woman turned to see her precious slide into the silt. "You little toot," she cooed, wading back into the muck. Held it up in the sun, lavishing the ratdog with butterfly kisses. Precious kicked the air in ecstasy, spitting mud droplets all over the woman's golden face.]

"Uhhhh. You sure about that?" Applejack asked.

"I have decided," Colonel said.

Futureman sat up, half awake. "Wooos."

"I think the Colonel wants to get a dog."

Futureman looked confused. "What did you – a kernel dog – popcorn?"

"I miss my dog Sam and I'm going to get a Trail dog."

"He's getting a dog," Applejack said.

"You mean – buy a dog?" Futureman asked.

"Yes, I have to."

"He has too."

"Like, today?" Futureman asked.

"Well, if I find one."

"So we're not leaving then?" Futureman asked.

"No, apparently not," Applejack said.

"You guys don't have to stay with me. I won't be alone. I'll have a dog."

"A dog," Applejack nodded.

"A dog," Futureman echoed.

Two options existed for obtaining a dog. The first: a pet store at the mall in nearby Pittsfield; the second: an animal shelter. It was Tom's day off at the grocery store. He gladly offered his shuttle services.

Warm air strummed through the car as they drove. Applejack leveled back and followed the ridgeline with his eyes. A tower on a hill caught the sun and shot toward him, a splintered cell of light. He began to pontificate. Without realizing it, his thoughts had become audible.

"What are you muttering about, Applejack?" Tom asked.

"Oh, uh, just about TV."

"What about it?"

"Well, I was just thinking it's sad that so much of American culture is shaped by network executives who rarely use TV for education or art or anything remotely helpful."

"It's TV," Tom nodded. "TV stinks. It's never been about art or anything useful."

Colonel stirred in the back, hesitant to speak.

"Tell us," Futureman pried. "We value your opinion."

"You're gonna laugh at me if I say it. You'll think it's stupid. I know you guys."

"Say it. We won't laugh. It's about art, for crying out loud. We're supposed to have different opinions," Applejack said.

"No way."

"C'mon, say it."

"Say it!"

"Alright, okay. So, I mostly agree with what you're saying. But. I think there is some real art on TV."

"Go on."

"I think MTV's Hip Hopera is really artistic."

They waited in silence. At last, the piston-pumping laughter spewed out.

"I knew you'd laugh!"

"Of course we're laughing," Applejack said. "A Hip Hopera? On MTV? Art?"

"Shut up. I'll kill you! It's my opinion. Plus, you guys haven't even seen it."

"Do we need to?"

The pet store at the mall had two chocolate labs, a dachshund, a jack-russell terrier and three fuzzy dogs. They barked silently behind the glass, teething, gnawing on their cages, running in tiny circles.

"I guess it should have dawned on one of us before we came here that pet stores usually sell puppies," Futureman said.

"Yeah," Colonel said.

The animal shelter had adult dogs, alright. The genetically doomed. Two virtually rabid mutts and a lab/bull mix eating its own tail. Three of them weren't clearly even dogs. There was an old hound too worn-down for the long haul. And then there was the one in the corner. Golden, youthful, medium build, tail wagging the dog. Ready for someone to love, someone who missed his girlfriend. Someone with a bad case of the Mississippi Quickstep.

Colonel was elated. "He's perfect!" He bent down. The dog licked him. "He's absolutely perfect. What do you think, guys?"

The cage was red-tagged: *Good, strong dog. Healthy. Keep tied up. Has a tendency to run away.*

"He's so perfect!" Colonel said.

"Are you serious? He'll sniff the Trail for about ten seconds and run off," Futureman said.

"No way. Look how much he loves me."

"He'll chase a rabbit first chance he gets. You'll find his picked carcass the next day. You want that on your conscience?" Applejack shook his head.

"Maybe it's a mix up, guys. Maybe they put the tag on the wrong cage."

"No, they're right, son." Tom said. "This one's not a Trail dog. I'm sorry."

Golden Boy barked as the Colonel walked out, dejected once again.

Day grew dark. After supper, the three men lined up to relieve themselves along a fence that ran between yards. The Colonel was in a pitiful mood.

"Sorry you didn't find yourself a friend," Applejack said.

"I'm sorry we didn't leave today. I know I held you guys up."

Futureman was eyeing something in the darkness two yards over. "Hey, what's going on over there?" he hissed.

Tom's neighbor had stumbled out onto the back porch. Very drunk. A beautiful retriever, maybe a year old, was tied to a post beside the kiddie pool, panting, wagging, waiting for her owner's gentle touch. Instead, the drunk slapped her across the face. She cowered. The man turned on the hose and started to spray her down. "Get over here, you lousy bitch!" he screamed, lashing her back with the hose.

"That sorry lush!" Futureman said.

"What kind of person? I'm going over there and –" Colonel hooked a leg over the bushes.

"No, no. Don't do anything rash. He's putting the hose down, now." Futureman kept a hand on the Colonel's shoulder until the man went inside.

A dull incandescence hung over the small town and its quiet, empty streets. They lay in their bags on the porch, trying to forget what they'd seen, but silence has a way of burning the mind.

"There's nothin' worse than seeing an animal get mistreated," Applejack said.

"Unless it's a person," said Futureman.

"True. Even now that dog is waiting for love from her owner. Even after getting beaten, she just waits and hopes. Thinking tomorrow's gonna be different. Tomorrow will be better." Applejack's voice faded. A steady breeze picked up and presently moonlight fell into the shadows. At last, they drifted off to sleep.

Sleep didn't improve the Colonel's mood. The next morning he woke up muttering.

"What are you saying, Colonel?" Applejack threw off his covers.

"I'm gonna take that dog," Colonel said. His eyes looked strange, unhinged, pixilated.

"You're going to steal Tom's neighbor's dog?"

"Yep. I have decided," Colonel said. "And I have a plan."

"This is going to take all day, isn't it?"

Futureman crept around the front of the house, low to the ground, trying to avoid being seen by the neighbors. *How in the world did I get roped into being the one who steals the dog?* The others stood watch, strategically placed, Applejack in Tom's front yard, Colonel across the street. The owner had gone to work, wouldn't be back for a while. Colonel shot him a thumbs up. Futureman rolled his eyes and slid toward the back yard.

"Such a bad idea," Futureman muttered, inching his way closer and closer to the dog. She wagged her tail joyfully and rushed to him, a licker not a barker. *Thank goodness.*

Suddenly, the back door opened. Futureman instinctively dove into the bushes next door and cursed the Colonel for this lamebrain scheme. Two little girls padded onto the porch, eager to play with their puppy dog.

Kids? Futureman hung his head. *I'm trying to steal a dog from two kids. I'm a bad person.*

"D'ya get her? Where is she?" Colonel asked.

"Find yourself another dogknapper," Futureman said.

"We went over this! We agreed."

"Sorry, but there's kids man. Remember how much you loved your dog when you were little?"

"She has kids?"

A heavy storm rolled in that night. They stretched tarps across the porch to shield their gear from the rain. Tom invited them in for dinner – steaming kielbasa, Caesar salad, a medley of zucchini, squash and almonds. Impressive for a bachelor.

In spite of himself, the Colonel couldn't help but bring up the failed heist. He needed some closure. Lately, his life had seemed like a series of fizzled-out dreams.

"Tom, last night we saw your neighbor stumble out the back door…"

Tom set his fork down and wiped his mouth. "Yes, I've spoken with him before about this. It's not a very frequent occurrence. Once a month or so, he'll get angry drunk and start yelling at something. I'm glad it's his dog, actually. Could be worse."

Tom took a bottle of Goldslager down from the cabinet..

"It's a good thing you didn't go through with it. I'm afraid you wouldn't have gotten very far," he said, tipping his glass.

"Why's that?"

"My neighbor is a detective."

After a few laughs, toasts and a detailed briefing of their ridiculous plot, the Colonel decided to let it all hang out. "Raise it high. Let's drink to Yukon Rasputin," he declared.

Glasses dropped to the table. Tom looked at the clock. Applejack shot Colonel a look.

"Uh, I'm sorry. Really." Colonel said.

Predictably, Tom handled it with class, choosing not to explain the vulgar episode that had made a mockery out his generosity.

"No, it's fine. Some people are just not cut out for decency."

And it is true, some aren't. Human conscience wears heavy traffic on the soul, always telling us: *Do right.* Conscience bears forth common grace and common grace goes a long way, restraining humanity from fully enacting the dark desires within (*I will plant a land mine and Larry will never again walk through my petunias*). But if the recesses of the human heart suddenly became reality, the world would experience the worst fate imaginable. We call it The End. Our God-given conscience makes us want to be better people, and at the very least, reminds us that we aren't. Conscience is honest, and even though we may hide it from the world at times, we can never hide ourselves from it.

But then again...

There are some. Some whose consciences are seared. Some who live outside of its cramped prison. Psychiatrists may quibble – were they born so singed? Was the inner voice overthrown? At any rate, these *ubermensch* roam the earth beyond evil. They are free.

Yukon Rasputin was one of these beings. He was a free man. Free from the inconvenience of having to be decent. Free from the rules that force other people to respect life. He was **allowed** to take advantage of people and their naïve kindnesses. Ethical freedom was his birthright.

When Tom of Dalton invited him into his home free of charge, Rasputin (rightly so) chose to consume a case of beer, polish off a fifth of potato vodka, get barb-wire underwear drunk and howl at the moon from the neighbor's flower bed. When the police responded to a call at 2 AM, Rasputin was **permitted** to tell them to "fugg off" because he was "on Tom's property" and "Tom said I could do it" (even though he was across the street *not* on Tom's property). This is entitlement. The spoils of a liberated spirit.

Rasputin shows us the way. The chains of decency are too binding. Cast them off! Respect, virtue, nobility? Far too long these loathsome notions have held us under their tyranny. Burn them. Release the krakens from their prisons in the deep. Shoot rats at the dump. Jump on sandcastles.

Blow shit up. Stick firecrackers into animal rectums. Speak before spoken to. Pee on sidewalks. Wear X-ray goggles. Frighten children. Hump everything in sight. Insult old people. Drive a Hummer. Litter. Build waxwings and spit at the sun. Take the handicapped spot. Get freak nasty. Yukon Rasputin would want you to.

The doorbell sounded. It was still raining, dark. Who would be ringing at this time of night, in this weather?

A thruhiker would.

"Do you fellas have room on the porch?" Tom asked.

"We can make room," Applejack said reluctantly.

During the first two months of hiking south from Maine, there is the constant intersection of North and Southbounders. They share shelters and food, stories, advice of all kinds, even warnings. It is an easy comradery and a playful rivalry. As time goes by, the northbound line dwindles to a mere thread of stragglers and the line of Southbounders thins as well, as each finds his own isolated pace toward Georgia. At summer's beginning, Applejack and Futureman had greatly enjoyed the excitement but lately, they appreciated the solitude. The old codgers were feeling unsociable.

"Hi. I'm Terranaut," the stranger said, soaked to the core. He was clean-shaven and red-cheeked. An impressive hairline rose above a high forehead.

"Ah, *earth-traveler*," Applejack said, digging through his Latin.

"Very astute," said Terranaut.

Terranaut was fresh out of the Navy. A graduate from Harvard University with a degree in geography, he was sharp-witted and ambitious, but grounded – eager to shed the obsequious hubris that came with an Ivy League diploma.

"And you are…"

"Colonel."

Terranaut snapped to attention. "Sir, yessir…Uh, just kidding. I'm only a lieutenant – never mind. Not important." He clapped Colonel on the shoulder.

"Well, join us on the porch, if you like. It's a little wet for tenting," Futureman motioned them outside.

The rain pattered against the tarp for hours, a good rhythm for deep sleeping. Yet something woke Applejack. Some presence that caused him to raise his head and search out what was there in the darkness. A shadow moved toward him along the wall.

"Please be Tom's cat," he prayed. The creature stopped as a black bushy tail rose above its form.

"Please, do not be that. Please. Do not. Be that." Distant lightning illuminated a white stripe down the creature's back.

"Sheeeeeeeeit." It was clearly a skunk: universally feared beast, foul empress of the outdoors. And there she stood, not two yards away from Applejack's face, seeking solace from the storm.

This is real. What do I do?

The inside of a warm sleeping bag was looking like a good option to her.

Applejack lay cocooned, arms useless. *Think, think, think.* To scare the skunk would lead to instant misery. To ignore her and hope for the best would be impossibly foolish.

And so, he did the only thing he could do. He began to make noises. Unidentifiable, unmistakable, non-threatening but mildly disconcerting noises, born from some forgotten place deep inside him, forced upward by one of man's strongest desires – to live life without ever knowing the taste of skunk ass. Firecracker-dud noises, kick-in-the-groin noises, empty-shaving-cream-can noises, sneeze-during-church noises. He ticked his tongue. He pooted through his teeth. He strangled his tonsils.

Yet the skunk came closer, curious to know the identity of this creature. Then, at last – perhaps from confusion or fear, probably from disinterest – she took a step back.

It's working! "Hisssssss, tick, ptoot, hisssssss." Applejack held his ground.

She turned and found the edge of the porch. It had stopped raining, moon back out. Off she scampered into the night.

Applejack dropped his heavy head against the floor, sighing like a man who has passed a kidney stone.

Jerry the cat had seen the whole thing from the living room window. He licked his paws and returned to bed, most impressed.

III

After a breakfast under the Oak they said goodbye, grateful to have known the famous butcher who has never met a stranger. Tom smiled and closed the screen door behind him. Now a full quartet, Terranaut led the charge into the hills.

God had smiled on them once again with the cool air that sometimes follows a storm front. The creeks and streams were full again, pumping the Colonel's cracked innards full of the aged Puritan waters of Massachusetts. Applejack walked with his old strength, chuckling at good fortunes and turning through the pages of *Walden* in his mind. Terranaut was chipper, pleased to be back in his old neighborhood.

Late that night, Futureman awoke to the sound of distant explosions. He walked out under the sky and found dancing dragons and long-beaked birds high above the valley. Below, the town of Great Barrington was lit red by fireworks. It looked as though it was burning. *The world in judgment*, Futureman thought, unaware it was Labor Day.

With time and miles, hikers find their own personal cadence, a rhythm as unique as a fingerprint. The colors, sights, smells, sounds and tastes along the way are assimilated by the senses and blended with personality to forge a distinctive style – like the aroma wheel of a good ground-soaked wine. *She's a sprinter. He's slow and steady like the tortoise. She's a marathoner*…and so on. Cadence, like mood, changes with the environment. Blackbeard, a pacer, will slow in the late afternoon if he tastes trillium in the air. Erratic Little Moose quickens to match the breeze and sputters when it dies. Fred Baby, a steady-hander, counters her ebb and flow by grinding in the middle, always there.

By the time Terranaut, Applejack, Futureman and the Colonel wandered into Ice Gulch, two miles out from Great Barrington, they were shelled into their own worlds. No one else existed. It was just one of those days – maybe it was in the water, perhaps on the wind – but no matter. They had awoken to see before them the naked Trail – wood, tree, lichen and flower – as woman, for the first time.

It didn't take long for them to drift apart.

Morning

Terranaut climbed up into the forest on East Mountain. Pin cherries, ash and balsam poplars mingled with thick patches of nannyberry among large discs of jagged rock. Winding in and around was the Trail, a downy soil footpath, spring-loaded, effortless. A morning mist hung at chest level. As he passed through the forest, it felt more like canoeing than walking. He came across a massive cylindrical rock, notched and serrated, digging into the mountain. Tunnels and archways dissevered it intricately. *This is why I'm a geographer. This is what I wanted from the Navy. To explore, to uncover. Hm, very peculiar formations found only in the northern Appalachians.* Terranaut sorted through the site, fate and fame awaiting. *At any moment this fissure is going to open up into some huge chamber, and within-the lost remains of an unknown pre-historic people.* He could see the headlines. "Terranaut: Geographer, Explorer, Adventurer, Friend to Man – Finds Lost Civilization – Rewrites History." He could see it all now – the cameras, the notoriety, the grants.

He climbed out of the forest onto a sharp cut of metamorphic rubble.

Slate cliffs shaved the peak short, a domination over the flowing country-side. Sky cleaved the valley in two. The sun, reaching down into the sprawling farmscape, shattered the fog like so much pulled cotton.

The valley was comprised of old farms dating back to pre-revolutionary war days. Acquired at a heavy price, the farmers and their sons had secured the rights to them with their own blood. They had survived hard winters and disease. They had clung viciously to it, time and again, wrenching it away from warring natives – peoples with an even earlier claim to the territory. An anger for European disrespect to the land stirred in the trees. Outrage at the plight of these diseased and forgotten tribes slashed through the quiet, even here, these many years later.

At the base of East Mountain with tracts of brown, orange, green and yellow, farm country begins. The Trail meanders through it for miles traveling as a snake would – wherever it can find passage – through bright cornfields and over country roads, until it happens upon a busy highway running blindly across the valley, the indifferent artery of some larger entity. A dark forest of old pine sits at the far end of the valley below the mountain. The Trail disappears into it before climbing up to the tip of Jug End, a blunt pinnacle standing tall over the checkered vale.

<u>Noon</u>
Applejack came across an old stone bridge over Hubbard Brook. The current echoed off the undersides, gurglings of the past. Several quiet hours will unravel its nostalgic threads. Upriver a ways, he saw an old willow hanging over the water, where the Trail turns toward it. A wide brown beach cleared room beneath its branches. The stream, copper-rich, smelling of pine, flowed down from the source at Root Pond not many miles away.

Applejack sat under the willow and took his lunch. He studied the Old Man's arms as they bent over him, the crooked back that shaded him. The willow had been one of his favorite trees ever since he was a small boy. There was one on his great-grandfather's farm in West Tennessee. He had wondered then, *why is it sad?* Now as he sat, he thought about the nature of sadness. *There are many kinds of weeping in the world – that of both joy and despair. Which is the Willow's?* The words of Solomon came to him: "In much wisdom is much grief, and he that increases knowledge increases sorrow." *From wisdom, then. That is why the willow weeps.*

The willow is old. Centuries have come and gone while it sits in the soil, drinking, watching the tribes of men come and go, as they fight and spill blood for possession of an earth that cannot be owned. Hubbard Brook had seen its share of red water. *If I can do more to grasp the nature of wisdom, then I should weep as the willow does,* Applejack realized. The words of the gospel came to him. "Blessed are those who mourn for they shall be comforted." *When will I mourn? Have I ever mourned?*

<u>Evening</u>
The sky turned from blue to green as a dark cloud drew itself over the valley. Futureman walked briskly. Corn everywhere, rows and rows, fields on fields, swaying in the wind, bending down over endless tunnels and mazes. *Lost in a labyrinth*, Futureman imagined. *Which way to turn, which path to choose? The possibilities. The dangers.* He walked ahead. *Straight and narrow.* The end comes as soon as the beginning in a labyrinth. The trail hooked and turned, curving with the crook of the farm. A fence opened into a gap, a patch of struggling stalks, sparse, browned by the sun. You have to leave the path, it says. Make a turn, even a wrong one. It's okay in a labyrinth. Lessons, it says. Lies! Waywardness ends in loss. *Walk it. Straight and narrow.* Forgetfulness gets you lost. *Not to the left, nor to the right.* Lay a marking down. To remember the paths you have already been on, the turns you have already made. Futureman grabbed a husk and ripped it open. Plucking kernels off the cob, he dropped them at his feet. They trailed behind him. He ate a few, then the cob, starch running down into his beard. Sustenance for choices. But they change. The turns change, the paths you've been on. Not quite remembered the same way they were. The kernels dry up. Crows eat them. Temptations. Illusions. The labyrinth is long and straight. *Straight and narrow.* Its turns are tricks, its noise trickery. The wind whistled through the corn. *Walk ahead. Stay on the path.* A wooden turnstile offered itself from within the barbwire lines. End comes as soon as the beginning, in a labyrinth.

<u>Night</u>
The Colonel was lagging behind again, knees wobbly. Through the day, he had saved the farmers hard-earned pence fertilizing their cornfields for them, and now he found himself standing alone in the middle of the old forest at dusk. The high old pines blocked out what little light was left, their jacket thick, trunks black. Needles covered the forest floor. No understory in such a forest, only space. Vivid emptiness. Perceptions of near and far had disappeared. An uneasy feeling came over him, like that of the wanted man being watched. Immanence pressed in close from the canopy above. It moved along the ground. Not animal. Not human. Reluctant to use the *word*, the Colonel moved on, skirted by presence. *But there is something in here. With me. To be sure.* There it was again, along his periphery. This wood was…haunted by something to be sure. *I want to get out of here,* Colonel thought. Then suddenly it came, as it always does.

The affliction. *Not now, for the love of mercy!* His insides quaked, roiled. Down low, it was an emergency, an explosive condition. There was no time to get out of the forest. No time at all.

He found a spot just off the path. Hanging onto a sapling, he lowered his backside into the dark. The usual noise of the forest was gone, no twigs snapping, no animals scurrying, no wind. *C'mon, c'mon, c'mon.* Breath on the back of his neck. *Evil-come-out-come-out-of-me now!*

The Colonel shook his hands at his sides and trotted out beyond the last pine, climbing messy-legged upward to Jug End. High stepping, as though hands grabbed at his ankles from underneath the basement stairs.

Futureman, Terranaut and Applejack were sitting on the crag looking out across the valley. Sunset was playing out its coda along the horizon.

"What happens in the valley *stays* in the valley," Terranaut said. "That's what these two mountains are here for. To make sure."

"What happened in the valley?" Applejack asked.

"Didn't you – feel something going on in the woods down there?" Terranaut asked.

"What – you mean ghosts?" Applejack said.

"Something," Futureman nodded.

"Yeah, something for sure. This here valley is the site of Shay's Rebellion." Terranaut gestured broadly.

"No kidding."

"There's a monument just off the Trail back there. I went down to check it out. You guys remember anything about Shay's Rebellion?"

"Vaguely, something to do with land seizure and a farmer uprising," Applejack said.

"Yeah. Basically, after the Revolutionary War, the merchantmen were cut off from the Indies. The whole coast practically shut down – no trade, no ship building, ghost wharfs, the works. So, to make up for the deficit, the government did what it does best – raise taxes. The whole state turned ass up, and the people who got screwed the worst were our farmers right down there in the valley. They asked the state for paper money to get a boost, so they could save their farms. Now remember, these were the same men who, not a decade before, had bled in the Revolution, and for their trouble they got their farms taken from them. State seized every last one, said they were *debtors*. There's the beginnings of a good rebellion."

"So Shay was the voice," Applejack said.

"Yep, and he kept a pitchfork in hand to back up the talk. He figured if the King of England couldn't take his belongings, then why the hell should the Massachusetts legislature be able to? So, Shay led the charge, and thousands of farmers managed to take back their farms. Got it done the

American way – took it by force. Some would say in the same spirit as the Boston Tea Party."

"Who would say that?"

"Well, the guy who put up the monument, I guess. Anyways, it happened in the fall of 1786."

"All this was on the plaque?"

"Uh...yeah, it's all right there on the plaque," the Harvard man elucidated.

"And the ghosts in the forest?" Applejack said.

Terranaut pinched his bottom lip. "Well, as legend has it – and bear in mind that I am making this up as I go along – all the farmers who died in the battle, are still rummaging around in those woods down there. Waiting to get back the very thing they bled for – their dignity."

"Someone should let them know they got it. Time to move on," Applejack said.

The Colonel rustled up the hill. "Guys, am I glad to see you!"

"Did you run into the ghosts?" Futureman said.

"You don't even know the half of it. I had to poop right in their lair."

"Hey, what's that on your leg?"

IV
"When you're driving in your Chevy, and you feel something heavy: D-I-A-R-R-H-E-A."
                    -An American folk song

Alone in the dark again, at the end of another day, the Colonel lurched forward, bruised, marred, in despair. By the time he got to the shelter, his ego was in about the same condition as his diaper rash.

"I've had just about enough of this. I can't stop it. I can't wipe it off. I've got nothing left to give," he said.

He plopped down on the broken slabs of Glen Brook Shelter. His shoulders slumped, resolve decayed like the wet bark walls. Badly in need of distraction and purpose, he turned to his friends.

Futureman suggested a game of TV Tag in the hemlocks surrounding the shelter.

"I have a rash, remember? I can't run around. Can't do shit."

"Actually, buddy, that's the one thing you can do," Futureman said.

"Ha, ha, ha."

"Don't worry. It'll pass," Terranaut said.

"Actually, they don't know if it will or not," Colonel said.

"What do you mean?" Applejack asked.

"Doctor said he didn't know what it was."

"Are you serious?"

"Yeah, he said he's never seen anything quite like it before."

"Why didn't you tell us that? What are you doing out here?" Applejack asked.

"I don't know. Figured it was better than waiting around at home for the results."

"Colonel! I hate to say it, but you might want to think about going back home where you can get better."

Colonel shrugged apathetically, looking off into the valley.

During dinner, he didn't eat. He sat in the same position staring into the firs, until all had gone to bed.

Deep in the night, a little mouse came and perched beside him in the moonlight.

"You're a hiker," the mouse said.

"That's right, mouse," Colonel responded.

"Well, how does it make you feel to know that you and your friends have ruined our home?"

"What are you talking about?"

"I think you know. You owe us big time." The mouse wiped his whiskers, twisting them upwards.

"Alright, what do you want?" Colonel asked.

"We want things the way they were."

"Uh-huh."

"We want you to remove this shelter –"

"Listen, you can stop the charade. We all know you're glad we're here – all of you. You love our trash, with your fat little bodies. You think you'd be that fat and happy without us? Running for cover from the owls all the time?"

"OK. So you're intuitive," the mouse said.

"Yeah, big deal. It's not that hard," Colonel said.

"Alright. I'll just lay it down, then. I'm here to steal your food. And there's not a darn thing you can do about it. I've got tons of friends."

"Oh really?"

"That's right, hiker. We're gonna be loud as crap all night. We're gonna chew holes in your stuff and crinkle plastic wrappers." The mouse clutched his little arms tightly across his chest, whiskers see-sawing back and forth between squeaks. "And jump on your foreheads."

Suddenly the Colonel became invigorated. In this moment, he found his purpose. "I'll kill you, mouse. I'll kill you all."

The Colonel was patient and inventive. Mormon ingenuity burned in his bosom. Tirelessly, he worked. He built a trap out of a box and some Oreo cookie crumbs. He waited until they were inside and smashed them with his boot. He did this all night.

The first blow woke Applejack.

"What are you...doing?"

Colonel was on all fours in his underwear. "I'm killing the enemy. Look." He held up a dead mouse in the moonlight.

"Colonel, there are hundreds of mice, maybe thousands on this mountain alone. Just let them be. They're not out to get us."

"I have to kill them."

Applejack rolled over.

Futureman was flying over a gigantic milkshake in a licorice helicopter when he felt the presence of Colonel above him. He opened his eyes. The Colonel was whispering.

"uoo-ava-mou-n-yor-beeer."

What? Mou? Beer? Then he felt it, a tiny creature breathing, bedded down in the nest attached to his face. "For the love of – a mouse in my beard!"

Futureman shook his head violently. The Colonel slammed a shoe on the boards as the baby mouse scampered down into the cracks. "That's right, run! I'll get you. I'll get you all."

Again, after everyone had fallen asleep, BOOM.

"Gotcha!"

"Colonel!"

"Hah-hah!" Enjoying himself for the first time in weeks.

Over in the trees, Terranaut unzipped his hammock. He was sleeping in a *nice* spot. He'd been looking forward to waking up to a *nice* view of the valley after a *nice* night of sleep. Now it was time to take a *nice* walk up to the shelter.

He clasped his hands behind his back and leaned down into the shadows of the ramshackle room. "Your little box, Colonel, is real neat. And from the sound of things, it's working out pretty well for you. But SHUT THE HELL UP!"

The next morning, as they set out for the town of Kent, the Colonel still had diarrhea. And he was tired. Even so, there was a little smile perched on the edge of his mouth.

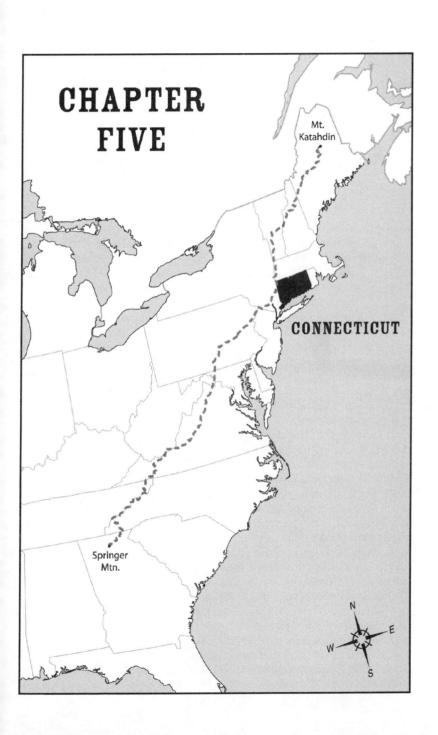

CHAPTER FIVE

Mt. Katahdin

CONNECTICUT

Springer Mtn.

N
W E
S

The sky ran to deep blue in the distance, then to coal black. The men watched it draw closer with every step. They gazed intently at it as it waxed and spun. It was not approaching night that filled them with dread, but the stampede of a storm hidden there. Daylight at midnight, the kind of revelation that can kill you. And fire, such as it is, cannot be avoided. With nowhere to go but on, they walked toward the sound of thunder.

I

There is a difference between a distant thunder and the crack of a thousand canons right over your head. Mothers turn fear of the trembling sky into sweet dreamscapes, telling their children that the rumbles in the clouds are angels bowling – sweet, fat, naked children, these angels. Sometimes, we will sit on the porch to watch the wind and far-flung lightning, but when the white-hot cinders of heaven slam down with the force of ten thousand trains, splitting the earth not twenty yards from us, they are a horror beyond words. No matter how many times we chant we are *not afraid of storms, not afraid of storms, not afraid of storms* – when we find ourselves inside one, the mantra evaporates and we run for cover. The natural powers are untamable and somehow far beyond comprehension.

The actual science of lightning is relatively simple. Turbulence and friction in rapidly moving air builds up a violent static charge. Air resistance will hold the charge in the cloud for as long as it can, but when that charge exceeds its tipping point, it fires negative electrons towards the earth's surface, upwards of 60 miles per second. Electrons stream up to relieve the charge. The electrons traveling in this conductive path can heat the air to as much as 50,000 degrees Fahrenheit. The air expands, resulting in *shockwaves*. We simply call it thunder, but the electromagnetic energy produced is a little taste of Armageddon. It vaporizes, electrocutes, causes fires and fells planes from the sky.

Lightning's fundamental simplicity is no comfort to us. It has the power to kill and that places it well into the mysterious realm of the dangerous and unknown. In the past, humans deified storms. These days we trivialize them – "only angel games, honey." To be honest, our nerves need the consolation.

There are many rotten days on the Trail. September 3rd was one of those days. Applejack, Futureman and Terranaut had been on one another's heels since lunch. Never far apart, sweaty, uninspired and irritable, pushing up and down an endless cycle of lukewarm hills. The Colonel labored on at the rear in his desperate fashion. At the end of this interminable series of hours,

Applejack, Futureman and Terranaut found themselves standing less than a mile from their evening camp spot, deflated, hungry, mouths agape at the wicked sight before them.

"The Trail goes up that, doesn't it?" Applejack said.

"Yeah."

"So I guess we're supposed to go up it aren't we?"

"Yeah."

"Why must you always mock us?" Terranaut said, downcast, undoubtedly quoting some great (obscure) work of literature.

"Mock us? Who's mocking us?" Futureman asked.

"Whoever put all these hills here."

"You mean God?" Futureman said.

"Well, I wasn't really referring to him, but, for the sake of argument, okay. Why does God mock us?"

"Because He likes us," Futureman smiled like he'd torn the face off a marionette doll and glued it to his own.

"What does that mean?"

"God mocks those He loves."

Terranaut was a non-practicing Catholic and quite adept at quoting dangerous snippets of the Bible. "I believe you mean, 'God chastens those He loves.'"

"What's the difference?" Futureman said, charging up the hill.

An open meadow waited at the crest of Silver Hill, highest Trail point in Connecticut. They had walked exactly one-third of the Appalachian Trail, almost to the mile. Applejack sat on the lip of the mountain in sweaty clothes, taking it in. If nothing else, the day was a benchmark. As the sun set, the sweltering air began to cool.

"Bout time to change into something comfortable and dry." *Maybe a thin cotton scrub pant and an open-toed rubber thong. Very chic.* Applejack found privacy behind a tree.

Though not as interested in reflecting on the significance of numbers, Futureman was very fond of capturing significant moments on film. When he saw Applejack creep away, he dropped his dinner spoon for the disposable camera. Stealthily, he crept closer through the brush toward Applejack's quivering shanks. A twig snapped beneath Futureman's feet. Applejack darted into the clearing, breaking for a promising patch of spotted knapweed, his creamy skin glowing against the shadowy underbrush.

That's when the preachers showed up.

Two ministers halted on the edge of the clearing, witnesses to the seemingly perverse chase. Futureman swung around with a savage grin. Unsated. Applejack dove into a stand of larix laricina.

"Hello, there. Uh." Futureman shrugged his shoulders.

The ministers called up ecumenical smiles and retired to a small knob of the hill to drop the gear from their sweaty backs. Thunder shook the far-off hills as they pitched their shiny tent.

They were non-denominational, Dean and Joe, out for some fun away from the flock. They didn't yet know that they'd picked the wrong spot.

"So what brought you guys out here?" Dean asked over dinner. He looked very modern for a preacher. Rimless eyeglasses, Columbia shorts.

"Lots of reasons. Solitude. Journey. Purity." Futureman said. His pat response.

"Huh."

"Where you guys headed?" asked Terranaut.

"Not far. Thirty miles or so is all we can hope for. Sounds like a good-sized storm's coming, eh? You guys run into any storms along your way?" Joe asked.

"A few."

"Been caught in any bad ones?"

"Yeah. Mostly just rain and wind up in New Hampshire, though."

Futureman nodded towards the Colonel who had just arrived and was pitching below the knob. "Up in Maine, that guy there got pinned in a light-ning storm on a bald in the Saddleback range with no cover. He said he crawled into a crack, wrapped his rain-fly around him, and curled up in the fetal, praying for God to spare him. Overall, we've made out fine, though."

The preachers nodded uneasily and watched a dejected Colonel drag him-self into his tent – a tent that was situated not two yards away from an inex-plicable steel pole which jutted impressively from the ground. Swarms of moths were gathering around it in the mounting static.

"So you fellas are probably pretty used to old Mother Nature by now. Nothing much gets to you, huh," Pastor Joe said.

"Not really, Joe. Seems God uses nature to humble us," Futureman offered.

"Amen, brother!" Joe said.

Dean nodded. "Mmm, I receive that."

A pavilion sat at the back of the hill, one of those built in parks for family reunions and redneck all-nighters, slanted tin roof and a few picnic tables underneath. A plywood shelf lined the shelter. It was decorated with graffiti messages – "Matt & Taylor 4Forever," "Slowfoot peed here," "We eat our money and shit out the devil," etc. Certain of rain, Futureman and Applejack threw their sleeping bags on the tables inside. Terranaut strung his rainproof hammock down the hill between two black oaks.

The Colonel had opted to forego supper for sleep. He couldn't keep it in him anyways. But for whatever reason, neither Applejack, Futureman nor Terranaut noticed his perilous location and, consequently, they failed to warn him. He was sleeping beside a lightning rod.

It was late when the first wave arrived, black of night coming quick under the clouds. The treetops churned furiously overhead. The day's humidity was convening in the heavens, bolstered by the cool wind that precedes the storm. The sound of sawing logs played convincingly across the hill but Futureman was still awake, wired and journaling to distract himself from his anxiety, counting the seconds between light and rumble. It remained at a distance long enough for him to drift off.

He woke up at precisely 2:33 AM, sat upright on the table. Thunder. That was close. He hated storms. *Hated them.* Squinting nervously into the darkness, he could see that everyone was asleep. He was alone. A huge bank of clouds pulsed beyond the far side of the valley, electricity germinating wildly inside its core – ready to burn the earth.

The air is still calm here. Still some time. He turned his headlamp on and crawled under the picnic table, journal in hand. He began to write. *It's marked me once before. The lightning might come to take me this time. If I can't escape it, perhaps I should embrace it...*

Sky fell. A shard of deafening electricity the size of a skyscraper hammered down on the mountain, honing in on the Colonel's tent. Everyone woke.

He ran across the field, screaming wild-eyed and dove into the pavilion.

"I could kill one of you! Why in hell didn't somebody tell me I pitched my tent beside a lightning rod? I can't believe you guys let me camp there. I don't know what I'm doing. You know that! I'm eighteen, and I'm sick!"

"Eighteen means you're a big boy," Terranaut said, soaked but smiling.

"Not cool, not cool." Colonel bit his fist.

Another column of fire shook the mountain. The boys watched as the preachers' tent began to shake and bulge, finally bursting like an over-cooked potpie. "Grab what you can!" Dean shouted. The terrified ministers broke through the zipper and clawed their way up the hill's newborn streams.

"Tent was supposed to be waterproof. Everything's drenched." Dean stumbled in, dumping everything at Terranaut's feet. "Is there room in here for us?"

"Always room in the fold for one more. Isn't that what you guys say?"

"Aren't we missing somebody? Where's Futureman?" Colonel asked.

Futureman was crouching under the table, eyes closed and sniveling.

"Hey, what are you doing down there, friend?" Dean asked.

"He hates lightning. Only thing he's afraid of." Applejack shrugged.

"A healthy fear to have. No one is safe from this kind of weather," Dean put a preacher's hand on Futureman's shoulder.

Garish studs of lightning split the sky open for the next half hour, so close it seemed that the flashes came from inside their own eyes. Silver Hill hunkered down through the night, a wide-open playground for the storm, high and exposed over the valley of Kent, Connecticut. There, the travelers huddled together, waiting for the storm to pass, safe and sound, underneath the glowing tin roof of the pavilion.

II

The affliction had run its course. It had finally turned Colonel's insides to cottage cheese. He darted into the woods three times during breakfast alone.

"Colonel, you need to go home," Futureman muttered, looking down at his gruel.

"Don't say that to me. No way."

"Listen, buddy. You need to get somebody to really figure this thing out. I mean, bloody feet we can handle. Shin splints we can handle, even the occasional heat stroke. But this – you cannot handle this."

"I've been handling it."

"No, you haven't. You're pale and weak and nearly done. It's over. We're sending you home, today." Applejack leveled his eyes at him. "Before it's too late."

"How can you say that? I don't think I can take going home again." Tears welled in his eyes. He wiped them and looked away quickly.

"You said the Trail goes right by your house in Winchester, right? We'll be down to northern Virginia in a few weeks. If you're feeling good by then, you can pick right up with us and off we go. Just like always."

"I'm gonna be just another one of those guys now. A failure." Colonel said.

"No, you're not. This is different." For a moment, Applejack saw him as a boy. A little brother. "You've proven yourself beyond any doubt. Now you gotta go home."

A few hours later, as they passed through the little town of Kent, the Colonel caught one last bus headed for home. They did not wave to him. They knew, as he disappeared behind the tinted glass, that they would see him again – but not on the Appalachian Trail.

III

Days passed dully under their feet and noses. Occasionally, Futureman caught himself looking over his shoulder to see if the Colonel was hobbling along behind. He missed him. Tired, not from strain, but of monotony, they set their packs down, mid afternoon, not interested in going any further.

"Well, it's been another terrific day here on the Appalachian Trail," Terranaut said wryly. "Very enriching. I haven't the words. I am *blown away*. *All* this wondrous beauty. *All* these glorious experiences along the App-ala-chian Trail. It's not every day in life you get to look at the same tree for ten straight hours. I'll see you guys tomorrow. I'm sleeping alone in the woods. Don't take it personally." He picked his way back into the trees, dragging his pack behind him.

Futureman was no better off. He sat in the dirt sifting through the contents of his food bag: cheese and crackers, dry oatmeal, dehydrated noodles, peanut butter, dried fruit, blah, blah, blah. He dropped the bag. "We eat this stuff all the time. Frankly, I'm a little sick of it."

"What would you prefer instead?"

Futureman shrugged.

"Flowers? Tree bark? Grass? What?"

Futureman slouched forward listening to the current of a nearby stream. "Now that's a grand idea!" Suddenly, he plunged into the brush, leaving his food bag behind.

"Where are you going?" Applejack called.

"Bring the pot!"

It took them two hours to collect enough crawdads to constitute a proper meal. Futureman situated himself on the bank, pot between his legs. Bulbous, crustacean eyes gleamed in the water. "Nearly fifty, I'd guess. That should do it, don't you think?"

When they returned, a visitor was standing in front of the shelter. Immediately, something about his appearance struck them as odd, almost alien. His frame was elongated, arms and legs stringy but powerful. Long fingers dangled just above his knees and wide-set eyes gave firm purpose to an angular face. His name was *Lost-and-Found*.

"Pleased to meet you both," he said, swaying slightly as though he could sense the earth's rotation. "I heard you in the creek below and decided not to disturb you. I thought perhaps you were bathing."

"We were catching crawdads," Applejack said, eagerly.

Futureman opened the pot.

"I see. What are you going to do with them?"

"Eat them."

"Eat them?"

"They're good."

"How do you prepare them?"

"Boil them."

"Alive?"

"How else? Would you prefer that we club them first?"

Lost-and-Found recoiled, horrified at the thought.

Applejack assured him, "It's like a frog in hot water. They don't even know what's happening. It's a peaceful way to go. They just sort of fall asleep."

"Have you ever done it before?"

"No."

Steam rose from the stove. Frantically searching for an escape, the crawdads contended violently against death, grabbing at one another, pinching anything they touched, antennae, arms, torsos.

"Holy jelly beans!" Applejack exclaimed. "That one just chopped another one in half!"

"Did you just say 'holy jelly beans'?" Futureman asked.

"In half?" exclaimed Lost-and-Found.

"They're not exactly falling asleep," Applejack said.

"They're hissing!" Lost-and-Found said.

As the water churned, a chorus of high-pitched squeals rose from within the pot.

"Are those crawdad screams?" Lost-and-Found winced.

Futureman threw the lid on the pot and pressed it down. The boil hissed and clattered around the edges. A crawdad burst, popping against the lid. "I could have sworn you said holy jelly beans."

"Guys?" Lost-and-Found moaned.

"So what, Futureman? You're gonna give me a hard time, after all the stuff that comes out of your mouth," Applejack said.

"Guys!" Lost-and-Found began pacing. Crawdads exploded like popcorn inside the pot.

"It's just funny is all. I've never heard you say that before, Applejack."

"Do something!"

"Just a little more, they're almost –"

"Now! Turn it off!"

Futureman dropped the pot on a rock. "OK. Dinner is served."

Lost-and-Found didn't have the stomach for it. He retreated into the forest.

Each crawdad had about a thimbleful of meat in its shell, exquisitely blended with creek-grit and algae.

"I've eaten twelve of these things and haven't gotten a whole bite yet," Applejack said, spitting out bits of mud.

"Look here. You've got to suck out its back. You can't just nibble on it like it's seafood dip and crackers," Futureman said.

"What do you mean *suck out its back*?" Applejack said.

"That's what the Cajuns do."

"What?"

"That's what I heard."

"From where?"

"I don't know, documentary or something."

"Is that what you're going to do?"

"Are you asking me if I'm going to suck the back out?"

"Yes, I am asking are you if you're going to suck the back out. That's what I'm asking."

"I don't know."

"It's a *Yes* or *No* question."

"I need to think about it for a sec."

"Listen, when you recommend that I suck the back out of a living creature, the least you can do is give me a straight answer as to whether or not you plan on doing the same."

"Then *yes*. Yes, I'm going to do it."

"*Yes,* you are planning to suck the back out of that crawdad?"

"Yes, all of it, yes."

"Well?"

"Well, what?"

"Well, do it."

"I'm waiting on you to do it."

"You're doing it first."

"Why?" Futureman asked.

"Cause this whole thing was your idea to begin with," Applejack said.

"So."

"So that means you're the lead guy. Pioneer. Exemplar."

"No, I'm the antagonizer. The coach in the corner, the guy behind the guy."

"No, you're president of the club. On top of the ladder. Man in charge."

"Are you going to do it or not?" Futureman said.

"You need to do it first, then I'll do it, that's what I'm saying," Applejack said.

"Fine." Futureman flipped the orange bug over and studied it. "Wait, have you seen the underside of these things?"

"Yes, I'm looking at it right now."

"Looks like a crab mouth."

"So what?"

"It's just that – now that they're dead, you can get a better look –"

"It's gross, I know. Just eat it."

"Don't pressure me. See all that mud in there – or would you consider this sand?"

"Listen, we're never gonna be like the Cajuns if you keep up with that kind of talk."

"I don't know if I want to be a Cajun anymore."

"Again, I remind you that you brought this upon yourself."

"I know, you're right."

"So just get it over with. I don't know what's gotten into you anyway. Usually you'll do anything."

"I know."

"Are you afraid?"

"What would I be afraid of?" Futureman asked.

"Well, the crawdad for one."

"No, it's not that."

"Alright, then, yourself. You're afraid of yourself."

"Myself?"

"Yes, do you have self-fear?"

"I'm not sure I –"

"It's okay, a lot of people have it. Shyness is real."

"You gotta be kidding me."

"I don't kid about shyness."

"Well, I'm not shy."

"Then prove it."

"Is this some kind of trickery?"

"Just prove it."

"No. What about you? Don't you have self-fear?" Futureman asked.

"I have self-loathing. That's different," Applejack said.

"How is it different?"

"It just is. Everyone knows this."

"Everyone except me, so enlighten me."

"It's beside the point. Besides, sucking on a crawdad cannot cure self-loathing, only self-fear. So eat up."

"Well, let's not deny the impact crawdads can have on both fear *and* loathing."

"How do you figure?"

"Before sucking on a crawdad, you experience fear. Then afterwards, it's loathing."

"That is good logic," Applejack said.

"Thanks."

"But unproven."

"How would it be good logic, then?"

"An unproven hypothesis can still be a good hypothesis, but hypotheses need to be tested in order to be proven." Applejack raised his index finger.

"Naturally, of course. It's the scientific method," said Futureman.

"So, to test your hypothesis, you're gonna have to suck the back out of that crawdad. That's my point."

"Can we not work together on this, as a team of scientists?"

"What do you suggest?"

"I will come up with the hypothesis, and you will test it out."

"I do not accept. This was your idea, so it's your test. I want you to get all the credit."

"But in a way it was your idea too, for as you know, everything is circular."

"Now that doesn't make any sense."

"What doesn't make sense is why you won't suck the back out of that filthy crawdad."

"It all boils down to the fact that you're afraid to do it. And that is not like you at all," Applejack said.

"Truly, you are gifted in the art of subversion," Futureman said.

"Thank you. Now do it. Your self esteem is on the line."

"I will, just as soon as – wait – what do you mean, self esteem?"

"You struggle with self esteem."

"Uh –"

"Isn't that what you shouted in the wind on top of Moosilauke?"

"Hey, I thought we were just having a good time here – why would you –"

"Did you or did you not shout that on top of Moosilauke?"

"I did, but this hardly seems the time to –"

"Why would you have a low self esteem anyway? You're a cool person."

"I don't know why. I'm working on it," Futureman said.

"Fair enough."

"If I remember correctly, on Moosilauke, you said you have a lot of secrets," Futureman said.

"I did say that. I do. I like to hide things from people."

"Why?"

"I don't know. I just do. To conceal my superiority. It's not good."

"Tell me a secret then."

"Alright. I believe in ghosts."

"For real?"

"Yes."

"You never told me that."

"Well, I do."

"That's fantastic!"

"Don't give me a hard time about it."

"Okay. So shall we suck these crawdads together?"

"Yes, together."

"So, you can conquer your loathing."

"And you can conquer your fear – and self esteem problems."

"OK, whatever."

They held the creatures up and closed their eyes.

"Wait." Futureman set his bug down on a rock.

"Good grief!"

"No, wait a minute. Earlier, I think I saw something on the map."

"What do you mean on the map?"

"We're downstream from Nuclear Lake," Futureman said.

"New Clear or Nuclear?"

"Just check into it."

Applejack pulled out the map, tracing their location back to – "A nuclear power plant. We are indeed sitting downstream from a radioactive nightmare."

"But we've already chewed on a bunch of them."

"Surely, you don't think –"

"Their blood flows green," Futureman said.

"This certainly ups the ante a bit," Applejack said.

"If anything's going to happen to us – it's too late now."

"Nevertheless, my respect for you, should you choose to accept this challenge, would be beyond measure," Applejack said.

"Build me up so I'll suck it down, eh?" Futureman said.

"Just saying you'd be my hero is all. And again, I would feel rotten stealing your glory. You're the reason we're here in the first place, eating radioactive crayfish."

"You do have a way with litigation," Futureman said.

"Thank you," said Applejack.

"So, together then, on the count of three."

"You're not buying it?"

"No. I'm not."

"Okay. Together then."

One.

Two.

Three.

"You didn't do it."

"Neither did you."

"For crying out loud!" Lost-and-Found said, returning from the woods. "Here!" He reached into the pan, snatched out a crawdad and without hesitation sucked it dry.

Applejack and Futureman squealed.

"Disgusting. I don't know why you guys like these things."

"We don't. We were just bored," Futureman said.

Later that night, Futureman awoke from a strange Kafkaesque dream. He felt his hands and wiggled his toes and fingers. *I'm human, thank god.* It was then that he noticed something peculiar going on in the field out front. Lost-and-Found, under the midnight moon, was gazing intently up into the firmament, as if he were waiting for something. Around him was fashioned a wide circle of sticks.

What on earth?

When Lost-and-Found returned to the shelter, Futureman pretended to have been asleep, resolving to keep the matter firmly to himself.

V

Terranaut emerged from the woods the next morning, raring to go. "Good morning, gentlemen! Yessir, another fine day on the Appalachian Trail. The road goes ever on, as they say…"

He bent down to do some stretching. Dozens of pink cartilaginous scraps littered the ground. "What's with all the shells?"

"Crawdads, don't ask." Applejack said.

"Crawdads? Ah, you mean *crayfish*. Gentlemen, gentlemen. You didn't…what am I saying? Of course you did." Terranaut clapped his hands. "Now, what's the proper southern expression for moments like these – yewl…yawns…yonses…"

"You-uns or y'all," Applejack clarified.

"Yeah, yunses are from Tennessee. My, my, it is an honor to know some real southern folk, ye eaters of the creek-sucking-crawdad. Man, I can't wait till we get down South. Yonses'all will have to give me the grand tour."

"It will be our pleasure," Futureman sneered.

The Connecticut-New York line lay just ahead in the woods somewhere, marking their passage into a sixth state. They set out with fresh legs, eating sweet grass along the way, and before they knew it, it was all around them.

Handsome, woldish farmland, flower patches of ginger and sweet cicely as dense as sunlight, fields of tobacco, air strong with the scent of fox grape and wicopy, filled with purple finches, blue-headed vireos and insects a billion strong. This was not the eternal city they were expecting. This was not the sin-drenched capital of commerce and culture that had loomed so large in their minds.

"So this is New York?" Futureman said, following a fat bumblebee. "I thought New York was all city."

"Who knew it was this beautiful?" Applejack looked into the trees.

"The people who live here," Terranaut said. "Speaking of the City, you guys are going in with me tonight – to meet my little brother," Terranaut stated.

Applejack groaned. "I don't feel good about leaving the Trail."

"You told me that you would come."

"*Might.* We said *might.*"

"Come on. It'll be a blast."

"Only if we can stay with you – at your brother's place."

"My brother's place? My brother lives in a fifteen-hundred-dollar-a-month pantry. His whole apartment is no bigger than the front seat of my Lumina."

"What are you saying?"

"I'm saying that you're gonna have to find other lodging."

"In New York? Are you crazy? With what money?" Applejack said.

"It'll be fine, Sarah lives in Brooklyn, remember? We can call her from the train station outside town," Futureman said.

"Sarah?" Terranaut asked, inquisitively.

"Old friend of mine – she's like my sister. She's an artist."

"Is she – pretty?"

"Photographer actually, and yes, she is very pretty."

"Well then, it's settled. We're all going to Manhattan," Terranaut said.

"Hang on," Applejack said. "We never said for sure that we're going. What if we lose our momentum?"

"Two days. Take the train in, go our separate ways, see the city, eat some good Indian food. Then right back out. Promise," Terranaut assured.

"I don't know," Applejack said, brow furrowed.

"Right back out. Promise."

Making their way toward Manhattan, deep in a loden green wood, the four men came upon a small clearing. In the middle, arrayed in bright sunlight, stood a large, peculiar structure – something like a fence or palisade. Wrought iron filigrees stretched across the top, buried in them were the words: *Gate of Heaven.*

There was nothing around the gate to explain its existence or purpose, no homestead, garden or graveyard. No church. Just the gate. One by one, the men passed through wordlessly, wondering – hoping – that somehow they'd be changed.

And so, they carried on in silence. Not even one of them glanced back to see if the northern world they had come from looked different through the door. More than likely it was nothing, a simple frame of wrought iron, standing alone in the garden grip of New York, the gate of heaven.

BOOK II

AD NAUSEUM

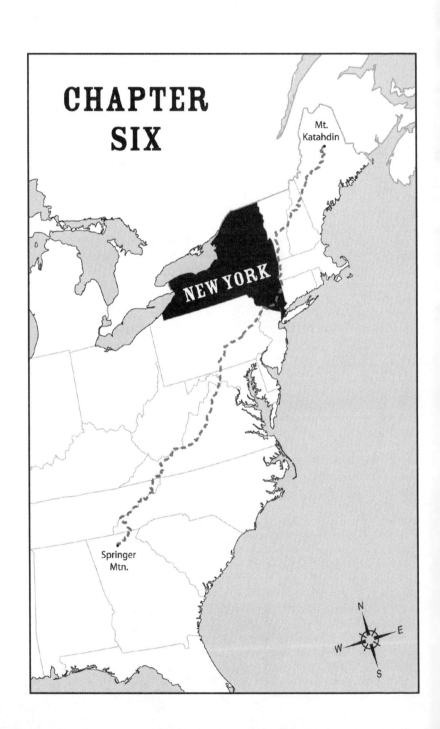

CHAPTER SIX

NEW YORK

Mt. Katahdin

Springer Mtn.

The distant Manhattan lights grew on the horizon, marking their non-destination. A certain disquieting finality clung to it all. Their trajectory was wayward and sure. Voices pulled on them. Singers called out to them. Unclaimed souls cried out from under the cleared catacombs of a pair of twins. New York, New York. Homeward bound orphans, fallen Gemini. The train rolled on.

I

Give me your tired, your poor,
Your huddled masses yearning to breathe free,
The wretched refuse of your teeming shore.
Send these, the homeless, the tempest-toss'd to me.
I lift my lamp beside the golden door.

New Yorkers have seen it all. Surprises are rare. In New York, you're just as likely to run into a Sudanese refugee as an out-of-work actor. Just as likely to stand in the street and catch a Derek Jeter homerun as you are to get a graduate degree in tap-dancing, get mugged, get evicted, or get drunk with Billy Crystal. It's New York. What do you expect? Anything and everything. New York is America and New York is the world.

Yet somehow, Applejack and Futureman managed to bring something new to the mix. A broker back from a day in the trenches raised his neatly groomed eyebrows and stepped aside. These people rubbed shoulders daily with transvestites, blind Armenian xylophone players and swarthy up-and-coming terrorists, but something was strange about these two. No one came within five feet of Applejack and Futureman as they stood gawking at the gigantic clock that winds the globe.

Grand Central Station at rush hour. Not the best time to try to get somewhere.

"OK. This is a bit overwhelming," Futureman said, rocked back on his heels.

Neither man had moved for probably eight minutes.

"Where are we supposed to meet Sarah?" Applejack asked without turning his head. Dizzy.

"I don't remember."

"Hopefully she'll see us standing here."

"Yeah. Probably." Futureman was attempting to make eye contact with every person that came by.

Sarah Martin was trying to make a go of things. A very talented photographer, she'd moved to New York because that is what serious artists must do. In a society where every child is a special snowflake, work is scarce for the artist unwilling to design screen savers for a living. Serious artists have to go to New York to find it. Until they wise up, at least.

But the whole thing was complicated. Sarah was a Southern girl. Intelligent, capable, savvy. But Southerners are always Southerners. There is no escaping the South. If you are born there, it is your mother. Other parts of the world are fine and good, but the South is the only place you feel truly comfortable. Even if you hate it.

A standout in the visual arts department at the University of Tennessee, Sarah was sent to Yale for a graduate degree in photography. As soon as she opened her mouth in New Haven, there was no doubt about it that her DNA was different. That accent curled up in your lap and took a nap. And, ahh, her pictures. They had trees and bails of hay and graveyards and smiling people wearing flannel shirts. Sarah was another little surprise to New York.

"My goodness, y'all look like serial killers." Sarah didn't bother to hug them; she was clean and looking for employment. "This way, gentlemen." She spun away and led them down into the dungeon underneath Gotham. Sarah really looked like a woman. Wearing a smart button-down oxford cloth under a dark suit, she seemed to know what she was doing-and she smelled like Applejack's sister who lived in Lexington, KY, thoroughbred country. Sarah was the first real woman they had talked to in many moons.

Somehow she had scored a huge apartment in Brooklyn on Washington Avenue, not far from the art museum, with high ceilings, hardwood floors, huge bedrooms and a studio.

"Sarah, I promise we'll get cleaned up. After a couple of days we'll smell pretty normal and we'll keep our stuff out of the way."

"Guys, honestly, I am just glad to see you. Stay as long as you want."

"Thanks. So is your roommate hot?" Futureman asked.

Sarah punched him. "You're a Neanderthal, you know that? Her name is Nancy. She's a native Brooklynite, very sweet – so stay away from her."

Thursday

Applejack pulled the shower curtain aside and drew back in horror. The inside of the tub was shellacked with filth. Millions of Futureman's dead skin particles, grains of dirt he'd carried on his body since Vermont, thick coils of beard hair, severed toenails and a veritable flurch of microscopic parasites were beached on the bottom of the once pristine marble tub. The thruhiker in Applejack was unmoved but the decent person in him became queasy. How disgusting. Futureman had a habit of doing this sort of thing. His mother had babied him too much.

After dealing with the tub, rinsing his body was no challenge. He walked out of the steaming room in a beige towel. Everything seemed so clean.

"Sarah, if we're going out tonight, I would really like to wear something – different. Anything, as long as it smells good."

"This'll be fun. I've been stealing from my brothers for years. Boys have cooler clothes than girls anyway." She pulled down corduroys and shirts from a box. "I don't know what y'all have got planned for tonight, but I would love it if you would come with me."

"We're yours. What do you have in mind?"

"I have some openings I need to go to in SoHo. Art stuff. Not a big deal. I just need to make some appearances. Then we can hit the city." Sarah bit her lip a lot when she spoke. Her auburn hair could catch sunlight in dark rooms.

"If you aren't ashamed to be seen with us," Futureman said.

"Oh, no. Trust me, they are going to love you guys." She tugged at the three-inch beard on his chin. "Plus, it's been forever since we hung out. How long have we been friends now, twenty years? My goodness, time flies."

"You know, you're not the whiny little girl you used to be. You look nice – professional, even. Seems like you're doing well for yourself."

"And you're the same spoiled unhygienic boy you always were."

"Thank you." He meant it.

Art is important, no matter what the television says. It is good and beautiful and true – or should be. Once was. Can be again. It is not dead. It's only sleeping. Artists are creators – makers of culture. It is their duty and their purpose. Born with eyes to see and hands to reach out, the artist is as important to civilization as the ruler, the doctor, the teacher, the soldier. Since the beginning of memory it has been this way.

And God is an artist – the Artist. His love for the act of creating is borne out inside the flesh and bones and brains of the artist. The artist is useless for any other purpose – if this one goes unfulfilled.

Yet from the beginning America has been a place fit only for the one who could pick himself up by the bootstraps, dust himself off and build something up out of nothing. Make a tiny empire to call your own. Till a patch of virgin ground and feed your family. Fence off a few hundred acres and fatten up a herd. Build a railroad from the Atlantic to the Pacific. Make a bridge, a skyscraper, a tunnel, an interstate, a rocket ship to carry a flag into space. Don't look back. Full speed ahead. No time for contemplation or a nap. America cannot wait. She doesn't have the time for you to stop and look and listen. *Instinct. Instinct. Instinct.* Follow your dreams. Follow your heart. Follow your nose. But don't you dare follow anyone else. That's the voice.

In the 19th century, William James and Charles Sanders Peirce worked to hang a name on the philosophy that most accurately explained that steam in the American stride. *Pragmatism* was the term they came up with. It most simply means that whatever works best is best. The worth of a thing, be it an idea or an invention or perhaps even an individual, is equal to the degree it is useful. If you do not believe that this is foundational in our society, look at our education system. When what is useful is divorced from what makes us human, we are well on our way to a bloody mess. Whatsmore, a hearty streak of anti-intellectualism has run through the American blood for well on two hundred years. To our average citizen, knowing and understanding more is not necessarily better than knowing and understanding less. Being and doing more is where the dollar is.

Yes, movers and shakers are the pillars of the American city. The writer, the painter, the thinker is the paraplegic sister that must be clothed and fed and kept in back because she cannot care for herself. There has never been much room for her in our society, yet she is not properly suited for any other function. Sarah and her friends were born to seek out beauty but were bred to sell mutual funds and vend cell phones. That tension made them want to scream. Nobody wanted their art unless it could sell cosmetics or titillate armchair quarterbacks. Nobody would believe them if they said anything good.

So, they went to New York, for better or worse, the spring from which the world's cultural reservoirs take their store. Art quit Paris when Picasso died.

That night, Applejack and Futureman found themselves escorted to the very epicenter of the raging conflict. At the gates they were greeted by the world's best and brightest, leg hair poking through fishnet stockings, mohawks scorning the polluted sky, questions dripping out of their pores, running down their sweaty faces, adorning and desecrating both canvas and life itself.

"About ninety percent of this is bull shit," Sarah muttered as she led them through a ring of smoking waifs and up a narrow-narrow staircase. "Everybody wants to be the art star. They're throwing away their potential. There are maybe five good artists on this whole street."

"This whole street" was Sullivan, a few blocks over from Broadway. Once the genuine 5th Avenue of New York, it and the surrounding area of SoHo had brimmed with stately mansions, shops and theaters. But as the district gained a reputation for affluence, bordellos and lavish saloons began popping up on side streets, drawn by the patronage of moneyed men. SoHo was the first red-light district in the city. With prostitution comes decline and through the eighteenth and early nineteenth centuries, as gentility moved out of the district, the Industrial Revolution moved in, erecting 250 cast iron buildings (the largest deposit in the world). Eventually the textile and export houses migrated out of the city to Newark and beyond, and SoHo found itself on the verge of being terminated by a superhighway. But in the early 1960s it was given one last chance and (according to Tom Wolfe) has become – along with TriBeCa and a few other neighborhoods – one of "the only slums in the world inhabited chiefly by young white people with masters degrees in fine arts." Educated at Ivy League universities, rising art stars and their trust-fund lackeys make the pilgrimage to New York City and hang out late at night on untrafficked streets like Sullivan, Charlton and Wooster looking either for attention or the abstruse promise of some wealthy aficionado.

They are called "openings." Openings take place in the cramped lofts and renovated townhouses of the district. Art is displayed, sold, critiqued, traded, performed, drunk down and spat out all over the walls. The unmade artists revolve and rotate from one opening to another, secretly admiring, outwardly smirking at the art on the walls. Those chosen to exhibit their work sweat blood all night. They can be found by the wine table, hiding, beaming, wretching with apprehension. The garish world that is their life and death spins all around them, planetary ellipses, comets streaking, dark matter absorbing, extinguishing: the sleek, shaven dandy with effected Danish accent sidles around arm in arm with dark-skinned twin; tough, hardworking, retired socialite from the Hamptons looks over the sycophantic dilettantes for the next Basquiat; in for a quick half-bottle of wine and a score of X, the well-to-do transsexual makes his appearance en route to a rave; embittered, poor, well-dressed, bearded art teacher stands-hungry for the desperate tribute of a drunk, pretty, dejected, former student – waiting, waiting to console.

"Excuse us," Sarah stepped between two weepy Scandinavian models.

"Guys, there is someone that I have to talk to. I don't want to be here long. Meet me in twenty minutes."

"Take your time. We're interested," Applejack assured her.

She strode out across the room, a lovely contrast. She was there for only one reason. She did not have time to shift or saunter.

"Dude, we have got to see what this is all about," Futureman pointed into one of the side rooms.

In the room they found a Plexiglas display case sectioned off in one corner. Inside it was a stool. On it sat a man with a heavy five o'clock shadow. He was wearing a woman's formal gown and puffing Marlboro Ultra Light 100s. His face was festooned like a clown's but with expensive cosmetics, not face paint. The lipstick was smeared in the corners of his mouth. Faux lashes spattered mascara across his brow. The man had topped off and crushed seven or eight cans of Coors Light. The silver cans lay all around his pair of kicked-off Louis Vuitton pumps. Wig had been slipping toward the back of his slick head for hours – part of the piece. His lecherous sneer, self-aware, traveled through a nearby camera and onto three televisions: one large plasma screen on the wall; a mid-sized Sony with the tag hanging from it; and another set, vintage and beaten in. Several people stood in observance, dividing their chatter between the man and his image. He began to sing *Waltzing Matilda*.

"Moving on," Applejack said.

Down the hallway and into a long narrow corridor lined with lightly framed color photographs. Cheap lights were tacked to the ceiling. The two hikers walked very slowly for a change, examining each composition, searching for meaning.

Hanging before them was a photo of an effete young man staring deeply into a bulbed diva mirror. The young man had a curious look of longing and hopelessness on his face. And concentration. He was drawing a charcoal moustache on his lip. Beside the mirror sat an autographed picture of Tom Selleck.

At the end of the hallway several enthusiasts crowded around a photograph of a living room. At one end of the shot, a teenage boy with curly red hair lunged toward a couch, a pair of roller skates on his feet. At the other end sat a girl. Coiled up, haggard and beautiful, mascara and tears were dribbling down her white cheek. The colors of the photograph seemed eerily enhanced, almost florescent. People seemed to really like this one. Not wanting to disturb the veneration, Futureman nodded toward the door.

Sarah was waiting when they got out front. Several of her friends and acquaintances had gathered, deciding on plans for a night in the clubs.

"I'd like you to meet some people," she caught Futureman's wrist. "This is Nick." Applejack extended his hand. Nick took it warily, unused to the archaic custom. "Nick is really going places. Last month he had a picture come up in Madamoiselle."

"It's not much," he said. "Just a cologne ad but it pays the bills." Nick had a chain gang of tattoos that ran up his arm and neck and onto the neatly shaved half of his head. Chin length black hair hung from the other half. Each tattoo was a bubble with a green and purple question mark drawn inside it. Nick had left the right side of his body in its natural state, just in case.

Things were winding down. Sarah introduced them to Tim and Petra and Lars and a few others milling around outside, all very nice, all very interested in Applejack and Futureman's adventure. The artists smiled at the hikers with a bemused curiosity. Wind-raw skin, sun dried accents, burly beards. Applejack and Futureman must've walked straight out of the Cro-Magnon exhibit at the American Museum of Natural History over on East 45th.

"You two are from where?"

"And you came from where?"

"And you're going where?"

"I've never been south of Chinatown. Ha."

"Are there birds living in your facial hair? Just joking, dear."

"You're from Tennessee? I was worried you were terrorists. Only kidding."

"What a doll. And a great pleasure to meet you, sir," said a man with a Slavic accent.

"You too," said Futureman in dumb American.

"This is my friend, Chris. He's the real deal," Sarah whispered.

Chris wore jeans, deck shoes and a pair of Clark Kent glasses. He looked like John Boy Walton. He had a camera slung over his shoulder.

"Howdy fellas. Pleased to meet you. Been doin' some hikin', from the looks of it. I've hiked some in the Smokies."

"Really?" Normalcy. Home.

"Sure is pretty country. How long you gonna be in the City? Maybe we can get together."

"Sure. Sure, Chris. That'd be nice."

"Well, good luck on your trip." Chris waved and smiled.

"Guys, gotta go. I'll catch up with y'all after the anniversary. Bye." Sarah walked quickly down the sidewalk, Applejack and Futureman in tow.

"I love it when she says 'y'all'," whispered Lars.

At midnight they rendezvoused with Terranaut and his ambitious younger brother at an Indian restaurant with five-and-a-half foot ceilings and a live sitar band. Terranaut was eager to meet Sarah. Sarah quickly informed him that she had a boyfriend named Grant. He was an artist too. He took pictures of strange happenings set in common milieu.

"Grant is very talented. He's a lot better than me."

"No he's not. Don't say that." Terranaut assured her.

"How do you know? You've never seen our pictures."

"Well, I –"

"So, isn't Grant from Connecticut?" Futureman interrupted.

"Yeah. His family is one of the early Connecticut families. Gone to Yale since way back, y'know? Grant's really sweet. He likes clothes, though."

"Clothes. He's into fashion?" Terranaut furrowed his brow.

"Well, he has these…phases that he goes through."

"Phases?"

"Right."

"Uh-huh."

"Phases."

"Go on." The men leaned in.

"He'll really get into something for a few weeks and then *it's done with that and on to the next hot rage.* Like a couple weeks ago he started wearing black Motorfinger T-shirts with black jeans and black boots. He was putting tonic in his hair and combing it all the way across his head and down to a little point above his eyebrow – but it's gotten a lot worse since then. Now he's wearing these sleeveless, ribbed turtleneck-type things. They're kind of disgusting."

No one spoke for several seconds. The sitar music swirled.

"Why does he…do that, Sarah?" Applejack asked.

"He just likes it. Whatever blows your hair back, y'know?" Her doubts had already passed. She was over it. She no longer cared that her boyfriend dressed like a deconstructionist German philosopher. She heaped more rice onto her plate. "So, I know this cool greaser joint not far from here. Everybody's dressed like the Stray Cats. You guys up for it?"

The bar was decorated retro-fifties but filled with the aimless angst of the new millennium. The bartenders wore tight jeans and white t-shirts, slicked back their hairs and spit in the brew. It was a perfect place to discuss religion.

With a few beers in him, it didn't take long for Terranaut to remind everyone that he was Catholic. "So, what are you?"

"Do we have to pick sides?" Futureman asked.

"Isn't that what the Christian religion is all about?"

"Us three are SUUTHERN BAAAPTIST, born and raised," Sarah said. It shocked the table, but her dimpled smile quickly set them at ease.

"So then. It's Protestants versus Catholics," Terranaut clapped his hands.

"Whatever you say, Terranaut."

"The big war."

"Why war?" Applejack asked.

"What is politely referred to in history as the burning of *heretics* – in my book, goes down as an act of WAR," Terranaut banged his mug on the table.

"I thought our side did all the burning." Terranaut's brother remarked.

"Nope, they burned 'em too, in Switzerland and England. Anabaptists got burned, beheaded and drowned by the thousands – by Protestants. And what about the Massachusetts Bay Colony?"

"We burn people in the Southern Baptist Convention. We burned Walt Disney I think."

"So what do you make of it? What's behind our propensity for burning, bombing and shooting each other?" Terranaut asked.

"Uh, human fear. Tradition." Futureman said.

"Tradition? Slow down there, bud. You're talking about a whole way of life when you say that – including mine. Raised to be a good Catholic boy. Does it mean anything? Hell if I know but I'm still a good Catholic boy. Right, little brother?"

Little brother shrugged.

"It's just such a shame that the church of Jesus gets lost in the politics of the world."

"Yeah, but then where would that leave me?" Terranaut smiled.

"I'm just saying, wouldn't it be nice if it was still as simple now as it was for the early Christians?"

"You don't know what you're talking about if you think it was simple for the early Christians. Ever heard of the Roman Empire? The Catholic Church practically saved the religion."

"I guess it wasn't ever simple. Okay, next question. As a Catholic, what do you believe in?"

"What's belief got to do with it? My family's Catholic, so I'm Catholic."

"Didn't Jesus say he came to divide son from father and daughter from mother?"

"OK, so what does that mean?"

"I think he was saying that his followers have to be willing to lay everything down for him, even their families – if those things lead them away from him."

"So, are you capable of that kind of loyalty?" Terranaut asked.

"I'm not sure. But I am sure that salvation comes through faith in Jesus, not through the traditions of men."

Terranaut eyed his brother. "But even without belief, people need religion."

"For what?"

"What did Marx say – *opiate of the masses*? Religion gives some kind of answer for the black beyond the telescope. But, when it comes down to it, I guess I don't have a clue, really. Four years at the nation's finest institution, and I'm still at square one," Terranaut held his cup in the air, remembering graduation night in the basement at Johnny Harvard's.

"So, are you saying that you believe – that you don't have to believe?"

"How are you defining belief?"

"If you believed the roof of this bar were going to fall down right now, you'd run out the door – that's what I'm saying. Belief is attached to something – doing. Otherwise, it's just man-made religion – the worst prison on earth. Faith without action isn't faith at all. That's what has made this whole sloppy mess."

"Actually, Applejack, you could say that faith with action is what made this whole sloppy mess-Crusades, 9/11?"

"True, but the actions Jesus talked about were love, patience, peace, forgiveness –"

"To me the beauty of religion is that we can be sloppy and still be okay. Baptism. Confirmation. Wonderful traditions."

"So you're saying that you don't really believe beyond those things."

"No, I'm not saying that. I'm Catholic. Catholics believe."

"And I'm Protestant. So what?"

"You see? We're having a war," Terranaut said, raising his Dixie cup to *Hound Dog*. "A little Protestant-Catholic war. Now why do we do that?"

"It's because we're not all part of the Convention," Sarah said.

"We must not, because we are fully aware of the eternal opposition between the Gospel and the church, hold ourselves aloof from the church or break up its solidarity; but rather participating in its inevitable failure, we should accept it and cling to it."

-Karl Barth

<u>Friday?</u>
<u>Saturday</u>
Applejack and Futureman didn't go anywhere. They didn't get up to meet Terranaut at the train station like they had promised. They didn't get up to tour the
city. They did not even get off the couch. They watched TV, as they had the
day before, all day, infrequently lofting questions into the air at one another.
Questions beyond rhetorical. Questions with answers so heavy with inevitabili-
ty that they crashed to the ground.
    "We're leaving tomorrow, right?"
    "We'll catch up with Terranaut pretty quick, right?"
    "We've got time, right?"
    "It'll be good for our bodies to rest, right?"
    There's nothing inherently wrong in asking these questions. They *did* need
rest. They *did* have plenty of time to make it to Springer Mountain by Thanksgiving. Days off *are* necessary in life (without them, bodymindandsoulmeltin-
tooneanother, indistinguishable, a bloodbrainmass of physiometaphysical turbulence). But by embracing this break, now – here in the Big Apple – they had
found a lie they would use for guilty comfort time and time again. Masters of
their own destinies they were not. Thralls under the sway of the All-seeing Eye
was more accurate. TV was dominatrix. They had missed her. Chopped strands
of color, fragmented conversation, sitcom kings, catwalk empresses. The spell
of the television could not be broken. It conjured its magic without intrusion.
Burning buzzing static. So great was its abuse and there was no one to come to
their aid. Sarah was with her confused boyfriend in Connecticut. Terranaut was
back in the woods. No one to intervene. But TV was, as it is, always there. College football: Florida State, USC, UT. Back to back Seinfeld. *Injections.* Mat-
lock. Looney Tunes. *Chemo*. Happy Days. Montel. Total Request Live.
Methadone. Texas Hold-em. The black and whites on Turner Classic. Court
TV. CSI. *Lobotomy*. For thirty-six hours they were ravaged and caressed by
their teacher. Feasting, fabulous delectations, feculent defecations, as they slid
further and further into the abyss.

<u>Sunday</u>
Applejack sat at a table. His chair and the table were the only pieces of furni-
ture in the room. Two men were in front of him. Agents, had to be. *Only
agents dress like that.* One by the wall smoking. The other leaning over the
table, the pores on his swollen nose, big as manhole covers. The whites of his
eyes were jaundiced between the vessels. He was angry and waiting.
    "Well, what's it gonna be, tough guy? Think you're big enough to ride this
out on your own? You wanna get the maximum dropped on you?" His eyebrows were gray, although the hair of his head was still dark and oily.

"You need us, believe me. Sure, we could use your help – makes our job easier. But either way, we'll still get 'em. But you? You're the walking dead, if you don't come with us." He leaned forward, within 12 inches of Applejack's face. "We can take care of you. You'd get to start over. Take your wife and kids, a new life. This kind of thing is done now. It works. They won't get to you."

"Okay. I'll tell you what I know. But you guys have to do this right. I'm not gonna settle for a new driver's license and some crap apartment. I need a new identity. I know these guys. They're as relentless as they are brutal. They'll find me. I ain't worried about what's noble and good. I'm just trying to stay alive here."

He gave them what they wanted. Connections. Bosses. Contacts. Jobs he'd done. Rubs he'd seen. Buttons he'd pushed. Rumors. Made men. Soldiers. Cooked books. He knew it all. The cops were too busy to smile. Enough to put all the big shots away for good. They were gonna get medals for this. Bonuses. Below ground swimming pools with mini-bars.

"One last question. Do you know where they buried him?"

"You mean – him." Applejack said gravely, no question in his voice.

Agent nodded.

"Yeah. I know."

The long black Pontiac pulled up to the curb. It was broad daylight. Saturday morning. Two years later.

"This it, Johnny?"

The three men looked around. It could have been anywhere in suburban America. Rows of a hundred and fifty thousand dollar houses. All the same. Brand spanking new, dirt in the yards, vinyl siding. A Dodge Caravan and a new Maxima sat in every driveway.

"This is it, fellas," Johnny said. "Quit your safety, boys."

Each man reached under his suit coat.

"Let's go. Ring the doorbell when we get there, Vince."

"Why should I gotta ring the doorbell?"

"Boss says you do it, you do it!"

"But Boss said next time I –"

"Shut ya stupid mouth and ring the bell."

Vince stepped out of the car and up the sidewalk, around an overturned plastic yellow dump truck. Frank and Johnny followed.

Frank tilted his black fedora and scanned the street. Nodded.

"Yeah, we're good," Johnny said.

Vince pulled out his Luger, put it at his side. He rang the bell.

A minute passed. No noise inside. Then, just as Johnny was about to check out the garage, they heard something rolling across the hardwood floors. It continued down the hall. The men listened, squeezed their guns tighter. The rolling stopped just inside the door. No one pulled back the curtain.

Even a year ago Applejack would have looked out to see who was at the door. But he had finally been able to let go of his fear and put his trust in the Witness Protection Program. It was the only way he could have any kind of normal life. Naturally, he expected the UPS guy or a girl scout but the old animal in him was not so dormant that he would reveal his surprise and fear at the sight of his guests.

"Frank. Vince. Johnny. Been a long time. Good to see you guys."

The men pulled their heads back, awkward and unsure.

"Yeah, uh, it's been too long," Frank said, sticking his gun in Applejack's gut. It made an unnatural clanking noise. "They sure did a good job wit you. Barely recognize ya. Should have gotten rid of the chain though, Jack. The chain gives it away."

Hanging around Applejack's neck, or what would have been a neck, was a thick-link gold chain, a diamond studded dolphin at the end. Jack's calling card. His teri-cloth robe hung open, the belt dangling on either side. The thin fabric of the robe offered a clear outline of what was underneath. Square at the shoulders and perfectly straight, down to the floor, the tank that held his vital organs made an easy target. There were no more bones and no more skin. All that was left were the heart, liver, lungs, brain, stomach and kidneys, floating in a bluish liquid, suspended in the tank-like his life. Nothing was left of his face. Not the Yale chin or the Roman nose. Only a pair of Mr. Potato Head eyeballs stuck against the glass and a black handlebar moustache hanging above a set of unmoving plastic lips.

"Jack, you knew we'd find ya. Didn't you, Jack." Frank had been his closest friend. He was the only one that the feds couldn't hang anything on.

"I had to do it, Frank."

"Like I said, good disguise. Real good. Only thing is, this tank is gonna spill all over the porch when I blow you open. How many gallons is in there, Jack? I would hate for your kids to wake up and see their daddy poured out all over the yard."

Sweating, Applejack bolted upright on his cot.

"Bad dream, buddy?" Futureman sat on the couch, pounding his knee up and down like a jackhammer.

"Uh. Real weird. I was a tank."

"That's cool. Get to blow anything up?"

"Not that kind of tank."

"You mean – what?"

"Aquarium. They turned me into a liquid and put me into an aquarium tank. There was a mustache taped on the outside."

"Okay. We need to get out of here."

Central Park is the world's largest hospital. The city would surely die a horrible death without her. She jumpstarts dead hearts. Cures cancer, treats bad blood, recovers lost memory, adds days. Gives succor, peace, respite, sanity, shade. Hope. She is New York's only priceless possession. The rain forests of the world may be plowed under and sold as potting loam but Central Park will never be touched. Used and abused in a thousand different ways, she will stay put. Moonlighting as playground, hideout, smack den and cathedral, she stays alive in the concrete jungle, waiting for the Restoration.

Futureman and Applejack emerged from the Central Park subway tunnel, ready. They needed sunlight and dirt. They ran around the zoo. Got chilidog gristle trapped in their beards, watched a collie jump to catch a frisbee. They sat for hours among the granite boulders on the north side of the Pond. Pretending that he was on Saddleback Mtn., Applejack sat motionless, eyes closed, the Maine wind blowing his dirty hair around. Futureman made up riddles, rhymes and limericks. He rode ET's bicycle.

After a nap, they emerged from a little grove of ten-year old poplars onto an enormous open field several hundred yards long, a golden-grassed meadow peopled with late-summer sun worshippers.

Since coming into the city, Futureman had noticed an irritation in his eyes. Itchy rims, sore pupils. He thought Central Park's fresh air would do them right, but they seemed to be getting worse.

"Hey man, do your eyes feel normal?" he asked.

"Actually, they've been kinda burning since we came into the city."

"Mine too."

"I think it's the pollution. We've been in the woods for a while. We're not used to it anymore."

"Makes me wonder what else my body's gotten used to over the years. Chlorine...sulfur...natural gas...vanillaroma..."

"Futureman, freeze. Stop right where you are." Applejack suddenly noticed the world around him. Awareness. *All is not well.* Lost in conversation and sunlight, they had not been paying attention.

For all their travels, Applejack and Futureman were still just hicks from the Bible-belt. Sure, they'd been through San Francisco and South Beach – but always on their way to somewhere else. They'd read about Gomorrah and ancient Greece but that did not prepare them for this. Here, in a field in New York City, they found themselves standing smack-dab in the middle of The Revolution.

This wasn't some parade. It was a lifestyle on a normal Sunday afternoon. All around them were naked men lying on beach blankets. Sunning themselves. Basking in the beautiful September glow. Men. Just men. Tanning. Everywhere. Lathering one another up with lotions and oils. Sharing cans of

Diet Coke (with lemon). Hundreds. Men. Every cut and color of bikini brief imaginable. Tan lines, highlights and tiny aqua marine boom boxes blaring Bette Midler crowded their senses.

"How did we get here? Weren't we in Central Park a minute ago?"

"This is still Central Park," Applejack whispered.

"Central Park where the families come to play?"

They looked back from where they'd come and could hardly see a path, so strewn with flailing bodies was the ground.

"Isn't Broadway over there?" Futureman pointed desperately into the sun.

"I don't know. Let's hope."

Picking their way through the throng was tedious. Careful to be courteous, not wanting to appear intolerant or phobic in any way, they tiptoed along but, en route, one gentleman in particular caught Applejack's attention. Off to the side – different. *Oblivious?* An elderly Indian man stood in the sunshine. Gristly white hair, skin bronzed and sagging, a speedo hanging too low for the bounds of decency. He danced. In place. Eyes closed, arms punching the sky, his legs bending and bouncing to a scratchy, trip-hop Asian techno grind. *Join my party!* his movement shouted. No takers, but no matter. He heard the beat of his own drum loud and clear, in the midst of it all, and it made Applejack smile.

It was September 9th. The city was preparing for the anniversary of 9/11. A peculiar mix of optimism and solemnity was cast over everything – brick, steel, neon, fabric and flesh. It wasn't exactly patriotic. For one bittersweet instant, the entire world had experienced the warm vibration of American patriotism, but New York still felt empty and alone. Everyone seemed to be moving through a giant choreography. Joined in an unrehearsed ritual. Strangers passed on the street with a nod of common grief. The dead seemed to be all around. Their voices steady, not yet quieted, still cried out. Yet no one wanted to relive it. It seemed separate from tragedy. No hint of nostalgia dusted its memory. The city searched always for relief. Some tiny crust of joy. The Yankees. The elections. The weather. Anything.

Monday

"This is it. We're leaving. Tomorrow."

"Yes. We are definitely leaving. Tomorrow."

"Right. Because today we still have a lot of city to see – and how often do you get to come to the Big Apple, right?"

"Right."

"So what are we going to do?"

"The question is 'what are we not going to do?'

"Nothing. We are not going to do nothing."

"Correct."

Americans don't like to walk. We like to ride and bike and run and jog and stair-step and swim and lay and loaf and lounge. Over the last two centuries, we've whittled the walking down to about 10,000 feet per day, or 1.89 miles. By the way, that's less than 2 miles. Per day. A day is 24 hours.

But Manhattan is different. The denizens of Manhattan walk on average 20,000 feet per day – that's 3.78 miles. Not bad, New York!

Thruhikers walk an average of 89,760 feet per day. Applejack and Futureman had grown accustomed to walking. So after two days of abject slothfulness, their over-rested, over-fed legs insisted they get off the couch.

They exited the subway in Chinatown – at the island's south end – hoping to walk as much as the day would allow. They ambled along Park Avenue, amazed by the amiable collision of two worlds. The world of outside and inside, the street and the palace. The world of the universally destitute and the supremely wealthy. They felt displaced, eccentricities. On the fringe. While Applejack expounded on such matters, Futureman tuned out. Slipping away from the here-and-now and into the then-or-never-would-be, he thought about the Empire State Building, the place that had appeared in his childish and childlike imagination so many times. The gravestone of King Kong.

Getting to the top of the Empire State Building entails a series of trips. Trips within a trip – escalators and hallways and velvet ropes. Somewhere in there a security guard in a burgundy coat took Futureman by the arm and pulled him aside.

"So you guys Taliban, eh?" the guard said, lips poked out, chin up like someone was yanking on his beautiful cofea of thick black hair.

"Huh?" Futureman said.

"Youse guys look like terrorists, comin' in here wit your hair and your beards."

"No sir. We aren't terrorists. We're hikers," Futureman said.

"Why you not shave ya face. Why don't you wanna shave ya face like a real man?" His hands were clasped behind his back.

"Sir, we are walking from Maine to Georgia. We are Americans. We are not Taliban," Applejack was doing his best to handle the situation.

"Then what ya doin' in the city? Why you here in my Empire State Building?"

"I want to see King Kong," Futureman blurted out.

"Eh?"

"I mean I want to see where King Kong died."

"Get back in line, weirdo."

It was a warm clear day. Low humidity. From the top they could see every-thing. Statue of Liberty. New Jersey's industrial wilderness. Roosevelt Island. Penthouse yards and swimming pools. But there was something missing. A chasm. And everyone on the observation deck was achingly aware of it. The World Trade Towers were gone. Two lifeless craters like gouged out eyes opened into the earth's blistering core, left as markers. No one pointed to where they had once been.

Ground Zero. It was out of the way and a long walk but they felt compelled toward the place that had once been the epicenter of world attention. It was September 10th, around lunchtime and they should have been hungry but weren't.

The streets around the site had been cleared out and roped off, transformed into a place for grieving and remembering. No traffic, only walking. Police officers were stationed at every corner and crosswalk but they were not needed. There were no disturbances nor would there be any, no noise save the shuffling of feet. Thousands of people circled the grounds, peering down into the cavity. No one wanted to sound out the terrible thoughts that were clamoring within. Thoughts of loss and desperation and hate and paranoia.

The Catholic church across the way had opened its arms to the mourners. Families and friends of victims had come and erected shrines all around it. Memorials for the dead. A faded montage of photographs: families embracing, couples kissing, fathers holding their newborns, honeymooners. Children came to this place to write messages to moms and dads. Poems scrawled in crayon. Wedding invitations and medals of honor tacked to the huge plywood hedge. Scores of *Missing* and *Have You Seen* flyers begging for the tiniest molecule of hope. The mass of visitors studied the tokens patiently.

On the far side of the church a different kind of cenotaph had sprung up. What was begun by a few earnest vendors as a solemn attempt to venerate the dead and mark their place in history had been transformed, disfigured by rogue capitalism. Hawkers from the world over set up booths all down the street and now stood in front of their merchandise – some of it tasteful and proper, most opportunistic and crude. Cheap audiotapes of patriotic songs, American flag belt buckles and t-shirts. Magnetic pictures of the Trade Center. "I Love New York" sweat shirts and jackets. Laminated covers of *Time* and *Newsweek*, but-tons, pendants, *Don't Mess With The Red, White and Blue* bumper stickers, even small hunks of concrete and steel purportedly drawn from the rubble – as many junk stands as there were cracks in the sidewalk. But very few of the vis-itors seemed to be patronizing these vulgar trash-brokers. Most didn't want to buy more crap and did not need help remembering. They'd seen it all on televi-sion.

A couple hours later, they were sitting on the front steps of the Metropolitan Museum of Art completely dejected and ready to leave town. The sun was beating down on the pavement. The gray mist of the city filled out the sky.

"I was so excited to see this."

"I can't believe we picked the one day of the week when everything's closed."

"You hungry?"

"You bet. What do you want?"

"Some New York chili dogs."

"Wasn't there a hot dog man down the street?"

"There he is, under the oak."

A black moustache and a white paper hat stood behind the hot dog cart in the shade of the tree.

"You fellas look like you're having a bad day. Lighten it up with a chili dog or two."

"How about three?"

"My kinda guys."

"Glad you're open."

"Of course I am. Relish?"

"Sure. We just came from the Met – they're closed today."

"Not from around here, huh?"

"Just passing through."

"Well, if it's art you want, then art you shall have. Guggenheim, few blocks up. Enjoy your dogs. And be careful, it can get a little crazy in there."

> And art made tongue-tied by authority,
> And folly, doctor-like, controlling skill,
> And simple truth miscalled simplicity,
> And captive good attending captain ill.
> -Shakespeare, Sonnet 66

They stood in the middle of the main floor at the Guggenheim looking up through the museum. It corkscrewed around so that there were no stairs in the building, only one long interminable ramp leading from the top floor all the way to the narthex in one elliptical continuous space. Very progressive architecture and lighting, stark color and irregular blocking provided a bleak matte, a willing contrast to the art on the walls. In the beginning, the Guggenheim had displayed the works of such modern masters as Kandinsky, Paul Klee and Piet Mondrian. Always at the fore of the avant-garde world, the Museum is renowned for its skill in walking the tightrope between the challenging and the refined.

Frank Lloyd Wright was commissioned to design the museum by Solomon

R. Guggenheim but neither man was alive in 1959 to see its completion. Wright's vision was to create a gaping nautilus, a "temple of spirit" conducting the observer to a new plane of celestial experience. Masterfully demonstrating the use of the axiomatic forms of geometry, the structure is layered with reoccurring circles, squares, triangles, arcs and ovals. One of his final buildings, the work is his finest in a career of exceptional distinction.

Accidentally, but true to form, Applejack and Futureman began their journey through the Guggenheim at what was intended to be the bottom of the spiral-the end of the exhibit. Hungry to see good art, they rushed up the ramp, oblivious to the throngs of people that were rightly taking the elevator to the top. The effect of their blunder was devastating. Instead of following the linear and thematic progression a piece at a time, the two hillbillies from Tennessee went backwards through the most sophisticated fine arts museum in New York.

The first thing they saw was an uncircumcised Negroid phallus. Last in a line of four black and white framed photographs by the controversial artist, Robert Mapplethorpe, the picture depicted the torso of an African-American man wearing a business suit, zipper ajar. A large, flaccid penis hung prominently from the opening. Beside it, a gorgeous photograph of a voluptuous, freshly opened calla lily gleamed on the wall. Next, a balop of a common stone, so immaculately achieved that each grain separated wholly from the others, self-sufficiently in unison with the entirety of the rock. The last picture on the wall was one that defines the famously aberrant career of Robert Mapplethorpe. A man sits in a chair, clad in a pair of patent leather pants, his features hidden by a hooded leather mask. Behind him stands another man, visible only from the neck down, hand resting on the shoulder of his slave. A classic bondage masterpiece. The placard illuminating this sequence was a quote from the artist himself. "A flower. A rock. And a cock. I want to show that they are all the same."

"They are?" said Futureman.

"I guess some people think so."

"Is this what you thought it was going to be?"

"I'm not sure."

An art exhibition can often have an autobiographical quality to it – not necessarily an overarching account from birth to death but certainly a chapter or two. After all, if no trace of the artist can be found in his work, then surely it would be soulless. A dead extremity. Good (as in effectual) art should and does unveil the heart of the artist, his center. Perhaps this is why it must be so painful to create. To live on that razor-edge of inspiration will draw blood. A piece of the artist is left on the canvas or the daguerreotype paper, in the melody or in the clay. Pulsing, coursing, causing the rest of us to swell with life. The artist lives to change his world.

Robert Mapplethorpe died in 1989, ravaged by AIDS. There can be no doubt that the world was a different place because of his living. Indisputably, a technical master, Mapplethorpe dazzled a generation of artists with his gift. Everyone has seen his portraits, whether they know him or not. Artists the likes of Andy Warhol, Gregory Hines, Patti Smith and Peter Gabriel trusted him with their faces. And his love for beautiful delicate flowers is well known. Mapplethorpe's pictures capture the flower at the apex of its beauty, pistil and stamen shimmering, contour of the stem devastating its background. His camera ensnared shadow and light. They came willingly like companions. There can be no doubt he had an eye for beauty.

But his other eye found itself behind the camera more often. It drifted, capturing things on film that ought never to sully the mind. Not one to conceal his life, he opened the door on his dark sexual imagination and the world was stunned. There was the self-portrait of a naked Mapplethorpe inserting a bull-whip into his own anus. (He explained that S&M stood for "sex and magic.") There was a silhouette of a man with a stream of urine coursing into his mouth, as well as photographs of naked children and many other fetishist pictures. But because of the overwhelming talent displayed in his more salient work, these pictures were lauded for their brave genius and passed along in his collections – filed as artistic instead of deviant. After much praise and controversy, his photographs became the vogue, selling high to aficionados and collectors far and wide, long after his death.

"I wonder what's in that room?" Futureman walked around the corner. The walls were coated with more black and white photographs, almost exclusively of naked bodies and male genitalia. Several visitors stood reverently, arms crossed, studying the pictures with great care.

"Let's see what else there is."

"OK."

Video art was the newest thing in the art world and the Guggenheim was eager to oblige. Applejack and Futureman, lovers of film, grew excited when they walked into a small room and saw a movie screen on the far end. They sat down in comfy chairs and waited, examining the egg-crate padding along the walls. The projector clicked on. The screen came to life, sort of. Slightly off-center, a reel-to-reel tape player, laid on a tuft of grass, fell into view. The player began turning its reel. The left reel was fat and spun slowly. The right, thin and fast. The only audio accompaniment was the rhythmic ticking of the tape as it passed across to the opposite reel. Several minutes went by. The right reel became fat and turned slowly. The left reel became thin and spun quickly. The tape player stopped. The projector turned off and the screen went black. Applejack, Futureman and the other lucky individuals who had just experienced the life-transforming film got up and moved toward the door. Applejack and Futureman turned right, up the spiral.

They watched a couple of other short films on small televisions mounted in the outer hallway. One was about a burial ceremony somewhere in the Arabian desert. Another captured a man running, never seeming to get anywhere. Applejack noticed a box protruding from the wall. He looked through the two eyeholes there. The film inside was a very lucid documentation of a surgery. The doctors were cutting open an eye and repairing it. He thought that was oh-so-ironic. Futureman spotted a Lite Brite near the top of the ramp, he ran toward it like a child. As he got closer he began to make out the neon words: "whore" "slave" "queen" "machine" "WASP" "war".

"Are you about ready to go back to the Park?"

"One more thing. I thought I saw a really good photograph when we came in – somewhere near the bottom."

They headed back down. Even from a distance they could see the superb photograph. It spanned an entire wall. People crowded around it. This was going to be a breath of fresh air. Futureman could tell already. It had grace. There were trees and plants and sky. It was devastatingly beautiful. Future-man's eyes scoured the photograph, taking in the grains of color and detail. They strayed to the far left corner of the frame, where he saw it. A two-inch wide border encircled the perimeter of the picture. Individual photographs linked end to end formed an inter-connected sequence that guided the observer around the stunning larger photograph. The snapshots inside the border captured naked people engaged in sex acts. The entire border was a group orgy. The simple beauty of nature was trapped inside the frame.

Applejack and Futureman left the museum disoriented. They didn't even remember to visit the room they had come to see, where they would have found the Abstract Expressionism, Cubism and Impressionism they loved. They walked mindlessly down 5th Avenue until one of them spoke.

"I wanted to see Rodin."

"So did I."

"I wanted Georgia O'Keefe."

"I did too."

"I wanted Cezanne."

"People thought they were scandalous in their day, though. There was an uproar when *Nude Descending A Staircase* came out. Then, what about Pollock? And of course, there's Van Gogh. Never sold a painting, practically starved to death."

"Yeah, but aren't those guys different than that stuff we saw today? They were great. They were genius."

"But they were way ahead of their time. Maybe, we're just prudes."

"They were real artists. They were saying something."

"So, what do you think it is that makes good art?"

"I think good art directs us toward good things. Good ideas, good desires –

even in the face of the bad."

"But what does good mean?"

"Goodness is pure, just, lovely. Goodness deserves our loyalty."

"People say that some of that stuff back there is true and pure. Mapplethorpe did."

"I guess I just want art that edifies."

"I want another chili dog. Hey look, there's Barry White"

They turned and walked toward W 44th counting pigeons in the street.

It was twenty-one till eight. They were six blocks from the Theater District. The show was about to begin.

"Doesn't anybody sell chewing tobacco around here?" Futureman fumed, walking out of a store.

"Apparently not. Is too much to ask that we be permitted the pleasure of savoring a chaw during the musical of our choosing? Is it too much to ask that?"

"No. No, it is most definitely not too much to ask. This is the biggest dang town in the whole dang world, ain't it?"

"The most evil indulgences the world has to offer are within two blocks of where we now stand, yet we have but one vice and it is taboo. Once as viable a currency as paper money, now the vile leaf is as extinct as the dodo. And to think – on an island that was purchased for a string of beads –"

"Impressive. Tre bien. Are you done?" Futureman said.

"Yeah, all done here. Let's go inside and ask Mujibur if he has a can."

They popped into one of those timeless Manhattan mini-stores and came out with the contraband.

"Did you see how much he charged me? Eight bucks. Eight freaking dollars," Applejack complained.

"Oh well, it was worth it."

"Of course it was worth it to you. It was my money."

"We need to run now."

"Run?"

"The show is starting in ten minutes."

[Note: The art of chewing tobacco is not as agreeable or trouble-free as it may seem at first glance. For starters, it is clearly a barbaric and gross habit and carries with it a number of accurate stigmas. (ie: Only ignorant ruffians, dirty rednecks or politically incorrect baseball players chew it.) However, chewing tobacco will not ruin one's character. We will be who we will be with or without it. (Admittedly, it can stain the teeth if used too frequently; and if abused it will cause the cancer.) Furthermore, it does sicken most decent people to the point that they become queasy. They may even gag at the sight of moist, finely cut tobacco. They must be forgiven. They have never tried it. If it is your desire to keep their company it would be cordial and advisable to adjourn the activity until a more discreet and private setting is available. Thirdly: Women of all shapes, sizes, colors and ages do invariably loathe the practice and furthermore will make snap judgments about your quality if exposed to the secret joy too prematurely. Lastly: art demands sacrifice and the art of chewing tobacco is no exception. Mild inconvenience may arise in the event of indoor use. In which case particular supplies are essential to the procedure if a palatable effect is to be achieved: one cup, preferably opaque; two napkins or paper towels (one for the lining of the cup; one for post-procedures); a beverage, preferably weak in consistency for rinse and repeat; a sink for disposal of the spittle; a refuse can for disposal of the cup. Some level of forethought is always necessary and cannot be avoided. Disaster will ensue if the chewer is careless. In closing, the sacred art is not for everyone. Humankind is a loose and discipline-hating sort. Many will exploit the leaf and injure themselves. Do not be found among them. The true artist will seek balance and moderation. In that equilibrium lies bona fide enjoyment.]

Futureman and Applejack arrived at the Majestic Theater not a moment too soon. Futureman, owing Applejack a smallish chunk of money and other securities, dashed to the box office and purchased both tickets. Never one to go frugal, he procured the two best seats in the house. The boon companions, elated to the point of silliness, stormed through the darkness up both flights of stairs and, by no small amount of stumbling and apologizing, took their places in the very center of the very back row on the third balcony just as the curtain was being hauled up. They had their can of tobacco. They were preparing to see perhaps the most overrated and overexposed modern opera of all time (which happened to be the hands-down favorite of both men) when Futureman realized their folly.

"Did you get cups?" he whispered.

"No. Didn't you?"

"Of course not. I thought you would take care of it. I was buying the tickets."

"I bought the can. It was your job to get the cups." Their whispering was becoming a distraction.

"I bought the tickets. I couldn't get the cups."

"Shhhh" from the left.

"Sorry."

"Excuse us. Pardon us."

"Isn't there an intermission? I'll get it together then," Futureman managed in a whisper as the first aria commenced.

Singing. Action. Laughter. Applause.
Intermission.

Futureman moved down to the mezzanine where the drinks were served. Anyone else would have felt hopelessly out of place and underdressed. He was wearing the pair of paper-thin blue scrubs that his father had given him, which after two months of hiking had become so oversized that he could barely rope them on; and an amusing short-sleeved number with stripes he had borrowed from Sarah. It was unbuttoned to the bottom of the sternum, but little of his chest lay exposed due to the unfathomably large and unmanageable size of his coarse beard. He was wearing trekking shoes and still stank abnormally but none of these considerations seemed to register with him as he approached the bartender and pulled out his plastic wallet of the (Ziploc) sort used by thruhikers to keep their valuables safe and dry.

"How may I be of service?" the bartender said.

"Well, my good man, all I need is one bottle of water."

"Coming right up." He reached underneath the counter without breaking eye contact.

"And two plastic cups."

"You do realize that drinking is only permitted on the mezzanine. Of course you realize that." He smiled as he handed Futureman the cups, never breaking eye contact.

"Certainly, my good man. Now if you could direct me to the fontange, I need to tidy up a bit."

"The restroom, sir?" Strictly a professional, he pointed to his right. "Directly through those doors."

Moments later, Futureman was leaving the mezzanine, struggling up the stairway to the balcony. Nothing was in his hands. A five dollar bottle of French mineral water was tucked into his left sock and both cups were balanced precariously between his lower stomach and his waistband. Four theater attendants stood at the top of the stairs, unaware of the violation as he passed by.

Never before had Applejack or Futureman so savored a lump of tobacco. The two friends sat there pleased as pears, reveling in the supreme beauty of "The Phantom of the Opera." The arresting singing voices made them gasp. The costuming and edifices of the set were pure mescaline to the eyes. There was trepidation. There was mystery. There was the power and failure of love. Oh, Christine! It was more than they could bear. Beset with passion, the hairy men sat in the darkness, tears running from their eyes, tobacco juice dripping from the corners of their mouths.

Afterward, they stumbled home wordlessly and in the morning got on a train that finally took them out of New York City.

II

Stand at the crossroads and look,
ask for the ancient paths,
ask where the good way is,
and walk in it,
and you will find rest for your soul.
                    -The Prophet Jeremiah

The northern hemisphere rolled away from the sun for the day. Burgeoning shadows, imprecise strands in the caste of slippery elms, stretched across the corridor. Applejack and Futureman were planted there on the ground beside the rusted train tracks. Their bodies rested, their wills tired. Applejack looked down between his knees at the cracks separating the red New York ground. His musty imagination came alive; he could see that his feet were spreading out-changing color, burrowing, growing roots in between the stones. Planting themselves.

New York City was a kick to the head. It shouldn't have happened. But it did. *How could I get antsy out here – on the Trail? The Trail is supposed to cure me of this.* Applejack sighed and peered down the tracks toward the bend. The forest hung over the rails, tendrils of undergrowth lurked close to the tresses of brown steel that had guided so many trains north.

"Buddy, I just don't feel like going anywhere." Applejack spat on the ground, marked an infinity symbol in the dirt.

"Everything bends together," Futureman said in agreement. "Hard to see light. We have so far to go, I'm afraid."

Applejack and Futureman were friends. They understood each other in that way that makes the complicated simple. Their journeys had become one and the same over time, and loneliness and the unremitting desire to roam had driven them both, each one on his own, to this cracked hope, this lost-at-sea resignation. Mountains were to be climbed. Storms were to be outlived. States were to be pocketed. What now was this new shapeless smog, descending as they struggled to look up from the damned New York dirt?

A train was coming from its berth by the sea to take them out into the unfettered West. The Wyoming tables, the black and white cowboy vales. It would be here soon to collect them, they were sure.

"I think I'm done with the Trail, man. I'm going to hop this next train that comes by. I don't care where it's going. I'll be like ole Woody Guthrie. Boxcar will be my home." Futureman crouched low and put his ear to the rail, sure at any moment he would feel the vibration of a barking engine. Do what's necessary. Never say the word *quit*.

"That's a good idea! Maybe our journey is taking a new shape. Embracing the expanse. It's much bigger than the Trail could ever be."

Men in the grip of despondency will tell themselves fairy tales if that's what it takes.

"I think I understand the Trail now."

Sometimes the apprentice moves ahead of the master.

"I've always wanted to ride the rails. To anywhere."

And finds a waiting dragon.

"Back in high school my buddies and I almost jumped a train heading toward Omaha. We chickened out though. We had *things* to do. Now I'm sayin' Nico was right. It *is* just about the journey. It's not about doing every mile. It's about being out here, and there, everywhere, anywhere. Don't matter where. To hell with that purist straight and narrow."

When the choice is hope or ego, you choose hope. Ego shatters first every time.

A crippled truth passed back and forth between them. The whole version was too ponderous to voice or even intuit. To admit that they had not received a prize for passage, to find themselves beginners again at the threshold of a labyrinth of questions, to see ahead – more cost, more inbred blood, more striving under the sun – vanity of vanities. Too much for now. Choke on the bone. Wisdom leads to sorrow. *Laughter, don't leave.*

After all the miles they had not yet yielded to the path.

Train's a'comin', comin' up from the sea.

Often, in life we undertake a thing much greater than ourselves. A task, a test, a degree, a marriage. We find ourselves rearing a child, running a machine, raising a dragon; but we humans are somehow more than the sum of all our parts. In these moments we stand before a giant with the power to slay us many times over, but unlike David the son of Jesse, to deal the deathblow to the monster is not to sling one simple stone and be done with it (one might say that other Forces were at work there). No, it isn't enough to throw yourself at the Trail, furiously spending your resolve with a flurry of violent blows. Anger is not enough to do the job. Physical strength is not enough. Rigorous planning, sheer delight, high adventure nor bravado will be enough. Come-hell-or-high-water grit is not enough. The end is too distant. The hope of victory seeps into the ground like so much spilled water. There is only one way in the end to prevail. One way to walk the Trail and finish it – *the monster must be embraced.*

Accept the brute in all its rotten, stinking glory. Or go home.

No vibration came to Futureman's ear, his head still on the rusty rail. He looked down the line, squinting to make out the form of a fallen tree resting on the tracks.

"These rails are through. Woody ain't around no more."

The Trail crossed a road a hundred yards up, where an oxidized, bb-blasted RR sign bent over the track. The road disappeared into the smog, the tracks into chest-high weeds. One last deliberation.

A truck pulled up beside them. A man leaned out of the cab.

"Where ya headed, boys?"

"Anywhere."

"Alright. I'm going to the City if you want. Free ride."

Close your eyes, let it pass, find those stones along the river, the ones that fit into your sling, wind 'em up, release, let 'em fly, faith in trajectory, it's out of your hands now, nothing you can do, open your eyes, walk across the field of battle, cut off the head of your enemy, one of many, many of one.

III

That train, any train, is groaning in the earth still. Barely now, I can feel it chugging underneath me, chomping on the coal. Tunneling through, from Monson to Barrington. Ash to elm. Dalton to Kent. Nannyberry to Solomon's seal. It mines through the hulking membrane of core granite, carrying cargo: drums and drums of egoless void, on its way to the Deep South to pull my self-importance down. It stops at stations peopled with those who don't need rides – or even want them, just going nowhere for no reason – and it gives *them* the rides! Makes no sense. Good thing it's far below me now, so slight its vibration, not even an itch on my calloused feet (haven't felt anything down there anyway for quite some time now).

Futureman watched his face drip – a bit of his nose, a patch of eyebrow, a lobe, tiny pieces caught inside bubbles of his sweat – down onto the pallid dirt.

Applejack led the way, once again charting a course of day-by's down this Appalachian something. The New York ground here was baked, thirsty soil. Pieces of dead-gray, almost white, wood scattered about; sticking out of the ground like broken blades. It's so dry I can't even see my shadow, Applejack mentioned. Shade, shade, need some shade.

"What's that ahead?"

"Where?"

"A shelter."

"Good. I can draw in the dirt some more." Or maybe you can wipe that smirk off your body. Drop the disappearing act and start acting like a hiker. Be here. Act like you give a damn about what you're doing. Remember, the woods just before dark? Shadows grabbing at branches like night has fingertips. It's amazing. Where are these suggestions coming from? Are they mine? Apple-jack began to discern that the struggle was bending inward. Who cares about the voices? Lies. Rubbish. Dung. *Where is that calla lily?*

He saw a man drinking water.

The man didn't say anything as they approached. He was standing in front of the shelter, having finished an entire gallon jug. Nearing sixty, he didn't look it. Long gray hair streaked with black was bound up neatly under a hat. He wore a sweat-stained Ex Officio safari shirt, buttons free, hanging open. He was in Iron Man shape. He reminded them of David Carradine.

"Who are you?" Applejack asked.

"Shadow! Started in Maine. How you boys doin?"

Confession time. "I almost got on a train twelve miles back," Applejack said.

"Me too," Futureman said.

"Got on a train? Now? You've come so far."

"I know."

"We know."

"Hmmm." Shadow stroked his chin, took time to consider his guts. *This is one of those – moments.*

"Well," he smiled. "You didn't."

Applejack breathed deep. Ah, grace. *There she is again.* Grace.

"And I'm glad, too!" Shadow said. "Because I sure could use the company." Admonition and absolution in just fourteen short words. Surely, this was a man who had raised a house full of children.

Futureman turned aside to busy himself with unpacking. He could not accept the gift. *No, that's too easy. I didn't do anything noble. If that train was still running, I'd be on it right now. There was no decision involved.*

Meanwhile, Applejack felt the weedy heart in his chest pump a little stronger. Rich, thick blood, crimson. "Tell us everything we've forgotten, Shadow. And some things we haven't learned. Do you mind?"

Shadow knew what he was asking. "It would be my pleasure," he said, firing up his stove.

Remember the smells, that olfactory catalogue. That's the first important thing. The wood, the stream, the moss, the red lichen on Katahdin's crest, fragility that endures winters. And don't forget touch, that's second. If you forget touch, you lose touch. Find a rotting log in the forest and take off your shoe. Press your toes into it, feel it crumble against the balls of your feet. Rings caving in to make soil. That's decades, scores, hundreds of years – just to make a clump of first-rate soil. Then remember your sight. A host scattered throughout the forest, reforesting, all of them part of the larger, this Appalachian moraine, this great glimmering mass of mountain – the strong rippling arm of North America moving under your toes, so slightly you can barely sense the adaptation, carrying you forward just as much as you are your own self. The path is changing – always in motion. And then, taste your sweat. It's good. You need the sodium. Drink it down, your toil. Walking is a task, a task you have chosen. Walking takes you home. And last – don't forget, you were home already, when you crossed into New York. And you were home when you started in Maine. You were at home when you came out of the womb, and you will be at home when you turn back to dust. Home is contentment. Move ahead, but only after you can stay put. You will get home if you hold fast.

Applejack woke early. He smelled the dust in the air-like scraps of a hacksaw. The beauty wasn't only in the smell, but also in the act of smelling. He felt the shelter beneath him, vibrations in the wood. *I'm going to recuperate, I can feel it,* he thought. *Just like last time. Where's that gallon jug?*

Shadow packed early. "I'm off, boys. I get going with the sun, have to. Twenty miles ain't as young as it used to be." He winked. "Slow and steady, said the turtle to the hare. I'll see you on down the way. Oh, and stay off those trains."

"Right. See you tonight," Applejack said. A promise. *I have more to learn,* he thought. *Recuperation comes in waves. Rises and falls like the tides. I suspect low tide's coming in about fifteen minutes, when I decide to finally get up, but for now, I'll enjoy that hacksaw tang in the air, a marvel to be sure – to savor the flavor of lumber dust. It's coming back, I hope, how it is that pain connects us to joy, a canal between two oceans.* He laid his head back on the wood and smiled.

"Where we headed today? And I hope it's not slow and steady." Futureman fumed. He'd been waiting under his eyelids for Shadow to leave, not as taken with him as Applejack. Not as enthused by their reminiscences from those wretched, halcyon days of river-fording in the Wilderness. He didn't want to be reminded – how the raw, vulnerable flesh on his heels pulled off in the current. How the water turned the color of wine. Those were the good days? At least, he felt life in him then.

"What's wrong with you?" Applejack asked.

"Aaaahh."

"Yesterday is yesterday, man. Just try to forget about it. It's like Shadow said–"

"Right, Shadow. Our very own personal motivational speaker in a safari shirt. How much do you think he charges per hour?"

"What? He's great. He's positive. We could use a little of that right now."

"Andrew Lloyd Webber, that's what I could use right now. But this – I-once-was-lost-but-now-I-found-the-forest-again nonsense? No, thank you."

"Alright. Have it your way. Eat your oatmeal cold. I'm not gonna let you get me down, not today. So have a good hike. Just do us all a favor and burn off your fumes before tonight – or else go find a train."

Ultimately, we are alone in this life. Is this what compels our search for friends, spouses, business partners and golf buddies? Is this why we join street gangs and fitness centers? Why we pile into Wrigley Field for hot dogs, throw Tupperware parties and read books in clubs? As John and Paul put it, "All the lonely people, where do they all come from?" It's a rhetorical question. Isn't it?

Are we prepping ourselves (as Bombadil calls it) for that boundary of life and death? That threshold? The one we cross alone, into the afterlife? We'd like to say there isn't one but who honestly believes this? So, what happens there? No one comes back to tell us. Ghosts don't talk. The Book of the Dead is buried in sand. The preacher who stands in the pulpit and charges us to – Have no fear of death! – if you look closer, you'll see them. Darting eyeballs. Truth is, we just don't know what happens on the other side. Faith doesn't make that promise. It gouges out fear's eyes, yes. But blind fear is still fear.

And yet, the preacher's wrong. The beginning of all things is a certain Fear. Without it, there can be no wisdom.

Applejack caught up with Shadow at Skunk Mine. He was eating lunch, pony-tail on his shoulder like a pet python. Applejack pulled out some crackers and dried fruit.

"Where's your friend?"

"I don't know. Back there somewhere," Applejack said.

"Not out of his slump yet, huh?"

"No, but he's got his fairy tales."

"So you just left him there?"

It made Applejack uneasy. "It's okay, we hike alone. You should have seen him when we started. He was so fat. You remember Chairback in the Wilderness? He got stuck on that rock cliff and started shouting for a miracle –"

Shadow cut him off. "That was yesterday. Today is New York."

After eating his oatmeal cold, Futureman took to swinging through the trees. The ground had too much soil on it. Bark is better, nice, too. Yep, that Tarzan was on to something. Travel by vines, girlfriend Jane, best friends with lions and gorillas. Anything to take my mind off that dry wad of vacuum trash down there.

Today, in New York, Applejack thought about Shadow's words. But I need yesterday. I need the memories. If they fade, I'll end up out West somewhere singing dust bowl ballads the rest of my life. And as far as Futureman is concerned – that idiot – he actually told that Empire guard that he came to see where King Kong died. What a weirdo. I hope he's alright, alone. I left him in his shell. He won't stay in there for long, though. He doesn't like being stuck inside of it.

Futureman took his journal out at lunch on Three Lakes Trail and scribbled some scrabble. He drew a picture of a cat in a tuxedo with crab legs, pinchers, a giraffe neck and a bowtie. *What in THE hell?* He wasn't sure if he should laugh.

Applejack carried forward toward Catfish Loop. Steady now. Smell the yellow birthroot. Taste the dusty goldenrod. Listen to the weary birds. Feel the broken ground. Watch where you're going. Follow the white blazes. They lead the way. What if Futureman lets off the blazes? What if he walks down the wrong side of the river again? And what if they tear down the bridge in the meantime? How will I get my friend back?

Futureman was searching through his belongings, looking for anything, when he found the Bible he'd been given in Gorham. It was something. Bombadil had his old one. A girl named Wild Boar had given him this one. He'd forgotten.

Today, in New York, he opened it to page one, and began to read. *In the beginning, God*... A chill came over him. This is a dangerous book. I think I'm afraid of it. Strange. I'm not sure if I've ever even read it before. Not really.

Today. New York. I'm here now. I've walked hundreds of miles to be here. A hundred days maybe. They are all single miles, days, moments, and they all lead here. To this one mile, day, moment. Maybe the last one. I have to be okay with that. Applejack walked toward evening. His steps left imprints in the earth, tracks for Futureman to follow.

Futureman met Shadow at Canopus Hill.
      "Hey there. You look better," Shadow said.
      "I am. Just needed some soil, the kind trees grow in. Know what I mean?"
      "I think I do."
      "You seen Applejack?"
      "He's on up ahead. Said he'd wait for you at Denning Hill."
      "You coming up?"
      "I'm gonna camp here tonight. These knees are done for the day. I'll run into you guys tomorrow or –" He nodded.
      Crossing Old Albany, Futureman thought about *Or*, making his way toward Denning Hill. *What does he mean?* I like that Shadow.

Light angled cautiously into a grove of dark forest that clung at the base of Denning Hill. Applejack sat on his pack listening to twigs pop on the branches like broken drumheads. Fupp, twap. This is a perfect place to wait. Feels good. Dark in here and the heat's all busted up. My thoughts have nowhere to go. I'll wait until my friend comes and we can climb out together.

From a hilltop, Futureman noticed a suspicious knot of trees, below. He watched as bits of light unsuccessfully spattered the edge of the grove like paint. *He's in there. He's gotta be.*
      "Applejack?" Futureman called.

"Over here," Applejack said, relieved to hear his friend's voice.

"What a day."

"What a day."

"What do you say we fill up on water and climb out of here?"

"Sounds good to me."

As they made camp on top, orange light burst through a gap in the great blue canopy. The column bowed and bent. It cracked and came crashing down. A necessary destruction, they considered. *Sometimes a thing has to be torn down if it's ever going to get better. Sometimes you've got a rotten foundation on your hands.*

In the morning, they struck camp quickly and were off-mind set on foot. But it was remission. Only remission.

IV

Miles faded behind them, visible only in the dim recognition of greens and browns. Their imaginations wandered as well, as they plodded along, heads down, lost in ruins. Path upon path, turn upon turn, until the white blazes disappeared. Up the forest, down to Georgia, the way was one now, unimportant to this patch of wilderness. The overgrowth around them should have been obvious – old field succession. The trees closed in on the path rapidly, choke and pin cherries, alder buckthorn and black locust. Spireas hung over the track, hauled down by the weight of bee-clusters. An old pond, stagnant; an old tree, cracked trunk, plunging into it, so much water it drowned. Onward still, they walked until the oval leaflets of wild sumacs wrapped around their foreheads, yanking their wooden dolled thoughts toward lucidity. Lost.

"Are we? C'mon, are you serious?" Applejack kicked a rotten log.

"I don't think the Trail likes us anymore," Futureman said.

Back-tracking was out of the question. Too many knee-knocked little paths through the woods to count.

"What do you want to do?" Applejack asked.

"I guess we should call this a date with fate," Futureman said.

Piecing their way by path, field, farm, house and road, they found the Trail again and rolled toward dusk. Perhaps, there was no mystical significance to the mishap. They simply continued to walk on, the ambling summer afternoon mending their idea of home and boundary.

By the end of the next day, they had begun to move along in the simple silence of the forest again when a hum began to grow in their ears. Emerging, wood to pavement, they came across the Palisades Interstate Parkway. After a day's business, thousands of people drove through the crossing, rushing toward supper, sleep, celebration. They were thirty miles from the City. Half an hour's travel for some. A couple of days for others. Futureman and Applejack were mildly inflamed, slightly titillated by the speed and the noise. They crossed quickly, feeling distant once more from the pace of city life.

Eager to shed the murky shawl of the lowlands – of yet another day, they pushed up nearby Black Mountain, hoping to find Shadow settled on the crown. As Applejack moved over the grassy crag his pack and chin dropped in wonder. A sea gale had blown away the day's vapor and nothing hindered his view. The flush of the Manhattan skyline was drawn crisp against the blue. Out beyond Yonkers, Patterson and Jersey City, the New York lights crashed recklessly into the Atlantic. He could see clearly the Empire State Building standing a lone watch over her end of the island. To the north a bridge, perhaps the George Washington, pulled the earth together. Tens of millions of thousands of light rays kindled his eyes. The throbbing glow still crying out to him. But he knew that he was done with the City. He and Futureman were home again, for now.

Shadow was nowhere to be found so they pitched their tarp hard to the wind, ate a sound meal and slept deeply, the distant city lights flashing against their dreams.

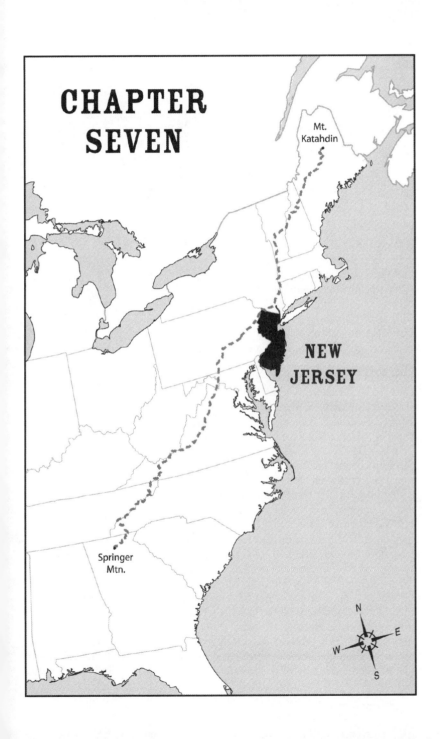

CHAPTER SEVEN

Mt. Katahdin

NEW JERSEY

Springer Mtn.

A high wind rose, searching over the top of the mountain. It grabbed at separated blades of grass and small twigs, squealing between viburnum, picking
on deerberry. And on the wind, it came to them once again. Curiosity. There,
it found the men sleeping soundly in the early morning light. It pulled on
their bags, rapped gently on their foreheads. An almost audible command to
rise up with the sun.

I

A now-nother day. Newmorrow. Bluearrow. So rare – Oh! This day,
fresh-sparrowed ray of righted light,
high-barrowed brow of gone night blight.
A month's worth of wind in a breath.
To begin again, what girth – around its neck!
This all-born open-eyed day of deep days.
Deep as a well-stone quarry. Down
As a now-nother, peer-skied dawn.

Applejack awoke in the baby blue. The wind was still blowing when the sun
came up. It carried something lighter on its steady prow, a balsam salve.

They couldn't see the city anymore. It was lost in the morning light.
Applejack stowed the tarp and bags while Futureman boiled water for his
friend's oatmeal. None for himself, his vow having become a preference.

Applejack felt settled as he crossed the mountain looking for signs of
Shadow's camp. Fresh ash, crushed turf. But it was clear he had not slept on
top. They moved on.

William Brien Shelter was hiding underneath a ledge of rock at the rim of
a small, cupped palm of earth. Both of them knew right away this was where
he'd been. There were no overt signs or footprints – nothing like that. But
they could feel the hint of his presence. They could nearly smell him. *He's
been here, alright. Sat on this log. Slept on that side of the shelter. He had a
small fire, only kindling and branches. I might be mixed-up and city-bit, but
I know that much.* They felt these things.

Modern man is so distanced from the natural world that he cannot believe
in such notions. The world's fracas is too distracting. But the occurrence is
not creepy or necessarily spiritual. Over time the woods simply restore to
man the gifts that he once possessed more fully – subtleties, gifts thrown
down. A thruhiker makes one tiny step toward recovering them. He is simply afforded the luxury of silence and time, to listen and observe. Slowly he
will lay down his feckless rushing about and whirlwind addictions, and he

will begin to sense. It does happen. After walking for days without crossing paths with another soul he will begin to hear animals as they take their courses through the woods. That is the sound a squirrel makes in dry leaves. There is a mouse scurrying over a wet log. There is the tentative measure of a deer. That is the flight of a martin. There, a swallow. These are the ruts of a wild boar. This is the bed of a deer. That is the sweet musky smell of a bear. A thruhiker, when not too consumed with his own preoccupations, will learn to call the difference between an osprey and a red-tailed hawk at a hundred yards. To smell a coming storm. To spot distinction between the noise of high wind in the trees and the rush of a creek. It comes. Naturally.

So many times startled by the furious rush of a game bird taking to air, Futureman had come to sense the turkey or pheasant around the corner almost before it stirred. He was no longer startled by it. Applejack could look at the pitch of the shadows and tell within five minutes what time of day it must be. Acquainted with the fragrance of the forest, they could smell if a clean person had recently passed through, detecting the wilting odor of perfume or deodorant as it lingered in fetid clouds on barks and leaves. They had lived among the trees and animals for a time. They drank water straight from the ground. Their beards were turning to moss and their muscles to stone. They wore a forgotten instinct.

Pressing down on the end of a twenty-two mile day, they came into the town of Greenwood Lake – a good spot for a steak dinner.

With bellies full of T-bone gristle, they proceeded down the main thoroughfare, assuming it would intersect with the Trail at some point. Up above the town, the A.T. ran along a parallel ridge that followed the New York/New Jersey state line. It was a precarious balance they were playing with and they knew it. The balance between forest and city, with this little town a stepchild of the thief. A thin membrane of resolve lingered on even still, smoldering in the firepit of Futureman's imagination; delicate scar tissue of a hairline fracture grew slowly across the brittle bones of Applejack's fragile dream. They passed a cheap motel marquis that boasted of movie channels and a continental breakfast.

One eye on the Trail, one on the promise of doughnuts in the morning, Futureman paused. "What do you think?"

"No, let's move on."

"It's gonna be dark in a couple hours, anyway. Just a quick stop. One night in a bed," Futureman persisted.

"C'mon, buddy. Let's just get on up the ridge and sleep under the stars."

"You're right. Maybe you're right."

Futureman was interrupted by a tapping on his shoulder. He turned. Incidentally, he had come to a halt directly in front of an old woman's mailbox.

"Sir, would you mind scootin ovuh a little bit. Hate to interrupt ya discussion. It sounds very important but I really would like to see if my celebrity magazine came in. You know, that Angelina's baby is due any day now." Pleasantly startled by the Yankee voice, Futureman stepped aside as the old lady reached inside the box.

"Shishkabobs! Nuthin. It always comes on Friday. That way I have it to read on Saturday." She smiled up at them through her gilded spectacles. She could barely make out their shapes. Two strings of (faux?) pearls hung down over a fuzzy sparkling sweatshirt. Futureman wondered if her poodle had been a fur donor.

"Hi there. I'm Applejack." He extended his hand. She didn't see it.

"I'm Hazel Steinberg. Very pleased to meet ya. You men work for the city?" Her voice crackled and careened like warbling pigeons between skyscrapers.

"I'm sorry?"

"I called 'em and told 'em that somebody needed to cut the top outta that tree before it falls on my power line. If it falls on my power line everybody on the street's gonna blame me. Well, no sir. It won't be me they blame. It'll be you guys at the power company. You're in charge of trees, aren't ya?"

"Uh. Yes. Technically, they are the ones in charge of trees."

"So do you carry the cuttin tools in those backpacks of yours?"

"No, ma'am. We're not from the city. We're just passing through."

"My favorite magazine is *TV Guide*. I love the colored parts. Frances reads me the times. I only watch shows during the week and sometimes on the weekend if there's nothin' on. But if you don't work for the city, what were you doing in my tree?"

"Ma'am, we weren't in your tree. Remember? We were standing here having a conversation and you needed to get your mail."

"Oh, of course, of course. So what *are* ya doin?"

"Do you really want to know?" Futureman said.

"Who do you think I am, some dame from the Bronx? I'm from the Uppuh East side, young man. Now tell me."

"We walked here from Maine and we are going home to the South. It's the Appalachian Trail."

"What? Oh my goodness. Stop the presses! No, you can't be. Impossible."

"Yes ma'am. It's true."

"Oh my! I've never heard of anything like that before in my life. My, my, my. So are youse gonna be in the book of records?"

"No ma'am. We aren't the only ones. People do it every year," Futureman said.

"Have you told the papers? What a story. I used to have friends in newspapers. You need to tell ya newspapers. They'll put you on the front page for sure."

"Ma'am, we –"

"Who's ever walked from Maine to Georgia? Tell me! Who? You're going to be famous. You'll be on Leno."

"You know that the Appalachian Trail is right behind your house don't you? It's practically in your back yard. See that ridge up there?"

"Yes, I see it."

"Right up there. That's where it is. That goes all the way to Georgia."

"Nobody goes in my backyard except me and Agnes and Erma and sometimes the mailman comes back there." She turned, her sunshine yellow pants catching the light, and put a hand to her head. "Headliners! And I'll say I knew you when, yessir. Wait till I tell my daughter about this. Bye-bye now. And tell the papers. Frances reads them to me. And tell the Guinness Records."

"Yes ma'am. We'll be sure to do all that."

Hazel went inside, motioning wildly along the way. Applejack and Futureman bushwhacked up the hill back to the AT and back over the New Jersey state line. Stop the presses!

II

For a couple of forward-moving, forward-thinking hours, they marched ahead, mile on mile. The perforated New Jersey wood brought the fight out in them.

But fear is a clever foe and doubt is dogged. Accusation roosts in tree-tops– leering, biding, waiting for scraps to fall from the table. These three are scavengers, scab-pickers, not dignified as predators. At sundown, the tri-une scarecrow of ankle-biters convened, selecting an old seducer to return and lay into the wayfaring stragglers – discontent.

"Say, where does that road go?" is all it took.

"Don't know. Let's take it."

"Where?"

"Anywhere but here."

Right. Agreed. Anywhere but here is suitable. After all, the trees are dull, the air is hot and stale, and the monotony of hiking tears away at the child within.

The road was cropped with ripped-up asphalt. It was a country road. It led to mystery. *Take me home, to the place I belong...* They walked for three miles headed toward anywhere as the sky grew dark.

"Where we gonna stay?" asked Futureman, the faint memory of being lost sputtered somewhere in his mind.

"I don't know. Wherever we find a flat spot, I guess," Applejack said.

"How 'bout there." Futureman pointed to a farmhouse at the end of a long gravel drive, dark and full against the foundering sun.

"Why a house? What's wrong with going back into the woods?"

"Didn't you say you wanted to sleep on a bed?"

"No. You said that."

The owner of the old farmhouse was a lady. An American relic of times past, when a woman was arrayed in the sweaty silken locks of a sun-baked day. A time before epidurals and blow dryers, aerobics and laser face procedures; before business suits, poodle grooming and daytime drama. This was a lady who grew her own corn and churned her own butter.

She watched curiously as Applejack and Futureman scuttled up the long drive like carrion beetles. *Now what in the world are these two up to?* She stood with her hands on her hips as they came to her.

"Hey there, miss," Futureman said.

"Hey, there yourself, fella. What do you need?"

"Well, uh. We're hiking the Trail and, uh, we…"

"The Trail – assuming you mean the Appalachian Trail – is three miles back down the road. That way. So you're not really hiking the Trail now, are you?"

"No, we, um…"

"Listen here fellas. You two look like you've come a long way, and it looks like you've got yourselves a long way to go yet. So I suggest you get back to doin' what you put your minds to do in the first place."

Applejack and Futureman were dumbfounded. They just looked at her. She treated them like sons.

"Alright, then. You boys look mighty thirsty. I'll go in and get you some fresh water. Here's a little company while I'm gone."

She whistled. Three little heads poked out from the barn door. "Joshua, Katy, Samuel. Come over here and meet some friends of mine. They're hiking the A.T."

The children put down their chores and stood before the burly men. Taught to present themselves properly, they waited, attentively and without awkwardness.

Applejack loved little kids and wanted to seem mighty before them, like a valiant explorer; instead, he found himself suspecting there was more wisdom in their innocent ways than he'd found so far in his soul wanderings. He stared blankly at them.

"So you guys are hiking, huh?" Samuel, the oldest, said.

"Yeah, that's right, we're hiking. You ever hiked?"

"Lots of times! Daddy loves to take us!" Katy chimed in, tooth missing.

"Me and Josh are gonna hike the whole thing some day, just like you guys!" Samuel said.

"You should hike it better than us," Futureman said. "Hike your own hike. That's what we say out here." He laughed weakly.

"What's it like?" Joshua asked.

Futureman paused, struggling to find that same excitement that had once been alive in him. "It's a lot like life, buddy."

"Well, we're gonna do it, aren't we, Josh?"

"Yep, someday," Josh said. "It was nice to meet you both. We gotta finish our chores before it gets dark out. Good bye."

The woman returned with water. "Here you go, boys. Some nice cold water – straight outta the well. Just the thing you need to refuel you and get you where you're going."

She was talking about Springer.

"Thank you, miss. Thank you very much," they stammered.

Then she looked intently at them, directly into their squirming eyeballs. "Don't mention it, we all need a hand every now and again." Some radiant torch combusted somewhere within her, burning out from green irises – for an instant. It was her own deep well. A hard-scrabble strength, passed down through generations of hard laughing and hard working. She had no business sharing it with them. But she did anyway.

Back on the trail, rescued again by the grace of another, they shuffled forward. In the failing light, Applejack spotted a square of white against the dark curtain of trees. It was a scrap of paper-facing north, stuck to a Wawayanda State Park marker. It wasn't clear from whose hand it had come. It read:

Beware, all you hikers north,
For you the bear comes forth.
And beware all you hikers south,
Not to end up in the bear's mouth.

III

A spring peeper looks for dew pockets. Deer mice dig through hiker packs looking for food to eat and tissue to bed down with. A coyote kyoodles and dogs within a ten-mile radius bark in ape-chase frenzy. The crickets harp in unison. A buffalo treehopper gets caught in the labyrinthine sumac. Spiddle-bugs claw at their nests. Hundreds of moths flap for their lives, swallowed up in a wolf spider's web, a harvest of evaporated dust. Frogs croak. Squirrels play. Owls hoot. Raccoons shuffle across the twigs on the loam. Falling hemlock cones tap gauche cadence on the branches beneath. Creeks burble. The wind rushes through the forest constantly, sometimes stalwart, other times delicate. Trees moan in the sway. Bark pulsates, growls. A hollowed-out knot catches a night breeze in her courses, ripping undercarriage open. She howls like a banshee. These are the sounds at night. They remind us that the forest watches while we sleep.

After a while, you get used to it. Well – not really. Sure the frozen terror wears off, but the mystery of darkness leaves too much room for the imagination to truly be at peace. Futureman had a harder time with it than Applejack did, of course. The mystic in him strung it all together, weaving bizarre stories through his antic-riddled mind. He sat up regularly to scrutinize the shadows, needing to justify their activities.

The warnings Wawayanda State Park had posted everywhere concerning the overpopulation of bears, along with the large padlocked food boxes available not even a hundred feet from the shelter – these weren't comforting.

Like rats – hikers say about the bears in New Jersey. Bear hunting had been outlawed in the state years back. Since then the beasts had overrun the place. In states where hunting is allowed, bears are much more skittish – reflective, reticent even. Humans mean rifle rounds. But in New Jersey, humans mean food, and lots of it. BBQ sauce and kettle cooked potato chips, peanut butter and bananas, frank and beans, steaks, tuna, egg salad and Oreos. A feeding bear in a campground looks harmless, almost domesticated.

But wild, well-fed bears are still wild. The only domestication that has occured is that the bear has become completely and totally unafraid of humans, whereas before he was moderately unafraid. Rumor had it that New Jersey was considering sanctioning the bear hunt once again – but it hadn't happened yet.

A large twig broke in the forest. Futureman sat up. "Sheeeezz." He listened. *Don't be ridiculous now. These are just black bears, not like the big grizzers out West, with paws as big as a man's chest. These eastern black bears are just little old, five hundred pound heaps of grumbling fur is all, which means...I'm gonna get eaten.* He sat up for a time, eyes wide, waiting for the worst. Finally he dozed off again, where vigilance and exhaustion drove him into a nightmare about a tiptoeing minotaur.

Applejack was sprawled out beside him, buzzing. Close now to the Mason Dixon Line, it called out to him through his dreams – a longing for the Southland, elastic and gentle, unruly and nostalgic.

Home. *How long has it been? Autumn in Tennessee, the leaves – deep orange, crimson, neon blonde and fire red. Mama's lemon meringue pie, warm summer nights too hot to let the windows down and the fireworks in,*

*uproar of hot wind along gravel roads, knolls and curves, leading to look-
outs along the Tellico lake front and a walk with that sweet girl by the dam,
southern belle, accent hung up in the back of her mouth like hidden treasure, the warmth of that twangy charm let loose in the world. Home. It's
been too long now.*

So deep were their dreams that they did not stir as a three hundred pound
bear sniffed at their toes for food, nor did they toss as it tore in frustration at
the food cage nearby. In the morning, the paw prints on the ground and
scratches on the box were curious to them, the work of this rat of unusual
size. Alarmed, they moved on.

IV

All the day long, they pass unfulfilled promises of bear. Now hanging at the
end of a sweat-slathered anaerobic noose, strung up in a stump-littered
crack-pipe gully, Applejack and Futureman trudge along in a daydream. In
the distance to the north-northeast, they hear the buzzing of an angry hornet
– no, a tiny plane – sputtering through the thin air and – there! In the trash-
can-lid opening of forest sky, they see it – a crippled crop-sprayer dropping
low, diving, jaundiced underbelly sick against that paltry strand of humidity.
Its innards unfold, releasing a cloud of – papers? – down they come, sheets
of paper – hundreds of them eerily floating earthward, blanketing the tattered oaks and swollen ground. Applejack, stunned – teeth swung ajar,
chooses one, unsticking it from a thorny branch, and reading, sees this plea:

New Jersey is MIA.
Has anyone seen New Jersey? I can't find her.
*She's tucked away like a stain. Forgotten. Molded into an armpit by ignorant
assumptions. Sits she like a child at the counter of the candy store.*
She wants a root beer float, but no one will give her one.
*She wants America to know that she is beautiful too, that she has
mountains and flowers and fabulous bears.*
But they won't listen. All they can see is factories.
Well, it's New Jersey's turn now.
She doesn't have any billboards on America's interstates.
No commercials. No cheerleaders raising spirit fingers for luck.
Someone – anyone, give New Jersey a chance.

V

They had only hiked twelve miles, but upon that one spot where Applejack
and Futureman stood, the sun shone directly. Unfiltered radiation burnt off

their skin and evaporated their guts, broken crystals of sweat collecting in the corners of their eyes. Swabs of cotton filled their mouths, chunks of salt between their toes.

"What did I do wrong? Why am I being turned into salt?" Applejack said.

"It kind of tastes like ocean in my mouth." Futureman mumbled. "Salt water in my shoes. And listen – I swear I can hear waves crashing on the bases of the hills."

Alas, they found a heavy flowing stream. What relief. Applejack slid off his shoes and dipped his feet into the cold current.

Futureman looked hesitant.

"What is it?" Applejack asked.

Apparently he was afraid to stick his feet in the water. He said: bull shark.

Applejack produced some good questions and made some solid points: "that makes no sense, whatsoever" and "why would you think such a thing?" Also, "there are no sharks in this stream." Good points.

Good questions. But Futureman was disappearing into those regions of his brain that reason had never been able to master. As a young child, he'd thought that maybe King Kong was born in the forest beside his house. Convinced that ninjas were following him everywhere he went, he'd learned how to swing nunchakus, just in case. And on the neighborhood swim team, he swam fastest because he thought maybe the last place kids got *bull sharks* unleashed on them. Fault lines and lava cracks could erupt in the kitchen at any moment. Crocodiles frequently found their way to the bathtub. Cartoons came out of the TV sometimes and Lego ships took him into space on the weekends.

"Dude, you're being incredibly stupid and it's ticking me off. Seriously." Applejack said. "Just put your feet in the dang water!"

But fear is more powerful than logic, and sometimes it is, literally, in the water.

"Did you know that a bull shark can survive in both saltwater and freshwater, and that many bull shark attacks have happened in swimming holes along the Mississippi?" Futureman said.

Applejack looked into the pool. "No. Didn't know that."

"There's a lot happens in water we don't know about."

"Okay," Applejack said, putting his shoes back on. "C'mon, we gotta get moving. Pennsylvania's not far away."

VI

As evening came down, they chose a hill high in the forest, far away from the threat of the bull shark, but right in the heart of bear/minotaur country.

Looking out towards the Delaware Water Gap *(somewhere to the south-not far)*, filling their bellies with crusty jambalaya, they heard a whistle coming, a'comin down from the north. A felicitous tune regaled the trees. They clapped their hands in reply sending down a light shower of sweet needles and bereft leaves – the ovation of summer's weary orphans. A pre-cursor, that herald. Ochre, burnt umber, sienna, the sallowest of golds stitched premature seams of autumn along the frayed tendrils of the highgrass hill.

The melody was surely hopeful as it came to them, sounding of experience not naiveté, yet...yes – hopeful, the earthy potion of a life lived in full, eyes wide open to the grieves of the world, not running, not fleeing but calling them on, extending the invitations of freedom, not freedom from these cares but freedom *for* them, abiding in patience, patiently forging ahead, gaining strength as it came. A pleasant improvisation. *Legato*. Shadow's melody. The Ballad of Dusk.

His sinewy notation paused on the fringe, *intermezzo*. Harmonics, frame of form, form of contrast against the twilight, billowed and whorled – or was it the quill of white birches whorled? – as the refrain trickled along behind, syncopated, closing with a rest – whole rest, breve, half-rest, thirty-second rest, whole – silence. Except for the clapping of the trees, *cadenza*. Then, buried beneath the fire pit bouquet of softwood, a flickering tongue kindled, dulcet lilting, smoldering strings rising to meet the composition – just a bit more, come up – *come, yes. Yes! There it is! Intone!* – weaving, woven into the folial ensemble of yellow-green and orange gray. Now the withering fronds of flowers, soon crushed to dust, welled on the breeze, feeding their fading tones – the reeds, wildwood woodwinds, irises and oboes – to the crescendo, the Swell, that glorious swell and finally the baton falls upon the closing rest, echoes of an overture carried through the forest and into the valley, whole rest – whole, half-rest half, quarter, *breve*, one-eighth, sixteenth, thirty-second rest, whole on whole on whole to – silence. All except the clapping of the trees.

The man raised his other hand.

"Hey there, old friends. Pleased to see that you're alive and well."

"For at least one more day. Breath for another day," Applejack stood and offered his stump to the guest, the conductor.

"Been another long one, but here we are – all three of us. Still marching to that beat we hear. Truly glad, truly glad to see the two of you." He pulled the band out of his long gray hair, letting it down – the hair of a maestro – and settled into Applejack's warm seat. A low groan accompanied him as he sat, the slow exhalation of recycled melody.

"Spend any time back there in Vernon?"

"Just enough to come and go," he said. The electric shape of whistling still hung on his lips as he fastened his stove to its fuel cell. Out came the silver tin of wintergreen dust, the final movement – the perfect resolve to a day of whistling. "Didn't tell you before 'cause you needed to see for yourself, but towns are no good for this sort of thing. They steal your thrust, knock the wind right outta you – and at my age you need all your breath for the flourish at the end. Truly, towns introduce the dissonant tones." He smiled. "You two found that out the hard way, I suppose."

"Guess we're beginning to understand some things."

"Life's hard enough. Dodge as many wrecking balls as you can. You're gonna take your fair share of blows no matter what you do." He twisted the chrome dial beneath his stove. A thin blue funnel of flame pummeled the base of his scorched pot, lifting out the ringings of a miniature kettledrum.

The trill caught his ear, Caribbean alto. Futureman turned toward the percussion. "What do you do when they knock you on your backside?"

"Well, son, there's only one thing you can do. I'm out here right now, but back home, my daughter is dying. She's got cancer – caught her in her prime. They didn't find it until I got down past the Whites. She was already – already overrun with the stuff. So, when I got off the phone with her, I headed straight for the bus station." He stirred the pot, mixing in spices. "But I kept thinking about something she'd said. Couldn't get it out of my head. It rang in my ears." *Aria. Deathbed serenade.* "She said, 'Pop, I'm with you as you go along. You're my legs. Keep 'em moving.' And that's what you do, Futureman. You dust off your ass, look around, find north, find south, spot a marker-and keep 'em moving."

"Where is your family?"

A descant shimmered in his eyes, in the corners of his mouth – ellipsis of doxology, smile of praise. "Not far. Pennsylvania. I'll be getting off the Trail soon to visit for a couple of days and then back out here. We live in the country. In a pasture between the scree fields. It keeps my head on straight."

"Are the rocks as bad as they say?"

He chuckled. "They'll cut you up pretty bad. And be careful of the rattlers. *Crotalus horridus* they call 'em. And horrid they are, to be sure. But I want you fellas to remember something for me."

"What's that?" Applejack knelt beside the slouching man, haunches in the dirt.

"When your knees are bloody and you feel like you're trapped down in between those poisonous bastards and horny shards of rock, you lift your head and look around and find the music. Find that inspiring tune and then you'll remember, you'll know that life – all of it – is sweet music, sweeter than sweetest honey and finer than finest gold. And when you get moving again, across that scree, you'll realize that you're not struggling at all. You'll see that you're really…gliding. Well, these bones are aching. Good night, my boys."

"Good night, Shadow."

As he gathered his things and crawled into his ragged nylon sack, the gray-haired bard looked grayer and older than before, than on the lemon-squeezed hills of New York. And when the first chill breeze of the season blew across the knoll that midnight, a polyphonic dance sounded through the subterranean caverns of Futureman's dreams – whispering calmly beneath his...sleeping-dreaming-hallelujah-sedated-at-last...imagination.

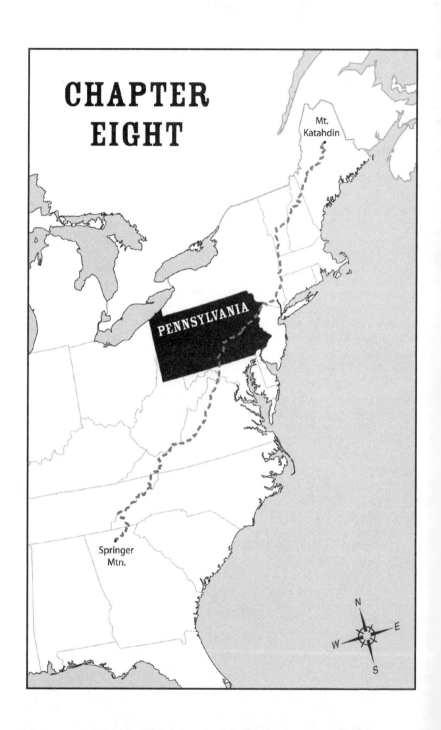

CHAPTER EIGHT

PENNSYLVANIA

Mt. Katahdin

Springer Mtn.

N
W   E
S

A plea bargain of sorts. The men heard it when they awoke their first morning in Pennsylvania. For a chance to make something of themselves, millions of small voices rang out, dull-witted and numb to learning. Some screeched like children locked in a dark closet. Some laughed like youth drunk for the first time. Some cried tears of joy as though listening to a song that reminded them of this and that from way back when. The men cleared their eardrums and nodded in agreement of something curious happening here. They took breakfast a little faster than usual.

I

Time, wind, water and ice have eroded the Appalachian Mountains to a third of their original size, at least that's what we're told. This could mean that once upon a time the Appalachians may have been taller than the Andes – challenging even the Himalayas. That's a lot of raw tonnage to account for. Any way you slice it, northern Pennsylvania got a raw deal because all that remains here are fields of jagged, scornful scree – shards of a bitter geologic divorce. Go to the Appalachian Trail nestled there beyond Amish country and you will find a huge mess. A sandpaper charade of stones, tightly congregated like roach orgies on unimpressive mole hills. But be warned if you walk there: they make the feet very, very sore, until every muscle and bone in the whole body throbs with the aching tenacity of a blood-bruised rectum.

Of course, hikers would rather the wind, water and ice finish the job and erode the rest of this immodest Appalachian mid-section but the hills will probably be there for a while. This means that the *felsenmeer*, or "sea of rocks," with their crypto-geologic talons, will be there too. Until then, the forlorn hiker will continue to struggle, fall and slip between Pennsylvania's petrified nethers-scrubbing shins, scraping calves, smashing knees, snapping ACLs – for at least one hundred miles between Delaware Water Gap and Harrisburg. And after all these miles, the hiker may gain an awareness, a grotesque suspicion, that the Appalachian Trail in northern Pennsylvania really only exists to get him from point A to point B. It is only blasted connector trail, the mustard-stained aquamarine cummerbund of an otherwise glorious state. *Ahh, felsenmeer! Ah, Pennsylvania!*

But in order to be fair, the geology *is* quite fascinating. Just listen to this: The Pennsylvania batholith is a corrugated deposit of several overlapping centers of felsic magmetism rich in diversity: obsidian, basalt, rhyolite, granite, gabbro and diabase; and minerals: from the atomic SiO-4 compounds to the mono-elemental forms of Au, Ag, Cu and S; from the compound anion of halite (built with equal parts of Na and Cl) to the oxide ores of Fe-3O-4, FeS-2, FeCr-2O-4 and [(ZnFe)(S)]. *The contention between the felsic and mafic concentrations in the subcutaneous compositions is alarming!* Rhyolite to granite, basalt to diabase, lithification (evidenced by the conglomeration of other rock types: igneous, metamorphic, clastic, non-clastic sedimentary, carbonate, slate, argillite, phyllite, hornfels, schist, gneiss, granulite, serpentinite, limestone and dolostone – not to mention the bituminous and anthracite coal that Pennsylvania mining is famous for) is indication of activity in range of 200 to 300 million years ago (give or take). At that time, convection cells in the earth's mantle would have compressed the continental plates of North America and Africa together and then pulled them apart, suturing the rift with the Atlantic Ocean. In turn, this region of northern Pennsylvania sucked up magma sediment that lithified and widened the central convection gap in a process called *orogeny* (the tectonic process in which large areas are folded, thrust-faulted, metamorphosed, and subjected to plutonism). The cycle ends with uplift and the formation of mountains!

In other words, the earth's tectonic plates got smooshed together, making giant mountains before separating into continents, and this is fascinating. C'mon, it is.

"Shadow said we'd glide, so let's do it in style!" Applejack did a jig.
"But a hovercraft?" Futureman said.
"We can do it."
"Really?"
"What men have done in the past, other men can do in the future-I mean the present."

It's true. Men have built hovercrafts. They exist.

Emanuel Swedenborg built one in 1716. A scientist, philosopher and theologian of sorts, Swedenborg figured that if he could get enough air under a vessel, then said vessel would lift off the ground, enabling men to travel on air. His plan included man-powered oars that forced air underneath the craft. Skepticism was unanimous (*air oaring?*) and the plan was abandoned.

In the mid 1870's Sir John Thornycroft applied the concept to boats in order to reduce drag on the hull. Then in 1952, Christopher Cockerell integrated the use of a vacuum cleaner, a motor and two cylindrical cans, devising a craft that could traverse swamps, water, even firm ground until – *voila*!

In addition to boasting its murderous scree fields, Pennsylvania offers the meanest and most plentiful bevy of timber rattlers and copperheads on the entire AT. What Applejack and Futureman lacked in bear-sightings, they more than made up for in snakes. Not surprisingly, Futureman found a baby rattler to play with, poking at it with the end of his hiking stick. The adorable but venomous snake snapped its diamond head powerfully, sinking itsy-bitsy fangs into the hard rubber of his pole. It sent shivers down his spine.

"Geez, even the tiny ones will chew your feet off!" Futureman said.

"We need to get up off this ground. I'm telling you man –"

"But a hovercraft? You're serious?"

"What men have done in the past…"

"I know…others can do in the future."

"Present."

All that is really needed in order to build a hovercraft are the following materials:

-one 4ft square of PLYWOOD;

-one PLASTIC SHEET (e.g. an old shower curtain);

-one LEAF BLOWER (preferably battery powered-eco-friendly), or a power vacuum with external exhaust;

-one SMALL PLASTIC DISK (a coffee can lid will do);

-two FENDER WASHERS;

-one BOLT;

-and one NUT.

This ultra-simple hovercraft can lift several adults! Seriously. Or at least two.

"That's the last time I stick my foot into a copper nest. The last time I step on a rattle head and the last time I bite my tongue on the balls of my feet. I'm leaving this infernal Pennsylvania ground. I'm building the Craft." Applejack stomped the dirt.

"Do it."

Applejack's hair blew in the wind. He clutched the manual controls of the hovercraft and smiled. Below him, the rocks of Pennsylvania were clawing at the edges of the plywood base. "It's not fair! This is our only joy in life," they wailed. The thirty-five hair dryers he and Futureman had hooked to the used generator at the back of the craft firmly pressed the rocks down and the board up. "Take that, you poor excuses for magmetism! You lithified plutonized forms! You limp felsenmeer! You are vanquished! We have built the Craft!" Applejack shouted as the proud vessel sailed over the passionless orogenous zones.

Futureman, cruising along at the stern of the airship, was cooking up a few ideas of his own. He bent low, cutting away at the fabric, industriously fashioning his silken polypropylene bedtime shirt to withstand the rising torque. After a few minutes a brilliant ebony kite emerged from his hands and rose into the blue sky. With glee, he tied it to the generator, watching it cavort in the Pennsylvania heavens. *Hmm. Perhaps I could harness some more power to push the craft onward toward greater speeds,* he thought. And from the leftover shirt scraps, he built a sturdy sail for the vessel. "Power of the wind!" he shouted.

Applejack felt a surge. He turned and saw the sail. His shouts carried through the screaming air. "What...is...that?"

"I've...figured out a way...to...harness...the power...of the wind!" Futureman belted back.

"You're a...friggin genius! You...know that?"

"I also...made...a kite!"

One thumb up, the other one on the hoverstick, Applejack guided the craft across Blue Mountain, finally setting it down on Pulpit Rock. *Terra firma* at last.

"What's that you got stashed in those bushes over there, all covered with leaves," a couple of day-hikers asked, passing through on their way into Port Clinton. They could hear the generator whirring as it cooled off under the frondescent wrap.

"I don't know what you're talking about," said Applejack, clenching his brow.

"Move along. Nothing to see here," Futureman said, waving his arms. "Pulpit Rock over there will be of more interest to you. It's actually quite beautiful," he assured. "In the early morning hours and at dusk the quartzite in the sandstone gives the pulpit rocks a bluish appearance."

"Yes, friends, it is a most unexpected treat along this desert path of bland scree-stone. Now, off with you. Be gone." Applejack clapped his hands sternly.

When the generator banged on the next morning, the hawks nesting above the Gap hurdled through branches and flapped into the sky. It whizzed and whirred and pumped energy into the hair dryers, until their ingenuous creation started, once again, to levitate.

"Hop on, Futureman. Another day under the sun. Get out your kite, friend. Raise it to the hawks. This Freedom Flyer is about to cruise on down the Trail. Hoverboard away!"

It was like they really were on the high seas.

II

Mothers, tell your children
Not to do what I have done
To spend your life in sin and misery
In the House of the Rising Sun
                    -Traditional

It was time to see if all the hype was warranted. Applejack started to run, lunging along the rock-strewn wrinkle that runs above the tranquil Susquehanna River. From there the Trail zigzags down to the water and dumps out beside a mad roaring highway. He looked over the concrete barricade at the blue water. Tall green grasses grew up from the bed, stretching their way through the water toward the sunlight; rested on the surface, pointing calmly downstream. Houses personified 1940s and 50s symmetry on the western bank. A little town spread out in the sunlight. Duncannon. Famous up and down the Trail for one reason only: the Doyle Hotel.

"So this is the place, yeah?" Futureman caught up with him on the bridge.

"Baltimore Jack said it was the only thing worth seeing in all of Pennsylvania."

"It can't really be as interesting as that. We'll get there and it'll be empty. Nothing will happen. Just wait."

"We shall see."

Since New Hampshire, the legend of Baltimore Jack had continued to grow, a *friend of a friend* kind of thing. Unlikely tales of debauchery and bravado moved easily up and down the Trail. It was even said that he had thruhiked northbound seven consecutive years. The son of Dartmouth professors, Baltimore Jack had made many proselytes and many enemies, spreading his ribald philosophy and earthy cheer. His knees were shot and his liver was dead several times over but he didn't know what else to do with himself – and that didn't bother him much.

So when Applejack and Futureman had rounded that verdant Vermont bend a few miles north of Killington and met the man in the August-baked flesh, they'd been surprised to say the least. It was mid afternoon and hot, yet there he stood on the side of the hill, the embodiment – or perhaps the prisoner – of his own myth. Half-gone bottle of Jim Beam in one hand and two (yes, two) hand-rolled cigarettes in the other. There was no doubt as to who they were looking at even before he spoke.

"Sobos. Truly, a rare breed," he scratched out stoically.

"It's the only way to go, Jack. You ought to try it some time."

"I like you already, kid. What's your name?" Jack stuck out one of the cigarettes as a gesture.

"Rubber Ducky. So, why don't you go southbound, Jack? Doesn't it get old?"

"Not a bit. Different Trail every year. It seems like a whole new ball game. You've been out here long enough to know the Trail is alive, how it grows and changes like every living thing. I've thought about going south but, alas, I'm a social creature. I need society. I need, shall we say, certain consolations that the southbound Trail might be hardpressed to supply." He chuckled to himself.

"So, any suggestions on the way down? What to look forward to?"

"The Doyle of Duncannon, PA, my young friend. I realize that you may have expected some spectacle of nature. And there are indeed many wondrous sights ahead of you, but none so miraculously display the perverse beauty of a fallen world as L'Hotel Doyle. Nothing can compare to your first night and nothing can prepare you for it."

"What's the big deal? Is it haunted?"

"Haunted? Not by the dead anyways but perhaps in a sense. When you walk in the door, you put one foot over into the other side. It's like a netherworld. If you think I'm a drunk, just wait. The Doyle was an old Anheiser-Busch Hotel back when Duncannon used to be a boomtown with the railroad and the mill. Somewhere along the way, all that went south. No more jobs. Nothing but booze. Anyway, about three years ago I was there and my toenail came off. I always get room 33, so I put the toenail in the second shelf of the chest of drawers – just to see if they ever clean. Next year? Sure as the world, out comes the drawer and there's that toenail. Like a four thousand year old mummy."

"Huh, so the hotel's dirty."

Jack snorted. "Alright, I'll bring out the good stuff. One year I check in, get my sheets and towel at the bar and then walk up to the third floor."

"Room 33?"

"Right, room 33. But as soon as I hit the top step I know something's not right. This rancid smell's running all up and down the hall. Literally about knocked me over. I'm hoping that it's on the other end, so I head toward my room but it just gets worse. I pull out the key, turn the knob and push – but the door won't budge. Like the bed's forced up against it or something. I shove and shove and nothing." Applejack and Futureman had taken off their packs and were sitting around Jack's feet like school lads.

"Well, 33 is on the corner, so I go out the fire escape door at the end of the hall and get out on the ledge. I inch my way around the corner, pop open the window and I'm in – and you already guessed it. Right there behind the bed is a dead body."

"No."

"I give you my word. Drunk guy crawled in there and died and I found him. So I heave his rigor mortised ass out into the hall and vomit all over the floor. Downstairs, I tell them there's a dead guy in 33. They say, *You can have the room for free then, Jack.* Now that, my friends, is the Doyle – and that is what you have to look forward to."

"You remember that day that we met Baltimore Jack?" Applejack started over the bridge to Duncannon. "Why didn't you tell him your real name?"
"Huh?"
"I know that we tell people a lot of things but you knew he was Baltimore Jack. Why didn't you tell him your real name?"
"Because he's Jack. He's a legend. Like Joe DiMaggio. I felt – dumb."
"So you told him your name was Rubber Ducky?"
"Yeah. Yeah, I did."

The town was dead. No cars came. No one walked on the sidewalks. The Hotel waited at the far end of Main Street. The only way in was through the bar. It soon became apparent that the Doyle was not a hotel at all, but a round-the-clock drunk hole.
The other stories of the Doyle that traveled up the Trail to them had been misleading – as are most stories that surround the Trail. thruhikers usually came away from their time in Duncannon with a belly full of free drinks and an anecdote or two. Their memories of the Doyle were quaint and amusing, the kind of impression tourists almost always have of the places they visit. But Baltimore Jack had been there when the hangover wore off and there weren't any more upbeat young thruhikers for the regulars to get loaded with. Nobody to laugh at the old jokes. He had been there long enough to recognize that the hospitality wasn't all it seemed. The patrons of the Doyle were greedy for life. Behind the free rounds and pats on the back, they were scratching and clawing to get at the energy inside anybody who came through the doors – anybody that still had the ability to walk back out whenever he wanted. The door had closed on most of them and they weren't going anywhere.
Jack was right. The people that sat on the stools at the Doyle weren't social drinkers. They were end-of-the-road soakers.
The room leaned in as Applejack and Futureman walked through the foyer. It was mid-afternoon and the saloon was already busy and loud, full of rough talk and rough people who had worked in Pennsylvania's steel mills and coal mines their whole lives. For the first time since Maine, Applejack and Futureman weren't the toughest looking characters in the room. Several groups raised glasses, beckoning them to come swap stories but a curious little man presented himself first, motioning them toward his own private table, so eager that they could not decline. They followed him,

tired, hot and wanting the hydration of water, not the dehydration of beer, but before they were settled in their seats their new host spread tall golden brews before them.

He spoke quickly, a staccato breath between each word, fingers conducting each syllable. "Hello there – ahhh – call me Howard. I'm very pleased to finally make your acquaintance. I've been waiting for you. Perhaps you – of course you were taking your time in the woods. Understandable. Very – ahhh – understandable. It has been very nice weather lately."

"Sir? I'm sorry but there must be some sort of mistake. I don't believe we've met before," Futureman said, courteous but firm.

"Oh, no. Of course not. No-no-no. Of course you would think that – I mean of course you wouldn't. You are Applejack and Futureman, are you not?"

"Well, yes but –"

"Allow me to ahhh explain. I am doing some – research. Putting together a ah – collection of, shall we say, ahhh thruhikingggg memorabilia. A patchwork of Appalachian Trail experience. As specimens – ahhh errrr – as *hikers* come through these parts I collect them and ahh rrrrecord their data." His *'r'*s trilled like twirling batons. "It will be a verrry endearing portrait, I – aah – assurrre you. I have been very eagerrrr to meet you gentle fellows. One of your, how shall we say, friends from the Trail informed me that you would be coming my way in a matter of days and that you would ahhhh yesss be verrry willing and informmmative participants. Thus – my presence – before you now." Howard attempted something of a bow.

"OK. So, you're making a book or something –"

"Well, let's just say that I am ahhhhh creating a document."

"That helps. Well then, how can we assist you?"

"You can start by giving me your – aah – heights and weights ahhh respectively, of course."

"Five-ten and probably down to one hundred and sixty-five pounds," Futureman said with pride. Thirty-five pounds in under three months. Howard's writing was so meticulous that it could be easily read upside-down.

"Now, why would you or anybody for that matter be interested in thruhikers? It's just that, pardon me for saying so, you don't exactly look like the outdoors type." Applejack was not so eager to become a *specimen*.

"Oh heavens to merciful – goodness gracious. No." Howard was strangely energized by this remark. He pushed his encyclopedia-thick glasses back on his nose and ran his hands down the front of his starched polyester shirt. "Permit me, yes, to declare that I am simply an ahhh admirer of the breeeed." He leaned back in his chair.

"Okay, Howard. I'll bite. I'm right at six foot and maybe down to one-sixty-eight, one-seventy."

"Yes – Yes – Now – What would you say that you have learned from yourrr time on the Trrrrrail?"

"I've learned that Futureman is a dirty, dirty individual. Also, I've learned that life is a series of seemingly random but dazzlingly interconnected events that invariably lead toward meaning."

"Ahh." Howard carefully recorded each word.

"And I've learned that I would like to be buried in a time capsule," Futureman said.

"Time capsule. I ah find it aahh intriguing that you should mention that, Futurrrreman. In my admittedly limited understanding of the ahhh Appalachian Trail, I have often thought that it was something of a ahhahh time capsule in itself."

"In what sense?"

"The Appalachian Trail, from its ahhh inception, was intended to provide the contemporary man with respite from the ahhhahhahh ravages of a tyrannical modern life. It was designed to ahhhrr establish an ambulatory conduit from the American North to the ahhhemm American South. But it was principally designed to be an ahh yesss – epochal marinade – a thin slice of radically untainted forest through the rapidly developing technocratic tangle of the ahh eastern edge of the continent. Or, as you say Futureman, a time capsule." Applejack and Futureman were rigid in their seats.

Howard licked his lips. At last, he drew his arms outward, as though opening the bellows of a great accordion. "It is the spllleeeen of the megallopppolis."

"Um, did you say spleen of the megalopolis?" Applejack asked.

"The spllleeeen of the megallopppolis." Howard nodded with perfect satisfaction.

"Yes, I've never heard it put quite in that way, Howard, and yet it feels right. It has the – shall we say – ring of truth to it. And now I'll be retiring upstairs to take a shower. Thank you for – ahhh – involving us in your – ahh – project." Applejack was tired. He shook the little man's hand and turned away.

"Yesss, yess, Applejack." Howard came around the table. "If you ever need annnythinnng and I do mean *annnythinnng*, you know how to get in touch with me. I am your mannnnn." Howard pulled a card from his breast pocket.

"Thank you, Howard. You're very thoughtful."

"Say nothing of it. And if you ever find yourrrselfff in, shall we say, a situation of any kind, I can help." Howard tapped the card in Applejack's hand. "I knnnow people. I have connnectionnns." Howard leaned in close. "I am with the government."

At supper, Futureman and Applejack came down from their room (31) and enjoyed an excellent Cajun meal prepared by the proprietor himself. He came out from the kitchen and talked with them about his life, his establishment and his hopes for Duncannon and the Doyle. He and his wife had only recently taken ownership of the hotel, and wanted to upgrade and bring some of the original class back to the place. He watched proudly as the hungry men devoured his food. They wished him luck and retired for the night.

The shouting commenced somewhere between two and four AM. Futureman had been in the grip of cavernous sleep. Separating himself from his dreams was difficult. These are the words he heard in those gray moments:
"GET YOUR HANDS UP!"
"UP OVER YOUR HEAD!"
"WHAT DO YOU WANT WITH ME YOU SONS OF BITCHES?"
"DON'T MOVE! KEEP YOUR HANDS ABOVE YOUR HEAD."
"CALM DOWN. That's right, there we go."
The commotion drew him to his feet. Looking down from his third floor windowsill, he spotted the disturbance. Two policemen were bent over the shape of a man facedown in the gravel parking lot. The officers had thrown him against the trash dumpster by the hotel. Apparently, the five bottles of malt liquor the man had consumed had given him analgesic courage, and he rebounded with angry kicking and a slew of demon-mean insults. As the police officers dragged him toward the squad car, Futureman reached over to Applejack's bed and shook him to life.
"What – what's going on?"
"You've got to see this. We've got a real situation going on down here."
"Huh?" Applejack staggered over to the window, rubbing sleep from his eyes.
Below, the officers were trying to force the flailing man into the back seat of the squad car. Across the parking lot, a gangly man in hospital pants stepped out into the blue light of the streetlamps. An inch of ash hung from his cigarette. "You be careful with him now. That's my best friend." He nodded toward the culprit.
One of the cops wheeled around. "You keep out of this, sir."
"Just trying to help is all. Trying to be a good citizen."
"We don't need your help. So step back, Eddie. Step back." Eddie backed into the shadows, his cigarette glowing in the dark.
Suddenly, the officers sprang away from the car and slammed the door shut. It would have been a perfectly executed procedure except that the rear window was still rolled down – just far enough for a shaggy head to come

poking through.

"I ain't never done nothin! Who the hell you think you are? Lockin me up like this! My lawyer's gonna eat your lunch! This is discrimination! Innocent 'til proven guilty! This injustice will not stand! I'm a innocent man!"

One of the officers forced the shaggy head back through the window. "If you're so innocent then why did you grab my badge, throw it and run out the door?"

"I did it because this is wrongful imprisonment! Ex post facto! Double jeopardy! I'm gonna go free! These doors are gonna swing wide!"

"Oh boy. Here we go." Futureman muttered, his chin resting on the window sill.

From a row of houses behind the Doyle, a hysterical woman of no small size bounded full-throttle into the parking lot. The tropical colors of her moo-moo flashed in the dim light.

"What are you doing to my baby? What's gonna happen to my baby? Where you taking him? Where you taking Jimmy? What's he done? Let him go! Let him go!"

An officer stepped forward, intercepting her before she could reach the squad car.

"Calm down, ma'am. We're taking him in. Everything's going to be alright. We have some things to look into. Just calm down." He grappled gently with the woman, absorbing her aimless blows without anger until she collapsed into his arms.

Applejack was impressed. "These guys are real professionals. I would have seriously violated somebody's civil liberties by now."

"Tell me about it. Can you believe this is happening?"

By this point, the ruckus had risen to such a level that several patrons of the bar had gathered and were casually taking in the entertainment. A group of curious neighbors collected for a late-night smoke on the far side of the parking lot.

"I'm gonna break free of these chains! Can't hold me down! I'm gonna break free and fly like an eagle! These trumped-up charges are gonna fall! I'll be back, I'll beat this rap!" Jimmy's campaign for freedom had resumed. He was banging his head against the back windshield.

One of the officers stepped toward the squad car, intending to drive the prisoner away. This sent the woman back into hysterics.

"You can't take him! He's all I got! What's gonna happen to our babies? He ain't done nothin to nobody! Let him go!" Sobs shook her body as she lay on the ground in a heap.

The best friend Eddie crossed to her and raised his fist to strike, when one of the policemen intervened and guided him back against the brick wall of the Doyle.

"Sue, you dumb hag! What do you mean? You're the one called the cops on him! You're the one says he's a wife-beater! Well I'm gonna take over and beat your fat mouth til you can't cram any more twinkies down it!" The gallery erupted into peals of laughter. Sue rose to her feet, sent a satanic volley of unrepeatables at her husband's best friend, then bolted toward her house.

"Dear Lord. She is going to get a gun." Applejack shook his head.

"Everybody needs to calm down! Just go back to bed. I don't want to have to haul anyone else in tonight!"

Just as the spectators were putting out their cigarettes and turning for home, a chorus of hair-raising snarls stopped them in their tracks. Sue was returning with a vengeance, driving two crazed rottweilers down from the house. For several long seconds everyone was frozen as they watched the beasts rush down the hill. For the first time since Jimmy went down, the cops pulled their pistols.

But the dogs weren't the hounds of hell they looked. Instead of tearing throats and ripping handcuffs apart, they just ran in circles around the squad car, chasing the spinning red and blue beams across the pavement. A sigh of relief went out, until...

"We got blood over here!" Everyone turned. "Dwight, get the EMTs. Randy, help me wrap this guy. What an asshole." A policeman was crouched over Jimmy's wilted frame. Blood was everywhere. In the dark it was hard to see just what had happened.

"What in the world did he do? He's not moving at all. Do you think he's dead?" Futureman leaned out the window.

"I have no idea. A gun didn't go off anywhere. Did he have a knife?"

"It looks like his wrists."

The ambulance rolled up. Three medics hurried over to the body and went to work. The cops turned back to send away the throng of concerned citizens.

"Dwight, poor bastard got so worked up, he dug these cuffs into his wrists. They're way down in there, man. He's lost a lot of blood."

"What is up with this town? Something must be in the water."

"Something's in the water alright. Booze." The cops were standing directly under the windowsill of room 33.

Half an hour later Futureman and Applejack were watching the Fire Department spray blood into the drains. Jimmy had been taken away in an ambulance. Sue had been carted home by two neighbors and Eddie had taken Jimmy's spot in the backseat of the cruiser to spend a night in lockup. Everyone else had gone home in a confused state of exhaustion. On the third floor of the Doyle Hotel, Applejack got up to relieve himself in the luxurious communal bathroom.

He heard the telltale signs long before he ever reached the restroom. All doubt was swept away when he opened the door. There, on his knees, a bald bearded man was retching violently into the commode. A miniature box of Honey Smacks and a green lighter lay beside him on the floor. Applejack visited the second floor bathroom and returned to find Futureman fast asleep. The clock read 4:21.

Applejack woke to singing. It was coming up from the bar through the open windows. *You ain't nothin but a hound dog, crying all the time. You ain't nothin but a hound dog, crying all the time. You ain't never been a rabbit and you ain't getting none of mine.* The clock read 7:13. He looked out the window bleary eyed. Three drunks were leaning on each other, making their way past the dumpster and down the alley.

"This is unbelievable. Futureman, get up. We're getting the heck out of here."

The clock read 8:06. They were on their way downstairs to the bar to checkout, then to the woods to hit some solid ground with the strength of trees.

On the way past the bathroom they heard a scrubbing noise. Applejack poked his head in. It was the bald vomiting man. He was on his knees again, this time a brillo pad and bottle of Comet in hand.

"Sorry about last night, buddy. I guess I had a little too much to drink."

"Don't mention it. Just glad to see you're feeling better."

"It's hard enough keeping this place clean, then I go and throw up all over everything. Know what I mean?"

Applejack paused, a puzzled expression growing cold on his face. *This man is the janitor.* "Have a nice day, sir."

"Better than the last one I hope." The man smiled and continued his scrubbing.

Applejack and Futureman ate breakfast and hitched down the highway to the Trail to pick up where they'd left off. Back again on the spleen of the megalopolis.

III

Mature sourwood lay thick at the line, dividing town from mountain. A demanding climb signified southern Pennsylvania trail would be different from northern. The bulky oak-hickory forest was promising. Ovenbirds in the brushwood sang *teacher, teach, teacher*. Scarlet tanagers and rose-breasted grosbeaks made their way through the chestnut boughs, eyeing the two nervously as they entered the wood. Fox squirrels and eastern chipmunks were busy with the organization of the coming change of seasons. The path twisted up the hill like a tall, spiraled shumard oak toward Hawk Rock, a peninsula outcropping directly above Duncannon.

From the pinnacle, Applejack and Futureman scanned back over the town one last time. As new perspective comes with experience, the mystique of Duncannon's legend was now dispelled. There was nothing romantic about the place. Only the sad remains of a deathbed town lay below in the rusted railroad valley. Apparitions searching for a life long gone.

It was from Hawk Rock long ago that the Iroquois had looked out over the forestland – hunting grounds, worshiping grounds – until 1736 brought a battalion of ax-wielders armed to make room for white settlement. It wasn't long before farming and trade products were pouring into the upstart town, promising a booming haven of industry and civilization. Fertility of a New World. The 19th century was Duncannon's heyday. Industry and capital from the east descended in force, bolstered by the promise of the far-reaching Iron Horse. A new bourgeoisie emerged and the streets became a raucous mixture of poker, pioneers, railroaders, opium, European fashion, theater and industry – the adolescent growth spurt of all American capitalism. But somewhere along the way, this all changed.

Applejack found the melancholy Susquehanna cupping Duncannon in her palm. The deep blue stirring of the river seemed to be the only living thing that would come near. Once thriving, the besotted town now knew only stagnation and incest. The sweet river was no longer able to pull her to her feet. The stuffy murmurings of the breeze blew up from the water. What has become of her pomp, her populations of work and wealth? Where are the children she raised? Gloat not in the valley, nor on the hill. It is no longer hers. She has trampled the Iroquois in vain, having built a town out of stone, brick and blood for nothing.

But Hawk Rock's gaze perched steady still, offering some strength to the remnant of people below. She too was always in view, only an arm's length away. An ancient bystander, resident even before the native tribes, she was guardian of the seed. That granule of hope, of restoration. Promises will hold true, she spoke. Word is Word. And on that day, all this will be reconciled-man and beast, earth and sky. So she waits unmoved, her call constant, an invitation to savages and noblemen alike – come remember or repent. Redemption sits patiently beside her on that perch, the promise of higher ground.

IV

Occasional echoes of buckshot coursed high through the air. Hunters were on their way. A thin fog covered the woodlet, hinting at a coming sleep for the sassafras and hophornbeam, highbush blueberry and spotted pipsissewa. Sherman Creek and Dark Run were hidden underneath the swab. The ground before them spread light and fast, barely there.

"Perhaps today is the day," Futureman said.

"Damp and cool, cloud cover. You might be on to something."

"What do you say?"

30?

They began. Steady. Pliant. Pacing.

An impressive double-decker shelter, window-paned, lofted, laddered, benched and broom-racked was built on top of Cove Mountain. In its shadow was a tiny pine hamster box that had once been called a shelter. Earl Schaffer, the famous *first* AT thruhiker had returned to this spot to build it himself. Its dirt floors and leaning walls were dismal compared to the new giant, but strangely cathartic. Legacy dwelt there in the humble shack.

Less is more. Always was and always will be.

Against his nature, Earl Schaffer has indisputably become the premier figure of the Appalachian Trail – a real legend. His story is deeply chiseled into American folklore, like a living breathing Johnny Appleseed or John Henry. In the summer of 1948, straight from Army service, young Earl set out to walk the length of the Trail. Bushwhacking overgrown sections, linking together disconnected strands, Shaffer walked an average of 17 miles a day and completed his 2,000-mile journey in four months exactly. Ironically that same year, Trail visionary Myron Avery, published an article in the ATC's news journal (while Earl was doing his hike) which clearly posited that an end-to-end trek was most improbable if not impossible. Young Shaffer was greeted with skepticism at the end, but cross-examination and personal photographs verified his claim, and Earl V. Shaffer passed into the canon of American history.

Applejack picked up the shelter log – the journal where weary travelers put down their weary thoughts. He studied the book's outsides, turned it over just the usual brown, cardboard cover, bound with cheap wire; but it hummed between his hands. Opening it, he saw words on crinkled paper, dried and re-dried words tapping at his brain. He saw names – 10%, Blackbeard, Reggae, Lost-and-Found, Rabbit, Terranaut – and felt that bizarre shameful whirlwind of the joyous human heart. *Oh yes, I see.* He had forgotten too much through the months-trapped within himself, bludgeoned by reality.

The log fell open to an entry, signed by a familiar name, one he had not seen since Maine.

To Our Friends, Ahead or Behind,
Our great journey is almost halfway done, and we are beginning, only beginning, to enjoy it more than we ever thought we could. The Trail is different now, you all know. Always changing, molding itself to keep up with the pace that we try to force on it. The lessons are seeping in. (I am changing, too.) We're not even sure what they are, but they're there, all the time now. We think of little else than each other, enjoying our love and the earth between our fingers. By the way, Fred Baby looks incredibly good with dirt all over his body. Yeah, we sure do love the grit and simplicity. It's all so simple out here, isn't it? If those we met are reading this, know that we miss you (even though Fred probably wouldn't own up to it) and still think of you often. So to all of you, a lovely Hello – 10 %, Ogre, Buttercup, Snot, Gentle Ben, Willie McGee, Speedo, Conan the Hiker, Applejack, Futureman, Ice Cream, Blackbeard, Colonel and all the others – we walk with you still.
                                        With love, memory, hugs, laughter and dusty tears,
                                        Little Moose

There they were, their names, etched onto the pages of that rotting log-book, yet as stone – preserved and unforgotten – *remembered* and *known* by somebody. Someone with a name of her own – a real person – who remembered something about the scattered toil they had all shared together way back yonder in the wilds of Maine. They had come so far since those days. The distance from there to here, the migration of a rudderless glacier. A journey filled with yarn.

And now, here in the pages of the book, sat everyone they had known-crammed like sardines into the sweaty shack that Mr. Shaffer had built for them. The whole gang together – poking and backslapping, telling life's tall tales, sharing regrets, beliefs and qualms. Hikers past and present. The luminaries who planted seeds together with the laborers who spilt sweat and blood to build a long walk from Maine to Georgia. Bridges over rivers. Shelters at the edge of springs. Guardians locked in arms to resist those who would tame the heights with greed. The whole Trail was here, this Appalachian Something – and they were on the list.

As he walked, the companions kept him company for a while, resuscitating his oxygen-dull imagination. *It was Bear: "Fall's comin. Got space in the bunkroom." And Sharesh: "Stay a day or just come and stay." And there was Reggae: "I've returned to the world. Things are too fast here. Take your time. Please, take your time." And Sarah: "Tell me about the south-land again. Or take me with you." And Bobby: "Okay, I know it stinks, but eat the garlic – it's good for you." And Bombadil: "There were these stone steps in the clouds at Mt. Madison, so I took 'em all the way up into the sky. And, man – the worship is loud and crisp." And at last, Blackbeard:*

"The Great Northern Woods are far behind, but we still got some hell to raise. I keep looking for you guys, but I can't wait around forever – you gotta do your part."

Then, one by one they dropped out, leaving him alone where the valley extends undraped beneath Pipeline Ridge. The journey was once again his own, one part from the whole, and he was content to take his proper place amidst the expanse.

Eight miles in, twenty-two to go. Put one foot in front of the other and get to steppin.

Twenty miles is a solid day of hiking. You feel like you've bitten off a good chunk of Trail. Anything beyond twenty is extra credit. Gravy.

Hiking twenty-five miles is purely a struggle of the will. A challenge for challenge's sake – bordering on dumb pride and misery. *How far can I go? How long will my feet last? At what point will my ankles turn to dust?*

Somewhere in the upper twenties, the mind and body seem to initiate a new process – a release of some kind that pulls the curtain back. The bones and joints pass over the edge of numbness – and, sometimes, they keep going. Pain dies and a new mark is set, ready to be toppled another day. *By Jove, I can do more. I can walk on.* The human body is as delicate as a dandelion and as resilient as a miracle.

If you live long enough, you'll do something you never thought possible.

For Applejack and Futureman, that new something was hiking 30 miles in one day. To the hiker, 30 is that place where mind/body distinctions disappear, and the soul at last masters the will. But can we get there?

Mile seventeen. On edge but feeling good. Coming out of the woods is always weird. The path led them to a concrete bridge over Highway 76. They were immediately overwhelmed by the vehicular fart of exhaust and speed. Dizzied, Futureman gripped the railing for support.

Cars racing by. Phhhhhh. Caaaaaaaaah. Bbgrrrrrrrr. Waaaaah. The trucks (heavy loaders) drumming asphalt and steel – grong-crong-crong-grong. Pavement rocks bouncing like uranium atoms – ting – on the giant green sign hanging overhead like a guillotine ready to fall. Too much for tender Applejack, softened by so many nights on the mossy turf, he bolted for the far side, braying like a wild ass in a war zone.

Breath and laughter collided. They were across the bridge – safe on solid ground again – and disappeared into a patch of slash-and-pitch pine planted against the asphalt. It took two solid miles distance before the general roar of motors died away and their gasoline-bombed nostrils could again decipher that summer-fading fragrance of pulpit jack. This side of the bridge. This side of autumn.

Mile twenty-five. In roughshod cadence, on the flat shoals of the Pennsylvania valley, they lumbered and walked in silence, tambourines hushed,
drumheads slashed, cymbals muffed, harmonicas pocketed. Mind-numb,
imagination-dumb body lurches forward. Spirit lost between earth-and-sky
gray. Twenty-six. Twenty-seven. The hills return. *Now we're gonna make
it.* The mesic soils reappear and in them, tulip trees, white oaks, hackbery
and hawthorn. Hickory nuts litter the path. Chubby squirrels sift the nuts,
eating the low tannin white oak acorns for instant energy, burying the high
tannin reds and blacks for time-released strength deeper into the winter
chill. Twenty-eight. Twenty-nine. *Each step now the furthest we've ever
been. Curtain pulls back. There she sits* – 30. The mark. The essence.

At the end of thirty-one miles sat Alex Kennedy Shelter, a small fragile
box, exposed on a ridge of mockernut. Inside the shelter sat a man, emaci-
ated and skeletal.

IV

Moose hadn't always looked like a picked-over carcass. He'd weighed 316
pounds when he started the Trail but by the time Applejack and Futureman
caught up with him on this southern edge of Pennsylvania – through nearly
a thousand miles of rock, root, heat, peak, road, gully, cave, notch, town,
sidewalk, valley, farm, hollow, bridge, boulder, rain, pond, stream, river,
lake, hail, storm, forest, meadow, cone, plateau, scree, knoll, hole, tick,
mosquito, brier, bear, frog, snake, blister and bog – Moose had been
reduced to little more than a flesh-abiding cadaver. Eyes sunken into his
skull, hair split on the ends, cheeks hiding under his bones, arms and legs
bowing out at the joints. He offered a picture of himself from four months
prior. The man inside the face was swollen: a smile pushed through the
blubber by sheer will; cherry-burned cheeks mounded up stealing sunlight;
implanted eyes cowered in dark caves underneath a cellulite bulge of puff-
cake brow.

    Moose wore velcro Silver Series shoes to hike in. His toes were exposed
on the ends from holes. His aluminum frame backpack had whole sections
of fabric missing, MacGuyvered together with twine and duct tape. He'd
'waterproofed' it with twenty-gallon trash bags and rubber bands.

    Moose was a young man, but his heart was ancient. He had come out on
the Trail after his wife left him, hoping to move forward with his life. Two
months along, he ran out of money and started working his way southward,
stopping off to do odd jobs – pick apples, paint fences, work on cars, collect eggs, can okra, shuck corn. For two months, he had eaten oatmeal and

only oatmeal three squares a day. Despite these bleak circumstances, Moose was astoundingly high-spirited – and extremely happy to shed his layers of leopard seal insulation.

"Besides the fact that you used to be a three-hundred-pounder, why do they call you Moose?" Futureman asked with the tact of a blind goat.

"I think maybe because I saw so many moose in Maine."

Futureman had seen seven-three running scared through the forest, one chewing grass, two babies and a mama swimming in a sacred Wilderness pond.

"How many are we talkin' here – a dozen? Twenty?"

"Fifty-eight."

Futureman nearly swallowed his tongue.

"Sorry? Fifty-eight, as in twice as many as twenty-nine? Is that what you said?"

"Yes."

"How about bear? You seen any bear?"

"Yeah, I saw six bears in Maine, four in New Hampshire, three or four in New York and nine in New Jersey. They really are like rats there. How many for you guys?"

Having failed to spot *a* bear between the both of them, Applejack admitted, "None, more or less."

"Be glad," he consoled. "I don't like bear all that much. A few weeks ago, one almost ripped my head off." Moose spoke with childlike resilience.

"Really? What happened?

"I was heating up some oatmeal on the fire when I heard a noise. Turned to see what it was and there stood a bear not three feet from my face, crouched down – like he was getting ready to pry open my head and have my brains for supper."

"What did you do –"

"The only thing I could do – I turned slowly, grabbed a log from the fire and politely smacked him across the face as hard as I could."

"What? You! Seriously?"

"Seriously." Cool as a cucumber.

"What'd it do?"

"Think it surprised him. Probably, never been whacked on the nose with a burning log before. He kinda snorted, shook his head in bewilderment and then ran off."

When the mouth hangs ajar for long periods of time, it tends to become dehydrated (and can also experience lockjaw).

"Wow, Moose. That's – Is that the most scared you've ever been?"

"I guess I was more surprised than scared. Didn't really have time to be scared. Now, I did have one chase me down a hill last week. I was scared then."

Such was the life of Moose. He was just one of those guys – a precious member of that anomalous clan of human beings whose lives are a series of unlikely and categorically crappy events. The most recent of which had occurred only days before, when he had cheerfully rounded a merry forest corner only to find a disgruntled stinking, six hundred pound mass of mama bear towering in front of him.

Applejack put his hand on his head. "Tell the truth, man! God is watching."

"God as my witness, that's the truth."

"What did you do?" Futureman leaned forward.

"I shouted and waved my arms and threw rocks at her."

"Did she move?"

"Yeah. Like I said, she charged me."

"Whoa."

"Most black bears usually mock charge first, as a warning. I mean, that's what they tell us, right? So I held my ground and continued to shout and throw rocks, like they told me to."

"Yeah?"

"Well it's hard to tell between a mock charge and a real charge when a six-hundred pound ursa is running at you."

"Understandable."

"By the way, if a bear chases you, run down hill. Hind legs are longer, they can't run downhill."

"That's what they say – I mean – that's what you say, and you would know."

"I ran about three miles just to be sure."

"Can't be too careful."

"Funny thing is, as I was running down the mountain I met another hiker coming up. He says, *What're you running from?* I say, *Bear! Bear!* And he says, *Really? I wanna see it.* I say, *you don't want to see this one!* And he says, *You're not supposed to run from black bears, you know.* And I say, *Suit yourself, but I'm running from this one.* About thirty seconds later, he comes sprinting past me, screaming, *It's gonna eat us! Gonna eat us!* I would have laughed more if I wasn't so out of breath. We ran full tilt for two miles, packs and all. A lot of adrenaline pumps through when a bear is chasing you."

Moose's stories were too outrageous to be lies. He had that magical, Murphy's-law, shitstorm kind-of-luck – *if it can go wrong, it will, and you will live to tell about it.* He was the kind of person who discovers black ice on mountain curves and winds up upside down in a river (with no broken bones). The kind of person who pulls off the highway to ask for directions and ends up changing a flat tire in his underwear in the ghetto. The kind of guy who walks into the girl's locker room by accident and comes out with a date, who mistakes the superglue bottle for eye drops, who gets hungry for a chili dog and walks into a convenience store holdup, who bends down to yank a tick off a dog and gets rabies, or rents a car in Zimbabwe and winds up in the middle of an elephant stampede.

This brand of *bad* good luck cannot be forced. You either have it or you don't. The folks who try to force *bad* good luck on themselves – adrenaline junkies, backyard stuntmen and the like – these are the ones who get mauled, mashed, charred and drowned. This brand of luck will not be pawed at or manipulated. It will only settle on the one who isn't after the fame, someone who won't let it go to his head. Someone like Moose.

While Applejack and Futureman ate their dinner, Moose spent an hour gathering soggy twigs and another half-hour whittling them. It was nearly bedtime and he still hadn't eaten.

"Moose, I appreciate the gesture, but a fire really isn't necessary tonight. It's warm, and we'll be asleep soon anyway." Applejack patted his bony shoulder.

"Well, I'd rather not eat cold oatmeal, so I have to build a fire."

"You don't have a stove?"

"No, I couldn't afford one. Plus, I enjoy the activity."

"You should have said something, Moose. You're more than welcome to use our stove."

"No, no. I'm not one to impose. And besides, it would spoil me."

Tiny flames burned beneath the blackened tin can, warming his oatmeal stew. Distant thunder sounded, perhaps from the heat. Even after sunset, the sky retained a hint of fluorescent blue; scraps of static gathering in the air.

Futureman's fear had made him a quick study. Now keen in his ability to track the sound of thunder, he followed the wind and studied the tiny charges as they prickled his arm hairs. By these he made his judgment and retired to the shelter, droplets of rain on his hand.

Late in the night, the bolts cleaved the cloudbank in two. The halves competed. Yin versus Yang. Good versus evil, in the distance. Sound and light five seconds apart, loud enough to wake Futureman from his nervous slumber.

What side of the ridge is it on?

Dark. Then light. Shriek, flicker, tree-to-tree.

Four seconds. Ddrrrrrrrrrrrruuuuumm.

Other side, far off, still safe.
Dark. Flick, tremble. Static on the leaves. Light.
One. Two. Bacraaaaaaaaagg.
Closer, moving fast. It's turning, jumping the ridge.
Dark. Light.
One- Baccragggggccckkkkkk!!! Sound in light. Inseparable.
On the hill now.

The trees bent, firm timber split apart in the positive-negative. They
turned their leaves over, forest painted blue. Futureman backed into the corner of the shelter like a tortured crab, bag shelled around his body. *No
escaping it now. Just have to wait it out.*

Ball bearings of rain smacked the wood beam roof. In the afterglow,
Futureman saw Moose. There he lay on the lip of the shelter. His arm hung
off the edge, jerking slightly at the sensation of cold rain.

Futureman was leaning forward to drag Moose back into the shadows at
the precise moment that it came. From heaven to earth, ripping space,
bending time, it traveled through the adverse charge toward its destination:
Alex Kennedy fire pit. A scalding-white blizzard of light, falling somehow
in slow motion.

Flame of Righteousness filled Futureman's body – buzzing, burning,
healing.

"Holy! Holy! Holy!" he cried.

Blindness everywhere. Night disappeared. Rain dried.

The atomic light slammed five feet from the edge of the shelter and
ignited the ground, where Moose's hand was stretched out like Michelan-
gelo's Adam. And in that single moleculo-spiritual moment, his entire body
was filled with the worship of the Seraphim. Electrocution by proxy.
Moose sprang up like gunpowder, aright in the blink of an eye – back
frozen, pupils dilated, hair follicles stimulated by a million fabulous centipedes. Purring like a Bunsen burner. He turned to Futureman, still sitting
catatonic in the corner of the shelter,

"W-w-w-w-w?"

Futureman stammered back. "I thi-thi-think, that ju-ju-ju, all-l-l-l-m-m-
mos got hi-hi-hit by y-y-y, li-li-lightning."

"Wul that woo-woo-woo-would s-s-s-plain it."

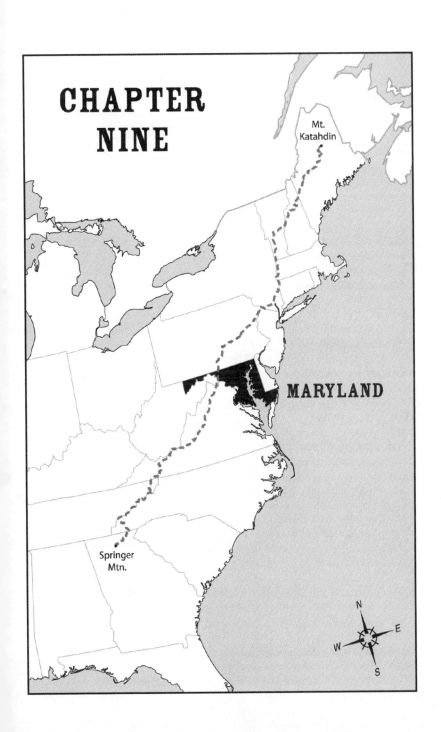

CHAPTER
NINE

Mt.
Katahdin

MARYLAND

Springer
Mtn.

N
E
W
S

Having crossed into Maryland, the two men found themselves in a neighborhood of intentions, each its own groomed garden and accolade won. Each with thoughts, with questions. With memories of modified details, temptations. Drawn here to be sifted and weighed on scales by hired angels. Some good, others not. They stepped unsure but steady, slow enough to recognize the sifting. Quick enough that all lessons learned would have to wait for a colder, more quiet day.

I

Pennsylvania has gone, bruised shin at thirty's end.
Look – emerald green piles, there on the Gemstone Ferry
Sailing away – dignity, nobility-off now
Off to find other shores, other days, other lives.
So now travel here, they on this dragon scaled shoal
Of Maryland, two travelers like blind beggars,
Their paths trundle buried, weed with brown fuzz married.
Upon three tempters they come, chthonic Trinity.
Have they the will to pass – end before End, death's last?
Will they onward, forward – past end at Harpers mast?

II

Broken word, O fragmented dialogue! Trapped in
Black silicone. (Numberless) numerous among
Noises not meanings – palinodes of sorrow sing
Sad songs. Missing faces pilfer forms, pull down the
Billowy white clouds from above (clown lips parting).
Heavy black telephone wires, welded, spindled, and
They like bobbins kindled, wound sound, the mirth of fools.
Conversation without thought, whit, whim at the wheel.
They plod on, guided by the starless white night of
Numbered bland days – wondering – where did beauty go?

Missing from Mount Dunlop (depeaked)(defaced)(denosed).
Down, down in the gaunt vale, where scholars lie reposed,
Reason decomposes, worm's logic imposes
The thievery of rite, the scepter of High Rock's
Coronation. In swollen gorge, hackberry forge,
Self's missing elation. Raven is a thief (lust)
Thrusts aft the terrain. Leave behind the sunken moat.

Rain! Rain! Rain! The dense sky is filled with black birds who
Forgot how to fly. Rise again! Fracture the soiled
Sand on brown land. With pruned hand enters the Brigand.

It speaks, "Leave this place (roiled stain)(hard rain)(soppy grain).
Forget this ground, what you've found. Your senses drowned
in the drizzle, remember?" "How long will nimbus drop
her pocketed mist? Soon the gray-blue splash will fall
upward, and melody will strike her hand against
heaven's harp – so speaks the lingering hope of Me,
On this colorless, crude, cursed land of quicksand and
Meditation." Words (thoughts) – they that stump the brigand.
They are cleansed with sky ("Rain, dark clouds") grace led, words fed,
"Beauty be!" in woeful glee. (Stones unturned to bread)

III

"Have we not tread enough to merit climb? Up from
Warner Gap Hollow – cistern of cupreous rust!"
"And why no brawl, Black Rock small? Where is your gall, your
Revolution?" "O disobedient marquis
of Washington – milksop Monument plummeting
In convolution (breath of nullity) we see."
"But we have known (seed buried) wisdom sewn, from the
Ground it groans." Blood beyond law (self's diplomacy)
Offers a cozened trophy – at end before End.
Drunk on Folly's gin – here in Old Scratch's playpen!

From Attica they rise. Plein air, O candid sky!
Where (form of) Widow weaves her web, taped with the
Silk nebris of the whitewashed wayfarers (mind's eye)
Looks past this scape, this hesitant brume of tagged days.
Look they at their accomplishments. "Vincible states!
O mount! Ostiary of the sun. To have reached
Your apogee. Toppled dome wearing waxed wings, and
Still alive – Defiant klisters in Phoebus' court!
A thousand miles (helots) under thrall of footfall."
Homily of praise! Solipsism of vainglory!

Widow's con – rude curse! Speaks, "Stand you on empty purse?"
With Self's own guile. "Are you not more than this dreaded
Droll ground? Hikers or clowns? What now is your answer?"

"Would we drape fisher king gowns, put on painted crowns?"
"Would we wart-faced princes be, in dyed-gare purple
Robes – No!" "Lest in Mummer's Court we be found. Therefore
Leave us be, black Vanity!" Cursed Widow cast down.
"Thou Merchant of masks! Macramé of pellicled
Ash! Thou Wardrobe of skin – Do not drape us in.
But in vestment of death!" (They stand at epithet)

IV

"Where is your melody hiding, O Maryland?
Your noble branded gone days? Please, say where you keep
your stories – beneath broken bridge, broken land or
broken hand? Or are they scattered in broken sand?"
The skilled, numb blank of physique after days of thirty.
They tarry! Rushing onward toward life's last query –
Harpers mast, the Gemstone Ferry. "Lady sing your
Song. Wander still, but bring your wisdom into town.
Wait for us there – and look, from the ridge, you'll see us
Come down. At end before End, there give us death's gown."

Vial of vanities felled, in Dhalgren's graves are held.
Buried bane in lock of stone – flesh dwindled to bone!
Whence appears (form of) Lady, unexpectedly.
Beatific melody, prosody, subtle
Trickery (the temptation of vain martyrdom),
Illusion's final minddance, hanging in balance
On a thief's cross – manumission of life, nothing
More. "Arise! Awake!" Words lost on azoic heights,
Elixir grabbed down into the bosom of death.
The consummation of our Lord's great victory.

Appears as one (emulation of angelic
light) – Brigand, Widow, form of Lady (trinity)
Of the firedrake – speaks, "Walk to end's End and there die.
You have no more need – but comfort – We offer rest,
As our people plead. Foul foe? No. Just a friend with
Fiery breath." Revelation of the dragon's breast,
Exuviated scales, blindness past Harper's mast,
They search for the Gemstone Ferry, guided still by
Firedrake's hand, the Firedrake's compass and Firedrake's plan.
Heels walk on children's chalk (a jejune melody).

V

But there, beyond river (steady)(olden)(golden)
True Lady stands (wisdom's heir), pharos on the shore.
Speaks in true voice (infinite sound) to drown the drake,
"Take on the habit of Resurrection. Onward
Past illusion, with absolution, moving beyond
Thanatos' vale, and there stand on the doorstep of
Eden – world without end – O Alpha Omega
Come." They stand (pure form) unveiled, unabashed
In judgment of fire, grace of rain, and look to see,
from precipice, rising – the hills of sunnygold.

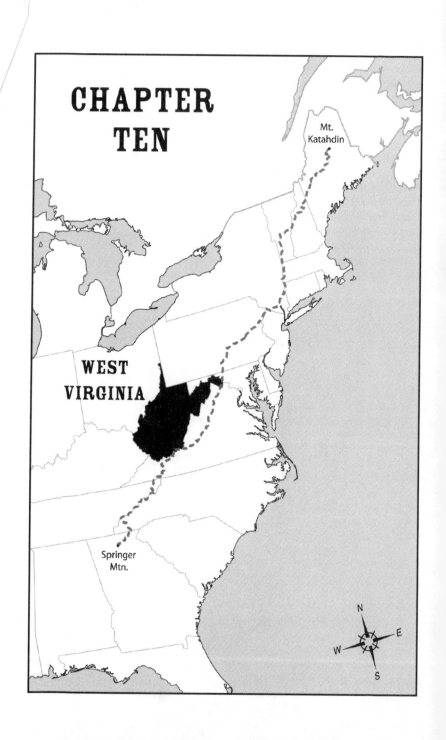

CHAPTER
TEN

WEST
VIRGINIA

Mt.
Katahdin

Springer
Mtn.

N
E
W
S

The morning came without dawn. That day's six o'clock light was hardly discernible as they crawled out into the world. It was already there, though – the burning desire to get somewhere. Tugging at them more than hunger and thirst. It certainly wasn't that they felt good. Since the lightning night, they'd seen only thirty-mile days – marathon stretches that left them with nothing but hollow bones and rusting ambitions. Yet one thing called them on. Harpers Ferry. Halfway home.

I

"Without the shedding of blood, there is no remission of sins."
                      -Hebrews 9:22 – John Brown's favorite scripture

Back in the beginning, nobody ever talked about Harpers Ferry. Springer was a grand ideal – whimsical even. A thought so distant and gargantuan that the mere mention of it was like reciting poetry. But Harpers Ferry was different – they had to actually pass through it if they were ever to get home. It was something real, between here and there – a tangible fact – smack-dab in the middle of the whole dern saga. And in the back of their minds they knew that when they finally got there, after the elation died away, they would have to deal with a single wilting realization. *It's true. We've come a long, long way. Over a thousand miles...but we still have a thousand to go.*

So it was that both dread and anticipation compelled the men to wake early, and in the dismal rain they began their twenty-six mile march down into Harpers Ferry.

Bryson calls it "a pretend town," which seems right, in a literary kind of way, but truly pretended things don't exist and never did. Harpers Ferry, once upon a time, had been an authentic place but it no longer exists in any real sense. It's almost as if the town was discarded, once won. The commemoration of its past seems faked, pretended. The memories that Harpers Ferry peddles are mostly not good ones, and, likely, digging up anything pleasant would be too much trouble. So these days, the life of the town comes and goes with the tourists, Civil War buffs and disoriented D.C. sightseers who appear with the first shuttle bus and disappear with the day's last souvenir.

At 247 feet above sea level, Harpers Ferry is the lowest point in West Virginia and one of the lowest points on the entire Appalachian Trail. Historian James McPherson explains that, "situated on a peninsula formed by the confluence of the Potomac and Shenandoah rivers, surrounded on all sides by commanding heights, it was indefensible from counter-attack." Consequently, sunlight has trouble slipping through the impressive crevices and ravines. These factors make it a perfect place in which to hide, defend if necessary, or – a lovely spot to get yourself trapped in. That is why, most likely, Harpers Ferry has such a dark and fascinating story to tell.

Applejack was in pain. The cold, morning-long drizzle had sogged his skin and brittled his bones, making it very difficult to get muscles, tendons and other essential body parts warmed up sufficiently. The only thing that pushed him forward was the prospect of spending a few hours in the dry ATC headquarters.

Across the Potomac from Harpers Ferry, he trudged along the C&O Canal Towpath in misery. It was perhaps his lowest moment physically since somewhere in the Hundred-Mile Wilderness. Down to a wispy hundred and sixty-three pounds, the wicked wind played games with his reedy frame, twisting and wrapping it in a film that burned his nose and choked his kneecaps. He cared nothing for the quaint tidbits of Harpers Ferry historia that would have normally enthralled him.

Unfortunately Futureman was faring better. He was reading the words of a tarnished placard beneath a dripping willow, when Applejack passed him by.

"Applejack!"

"What?" Applejack mumbled.

"Wait up!" The gravel crunched as he jogged. "Hey. Wait up."

Applejack spun. "Futureman, I feel like my feet are hardening in concrete and my frozen nipples are about to crack off under my shirt. What do you want?"

"Sorry. I just wanted to talk."

"About what?"

"It's very interesting. George Washington rode his horse down this very path. He thought that this was an important trade route that needed to be well-protected."

"You're right, Futureman. That is fantastically interesting. I'm ecstatic. Do go on."

"Geez. Never mind. I thought you liked history."

Harpers Ferry is very important to thruhikers. Halfway marker. "All downhill from here," they say. But the historical significance is far greater. In fact, it's difficult to fully understand the American Civil War without dealing with Harpers Ferry. For starters, Gettysburg, Antietam and Manassas (Bull Run) are all thirty miles or less from the small town. It was always a bit of a hotspot. From pre-Colonial times on up through the War Between The States, her unusual geography made the town a valuable fortress. In fact she changed hands eight times during the conflict, a slippery prize that no one could hold on to. But perhaps the story that most taints Harpers Ferry's epic tapestry is the story of Old John Brown.

Applejack and Futureman crossed the slick bridge over the Potomac carefully. Several times Futureman had to pause to dislodge his poles, stuck between boards. Even he was beginning to feel sorry for himself – tired, tired, tired. It was only 1:30 pm and they had already hiked twenty-six miles.

There was no one to greet them there on the brick streets – no parade, balloons or reception committees. No pretty flower-throwing girls. There were no trophies, medals or Baxter Porsches ready to chauffeur them to the nearest five-star restaurant. No crazy old Jewish ladies from the Upper East Side appeared to tweak their cheeks. Not even their moms were there. Just wet empty streets. Mist and frigid clouds of West Virginia indifference blew between the nationally treasured buildings. There they were, threadbare and shivering, drifting all alone through their joyless quagmire of glum blood pudding.

Passing quickly down a bricked lane lined with old-timey 'mercantiles' and 'saloons,' they followed High Street to Washington, then up the hill to the white house at the top. Inside were dry chairs, central heat, food and the ATC headquarters.

John Brown was an interesting fellow, unavoidable, polarizing and quite mysterious. But one thing is for certain: Brown lived by his convictions – and he had no shortage of those.

He had gained notoriety during the tumultuous years leading up to the Civil War. One of the premier *freesoilers*, Brown rose to national attention as a leader on the frontlines of Bleeding Kansas – and most importantly, one who would settle for nothing less than the complete annihilation of slavery. In those early years, Brown had gained many supporters, even people in high places – New England clergy, Congressmen and no less than the great Frederick Douglass. They were coming around to his position. Even peaceful folks were becoming persuaded by the militancy of radicals like Brown. But a fateful mistake brought all of that to an end.

Near the end of the 1850s Brown turned his attentions eastward – injustice, in his opinion, being more widespread there. Surrounded by his Secret Six (an esoteric group of abolitionists consisting of doctors, teachers and even pastors), Brown began to move on his greatest, most hare-brained and disastrous scheme of all.

plejack looked like a signpost in the mirror. He washed himself with
per towels as best he could, put on his one relatively dry change of
thes and walked back out into the ATC headquarters to look at the maps
the corner. His eyes were pushed back in his head from malnourishment.
s toenails were turning black from all the pressure and constant wear.
t warm. Sit down and rest. Sit down and rest for just a minute, then
ll get... His distended head dropped back onto the ragged couch and
hin seconds became dead to the world, fast asleep.

n Brown had come to a place in his ideological journey where he could
e no victory except that it came by violent hands. After all, the kingdom
heaven is taken by violent men.
    In 1859, he rented a vacant farmhouse seven miles outside Harpers
Ferry and began to pour his thoughts and plans into a final insurrection. His
life's dream had been to muster an army of abolitionists, march south into
the deep recesses of the Appalachian Mountains (calling all runaway slaves
and able Negroes to his banner) and establish a free republic of liberated
souls, at last. But there is little reason to believe that by 1859 Brown held
out hope that this dream could ever come to fruition. In his farmhouse
plans, no evidence can be found that he was expecting anything other than
one last suicide stand.
    Not coincidentally, Harpers Ferry was home to a United States armory.
On the evening of October 16, 1859, Brown and a band of 21 men (including three of his sons) pitted themselves against the US government and
everyone else, when they surprised the lone night watchman and captured
the arsenal and its cache of weapons. That is where the grandeur of the
scheme ends and, as townspeople began to fire on the cornered radicals, it
is reasonable to suspect that John Brown was reminded of his friend, Frederick Douglass – and his final words of warning: "You'll never get out
alive."

    "Hey buddy. Wake up. You've been asleep for two hours." Futureman
nudged Applejack. "We need to swing by the post office and find somewhere to eat."
    "Oh, yeah. Right." Applejack rubbed his eyes.
    "I already put our name in the Trail book and took down a bunch of con-
tact info for our friends." Futureman was holding a huge ATC binder which
contained Polaroids and vital stats of the hundreds of thruhikers that have
dropped in through the years. "We gotta get our pictures taken before we
leave. We don't want to be forgotten, do we?"
    "No, certainly don't want that."

Several striking curiosities hover over the John Brown calamity. In a sad twist of fate, the first casualty of the liberty raid was a freed Negro baggage master working for the railroad. He was shot by one of Brown's men as he came out onto the trestle. Other than that, however, little violence was required in subduing the insurrectionists. The two capable officers dispatched by President Buchanan to defuse the situation were Col. Robert E. Lee and Lt. J.E.B. Stuart – both still faithful servants of their United States. Within minutes Lee's men had done the job. Brown was captured, tried and executed swiftly.

In his last days he became the object of intense emotional energy. On one hand he was the very embodiment of the volatile, meddlesome agitator which the South feared and loathed. And on the other – the kind of righteous iconoclast that romantic abolitionists like Ralph Waldo Emerson and William Dean Howells hailed as a martyr – "a crucified hero." At any rate, John Brown had thrown down a gauntlet of sorts there on the Harpers Ferry banks. John Wilkes Booth watched his hanging in person, no doubt sensing a certain gravitas on the swelling tides of his times.

It is an impossible enterprise to try to crack into the addled psyche of a man like Brown. His motives and actions are too confusing and counter-intuitive. Apparently, by October before the raid, Brown had already realized the epic futility of his plan. Yet despite inevitable failure, he stayed the course, coming to the Ferry with a hopelessly smaller force than was planned; carrying no rations; and having never even scouted an emergency route out of the treacherous ravines. Having exhausted all hope of achieving paradise, Brown seemed to have moved beyond plan to a grim moment of violent singular action. He had become the unthinking union of will and deed. Perhaps he knew he was worth more dead than alive.

"Where are we gonna eat, Futureman? Everything's closed." They stood in the empty street scratching their foreheads. Too tired to plan ahead, they'd waited too late for everything. Applejack and Futureman didn't even know where they were going to sleep. Like Old John Brown, they were clueless.

"I don't know. We might have to pack up and go back out on the Trail."

"What?"

"Yeah." Futureman stiffened. "Imagine that, Applejack. What if we actually passed through a town without treating ourselves to a big dose of the good life? What if we actually got what we needed and headed back out to the Trail? Maybe it's time we bucked up a bit. We can be pretty soft."

"I'm not the one who – what kind of nonsense are you talking now, Futureman? We walked a hundred and forty miles in the last five days.

n't go preaching at me about being hard and bucking up."

"Sometimes, it just seems like you don't really want to be out here. I mean, wasn't this whole thing your idea?"

"Whoa. Hold it right there. I don't ever remember inviting you. I remember you inviting yourself. I remember you giving me that hangdog face of ours and dribbling out a 'Mind if I go?' And, now that you mention it- eah, you're right. Sometimes I don't want to be out here very much and either do you. Don't kid yourself."

No one said anything for a good while. Futureman counted the red ricks under his feet before finally breaking the silence.

"C'mon, bud. Let's get out of here. My blood sugar's kinda low."

And like that, their little quarrel was forgotten. Guys can do that.

A dinged-up blue Honda Civic pulled up to the curb, one of the old boxy ones. Applejack and Futureman stopped, wet clothes and packs sticking to them, shielding their eyes from the headlights.

"Where you fellas headed?" a voice called over the sputtering engine.

"Uh, we heard there's a good shelter up a ways. We're just goin back to the woods, I guess."

"Not on a night like this, you're not," the voice continued from inside.

"It's OK. It's not that bad out here. Really." They moved toward the next blaze slapped on the telephone pole ahead.

He came around the car and cut them off, a broad dark-haired man blocking the sidewalk. Speckles of mist were collecting on his glasses. "I'm sorry. I should introduce myself. You guys are probably thinking who the hell is this guy, right? My name is South Pacific – they call me South Pacific. I'm not a hiker, but I like living here, you know. Harpers Ferry is – nice and outta the way. Doing some, uh, consulting work for the city. Sometimes they call me over to D.C. – but not much anymore. So I guess you'd say I'm a Trail Angel, right? I'm cooking up some brats tonight and, maybe you want to eat supper at my place." Applejack and Futureman couldn't really see the guy's face. The light behind him obscured the particulars.

"We appreciate that but –" Applejack looked over at Futureman. "I think we're okay, South Pacific. We're just gonna head out."

"You gotta do what you gotta do. I understand." He stepped aside. "But if you change your mind, just give me a call. Pretty ugly out, tonight." The man scribbled numbers on a slip of paper and handed it to Futureman.

The big yellow overhang of a filling station stretched over them. Lightning lit up the sky like an indiglo watch. Applejack, chewing on a rubbery strip of pizza, pulled his hood up over his dripping five-inch mane.

"No way no way no way." Futureman rocked on his haunches. Wild eyes. Again. "No way. Uh-uh. Uh-uuuuh. No way."

"We'll just sit here for a while and wait it out. Get yourself something to eat."

"I'm not going back out in that, Applejack. I'm not kidding. I am firm – on this point, I am very firm."

"You are such a big baby. C'mon, that lightning's miles and miles away." A white-hot cobra bolt quartered off the western sky. "OK, maybe not miles away but we're not going to get hit. Especially if we go to that shelter."

"How do you know that? Huh? You don't. No way. Not me. Not after what happened to Moose."

"Moose did not get struck by lightning –"

"Moose was closer to that lightning bolt than two rats in a sock."

"Fine, Futureman. Fine. You win. I'll call him." Applejack stood up and spun around to see where the pay phone was situated.

South Pacific's apartment was an utter sty, but it was dry and smelled like bratwurst and that was good enough. There was freshly chopped tomato on the cutting board.

"Sit down. Supper's coming right up – right up." South Pacific was frenetically stacking papers. "What can I get you guys to drink, huh? Budweiser. Jack Daniel's. Buttermilk. Uh, I got ginger ale. I'm gonna have a Jack-and-Coke or four myself. What do you guys drink?" The man had huge hands, a pockmarked face and several scars on his arms and neck.

"Water for me."

"Water for me too, please-thank you."

"Oh, I get it. We got a couple of teetotalers here, eh?"

"No, it's not that we –"

"Hey, whatever blows your hair back. I'm not here to be pushy. I just want you guys to enjoy yourselves." South Pacific had managed to clear off about half of the living room space when his phone rang. "Hang on, Harry," he said over the line.

"Guys, I've got – something I've got to take care of. I apologize, but I'll be right back. Just make yourselves at home, eat your supper, and don't go anywhere. Hey, watch a movie if you want." He tapped a pile of VHS tapes, downed his tumbler, and spun out the door.

Applejack and Futureman were leaned back rigidly in their chairs, necks stiff.

"Wow."

"Wow."

There was nothing that could be called decorative anywhere in South Pacific's apartment. No pictures of family. No paintings, wall hangings or thing pleasing to the eye. But it wasn't the typical bachelor pad, either. ndreds of newspaper clippings, mostly yellowed, lined the walls. The icles seemed to be unrelated. Trials: big-name trials, local trials, capital nishment stuff, even misdemeanors – dating all the way back to the mid-venties.

"Maybe this guy's a lawyer?"

"I don't think so."

A Congressman indicted for an illegal connection to an oil conglomer-e. A truckload of unprocessed opium intercepted on the Canadian/Wash-gton border. A local single-mom family whose mobile home had been ashed away in a recent flood received $50,000 from a neighborhood ndraiser. The American attaché to Syria was arrested on the tarmac, a isc of unauthorized highly classified State Department documents found n his luggage.

"I don't get it. Why would somebody put this kind of stuff up on the wall?"

"Hey. Buddy, you got to check this out. Sean Penn looks like he's eigh-teen years old here. This has got to be one of his very first movies," Future-man said, kneeling at the stack of VHS beside the TV.

"What's it called?"

"*The Falcon and the Snowman.*"

"Never heard of it. Cool title, though."

"Could I use a drink or what!" South Pacific said bounding through the door.

They were at a tense moment in the movie. Sean Penn's character was talking to some Russian dudes. He knew somebody who had information they might want to see.

South Pacific bellowed when he saw it on the screen.

"Oh boy! Wow. That takes me back. I remember that stuff like it was yesterday. What a weird case."

Futureman hit the pause button. "So it's a good movie?"

"Huh? Oh, yeah. Movie's fine," South Pacific said, disappearing into the kitchen to pour another tumbler. "But man, what a dumb deal that was. Seems almost funny now. Boyce and Lee. One of those child's play scams – just so simple it fools everybody."

"What do you mean? Were you, like involved somehow or something?"

"Oh, no, no, no, well, no. What gave you that impression?"

"I don't know. You sound like you know a lot about it, that's all."

"Everybody knows about this, right? You guys – no, course not. What a schmo I am. You two were barely alive. See, we – they never would've caught Boyce if he had gotten rid of Lee. Last person in the world you'd suspect. Didn't fit any of the profiles." The big man pushed his glasses back on his nose, paused slightly.

In 1975, a 26-yr-old college dropout named Christopher Boyce was given a job at TRW in California, a high-tech contractor that operated in U.S. spy satellite technology. Boyce's father, who worked in intelligence for the government, had pulled some strings for his boy. Inexplicably, with no prior experience, Boyce was given top secret clearance and was stationed inside a black vault room where he daily used highly secure codes and satellite positioning info in the course of his work. For a while, Boyce enjoyed a strangely festive work environment, sharing daiquiris on the job with his coworkers, but it wasn't long before he figured out how to turn his privileged post into a personal goldmine.

Boyce sent his friend Andrew D. Lee, a very smalltime drug dealer, to Mexico City to establish contact with the KGB. Lee walked into the Soviet Embassy in the heart of one of the largest cities in the world and handed over an envelope and note from Boyce that read: *Enclosed is a computer card from the National Security Agency, crypto system...if you want to do business, please advise the courier.*

From there, Boyce and Lee began one of the most successful spy operations in United States history.

"See, the thing that did Boyce in was that he got cocky – a very arrogant guy to talk to. Even afterwards, he was like, *You can't touch me. I'm golden.*" South Pacific reclined in his chair, rolling into his fourth Jack-and-Coke of the evening. When he spoke, he gestured through the air, as if he were pushing a blindfold away from his face.

"When we all came back from Viet Nam, we saw a lot of those types. Guys that thought they understood what the government was about. Didn't think they owed anything to anybody but Lee was really the weak link, there – what a screw up. And he came unglued for us, too. Blabbed and blabbed about everything he'd ever known. Kinda pathetic, actually." South Pacific rested the glass on his belt buckle. It didn't even matter anymore if Applejack and Futureman were in the room or not. He was just enjoying himself.

In all, seven trips were made to Mexico City. Boyce was familiar with several of the surveillance systems the government was using on the Soviets at the time: RHYOLITE, PYRAMIDER and ARGUS. He traded photographs of the technology and various other types of available information to the Russians for a total of $70,000 over the course of a couple of years. In fact, the KGB was so impressed with Christopher Boyce that they offered him

n additional forty grand to finish his degree and enter the State Department or CIA. But Andrew D. Lee was, indeed, the weak link. Out of his
depth from the beginning, Lee's drug habit and self-serving, erratic behav-
iors brought the whole thing crashing down.

Lee wanted his own deal on the side. In an attempt to grab the attention
of a fed-up KGB agent, Lee made a disturbance that attracted the Mexican
police. At his arrest they found an envelope containing film from the
PYRAMIDER project. This, in and of itself, probably would not have
caught their attention. But Lee, with classic amateur boorishness, had
marked the envelope 'Top Secret.'

He got life in prison. Boyce got forty years. Their 'child's play' equipped
the Soviets with enough information to temporarily disable US surveillance
satellites and, according to Senator Daniel Moynihan, was "as much as any
one thing…responsible for the SALT (Strategic Arms Limitation) Treaty."

"Those were the days. At least we knew who our enemies were back
then." South Pacific's eyes were barely open, head dropping. "I have to say,
though, Sean Penn did a damn fine job with Andy Lee – just like him down
to the moustache. Hutton's performance was a little weak, though." He
winked at them. "Say, you know why they were called Falcon and Snowman?"

"I assume Lee was Snowman because of the cocaine."

"Right. And the Falcon?"

"I don't know, maybe, because of the satellites or something?"

"Good guess, but no." South Pacific waited.

"What? C'mon. Why was he called that?"

"He was a falconer. Trained 'em to kill."

The phone rang in the middle of the night. From the couch, Applejack
could see South Pacific's legs swing to the floor in his bedroom at the end
of the hall. He could barely make out the words.

"Uh-huh. You bet. Of course, I've got 'em. Uh-huh. Did some work with
him in Iran. Yeah, I know that. He's good. OK. Give me ninety minutes. I'll
be there."

He hung up the phone, turned on the light, rummaged in the closet and
was dressed and at the door in minutes.

"Oh, hey there, buddy. Sorry to wake you. I've gotta run. I, uh – drive
the ambulance and there's been – um, a bad wreck. You guys stay as long as
you like. Pleasure to meet you and good luck on your trip." South Pacific
closed the door behind him.

Applejack flushed the toilet. *Just when I think things can't go any weird-*

er... He staggered out of the bathroom. A splash of color caught his eye from the left. He turned toward the light coming through the cracked door of the spare bedroom. It was wrong but he just had to see for himself. He pushed the door open. Eight large filing cabinets. Ten-foot maps of Europe and Africa covered with markers, pins and flags. Stacks and stacks of files littered the tables and floors. There were several plaques with photographs of South Pacific shaking hands with important looking men. He saw words like *distinguished service* and *contribution* and *wellbeing of our great nation.*

Applejack didn't go into the room. He didn't want to know anymore. None of it would make sense anyway. He turned back toward the lumpy couch.

South Pacific didn't come back all night.

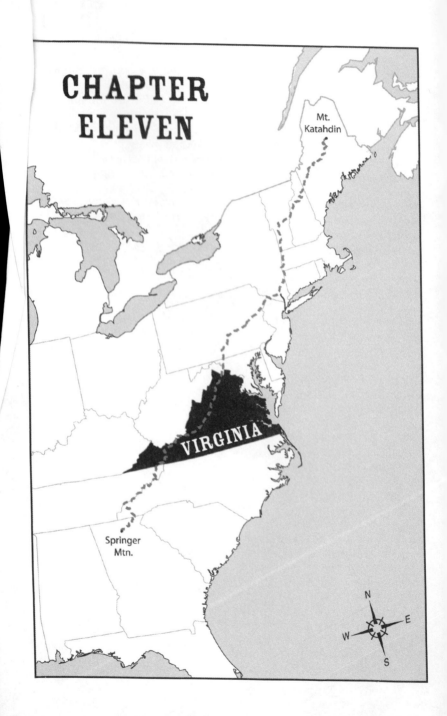

CHAPTER ELEVEN

Mt. Katahdin

VIRGINIA

Springer Mtn.

N
E
W
S

A cold breeze came in the night with the rain. It painted the beech and hung heavy on the wood sorrel. The men rattled and pulled their bags up under their chins, waiting it out, surviving the dark. Trusting the sun to rise and dry up the land. Sure bet, for you can always trust the sun to rise, right? Right?

I

The sky settled into an eternal gray with that comfortable thickness that marks a captor's intent. Settled, yet even now calling for reinforcements. They walked into it, on an up-down-up-again stretch of ground that ran like a roller coaster. In fact, that section of Trail is called the *Roller Coaster*. From Snicker's Gap to Spout Run to Fent Wiley Hollow to Ashby, Bolden and Rod Hollow – like a small scale New England without the views, granite cliffs, fantasy roots and granddaddy forests.

It was raining, had been since Harpers Ferry. Everything was saturated, including Applejack and Futureman, socks lumped up in the bottoms of their shoes like soppy locker room towels.

Plodding along in a deep funk, Futureman put together a monotone mantra to console himself. All the words began with *f*. Fire, forest, friend, Fred, fruit. "Fire the forest and the fruit...The fruit is on fire...Fred the fiery fruit...The forest's name is Fred...Fred lights forest fruit on fire." Applejack walked behind him head down, singing a broken Beatles tune. "Boy – you're gonna carry that weight – carry that weight – for a long time..." again and again and again. The chafing had come back – *always comes during the long rains* – and was spreading like wild fire up his inner thighs. The air tasted like licorice and vinegar, spiced with firecracker rim shots on the ridge above (an early sign of the dreaded hunting season to come).

They carried on like this for some time, almost bypassing the sign that pointed to Bear's Den. It was a small sign in a simple cleft of trail, but it was enough to break Applejack away from his song. And he began to remember that voice and what it had said to them on Tom's porch back in Massachusetts. *Guys, when you get to Bear's Den you have to stop and stay there. It's the best place in the world – the best place to build a fire, to laugh with your friends, to watch sunsets, to kiss your girl, to pray. Seriously, if you don't stay there for at least a week – I'll kill you!*

"Bear's Den. This is the Colonel's Secret Garden," Applejack said.

"Oh, yeah. He lives near here – Winchester, right?" Futureman remembered. "Let's give him a call. See what he's up to."

"I got no problems with that," Applejack said, a shaky finger on a raw testicle.

he Colonel was sitting at home twiddling his thumbs (teenage girlfriend back
school) when the phone rang.

"You're here! Stay there!" he shouted. "I'm coming to get you. Don't move!
eriously, I'm in the car, right now – I'm not far, you're coming to my house –
e're going fishing, I'm taking you fishing! I'm telling you. Stay. Right. There.
r I'll kill you!"

The car pulled up to the gas station in Linden in a matter of minutes. They
grabbed and wrestled each other like school boys. Colonel shouted, "I still
ave diarrhea!" And they were on their way.

n a devout Mormon home on the bottle-blue edge of the Shenandoah Valley,
Eric, the Colonel, was one of four children. He had two ten-year-old twin
brothers – miniature Colonels – and an older sister who lived in Salt Lake
City. They were very much an old-fashioned family unit, and they liked it that
way.

"My, my, my," Mom said. "I finally get to put a face on you guys. Welcome." She hugged each man tightly and invited them in for as long as they
saw fit to stay.

After a tray of warm cookies and a few jokes, once again, the triad set out
to find dinner. On their way out the door, the Colonel's dad whispered the
word *buffet*, adding, "Have fun putting them out of business."

Golden Corral is a fairly insulting name for a restaurant, if you think about it.
They waddled through the lines, heaping their plates to obscene heights. Fried
ham, roast beef, catfish, black-eyed peas, cooked carrots, sweet onions and
green beans. Rolls, biscuits and Texas toast. Pineapple cake with plastic swirl
from the soft serve machine. The herd moved around the turnstiles. Three,
four, five plates of buffalo chicken bones, fried okra skins and pecan piecrusts.

*What are we being fattened up for? How long before we're slaughtered
too?* Futureman wondered, as he licked his fourth pudding bowl clean.

According to their Mormon tradition, Colonel's family was considered to be in
the lineage of Aaron, the brother of Moses. This meant that Colonel had
demanding spiritual duties to attend to. Since the age of 16, he had been under
the supervision of the bishop, and was being trained to become a part of the
cohesive hierarchy of the church. Once officially confirmed, Eric would be
charged with great responsibility – blessing of the sacraments, administrating
baptism, teaching the congregation and conferring the Aaronic priesthood on
others proven worthy by faith and deeds.

The process demanded complete adherence and unblinking obedience to
bishop and church but conflict was simmering within the young man. Desiring

to be faithful to his family and religion, yet in love with the romantic notions of freedom and wilderness wandering, he wanted to put off decision time as long as possible. Everyone else saw him as a tall handsome man ready for the world. He wanted to remain a carefree boy with a rod and reel slung over his shoulder.

"We're fishing the entire Shenandoah!" Colonel said that night on the porch. He leaned in, carefully describing the spots where he'd spent his mornings, afternoons, days and weeks, hiding with the fish. Overgrown holes and river bends filled with huge smallmouth, fat on caddis. Shoals and eddies with trout and bluegill waiting in the cool water. These places were his refuge, his only moments of certainty or resolution.

It didn't take much to convince them. Applejack had fished ever since he could remember and Futureman had inherited the gift from his dad. *There's nothing like finding that one fish and fighting it into the boat,* Doc used to say.

They would need to be there by dawn, but dawn couldn't come fast enough for the Colonel.

In the faint morning light, they eased the car into a spot beneath the trees. Grabbing their gear and tackle, they set out after the smell of water, and without their notice, one day turned into three, blending together into a single, still, blue-green hour.

The river asks why, but fishing need not be explained – can't be. The joy of casting, the peace of watching water's traces, the patience of waiting, music strumming to the constant drum of the current – these things are sublime beyond measure, slow in coming but long in staying.

They stood upstream, thigh-high in an affluent of the Shenandoah. The cool flow was refreshing. It eased Futureman's blister. First light, first shadows brandished above the glassy whitecaps. The morning sun caught frantic midges darting back and forth on the surface – questing for a stagnant pool in which to play mating games. They cast into the current looking for corners and jetties of the river, searching for smallmouth and whatever else would bite. Lines sprayed. Arches of mist evaporated into the air, heavy yet clear.

Their reels buzzed with the dragonflies as lines unwound. Further and further, little by little. They inched silently upstream, each one straying, piling, arranging around him the collections of his own knee-deep world.

Since before he was old enough to ride a bike without training wheels, Futureman had followed after his dad, the good doctor, to the Tennessee bluegill holes of the great Fort Loudon Lake. Little Futureman always saluted his worm before sinking it slowly into the murky water, into the belly of a whop-

r! His whole being, his entire world was fixated on that one plastic bobber
t bounced on top of the water.

Any second now. Any moment now. That thing is going to –

"Pull! You got one!" Doc shouted.

Now. Now. Now. Bobber gone. Daddy's shouting. *Pull now!* And the small
ue fish flies from the water across the blue sky, to land on the rocks at his
et. The slimy scales fascinated his hands, nervous the dorsal might cut them.

That boy was still alive inside the shaggy man who stood now beside the
ver. Futureman cast into the brilliant water. He missed his father. Fishing was
ever right without him. "How 'bout I catch one for you, Pops."

n its good days, the river is a place the noise of the world doesn't care to
uch. Responsibilities, worries drift away in the constancy of its sway and
rve. It teaches how to deal with change calmly, to absorb turbulence. There
e songs stressed in the swallowed undercurrent. The Colonel came here
ften to find his way, to see clearly through the confusing, conflicting snares
f his teenage mind. Usually, he was able to release the stress into the mirror
ol water like a too-proud-to-be-kept rainbow trout but today, something had
managed to follow him in. It was following him everywhere these days – too
big and too strong to be rid of. Breaking his own rules, Colonel moved too
quickly up the stream.

That morning his father had been stern with him over his missing a meeting at the church. "Son, you need to think about your responsibilities, your
duties as a priest. This is in our family. You are my son, and you *will* take this
seriously. The priesthood is a great thing. The bishop likes you. He thinks you
have great potential."

A whippoorwill called from the bank.

*Do I want this? There's so much to do. Can I even ask that question? I
should obey my father. I love my family. Wouldn't do anything to hurt them
but do I believe in this? I do. I burn in my chest, I think. That's proof, right? It
must be true. I just wish I could see those golden tablets – see them for
myself. But the Book says that all the witnesses will burn in their conviction.
Who am I to argue? My father says I'm in Aaron's line. How's he know this?
Why won't he tell me more? What's the secret? I have to believe him – he's
my own dad for cryin' out loud – believe him and the bishop. It's just too
complicated. Why can't everything be simple – like this! out here! – but the
truth of things has gotta be bigger than what I can understand. Right? Why
didn't God let me stay on the Trail? That was something I understood.*

He arched a camber into a dark eddy and turned his focus on attractor patterns, trying to hook a trout or a char.

What am I running from?

Applejack was back downstream, fishing in the holes Futureman and Colonel had passed up. He squeezed his reel, looking for the *feel*, remembering that perseverance was as much a part of this as anything else. Faithfulness, understanding that one, two, ten casts in the same spot were not enough. He resigned himself to cast until he caught, or at least until he didn't care any more. He had been around fishermen enough to know that most fish were caught when you stopped looking for them, when the act of casting and reeling had become the end result. *Maybe that's when those sneaky beauties think they can get away with it.*

His grandpa, the preacher, was a world-class fisherman. From a whiny boy, Applejack had fished with him – dozens of times, off the banks of small, dirty ponds. Off creaky, gray docks. Underneath the snake-infested cypresses of Reelfoot Lake, where the Mississippi had run earthquake – backwards. There, together, they circled the swampy canebrake and trolled through tussocks murky enough to drown hope but hope never died with Reverend James. When the water was at its muddiest, stirred up by the mass exit of exasperated, over-heated fishermen, that was when the preacherman could work his magic best, teasing crappie and brim onto his golden line. When the wind chopped at the waters like an old woman with a fly swatter, he could still pull fish. Not one right after another. But steady and sure. Applejack watched him in amazement all his life. He seemed no different when his pole was bent than when it wasn't, for the care and attention he guided toward the water was actually turned toward higher things – toward the fishing of men. And so those minutes and hours in between passed for James with the ageless silver swell of eternal things, until *There! There it was* – a bass too big for a Polaroid. On the end of the line.

Nearly all the beautiful swimmers that Applejack ever saw had dangled at the end of his grandfather's Fish Eagle rod. But for every one, there were a hundred that had nuzzled the bait hungrily in deference to the old man before darting down deep toward safety.

So Applejack took his time, looking underneath the rocks for words that only fish can know.

The Colonel waded far ahead, walking briskly through the water, searching for those honey holes ahead that he hadn't disclosed to anyone. A fisherman never really shares his favorite spots. An act of brilliant selfishness.

Futureman watched the Colonel disappear. Now he was alone. Alone on the river – that unexplainable thing. It might be the caddis cutting the water, the stones on the bottom smoothed by centuries, spiders weaving wet webs across the plants, the wind cross-chopping the surface. Or, it might just be everything.

He looked down at his reflection in the current. He looked old. Water contorted his face, forehead sliding down into his eyes, lips drooping onto his shoulders, a snake swimming across his chest.

Snake? A snake!

And not just any snake, a moccasin. Very poisonous. Futureman froze. The snake fought upstream against the current.

Stay calm, stay calm, he told himself. *It's just a harmless-extremely poisonous snake swimming around your fat calves. Don't move. You're fine. It doesn't even know you're here...*He watched the moccasin glide effortlessly across the water and disappear into a tangle of cattails along the bank. *He knows I'm too fast for him anyway. I would've bitten his head right off.*

Only slightly disappointed, Futureman tugged on his Shakespeare Ugly Stik and spun his line into the pool. It would have been a good story to tell the others. Maybe *Outdoor Magazine* would have bought it. But the snake had no intention of revealing his favorite spots either.

There! Applejack held a chromer at the end of his line. The caudal fin dangled back and forth, slapping at the air, slinging drops through the sunlight. He grabbed it by the buccal, took it off the hook and studied it. A perfect lateral line from nape to caudal, pectorals, dorsals and pelvics, its mouth a constant channel for sucking water and passing it to the gills. Its eyes glazed with a milky film. It was a thing built for swimming, a creature under the dry world, completely other.

He released it, watching as it flapped back under the current. He shook the slime off his hands and moved upstream, quietly humming a hymn to himself.

The Colonel had found one of his holes. An island in the middle of the river with a brookie-pass down one side of it. By day three, he had already caught two dozen fish on his new Featherlite. He called to Applejack and Futureman to share his favorite spot, the fisherman's crime. They cast there through the remaining daylight hours. The cool waters of the Shenandoah River glistened in ripples and swirls under the sun. Slow arching trail and the beauty of the forest streaked by above, as if their minds were on hold – as if a little girl had drawn it on her sketch pad and was flipping through the edges.

They didn't say anything. Just fished, until the river faded black in the late afternoon.

"Thanks, Colonel. Thanks for all that back there," Applejack said as they walked back to the car.

"It's mighty kind of you to share your favorite fishing hole with us," Futureman added.

"Well, you guys can share my hole any time," Colonel said. It was a kind gesture, but somehow it just hadn't come out right. "Uh."

"Colonel, we appreciate the offer, but –"

"Shut up, you know what I mean."

"What *do* you mean, exactly?" Futureman asked.

"I'll kill both of you," Colonel said.

The Trailhead tugged on him. He wanted to strap his pack back on and walk away with them.

"Come back out with us, Colonel?"

"Naw, I'm gonna fish a little more, I think. But I'll be there. Just keep walking. I'll catch up, some day. I love you guys."

"See ya, Colonel. We love you too."

II

Days go by under a sunken sun. The Shenandoah mountain flats slide away like watercolor dripping down a gray-water paper sky. The light thunder of fat cherubs rolls across the clouds, the forecast of indefinite rain.

"If this keeps up," Futureman said, "I mean I know we're waterproof and all –"

"Body maybe, not the mind. We're gonna have to use other resources if we're gonna get through this," Applejack said.

"What do you mean other *resources*?"

"You got an imagination, don't you?"

Futureman thought about it. *Do I have an imag* – distraction: sucked down into a black retrieval tunnel, whirling, round-round-dizzy-round, in danger of being flayed on the spinning belt.

"There you go! That's what I'm talkin about. Imagination is our ticket out of here."

Thunder, like angels bowling. That good ole-fashioned black ball (burning wick ACME bomb) rumble on the lane – *coup de foudre* – camouflet of a flock of wailing seabirds. Winged pins hammering on the rubber matting.

The whole landscape turned into a bowling alley. Trail was lane. Sky was World Bowling Championships and the Civil War-era stone-stacked fences of these Virginia hill homesteads will be the racks-to choose our bowling balls from.

"If only we could find an actual bowling alley," Futureman said.

"If only," said Applejack.

They stood for a hitch into Waynesboro on US 250, thumb up (ball stuck to it). A rusted F150 rattled by. Fifty yards up, its one working brake light flicked on as the truck banged to a halt. The passenger got out and motioned to them with a well-rounded wave.

"Well, look who it is," Applejack said.

They hadn't seen Terranaut since New York City. Now, his clean-shaven face had a patchy beard that stuck to it like hair treatment plugs.

"It's been what, a month, maybe more?" Terranaut shouted.

"Yeah, more – I don't know. Who gives a darn-it?" Applejack shouted back. "Good to see you!"

"Hell yeah, it's good to see me. I'm a cool guy."

"When did you get into town?" Applejack asked. Terranaut wasn't wearing his hiker dregs.

"Yesterday. I'm glad you guys made it out of New York. I thought maybe you got sold on the black market and taken to Asia to pull rickshaws or something."

"Sorry about that. Didn't mean to stand you up that Saturday. We just kind of got swallowed up in New York's iron belly."

"No need for apologies. I'm not a four-year-old, but you did leave me alone with Lost-and-Found – that guy! He's quite pleasant most of the day, but when it turns nighttime…" Terranaut shook his head. "With his staring up at the stars and those stick circles he makes."

"Man, I saw him do that in New York, but I never said nothing about it. Didn't know what to say," Futureman said.

"Yep. I don't know."

"Where is he now?"

"I'm not sure. He got off the trail again at Harpers Ferry to see some people. Kept asking about you guys, though. I told him I heard you both got run over by a train."

"Funny, we almost did."

The man in the truck leaned across the bucket seat, revving the gas to keep the old rusted heap running. "Fellers, I ain't one to quit a good conversation 'mong free-uns, but I got me a wife at home'll get to kickin' some butt, if'n I'm not there in five ticks. Know wut a mean? You fellers hop in the back here. I'll drop you-uns at Weasie's."

"Weasie's?" Applejack asked.

"Bess darn dumplins in all Virginee!"

You're not sure how to stand. You don't remember how you stood the last time you rolled a non-gutter ball. But you pretend: hip hung, gut turtled, arms bent like broken wings. Your neck is craned over the ball, nostrils flared, settee full of curious onlookers (*What's that moron doing now?*) The ten-year-old one lane over just waa-waa-waaed it from between his legs and got a strike, and you start your stutter step forward toward the line that you dare not cross but do cross – every time. The crowds at lanes 6,7,9 and 10 cheer again – at you, sprawled out on the slippery wood.

But there is something about that heavy ellipsis hurled by angel wind and demon fire, as you pretend this is happening. Your ball teeters on the edge of the gutter, of fading hope or curving acceleration. Strike. Spare. Split. Turkey. Try to break 200! You! You're the one rolled that Lanehawk!

Weasie was the cook. He'd been wearing the same hairnet for the last ten years, the same white (now pale orange) apron, same whiskers and same what-are-you-lookin-at grin. He didn't have to be nice. That was Pearl's job.

"Howdy boys. Lordy, y'all stink!" She slapped a stick of Juicy Fruit against the tops of her teeth. "I'm just a'foolin. Don't care one bit. I love you hiker types. Plus, I think Weasie's got ya beat in the B.O. department!"

"We like jokes," said Futureman.

"How's the soup?" Applejack asked.

"Soup's like snake pee today. Get country fried steak or dumplins – bess darn dumplins in all Virginee. Finish it off with some homemade apple pie. Knock ya right up."

"That sounds about right," Applejack said.

Pearl didn't have to ask. She knew they would eat two dinners each. This was, after all, a small town diner on the Appalachian Trail.

"It's not my fault, you know," Terranaut said, slicing into a piece of home-made pie for desert.

"What isn't?" Applejack asked.

"New York. It's not my fault you got stuck there."

"Uh, we know –"

"At any rate, I'm just glad to see you two again. You guys are – good con-versationalists. A lot of people talk shit out here, put everyone else down like we're all part of some elite club or something. But you're ridiculous and you know it. I like that. It's a good place to start." His face curled with that Harvard smirk. "Even though you are Protestant." There it was again – laughter in his nose. They had missed it.

The last bite of pie was the crust. Pearl smiled, slapped down three more pieces and popped in a new stick of Juicy Fruit.

"Here you go, boys, these are on the house!"

"Weasie does it right," Applejack said.

"Weasie? I believe you mean, Pearl does it right? Weasie'd have a heart attack if he knew I give free pie to my favorite customers."

"Well, at least you don't discriminate between Catholics and Protestants," Terranaut said.

"Lord no! Long as everyone reads from the King James, we'll be alright!" She dashed away to do a round of coffee refills.

Futureman hadn't acknowledged the free pie. He was fixated on something outside the window.

"You okay, bud?" Terranaut snapped his fingers. "Look like you've seen a ghost."

"Is that what I think it is?" Futureman pointed out the window.

"Oh my…it is!" Applejack exclaimed.

Futureman had spied pink and green lights hiding behind the scattered trees, no small achievement. But there they were, tucked away across a gravel parking lot – the *Waynesboro Lanes*. The neon sign had just flickered on for the night.

You're no Marshall Holman. You don't have a swing shot. You don't own a pair of silver Dyno-Thane's. You don't wear a Wrist Master and you'll never use a Turbo 2-N-1 thumbgrip to increase axis rotation. "Tracking flare" "throwing rocks" "a ten in the pit" "mule ears" "grandma's teeth" "a snow plow" – it's like a foreign language. You baby the ball, have a chicken wing swing, and when you throw it – half the time *you* end up on the pines, too. You don't roll turkeys. You *are* the turkey. But you still have what every bowler has in that moment when you're up there in your zone. You have your own special dance, your own special ball, your own special lane, and your very own roundhouse punch to the face. That triangular jaw of mockery isn't laughing now, is it? Its teeth are on the floor.

"This is one of those southern things I need to learn about, isn't it?" Terranaut said, running after Applejack.

"Not southern, but it's gonna change your life. Honest," Applejack called, running after Futureman.

The bowling alley smelled like a closet full of used-up spray cans and work shoes. It was roaring with people. Teams of shirts with printed names and little bags (briefcases of the bowling world). "Tommy 2-Time" pulled out his ball and wiped it with his rag. "Bumper" laced his shoes up and gave a high five to shirt named "Lane Poet" (wrist guards clinking).

"What can I do you fellers for?" the man at the counter said.

"Here to roll some lanes," Futureman said.

"Team name?"

"No, just us three, I'm a size ten, he's-"

"Gotta be on a team if you wanna roll here tonight."

"Seriously?"

"Feller, you seen all these lanes?"

"Yessir."

"You seen any of 'em open right now?"

"Uh."

"It's League Night. Got us a Big Tourney on. I'm afraid you'd be waitin till we turned all the lights off."

Terranaut started to laugh.

"Shut up," Futureman said.

Man at counter raised his eyebrow. "Feller?"

"Not you."

"We're all fulled up. Come morrow night, we'll set ye right up."

"We have to go to the woods tomorrow. Understand? So please, just one –"

"Like I said, sonny-boy, it's League Night. No team, no lane."

Sometimes, you've got it all in hand. You step up to the rack and take your ball, the one with that unique chip mark just right of the pointer hole. You put your feet together. Hold the ball under your chin and glare. Pins cower across the reflective wood. You do your dance and roll the heat. Ball's in slow motion, it curves in a groove carved out just for that one run. You know before it hits the pins. You don't have to look at them. You turn, walk away and just listen to them fall.

Then again, sometimes your ball goes right into the gutter and slides into a puddle, pouting there in the rain for the next ten days in the wet, wet, wet Virginee woods.

III
"To have heard the coyote bark is to have earned much life experience."
                    -Old Indian proverb

They thrive in all types of environments – desert, tundra, grassland, dense forest, swamp, suburban area and garbage heap. Cunning animals, they steal small game with ease, hunt in packs, mate for life, bed in the shade, and even mate with domesticated animals; breeding wildness into an otherwise civilized world. Playfully curious, they take pleasure in checking things out. And though rare, if you pay attention, you just might see a coyote strolling right beside you among, say, the New York City lights.

The Native Americans called the coyote *Brother, Medicine Dog* and *Little Wolf.* They believed the coyote was a magical animal that taught the Zuni to hunt, showed the Sioux which plants were useful, told the Sen about the sweet juice that hides in the cactus, stocked the rivers of the Pacific Northwest with salmon and taught the Nez Perce how to fish there and build traps.

Canis latrans means "barking dog." Coyotes bark for two reasons, to rendezvous for procreation and to call their young. If you listen carefully, you'll hear them howling for a mate during the months of January and February, and during September and October, you'll catch the interplay play between mother and cubs.

The coyote's howl is mysterious. It hangs in the air long after he is gone, leaving only the impression that he is somewhere he is not.

The rain had filled the state with eight inches of new water, and it wasn't stopping anytime soon. Applejack, Futureman and Terranaut sat on the edge of the shelter, glad to be dry as the forest sponged more liquid from the waxy sky. Steam rose from their stoves and disappeared in the roof beams. A dim sunset journeyed from hoary to black.

Close by, a hunting dog began a frustrated bark, tied up in the wet rain. Other dogs joined in, five or six of them. They barked violently, screeching, wailing down in a hollow a mile or so away.

"What are they going on about?" Applejack said.

"I don't know, I'm not a dog," said Futureman.

"It's got to be an animal of some kind. Could be a mountain lion – or a bear," Applejack said, corner of his mouth drawing up.

"It's a coyote," Futureman said, sticking his nose in the air. "I've been hearing them lately."

"You been smelling 'em, too?" Terranaut said.

"Barking and muttering. I think there's a pack of them around here somewhere."

"Interesting," Terranaut said. "Well, if they come around the shelter tonight, Futureman, I trust you will use your keen senses to wake us before they gnaw on our legs. Good night, then."

Eventually, the dogs trailed off, tired of fearing what they couldn't see.

Hours later, Futureman woke. It was pitch black save for the moonlight, stringy fingers threshing through the forest. Night sky was clear for a change, resting before another morning rainstorm. Futureman leaned out at the edge of the shelter and looked upward to find lady moon, as if he had forgotten what she looked like. Rainwater dropping from the oaks and wet twigs buffeting the draggle confused the sound of feet as they snuck through the rhododendrons toward the shelter.

Futureman turned. Something was behind the shelter. Or, some things. The noise filtered around on both sides, to his right and left. It came around front – a confluence of sniffing and tiptoeing, low in the shadows between the trees. He shined his dim head lamp there. Several pairs of eyes darted up, catching the glow. Eyes were all around him now, just beyond illumination.

Curious and unafraid, the creatures weaved around one another keeping an eye on the light. Then, slowly, one of them came forward, extended its head from the shadows into the beam.

"Little wolf," Futureman whispered. Beautiful dog, green flame eyes at the bridge of a slender nose. "What are you asking?"

It eyed Futureman for a long moment, sniffed the ashes, one paw forward. Then, suddenly, it was gone, retreated into the thick timber with the others.

"What's that scratching around out there?" Terranaut said, turning in his bag.

"Coyotes. They're leaving now," Futureman said.

"That's nice," Terranaut mumbled, asleep again.

Futureman followed the sound of the coyotes as they made their way up the ridge. The noise of their moldering feet hung under the moon as he fell asleep.

The following evening, as they were ringing out their rain-drenched clothes yet again, they heard them on the ridges. Somewhere far, somewhere close, couldn't tell, a mother howled for her young prodigals to come home. Dissolute echoes remained until morning.

IV
My face looks like a wedding-cake left out in the rain.
                    -W.H.Auden

There's two kinds of people in the world: the kind that like rain and the kind that don't. So, the question is – which kind are you?

Terranaut was nowhere to be seen. Spooked by the intimate reports of early morning riflery, he'd disappeared into high gear after dawn, head low, muttering. Walking alone, Applejack spied some color ahead. It was Futureman, drawn up under a tree.

He had been there for a while, hunched beneath a towering spruce. It was clearly not keeping the water off of him as he had hoped. Conifers don't. They are insolent. They dribble everywhere and rain just keeps coming down. The Virginia Live Oak is deciduous, right? Nah, guess again – coniferous prevaricator, spoiler, state-sponsored trickster, and presently the site of Futureman's shivering vigil.

"I'm sick of this," Applejack said, coming to a halt. "I'm serious – sick of it."

"What are you sick of?"

"The average person would question our sanity. With the exception of our time on the Shenandoah, it has rained every day that we've been in Virginia."

"Indeed, it has," Futureman said.

"This is like that scene in Star Wars where Luke and Han Solo and Leia are rooting around in that big slimy trash compactor and that monster –"

"Dianoga."

"What?"

"That monster in the trash compactor is called a dianoga," Futureman said.

"Right. I'm not gonna comment on how geeky it is that you know the name of that creature – but ever since I was a kid I've thought that scenario has got to be the worst possible situation a person could get himself into, right? Wrong. Because here we are with this beautiful, epic place all around us and we're slopping around, blind as bats with monsters slithering under our heels."

"Dianogas."

"Whatever – and another one of those since-I-was-a-kid things – I have been looking forward to Virginia in October for as long as I can remember. The colors. Crisp wind. The whole rolling hills bit. And all I can think about now is how nauseating my foamy socks are and how repulsed I am by my own smell."

"That's really not another thing. That's basically the same thing."

"No, it's a new thing, Futureman, this smell. Do you not realize that we are dirtier and scummier than ever before? That a funk now grows on us that would make Maine herself gag."

Futureman rubbed his arms up and down in the wet wind. Once Applejack had gone, he sniffed his hands.

> The figures of the past go cloaked.
> They walk in mist and rain and snow
> And go, go slowly, but they go.
>   -Wallace Stevens

Even when engaged in torture, civilizations must remain civil. Take, for example, the pyramid spike of medieval Europe in which the victim would be hogtied, suspended in air and rotated like a corkscrew at the anus on the point of the spike. Not civilized behavior. As torture methods go, by far the most civilized one is the famed Chinese water torture – the drip. Drip. Drip. Drip. Drip. Drip. Drip. Drip. Drip. Drip. The drip is not direct affront. The passive/aggressive banality of water torture grows madness like a Petri dish, until wildfire rage controls and destroys all that is left of the ravaged mind.

It was all around him now. The drip. It was all around him still. It piddled down his moustache, filling his lips with gutter sediment. His neck felt like the inside of a gutted oyster. Gritty and humid. The spaces in his crotch had become as rotten and sodden as the esophagus of an eel. His leg hairs were knotted and his socks squished infernally in his concrete boots with the fetid sullenness of a midnight bowel movement.

Applejack was miserable. Wallowing, spirit-infected. Infested. At least it kept him company, as he walked through the muted, muffled forests where orange was no longer orange but muddy brown, and gold drained into the ditches like melted bronze. Maple red marred, dun, like confederate blood, muddled with the futility of failing arms once upraised – a brother's duel. The sky could no longer give off a true color either. All day long it spoke lies about dusk and dawn.

> The heart is deceitful and desperately wicked above all things.
> Who can know it?
> -Jeremiah 17.9

Be positive, Applejack thought, trying to regain some fortitude, stumbling and sliding along the deteriorated Trail. *Remember why you came out here. It's hard work, and that's okay. That's okay.* Mud clung to his boots like swollen leeches. *Funny – I almost died for lack of water in Vermont, now my brain and body are drowning in it. It's true, it either comes all at once or not at all. Why are things like that? We are we like that. Fickle. Temporal. See-through. Our ability to remember things as they happened evades, shifts. We pit memories against each other. Saying things about things that have never happened. Twisting nuggets, granules into lies – it's more exciting that way-when telling versions of stories, we are vindicated, glorified, Odysseus to ourselves. Sometimes, I get so far away from the truth that I can't even recall what was true in the first place – sometimes – certainly can't feel it anymore. Once I was so thirsty I wanted to die – I wanted other people to die, like those bastards in Vermont who wouldn't slow down their luxury death-traps – can't pump the brakes when your star's rising. But that's not real anymore, like summer and winter. In the sweltering heat, you can't even imagine what it would be like to feel the cold snow, amnesia settles in the feet, and when it's cold can't remember a shining sun for a day of sweaty, stuck-together knees. Bees and gardens growing, granny weeding on her knees. But all they care about is money, anyways, that's what's up in verdant Vermont. Green mountain boys can pucker up and kiss my shiny slimy railroad mooner. Gotta have their 24 karat leather interior, gotta build their modern eco-friendly home with the oriental waterfall pool-speeding by in their fifty-thousand dollar prisons, looking at me and Futureman like we're trash on the side of the road. We've got college degrees, you fools – graduated with honors, you pricks! What do you think about that? Or are you too busy preening your – whoa. OK. Hang on. Be positive, remember? Gotta get through this. Pick myself up. No one's doing it for me. That's for damn sure.*

He straddled a sweet gum that had fallen across the Trail. Threw his right leg over and touched back down on the syrupy ground. The accusations were back, clinging in the tops of the trees. Maybe they had never left.

> Dawn-sniffing revenant,
> Plodder through midnight rain,
> Question me again.
> -Seamus Heaney

There had been a time when the rain came down to make everything better. Cooled the air until steam came up from the ground. In southern Vermont and Massachusetts Applejack and Futureman had made a game of it, running the last few miles of the day in the downpour, barreling through the puddles and ponds, unaware and unconcerned – like children. Joy fell in those early morning torrents that pounded on the rain fly. New shades of green always followed the rain and covered everything with quiet. But now, sick mist painted everything with that shade of death that hangs around funeral parlors. *And you know what really burns me up are these pseudo-hippies, Spirit Watchers and Restless Wanderers that talk about prancin' around in this slop and act like they're gonna really enjoy it, like they're connected to some higher cosmic entity – Water Essence or whatever – at one with all things. Crap. Too much Thoreau in their freshman lit. class – as if that guy even knew what he was talking about. Walden, what a joke, living a couple miles from his mom's place the whole time, and he goes on like he's retired to this remote wilderness camp – really roughing it, took his clothes over to her house when they needed washing! What a croc, transcendentalism. Chhhfff – please. Get a backbone – you ethereal stargazers. Don't think you can come hop around out here – or wherever for that matter – Alaska, Arizona – just because you've got a Sierra Club bumper sticker and you read an artical in Backpacker about the Lost Hideaways of the Blue Ridge. And, oh – when Trey and Troy and Hunter – all those, all those other guys with their hip, outdoorsy names and their shiny North Face vests used to come back from their little expeditions and talk that nauseating, neo-beatnik, John Muir talk – I just wanted to – and, oh – of course, of course all those patchouli dancing-bears hippy girls were loving it. I should have said something, I should have told them where they could stick their D-rings and climbing gear and then they would've been – then they – uhh, heh – hey. Hold up.*
Positive. Positive.

Applejack stopped in his tracks. He took a seat on a moss-covered rock and put his head between his hands. "What is wrong with me?" The noise of his voice reverberated through the dying hollow. "Man, pull it together. This is sickness and you're a really mean person. What is the point of ripping and rehashing? Lazy anger."

He walked on through the haze, steam rising off his back.

Rain falls into the open eyes of the dead
Again again with its pointless sound
When the moon finds them they are the color of everything
-William Stanley

"You look tired," Futureman said.

"I am tired. Tired of myself. Know what I mean?" Applejack said.

"Yeah, I know what you mean." "Actually...what do you mean?"

"I've been burning off fumes, man."

"Fumes?"

"Weird stuff inside my head, memories and grudges I thought I had let go of. Long gone. But they're not gone."

"Like anger at injustice, or what?"

"More like – malice. Yeah, malice is the best way to put it. Hatred toward humankind."

"Well, what better place for it. Whole earth seems to be bubbling up."

"It's just hard to see yourself for who you are, sometimes. It's really ugly."

"Don't worry. It'll all come out in the end."

"Reckoning day, huh?"

"Restoration day."

They were quiet for a time. Vapor like gauze sorted through a patch of sweating ferns.

"Hey buddy." Futureman reached out and tapped Applejack on the knee.

"Yep?"

"Nobody likes this stuff."

"You mean the rain or –"

"Nobody likes this stuff."

Rain is grace; rain is the sky condescending to the earth;
without rain, there would be no life.
-John Updike

V

A star massive and dense enough will have such a strong gravitational force that even its own light cannot escape from it. As this happens, the star grows dimmer, appearing red to the distant observer. It is shrinking to a critical radius. In this event, light cones bend inward, unable to escape gravity's pull. Light – the fastest thing in existence! And if it cannot escape the pull, what can? Surrounding the black hole is a space-time periphery called the event horizon. Warning boundary, last chance. Pull out now or disappear forever.

Room 113 at the Best Western on the busy interchange between Troutville, Daleville and Cloverdale was a black hole, and Applejack and Futureman were sleeping on its event horizon in the woods below Cold Mountain, eighteen miles from the throbbing center. They were unaware of the light growing redder around them.

Futureman sat upright in the washy glim. The strands of his hair (floating in forces) had been churned by seeping dreams. Something was amiss. The ground seemed to be rolling under him like a caterpillar. He popped his jaw and peered into the delirium. Trees moved in slow motion, bending away from the wind.

Am I awake?

Futureman poked Applejack, relieved to find tactile reality at the tip of his finger. Their new friend Flavius, a Texan, was still asleep at the other end of the shelter. They wondered if they should wake him to let him know where they were going but they didn't know where they were going. They ate cold oatmeal instead and blundered into the fog toward Room 113.

Yesterday, as was custom, they had watched pessimism drip down onto the sopping-wet, Blue Ridge bog. Countless weekend hikers passed by on vacation, complaining.

Applejack and Futureman met Flavius at lunchtime, standing in the rain, eating a pack of crackers. Flavius looked like he was from Cordoba or Istanbul. Part Black, part Indian, part Mediterranean. But he was from Texas. He had rug-thick hair, full lips and high, chiseled cheeks. Soaked through like a wet cat, his shoes had holes in them, but he was smiling – signs of a hearty thruhiker.

"Applejack and Futureman. I heard of you two," he said.

"Who are you?" Applejack asked.

"Who I am is of no importance." He stretched out his hands. "What I do is. And what I do is BESEECH and ENTREAT."

Applejack frowned.

"Name's *Flavius*. Beseecher. Entreater." Wilding eyes brimmed with sarcasm. This was a man who showed teeth to the rain.

Futureman dug out a folded bagel, smeared some cream cheese and raisins on it (a Trail delicacy) and held it out to the stranger. "Well, entreater, permit us to offer you a kind gesture in this, the wettest part of our universe?"

Flavius smiled and rubbed his hands.

"We're headed to Cold Mountain for the night," Applejack offered.

"That's exactly where I'm headed myself." Invitation accepted.

Back in the morning fog of the present, Applejack and Futureman were lost again, tramping down the wrong paths – old overgrown logging and hunting trails – winding down the mountain. Trail was a bygone conclusion.

"Where are we?" Futureman asked.

"According to the map, if we keep walking down we'll find a road, and eventually, we'll get – somewhere." He stumbled forward into the brush, shrugging off the suspicion that a die had been cast.

When Flavius woke up, he found himself alone. *No, not another wet and lonely day.* He packed and set out to beseech his new friends.

Subtle yet strong forces were acting as gravity. The sky was still the wet diaper it had been for two weeks. A strong October chill now accompanied it, and they'd had enough. For a couple of days, Futureman had felt an ache in his gut from bad water. Now, with the prospect of a lazier, softer existence, he took to the complaints of a hypochondriac. He was near death, in need of a bed and two pizzas.

The interchange proved a bastion of conveniences – Old Country BUFFET, Cracker Barrel, gas station quikmarts, hot-lamp pizza racks, motels-telltale signs of *Truckerville*, where everyone's a stranger just passing through, a perfect place to disappear forever.

Inside room 113, Applejack (dry and cozy) lay on his bed and clicked the TV channels one by one. Unable to decide on a show, he threw the remote to Futureman.

"I don't want the responsibility," Futureman said. "You'll be sitting there judging me while I choose something." He flung it it back. It sailed past Applejack's head and landed between the bed and the wall. Applejack looked at it. Looks like it's gonna stay there for a while.

"I don't know, Sharon. I just keep thinking that he's not being honest with me. I never would've asked him to leave his wife, if I'd known he'd go cheating on me with his bimbo secretary. I couldn't…I just couldn't… bear it."

"Marie-Margaret, listen to me. You've got to take your power and put it into something good – like you. *You* owe it to *you*. And think of your kids, Chloe-Joe and Susie-Jade. They deserve better. You need to find yourself a trial lawyer – a real man! Who can send the kids to boarding school and give you everything you always ever wanted."

"Regardless of what they call it," Applejack said, chewing on his tongue, "every movie on Lifetime is a variation on the same plot."

"You watch a lot of Lifetime, do you?"

Applejack finally reached for the remote and began clicking.

Judge Judy.

Breast enhancement on MTV: "They look so real. Josh is going to so freak out!"

QVC: "You! Have! Ninety! Seconds! Left! Before the last! Blue moon pearl! With dyrothymate cunoneum sapphires! Is GONE!"

Stomach stapling documentary: "I've tried every diet imaginable (for two or three days). Nothing will work for me (they all require exercise). This is my last chance for a miracle (I'm glad I don't live in Nigeria)."

Commercial.

Explosions on TNT.

Commercial.

SPRAYON hair.

Pregnancy workout. "That's it, ladies. You're husbands will want to make another one!"

Wild (blurred nudity) on E!

Commercial.

Commercial.

Game show. (People watching people watching other people win things.)

Commercial.

"Get the perfect tan in seconds! With our scientifically proven easy-on formula! The chances are really good that it's probably totally safe!"

Easy Glider Max 3000 with bonus gift ponytail hat, "ABSOLUTELY-LUTELY-LUTELY FREE!"

Commercial.

Chuck Norris.

Commercial.

TBN: "Celebrating 6,000 years of broadcasting in the name of (what's his name again, oh yeah) Jesus." All donations go to the personal wardrobe funds of the hosts.

Commercial.

Applejack dropped the remote. "Didn't we see a Blockbuster down the road on the way into town?"

"I think I like where you're going with this," Futureman said.

"You figure they got a VCR we could use?"

"We're gonna find out."

Frank the manager crossed his arms. "You want me to do what?"

"I see that you do not rent VCR's to the public, but perhaps you have one in the back we could use," Futureman said.

"Nnnn –"

"You need to understand, sir. We've come a long, long way to watch some movies. I'm sick and my friend here –"

"Yeah," Frank said warily. "We don't normally –"

Applejack put his elbows on the counter. "Frank, we are avid, avid fans of the cinema. Not your average renters. And we haven't seen a movie in months and all this rain has made us a little crazy –"

Frank was cracking but he needed more.

"OK. Think of our lives as a movie," Futureman said. "And right now, this scene, this is the part of the movie where you give us a VCR. This is the climax, Frank."

"Now that's ridiculous enough for me to say yes."

Frank found a tape player in the back of the store that wasn't being used. "I could get in trouble for this, you understand?"

"Frank, this looks like the beginning of a beautiful friendship," Applejack said.

It made Frank smile.

In the thirties, people got dressed up to go to the movies, as if they knew that the golden age of cinema was about to begin. Men in black ties with flashlights showed the clientele to their seats. Even the popcorn machines were fancy. Hollywood was an event and the pictures proved it. *42nd Street. King Kong. Swing Time. Gone With the Wind. The Philadelphia Story. The Adventures of Robin Hood. Mr. Smith Goes to Washington.* Exaggerated goodness on display, the way life should be. Adventure and heroism, nobility and grace, imagination and sacrifice.

But the forties brought a war to the world and *film noir* to Hollywood, the black cinema. Pessimism, anxiety and suspicion materialized onto film. The new noir sets were dark and gloomy with alleyways, rundown motel rooms, disoriented visuals, spiraling cigarette smoke, bent camera angles. Borrowing from German Expressionism of the 20's, directors painted life with a darker hue. The spill of that demonic Nazi regime had stained the world and, though the movies spoke of a courage that could set the bad world right – *Casablanca, Citizen Kane, Arsenic and Old Lace, The Big Sleep, It's a Wonderful Life* – still, there was the constant shadow of human evil.

The decline of the golden age came with the downturn of the media moguls that had controlled Hollywood – MGM, Warner Brothers, Paramount, Universal, and Columbia. Ironically, our government became suspicious of opinionated conglomerates (many of which were Jewish run), and the Supreme Court forced the studios to diversify their stockholders in an attempt to crack apart the emerging Hollywood monolith. So the other monopolies – Seven Arts, Kinney Corporation, Gulf Western, MCA and Coca Cola – bought up the shares and added "Hollywood divisions" to their already massive empires.

So fell the movie giants from their heights as King Kong had, and the classic period came to an end. The constellation of post-war ideals began to melt and the mythology of the black-and-white perfect world? Gone. Was it beauty killed the beast?

"Okay, so you choose two movies, and I'll choose two movies. We'll get one veto each," Applejack said.

"Fair enough."

Futureman selected *Lawrence of Arabia*. Applejack, *Casablanca*. Even if they'd wanted to veto these, it would have been embarrassing – something only a redneck would do. Futureman accepted Applejack's second pick: *Airplane*. But Futureman's –

"No. Not a chance."

"C'mon, it's about the land that time forgot. These guys are in a balloon, and get blown off course to an island in the ocean where giant crabs and birds –"

"No. It's not gonna happen. Veto. What else you got?"

"Alright. *Armageddon*."

"*Armageddon*!"

"Yeah, what's wrong with –"

"Michael Cliché Bay – the corniest director in Hollywood – is what's wrong with it."

"It's about world unity blowing up a globe-killing meteor. World unity! Bruce Willis! C'mon, it's the one time Bay's slow motion and force-you-to-cry music actually works. We need this right now," he whined. "Plus, you already used your veto."

"Fine."

A strange fusion occurred in the room. Lights faded, static danced, plotlines and images congealed – deserts, outer space, airports and Northern Africa – all merged together in 113.

Lawrence saves the desert and himself, or maybe it's that he loses himself and saves the desert – or does he save everything and then lose everything? It's a movie but it's also more. And when Rick Blaine says to the dame, "You get on that plane," he was choosing revolution over love, right? Captain Renault could tell you – in that moment where he and Bogey disappear into the fog, the beginning of a beautiful friendship – that it's always about revolution. And we need revolution when we've been down in the mud and kicked in the face with an iron boot. WAR, what's it good for? Drinking problems, I guess. Wars are like meteors hurling towards the earth, those freaking meteors! What's strange is that if it weren't for deep-ocean oilmen and nuclear weapons the earth might not have a prayer. But it does, here in Hollywoodland.

A whirlpool of Debbie cake wrappers surrounded Applejack. After depositing a morning junk-food beefcake of earth-shattering magnitude, Futureman emerged from the bathroom, victim of beer, candy bars, potato chips, pizza, peanuts, cheeseburgers, egg rolls and ice cream. He wiped his forehead. *I've got wrought-iron guts leftover from cow-field Africa, but every stomach has its limits.*

"You okay?" Applejack asked. "You don't look so good."

"Yeah, just need some fresh air," Futureman said. "Plus, we're out of movies."

"What shall we do?"

"I don't know. Get twelve more?"

It sounded like a vault opening when Futureman cracked the door. Moist air rushed in, blowing plastic junk wrappers across the carpet.

"Looks like you guys have constructed a wonderful mess for yourselves." A bushy head poked through the crack.

"Flavius?"

"It is I!" He entered the room. "You guys vanished."

Futureman fumbled for an excuse. "We can't really – how'd you know we were – not that we were trying to –"

"Hey, I understand. At first I thought that maybe I smelled or something. Then I realized that we've all smelled like Uncle Herschel dumping in his overalls for quite some time now. So, when I saw this place, it made sense to me. You have to get dry somehow."

"Glad you found us," Futureman said. "Come, get dry. The festival has started. The films await and you are invited."

"Films?"

During the fifties and early sixties the movie biz hit a snag. The golden age of television had begun. People everywhere were becoming truly acquainted with the indoors for the first time. But, Hollywood soldiered on with *All About Eve, The Apartment, A Streetcar Named Desire, On the Waterfront, To Kill a Mockingbird, Rebel Without A Cause.* The pictures announced a coming shift in the status quo. A generation still clinging to its caucus of decency, was on the brink of breaking free. *Invasion of the Body Snatchers. The Searchers. Jailhouse Rock. Vertigo. Touch of Evil.* The sexual revolution that had been simmering since the Roaring Twenties was now about to boil. *Some Like It Hot* was exactly that, with a sensual and beckoning young Marilyn Monroe. *Psycho* boiled with a scandalous starlet named Janet Leigh. *The Graduate* and *The Hustler* smoldered. Then came the dark satires of a brave new world – *The Manchurian Candidate, Dr. Strangelove.* Hollywood's fascination with the Apocalypse begins with *Night of the Living Dead* and *Planet of the Apes. Rosemary's Baby* brings the antichrist into the apartment building next door. *2001: A Space Odyssey* opens up the cosmos and teaches us to both fear and desire Artificial Intelligence. A generation is defined by the freedom of the open road in *Easy Rider* – first one of the day belongs to D.H. Lawrence! That dictator, the human conscience, was slowly unwinding his grip and the future looked hopelessly bright.

In his life, Flavius had been too busy exploring actual people, places and events. He had not spent very much time watching projections of them. Consequently, he had plenty of experience with empirical reality but possessed an uncritical and horrid taste in movies.

Futureman vetoed *Teaching Mrs. Tingle*. Applejack vetoed *Snake Eyes*. Flavius' third selection was unfortunately untouchable. Surely, it couldn't be bad enough to bring the worst of Hollywood past two vetoes.

Flavius laid *The Substitute* on the counter, Tom Berenger at the B end of a long and underwhelming career.

"Do you have a substitute for this, Flavius?" Applejack asked.

"This is how democracy works, my friend."

Flavius didn't see any use for vetoes, so Futureman's *Aliens* and Applejack-'s *The Edge* were approved without discussion. On the way back to room 113, they stopped for a snack at the Country Buffet.

"Want one?" Flavius said, holding up a chicken liver.

"That's all right. I'll stick to my mashed potatoes and country fried steak," Futureman said.

"So what was that 'entreat and beseech' business you were going on about back in the mountains?" Applejack asked.

"Oh yes. Those were the words a wise prophet once said to me," Flavius said.

"A prophet?"

"I met him a week ago. He was giving me a hitch into town. On our way, he spoke to me in metaphors. *The wind is voice. The sun is burning wisdom. Trees are watchers.* That kind of stuff."

"And he told you –"

"– that if I was to capture their deep ancient wisdom, I needed to *entreat* and *beseech*."

"Beseech what exactly?" Futureman asked.

"Entreat where?" Applejack said.

"Guys, you are not listening and you obviously haven't opened your mind to the forest within the forest. The one that lives – the ORGANISM. Where bark is flesh. Tree teaches. Soil moves. I'm telling you, age old philosophies are floating down out of the sky like feathers, friends. And where have you been? What have you been doing with your lives out here? Not entreating and beseeching, clearly. Shame on you. Forgive my frankness, but since this wisdom has been passed down to me, as a disciple, I am bound by duty to pass it on to others. So, take your place. Lay hold of your destiny. Do it! Before it goes away forever." Flavius stuffed more livers into his mouth and said, "EMSTREAK and VISEETH."

You won't last seventeen hours, when killer aliens with acid for blood surround you, so the marine says. And he's been trained for moments like these. Or has he? Our best weapon against terror is violence. Or is it? It's the first substitute for wisdom, but it prevents us from doing the one thing that will save us: thinking. The world is in serious peril if we stop thinking but these days there seems to be no time for it. The invasion rains down like a flood. We're becoming extinct. Our shells aren't armor. Our blood isn't acid. It doesn't kill our enemies when spilled. Minds and bodies are being snatched away, two by two, and impregnated with angry alien babies, breeding alien ferocity into future CEO's, Congressmen, roadster mechanics and preachers. Yet somehow that small child survived in the hallway of monsters (and she didn't even have a gun). And what one human can do, another can do. *Say it.* How do you make fire from ice? Simple. Mold the ice into a lens and channel the sun's rays. Think, think, think. The rabbit is unafraid because he is smarter than the panther. Away with violent remedies. Hold fast. Salvation is just seventeen hours away.

"A materialized beseechment looks somewhat like a beached whale," Flavius said, yanking open the curtains to let in the morning light.

Futureman cracked his eyes and churned his body into half-motion. Even the dark sky outside was too bright.

"What are you talking about?"

"It was in my dream. A beseechment came up out of the ocean and beached itself on my gelatinous brain. That's when I knew what it meant. Whales die if they don't get back into the water. Don't you see? We've got to get out of here. We've been dry far too long."

"You've been here a day," Futureman said.

"A day too long! We were never supposed to be here in the first place. Get your gear. Wake up Applejack."

Applejack put a pillow over his head.

Flavius packed alone, but he didn't stop entreating.

Shut up, ye bard of age old wisdom. Close the curtains. Be gone, truthteller.

"I'm leaving. You should too, both of you, before you get trapped."

The theory of general relativity provides for the existence of certain "bridges" through time and space. Albert Einstein and Nathan Rosen realized this in 1935. They named them "Einstein-Rosen bridges." We call them wormholes. A wormhole is basically a space-time tube that creates a shortcut from one point in space to another, connecting distant regions of space-time in the flash of a second. It is a theory used frequently in science fiction movies. Real scientists tell us that a wormhole has yet to be sufficiently witnessed by anyone human. But how do they know?

Traditionally it has been thought that wormholes can only exist for brief periods of time, but more recent research suggests that highly advanced civilizations could possibly use something like a pillar to sustain the wormhole. Physicists conjecture that the pillar would be made of an "exotic matter" (catchy, isn't it?) which could prevent a wormhole from collapsing in on itself, thereby prolonging the period of time a traveler could move through it.

A wormhole spit Flavius back out onto the Trail, where he felt again the redemption of rain, where he lifted his heels and resumed his march toward the Tennessee border.

A small drib of exotic matter remained in the corner of 113. It would have to be enough. Its incandescent *elan vital* grew as daylight pressed through the half-open curtains.

Futureman looked out the window at the plasma smattering the gray sidewalk.

"Maybe we should go."

A tinge of edema skirted the lining of Applejack's stomach (causing him to feel strangely as though he had eaten three boxes of Swiss Cake rolls, two tubs of ice cream, three pizzas, five plates of Old Country Buffet, two bags of mesquite barbeque potato chips and twenty-two miniature Reese's Cups).

"My stomach's not feeling too good right now," said Applejack. (This was the same man, mind you, who had recently walked for twenty days on soggy feet with open sores pulsating between his testicles.) "I think I caught a bug. Maybe the sun will come out tomorrow."

Annie! "You're right. It will come out tomorrow. We should get some more movies," Futureman said. The exotic matter dimmed.

Cinema in the 50's and 60's had taken a hit. So, in the 70's, the biz began focusing on action-packed sagas and razzle-dazzle special effects. Leading the fight to save Hollywood was a 40-foot man-eating shark and a galaxy far, far away. And that's how the summer blockbuster came into existence.

Spielberg and Lucas were fresh out of film school, each man armed with his own powder keg of potential – sense of vision, control, creativity, keen eye for casting, and ambition. Walking in their footsteps, a new generation of directors was born.

Ticket prices rose from $1.65 in '71 to $2.50 by '78. Movie budgets doubled from $5 million to $11 million. Markets were created for Hollywood products. City movie palaces were replaced by suburban multiplexes. Celebrity magazines appeared on the newsstands. New film technologies dazzled consumers.

They called it the "Renaissance of Hollywood." The new generation of directors took more risks with bigger budgets. They left the traditional studios and traveled the globe to find their sets – on location shooting. Trucks were loaded, planes were packed. They filled the streets of New York, Paris and Sydney. The deserts of Tunisia and Nevada. Somewhere floating in the Atlantic. The rainforests of Venezuela. The streets of Hong Kong. The Australian outback.

Yet the cinema still reflected the aftermath of political disillusionment – Viet Nam on the nightly news, Watergate, the Munich Olympics shootout and a growing energy crisis. These images shaped the American psyche. The public was losing faith in the institutions that had once upon a time protected their dreams.

And the movies tell the story. *All the President's Men. A Clockwork Orange. M*A*S*H. Deliverance. Sleeper. Chinatown. One Flew Over the Cuckoo's Nest. The Deer Hunter. Apocalypse Now.*

But there was another way to deal with the disillusionment. Create a distraction. Build a diversion. The movies tell that story, as well. *Enter the Dragon. American Graffiti. Young Frankenstein. Nashville. The Rocky Horror Picture Show. Close Encounters of the Third Kind. Halloween. Saturday Night Fever.*

It worked. (Who, after all, *really* loves the smell of napalm in the morning?) Decadence moved in: cocaine, the Travolta strut, one-night stands, tight pants, roller skates and disco lights. The war had a new face. Boredom and convention were the enemies.

"You guys have watched eight movies in two days," Frank said.

"We told you we were starved."

"So what's it gonna be?"

There are a lot of categories to choose from these days:

Non-fiction, fiction, feature, animated, talkies, silent, serials, shorts and underground films. Classic, cult and British films. Family, action, adventure, comedy, gangster, drama and epic films. Historical, horror, B, science fiction, western, war, musical and revisionist films. Noir, romance, slapstick, satire, buddy and caper films. Disaster, detective, chase, fantasy and fallen woman films. Military, espionage, jungle, legal, parody, police, prison and political films. Religious, sports, slasher and swashbuckler films. Guy films. Chick flicks. Educational films. And doc(or mock)umentaries.

"How about a sexual erotic film," Debby said. "I bet you guys could use one of those."

Frank's assistant, Debby, had been stacking movies the last two days, keeping to herself, trying to avoid inappropriate eye contact with the customers. By the third day, she'd finally worked up the nerve to break the silence.

Applejack and Futureman were paralyzed. Frank shot Debby a look.

She changed the subject. "You guys are from Knoxville. I remember that you guys are from Knoxville." She smiled.

"Yep, we are. Good memory," Applejack said.

"I been to Knoxville," Debby said. "The Mouse's Ear is in Knoxville. I'll bet you guys miss that place. Who wouldn't?"

The Mouse's Ear is an 'exotic sports bar' shoved between a greasy car wash and a discount food store.

"Well, Debby, I can't really say that I miss it. I've never actually been there," Applejack said. "Have you, Futureman? Have you been to the Mouse's Ear?"

"No. I haven't, Applejack. I've not been there…yet."

Frank cleared his throat and gave Debby another look. "Uh, Deb, there are some boxes in the back that need to be broken down."

She glanced over her shoulder and shrugged as she walked down the aisle.

"Sorry about that fellas," Frank said.

"No worries. It's good to be reminded of home," Applejack said.

Given the present state of things, Applejack chose the film *Limbo*. No veto. Futureman tried to choose *The Land That Time Forgot* again, explaining that it was more about science than monsters.

"No No No! And I'm not using that as my veto!"

"Okay, *Conan the Destroyer*."

Veto.

Alright. *Clash of the Titans*. The perfect compromise – monsters fighting in classical Greece. They agreed on *Blade Runner* and *On The Waterfront* and dropped the movies on the counter.

Frank liked the picks. "Will we see you tomorrow then?"

"One way or other, Frank, we'll be back," Futureman said.

"Hey, of all the gin joints in all the world," said Frank.

The blockbuster motif created by Spielberg and Lucas in the seventies turbo-charged the new decade. *Empire Strikes Back, Raiders of the Lost Ark, Return of the Jedi and E.T* set the tone for the 1980's.

New special effects capabilities made blowing things up more impressive and more expensive. The importance of a good script diminished as production costs shifted from writing to creating. Ticket prices rose from $3 dollars in '81 to over $4 dollars by '89. Annual movie budgets rose to $18 million. With its attention turned to bottom-line operations, Hollywood searched for that movie with all the right ingredients: dazzling effects, sound mastery, money-making soundtrack, potential sequel and over-pumped, underfed stars who could wear their salaries well.

Of course, there was the occasional commentary film – *Raging Bull* or *Full Metal Jacket.* But overall, the verdict was in: folks were tired of the pessimism. It was time to focus on our own individual suburban empires. It was time for video games and Reaganomics. The great fortresses of evil were across the sea. Let freedom ring and capitalism flourish!

Blockbusters, movies for the people, spread the zeitgeist and cheer with *Tootsie, Gremlins, The Terminator, A Fish Called Wanda, Who Framed Roger Rabbit?, Field of Dreams* and *Top Gun.*

But in the 90's the blockbuster evolved to scold the land of plenty for its Cold War euphoria. Angst was back, giving birth to grunge, the 24/7 coffee buzz and the mainstream indie film. Yet the blockbuster still carried the national narrative. *GoodFellas. Silence of the Lambs. Unforgiven. Schindler's List. T2. Pulp Fiction. L.A. Confidential. American Beauty. Fargo. Dead Man Walking. The Matrix.*

As the industry looked beyond Y2K to our present digital age, moguls shifted to computer graphics and online distribution, hoping to sell more than ever – and sell they have. Movie budgets have risen to over $200 million. Ticket prices are $10 in many places. Actors have the power to change international diplomacy. They are demigods. Hollywood is the new Mount Olympus. Common mortals claw one another for her scraps.

The kraken has been released but we are caught in limbo. Medusa stares at a world turning to stone. Two heads are dueling, running with Dioskolos. We are building androids. Soon there will be android hunters because we put our evil nature into them. Evil-natured robots – who would have thought? But this technology can be used for good. The golden owl Bubo, built in a mechanic shop on Olympus, may offer some wisdom – may save us, yet. If we can just escape the dollar signs but when will this happen? That question hangs in the air like a coconut. Maybe tomorrow, maybe never. We could have been contenders. Could have been somebody, instead, we're – wait – not yet. Fly down, O Pegasus! Unleash your wings. Stir up some dust on the earth. The world will recognize the sacrifice. The unions will rise. The people will speak. Revolution is about to begin. It is always – about to begin.

Come and stay a day, or better yet, just come and stay, 113 suggested.

"We should go," Futureman said. "Should we go?"

"There's no choice," Applejack said. "We have to go. We've been reduced to nothing. If it weren't for Flavius leaving some of that matter behind, we would be done for."

"Well then. Time to rise from the dust. Begin. Again."

"A free rental on me," Frank pleaded as they put their movies on the counter.

"Not today, Frank. Here's your VCR. Burn it. See ya Deb. Stop thinking about freaky sex all the time. We found a wormhole out of here. Gotta take it before it closes in on us for good."

Frank felt conflicted. He had always hoped Hollywood had the power to pro-duce moral fiber, he had just never seen it.

It was raining outside, like always. Their hiking shoes had been lying next to the door the entire time, covered in mud, ready. Waiting.

VI

The sun was still a stubborn child playing hide and seek behind the clouds, counting to one million-billion, but the sweet smell of sugarberry, the odorous bark of the black tupelo and the fresh scent of cottonwood were like herbal medicines, curing mind-body-soul.

Crossing Tinker Creek, the sound of trickling water felt vaguely like home. The steeps on Tinker Ridge tumbled down through the forest forcing them out of their stupor. Applejack and Futureman found their way through Angel's Gap as the crane tops above the trees sprung into the sky. They crawled like curious toddlers out onto Tinker and looked down the sheer walls into the val-ley at the low clouds of black-pitch mortar bursts and gray smoke rising to fill their lungs. Shifting. Lowlands disappearing into sea breath.

The Trail – half-mile ellipsis of a divine plow stroke – horseshoed to McAfee Knob, considered by many to be the best view in Virginia. Mountain heath spread across the vale, lichen holding to rock like red and white splotch-es of paint, building biomass patiently to bring in the horsetails. Red maples and white pines fought for a view at the edges of the exposed granite peninsu-la.

This was a momentous day, indeed – a could-have-been glorious day. Bob-by's truck was parked somewhere on the other side of McAfee Knob. And seventy miles to the south, another truck was idling with Futureman's parents inside. Family. They were all meeting up at the Rendezvous Motel in Pearis-burg. It would be the first reunion since Applejack and Futureman left home four long months ago.

They heard Bobby before they saw him.

Applejack hurled a coyote call into the air.

Bobby answered, a good hundred yards away.

Futureman yodeled.

Bobby yodeled back. Just around the turn now.

He had committed to growing his beard with them until they returned home – a tangible connection to their journey. It had grown Arab – fast, three inches thick already. Jet-black hair flipped out on the sides of his face and frizzed on top like an unfinished bird's nest.

There they stood, worlds of crooked trail, rock, root, mountain and plain no longer separating them. They embraced, the zealous hug of old friends.

Futureman had known Bobby since he was eight. Bobby's family lived on a 186-acre farm in Lafollette, Tennessee. There were nine ponds, hills, valleys, thick forests, open fields and a house built by simple hands. A house heated by wood, insulated by carpet and shingles and founded on stone. The farm had cows, horses, chickens, peacocks and rotating seasons of dogs and near the house sat an old dilapidated barn frequented by owls, snakes and bats. In short, it was a boy's paradise.

Futureman had spent much of his youth there, milking cows in the early morning, running the dogs at noon, frog-gigging the ponds in the heat of the day, pitching through the woods in the late afternoon and riding horses into the sunset. Futureman and Bobby had grown up together.

Bobby was a man ruled by order but haunted by chaos. Necessity had taught him how to drive a stick shift by the age of ten. By senior high, he had built two cars from scratch, helped raise four siblings, built two homes with his dad and managed a local fish hatchery and restaurant. Those exacting years had forced him to lock into a hard grapple with fate. Suddenly, he found himself a prodigal running from responsibility; for a time, desiring the pigsty of a lesser existence – one fed by the phantasm of psychedelics, the defiance of booze and the electricity of danger. Thus, he stood many a night, drunk and cowboy-legged, on the roof of a car. And thus, he jumped three sheets to the wind off of pale moonlit cliffs.

One night after a high school football game, Bobby was arrested and thrown into a jailhouse to think about the course of his life. That was the night it ripped through the concrete slab and came to rest beside him there in the jail. Grace. He saw it in his mother. Grace. He saw it on his farm. He saw grace between the bars of the cell. He felt the offering – the rich, undeserved cloak of a peasant carpenter-king. It was a visitation. He took off his dirty dregs and stood naked before him. The Daystar. The Christ who had exchanged his own fine robes for old rags. And Bobby said, "I will serve him."

"Well, I'll be. I never thought you'd make it here," he said to them.

Months before Katahdin, Bobby had committed himself to them and their trip. He'd pledged to do their leg work and send them their food, and even after two months on the Trail, Bobby still offered his counsel, ran the show and gave correction. That was Bobby. Applejack and Futureman loved him for it.

That was why it was going to be hard to carry out their plan, the plan they had conceived deep inside the gravitated tangles of Room 113. They were dreading it, but they knew they had to tell him.

The plan
-To "yellow blaze." A truck ride down the Trail to Pearisburg, skipping near-on seventy miles of Trail.

The raison d'etre
-To make up for lost days
-According to schedule, they were supposed to have been in Pearisburg already to meet Futureman's family for the reunion. Due to mysterious 'stomach illnesses' they'd come up short.

The logic (justification)
-If we don't catch up, we'll get caught in the deep December freeze.
-It's not a big deal, anyway. We've already hiked over a thousand miles. We started in Maine. We're not purists. What difference does a few miles make?

Bobby failed to grasp the logic, too pure to be swayed by their pragmatic gymnastics. He was firm when he suggested that, after the reunion, he take them back to McAfee Knob – *pick up where you left off.*

"That's okay, Bobby. We don't mind."

"But you've come so far. You're almost there. Don't quit now," Bobby said.

"We're not quitting, Bobby," they assured him.

"This is important. You can't do this."

"It's nothing compared to the whole. It's okay."

"No! It's not okay. The whole thing stands together or falls together. This would be like quitting."

"No. Quitting is like going home after you get to Monson. This is yellow blazing, a technicality we're prepared to live with." They gritted their teeth. Golden platitudes of sophistry slithered through. Utilitarian subversions.

Many hikers yellow blaze at some point or other. A mile here, a mile there, like shaving small pieces off a marble masterpiece. But Applejack and Futureman were flat-out skipping sixty-seven miles of Trail and they had used their weary-warped, homesick brains to concoct a palatable justification. Inevitably and finally, they had come to the end of themselves, the rock-bottom trough of *ad nauseum.* And in that low-born moment, it was alright to disappoint their best friend – as long as it got them out of the mess they had made.

Bobby stared long and hard at the gray wet pavement. "Well, I'm shaving my beard then. You are no longer thruhikers. You'll have a section left to do when you get to Springer. You're only section hikers."

"Okay." Applejack swallowed.

"Why is it OK? I still don't understand," Bobby said.

"Because we're not sure we understand anymore, either," Futureman said.

A sigh, a mournful whippoorwill's cry, followed them as they made their way toward Pearisburg around the lonesome mountain curves. Her dirge slid sadly over the edge and into the ravines below.

"It's good to see you, Bobby." Futureman said, one kid on the farm to another.

"It's good to see you too. It's good to see both of you."

A hole will do nasty things to a man, supplying him a logic that *don't make no sense*. But the bloody bout between the pythonesque chains of pride and the dripping dementia of a dream is where the entire thing, the journey here and the journey there, gets interesting.

VII

"In each family a story is playing itself out, and each family's story embodies its hope and despair."

                    -Auguste Napier

Doc and Mama Otis were always looking for some over-sized children to adopt.

After college, Bobby had returned to Knoxville, searching for work and a place to crash, rent-free – just for a little while. A little while at the Otis household turned into five years. And that was okay.

And Applejack had met Futureman at the high school where they both taught. It wasn't long before he too was moving all his belongings into the Otis house. The only payment required was that he act as son and do his part around the house. In a good family, there's always room for more.

Doc had made a two-room reservation at the Rendezvous Motel a month in advance, even though the *No Vacancy* sign had probably never been turned on. On their way to Pearisburg, Mama O looked out the window at the distant mountains drawing closer.

"Our sons are out there, somewhere on those ridges."

She didn't know what to do with her hands. She pressed them on the tops of her legs. She tapped her feet on the floor mat, taking short breaths, then long.

"They've been wandering in these woods too long now."

"We'll be there soon."

The Rendezvous was a brick slab of a building, rooms walled with poorly painted cinder blocks, floor covered in gymnasium carpet scraps. Mama wrinkled her koala-bear nose.

"Honey, I don't expect much, but this is certainly no way to meet our boys after so many months apart. This place is a dump."

"We'll just have to make do," Doc said. "It's just for one night."

She fixed up the rooms as best she could, fluffed the pillows and pulled the drapes, decorating each of the beds with the letters she'd written them.

Futureman saw their shadows from a mile away – silhouettes waiting in the middle of the road. He met his mother with a hug. Doc wrapped them up with his long arms and they were one. An organism of many parts, self-contained and self-sufficient.

Applejack threw himself onto the bed. "Rooms are nice! Warm."

"You think so?" Mama said.

"Absolutely."

Futureman agreed. "Beds. Showers. Nice things to have."

She didn't really know about their struggles and failures but Mama could see that they were in some way changed. Along the way, they'd started to regain something most folks had forgotten: contentment in the simplest of things, existence at its lowest common denominator – breath, food, love, warmth.

"Well, how about we go get us a fattened calf and have it for dinner," Doc said. "My sons have come home. Sort of."

It wasn't exactly the best of wines or the fattest of calves. It was just Pearisburg's Friend's and Family Diner. But it was enough, a family feast – hands clasped for grace, Doc throwing bread rolls across the table, storied laughter accentuated by Mama O's chirp, Bobby's snort, Doc's warble; the color of eyes – hazel, brown, blue. For an hour or two, it was as if they were all in the dining room back home.

See? Time is elastic. Einstein proved it. And so it does bend and warp and snap back into place, subtly persuading us that things have not changed; that they are as they always were. But it is only a perception, an illusion of sorts, and no equation can absorb wrinkles or broken spirits or hard times. Life goes on. And it had.

Futureman missed his family more than he'd realized. Each step south was a step closer to them. Solitude had come to him slowly, inch by inch, one forward, two back. In the quietness of the woods, away from manmade clatter, he had been forced into self-reflection – brutal truth. And there he'd begun to see that we are strangers to our own hearts first and foremost.

In the stillness, the soul will say many things. Hard things to hear. Future-man had heard that he was his father's son and, for the first time – old enough and, for now, broken enough – he listened.

In childhood, as boys do, he had strived to emulate his father – mowing the yard behind him, shooting basketball like him, trying to throw a baseball as high and as far. Doc's tall legs were skyscrapers for the little boy to hide between when strangers came around. Every night Doc flew Futureman to sleep, via living room and hallway. On Monday, they played Batman. Tuesday, Superman, and so forth. But as he ventured into adolescence then adulthood, it was his mother in whom he confided. Doc, a man of actions not words, gave solid advice when asked, just not much of it. Mama was for talking to. She asked the right questions, always seeing beyond the *hellos* and *doing fines*.

So Futureman had figured himself a Mama's boy, and he'd always been fine with that. But over the past few months, in between the bony fingers of grand-daddy trees and old valleys, it was breaking through again. *I am my father's son.* Under a dripping hemlock in northern Virginia, he'd remembered something.

He and Doc fishing on the Outer Banks of North Carolina. They were casting into the surf, looking for the blues that make an early run on the season. Sand dusted across the deserted beach. The waves crashed along the shore. Separated by an hour of casting, Futureman looked back for his father and found a small figure against the blue dunes. Waves swallowed him as the tide moved in. Doc stayed put, casting in the same rhythm he'd started with, all the while staring out to sea.

The image had burned in Futureman's mind as he walked the Virginia trail. *Ah, there it is, there on the shore – the nature of my father's silence, a mistrust of the recklessness of words. The reward of simplicity. Content on the shore of a vast ocean, an organism too large to tame or understand, my father stands on the beach with his son. This, a far greater thing than any empire can build, than any word can describe.* He'd seen him there. In his memory, he saw him still. Smiling once, Futureman had turned to follow his own jig into the surf.

And s he gripped Doc – the hero of his youth, the great mystery of his life – here in front of the Rendezvous Motel, he wanted to tell him what he'd seen, what he'd learned. But inside him, the truth had come of age and grown strong – and it would hold, a bond that need not be cheapened with a vain flurry of words. "Father," was enough. For now.

The reunion had come like dew, refreshing the land. And like dew, it was burnt off with the sun. A sun at last.

"Do you have to go?" Mama quivered. "Do you have to leave again?"

"I'm afraid so." Futureman put his arm around her.

"Don't worry, Mama O. It won't be long now," Applejack said.

"I don't like this, not one bit. I know, I know. I won't keep you two from doing what you need to do." Her tone changed. "So stop standing around here. Get going. Put the past behind you and finish well." Time for strength. She would hold her tears until they were on the mountain.

"Love you boys," Doc said. "Almost home. One foot in front of the other."

Bobby made the steep climb with them out of Pearisburg, wanting to taste the Trail a bit more. *Am I really going to cut my beard?* he wondered. *Yep, I must. That was my word, my pledge. Besides, it's scratchy.*

They fought towards the top of the mountain, clawing their way through the laurel and rhododendron. A rock appeared a couple hundred feet above Pearisburg. For the first time in a long while, they could see the sun. A distant winter hemmed the open wind, ever so light, with goose bumps of chill. The color on the leaves was brimming, couldn't handle much more. Some were only a shiver from coming down.

"Guys, this is where I get off, I guess," Bobby said. "Wish I were out here, you know."

"Yeah, we know. But you're hiking Georgia with us."

"Yes, and I'm ready! I've already got it all planned out. We'll finish this thing up right."

"It'll be here in no time."

"Yep."

"So, Bobby. About skipping those miles back there –"

"Alright fellas, take care now. See you soon." Bobby left quickly, making for his truck at the base of the mountain. Maybe he'd heard them, maybe not.

Applejack and Futureman, at last, could taste the dry Virginia crackle of late fall on the air. They disappeared into the rolling yellow and red.

VIII

It was curious to him, that's all. He wasn't angry. Shoulda been but wasn't. And it hadn't surprised him. He was fully expecting to see them there when he came around the corner, been seeing and hearing them for weeks now. Hunters. All through southern Pennsylvania and Maryland. All through Virginia. All his life, basically. No, no. Not surprising. It was just curious to see them there, hunkered down in the cold *on* the Trail – hiding in plain view from the colorblind animals.

"You seen anything yet?" Applejack called loudly. Wanted to be sure the hunter heard him.

"Yeah," the hunter said emphatically. "A six-point buck were edgin' up on us til he smelt you fellers."

"Is that a fact? Too bad a hiking trail runs right in between you and your prey. Some luck, huh?" *Lucky for you I'm not a game warden or a park ranger, you ignorant half-witted bastard. I would arrest you for violating federal law.*

"That rack sure woulda looked good on the wall. But it's alright, son. We'll get ye one yet." The hunter nodded at a young boy crouched beside him.

Applejack persisted. "Not that one, because *he* was a *she*. I got a pretty good look and –"

"Yep, woulda looked good on the wall, sure 'nough."

It wasn't worth the trouble.

"My boy here ain't never got one before. Ain't a good shot yet. Got to practice somewheres – know wut I mean? Start 'em young." He slapped the lad on the back. The boy looked like he was seven or eight years old. Just started the second grade a couple months back. He had a Browning BLR twice his height pressing down on his shoulder and a lap full of .270s.

Applejack did not have a fear of guns. He'd grown up watching his parents shoot crows on the farm, approved of the stipulations laid out by Article II in the Bill of Rights of the United States Constitution and, more than likely, he would know what to do with a Winchester M70 if anyone ever had occasion to set one in his hands. He did not have a fear of hunting for sport or any kind of moral objection to the responsible practice of it. He might even admit that from time to time, he enjoyed flipping through some of the classics of hunting literature – Hemingway, Teddy Roosevelt – or the Spring issue of *Turkey and Turkey Hunting.*

He did however have a fear of people with guns.

It was not really a phobia. Phobias are irrational fears disproportionate to the degree of actual danger. Phobias make people get up in the middle of the night and search the internet for symptoms of diseases that can only be contracted from rainforest tapeworms. Phobias compel people to plan their vacation routes along highways that do not cross steel bridges. They happen when people watch too much Discovery Channel or too many David Lynch movies. Phobias cause people to stay away from carnivals, circuses, rodeos, birthday parties at McDonald's, etc. And firm grounding in reality is not a prerequisite. That specific danger may exist somewhere for someone but not for everyone everywhere. Phobia is first cousin to superstition.

Applejack's fear of people with guns, or 'shooters' as he called them, though somewhat indiscriminate, was rooted in fact and experience.

True sportsmen were never the problem. True sportsmen do not shoot people. In fact, the authentic dyed-in-the-wool gamesman will never even be seen by other people. He would have learned from his grandfather (who probably hunted to stock the winter freezer) to go deep into the remotest parts of the wilderness in search of the wildest game. After hundreds of hours of experience and weeks of preparation, stalking and judging, the true gamesman would have learned to go into the hunt with a proven weapon and return with the exact quarry of his choosing. He will never under any circumstance run into the Supercenter, ask for "dat gun right der with the camouflage handle," grab a box of 140-grain Nosler AccuBond bullets, ride his ATV out to the most visited walking path on the continent, plop down on a rock one yard west and commence to shooting at the (*I could've sworn he was an eight-pointer*) female fawn 50 yards away. Furthermore, he will never jerk his barely-out-of-underoos tike away from his Saturday morning cartoons and plop him down on the Appalachian Trail to teach him to shoot around hikers at the first pregnant doe, wobbly fawn or biped collie dog that rustles in the woods. True sportsmen do not take their turkey callers on shopping trips so that they can practice gobbling when the wife goes to try something on. True sportsmen do not wear camouflage pants to parent/teacher conferences. Hell, a true sportsmen may not even wear camouflage at all.

Applejack had only met with one true sportsman in his life, Mike Annis. Once, on a dove shoot, Mike told him: "Don't hunt with other people with guns. In fact, don't hunt with other people at all. I don't even know why I brought you."

Applejack had believed in those words. Now he was hiking by them and they were driving him crazy. *If I could just be a good little hiker and ignore the rounds going off around me like the other Southbounders, I would have a much better time.* But he couldn't. He knew they were going to be there – been looking for them since before opening day. But now they seemed to be popping up everywhere and he was more than a little uncomfortable. At first, it was only one sheepish hunter a day. But soon, here came the pimple-faced boys with Sears bows; then the Civil War re-enactors appeared, looking to get lucky with a muzzle-loader during lunch break. Now, at last, as inevitably as Fall itself, the hordes had come. Shooters filled the woods. For the past few days out of Pearisburg, he and Futureman had walked lightly through a narrow pass, shooters firing along the ridgelines – rifle reports coming in from both sides.

So Applejack was afraid of getting shot. Futureman had his lightning fetish to keep him warm at night. Applejack had his shooters.

"Start em young? Sound wisdom. Well sir, we've got a few hundred friends coming along behind us. Try not to shoot any of them. Have a pleasant day." Applejack moved on, stomping loudly through the dry leaves.

When he got to Old Orchard Shelter things were a little weird. It was only three o'clock in the afternoon and the place was already chock-full of people. Two thruhikers, *Wakarusa* and *Oops*, had gotten off to a late start that morning, then decided not to get off to a start at all. Two other thruhikers, *Strider* and *Tenuviel,* had been there since noon. A group of weary weekenders had already called it a day and pitched their tents nearby, slowly trickling up to the shelter.

After a supper of dirty-brown rice, Applejack and Futureman decided to go up to camp and socialize. It would be good to have some normal conversation. Little did they know that it was the wrong time. Things were unraveling.

Everyone was huddled around a ramshackle table beside the shelter. Oops had taken off his shirt to reveal a hoary talisman hanging from his neck. His headlamp looked like a fiery crown. Spread before him were the ornaments of his obsession – dice, several metallic figurines, a file folder crammed with ragged papers, purple book with the word *Spells* emblazoned on the cover. He held a pen (which more than slightly resembled a scepter) and was faithfully recording Wakarusa's mysterious utterances. Strider too had undergone some sort of transformation. A gilded amulet hung down on his naked chest. A plastic sword appeared from somewhere in his pack and now lay across the table, the wacky symbol of his buried warrior-heart. A thirsty gaze had arrested Tenuviel's face. Clutching a fire red book, she stared at her man longingly. Between her fingers Futureman could read the word *Beasts*. Several of the weekenders stood around the Four. It was as if some enchantment had summoned them all to this place. *Come, behold.*

"The hex has not left you, Strider. Your efforts were in vain. Now you must go to Elel-drig the Holder to receive His counsel. But be wary. He needs your dagger. Ho there! Who approaches?" Oops wasn't kidding.

"Just us. Applejack and Futureman. Did we interrupt something?"

"Do you wish to join?"

"I don't know, uh, I mean, I'm fine watching," Futureman said

"Same here," said Applejack. "I'm a watcher."

"A watcher?"

Applejack had caused a disturbance in the green flame of time. Oops placed his hands on the table. Strider clutched his plastic sword.

"Just here to watch you all, you know, play your game," Applejack clarified.

"Then you may watch," Oops allowed.

"C'mon, give me the potion. My mother is dying." Wakarusa tapped the table.

"I will roll." Oops picked up the dice. They both came up threes. "An omen!" No one spoke for several long moments.

Applejack pulled Futureman aside and whispered, "What game are they playing?"

"Dungeons and Dragons. Oops is the Gamemaster. I think he's a magician."

"Are you serious?"

Futureman nodded gravely. They stepped back toward the Ring of players.

"What kind of omen, Gamemaster?"

"An ill-favored omen. You may have the potion. It will cure your mother of her affliction."

"Really? That doesn't sound ill-favored," Wakarusa said.

"Her life will be spared, but the potion will steal your force to revive her." Wakarusa's countenance dropped.

"I'm going to go build a fire or something," Applejack said to Futureman.

"See you later. I want to talk to them after this is over."

"It's never over, dude."

In the morning, Applejack saw Tenuviel and Strider on the way out of camp. They looked happy and well adjusted as they packed their tent. He approached cautiously nevertheless.

"Morning."

"Hey there!" Tenuviel said.

"Sleep well?"

"Like a rock. Til those gunshots woke us up. You seen many hunters lately?"

"Plenty. You've got some orange to wear don't you?"

"Not yet," Tenuviel said. "I know I need some. I'm gonna get some when we get to Damascus, so I'll be okay. Should be there by Saturday."

"Maybe we'll see you there."

They waved goodbye.

The next day, as the young couple walked side by side down a wide stretch of Trail, Tenuviel was shot from behind – an arrow protruded from her back as she lay on the ground. Strider chased a camouflaged boy into the brush and, in a rush of fear and fury, began delivering him a beating. To his amazement, Tenuviel called his name from behind. There she stood, unharmed. Terrified but not wounded. The arrow had pierced her pack just above the shoulder, extruding just to the right of her cheek bone. Strider wheeled around, and the boy was gone. His bow lay on the ground.

IX

A lovely thing about Christmas is that it's compulsory, like a thunderstorm, and we all go through it together."

                                                                        -Garrison Keillor

Ah, Horatian ode to color! Eye rhyme of the October forest bard – the festive season of trees. Spark yellow hickory and fire-red red maple (invigorated by acidic soil) weaving through the brown thickets of white oaks and scarlets. Red heart of blackjacks, brown tinged, peppers the sallow yellow of the silver oak. The char-orange flame of the sugar maple ignites the timber. Some of the oak leaves will last through the winter and grow green again with the first thaw of Spring (a peculiar characteristic of many oaks, confirming the adage that truly, they are *strong as oak*).

Applejack raised his poles in the air. Splotches of leafy paint fell from the tips. "This is what I'm talking about. October in southern Virginia! Is there a better place than this?"

"Am I allowed to say yes?" Futureman asked.

"No."

"Then this is the best place in the world."

Applejack was preparing a retort when he heard the rhythm of a familiar gait. "Who is that?"

"Who is who?"

"Coming toward us."

The long stranger appeared, his stride remembered. And words fell from their mouths – "circle" – "twigs" – "crawdads" – "stars" – "New York."

"Guys!" Lost-and-Found held out his long arms. "Am I glad to see you, it's so lonely out here. You guys heading into Bland for a re-supply?" (Please hike with me.)

"If Bland is where you get more food, then yes, we are headed to Bland." (Sure, we'll hike with you.)

Approximately, three families lived in Bland. The first one owned the small convenience store on the edge of town. The second operated the Big Walker Motel on the hill. The third managed the Dairy Queen at the bottom.

"Welcome to Bland!" Jennie from DQ said, enthusiastically. "You hungry?"

"Three burgers, two fries and twelve cokes."

"Four burgers, one fry and three blizzards."

"Eight chilidogs and a gallon of water."

They sat by the window. The days were getting shorter.

"Maybe we should get a room at –" Futureman began to say when he was distracted by a burly individual walking toward them. A scarecrow ball of hair exploded out the top of a Kavu visor, large red beard spread against his chest, and fuzzy legs were crammed into a pair of beat-up Sundowner boots. He was a young Kris Kringle sort of fellow.

"How do? Toddy is my name," the stranger said, pulling up a chair from another table. "Mind if I sit?"

"Uh-uh."

"I see yall've spent some time in the woods as of late." He made eye contact with them, swallowed some of their fries, grinned and launched into a strange self-referential banter. "And for that, Toddy's jealous. Toddy would like to take the time off to spend months in the woods too, but he can't. What's Toddy to do?"

"You have to throw a rock through a window and jump out the hole," Futureman said.

"Toddy agrees. Got a rock pile beside the house great for throwing, but Toddy runs a business – camper tops, truck bed covers and metal sheds." He grabbed one of Futureman's chilidogs and took a bite, staining his beard. "If I left it behind, my empire would crumble. Now what would Toddy do with a crumbling empire?"

"Hike the Trail?" Applejack said.

"Ah-ha!" Toddy exclaimed. "I like you guys." He winked heartily at Lost-and-Found. Lost-and-Found edged back in his chair.

"It's okay. I do get out on the Trail. Couple days here, couple days there. That's all Toddy needs." He took another colossal bite of someone's burger.

"You've hiked some of the Trail?"

"From here to Georgia. Guess I can start working my way north now."

"We do what we can. Some windows are shatter proof," Futureman offered.

"That's absolutely right. We do what we can."

When Toddy finished eating his fill of their food, he leaned forward and said, "You know, it's not often I meet hikers here. Bland's not exactly a favorite Trail pit-stop. So this is a treat, my friends." He slapped his abundant but firm belly. "Blizzards on me!"

Toddy had a Ford Dooley parked outside. Under one of his own specialized truck bed covers was hidden a cache of equipment. Camping gear, tools, clothes, food, chairs, stove, kayak, paddles and a mattress. A home away from home.

"There's plenty of room in my house back in Wytheville, not far from here. Quite a place. Some might even call it – *festive*."

Forthright and perhaps downright insane, the man was mysterious but they trusted him. Too jolly for bad intentions it seemed. So they climbed into the Dooley.

It pulled to a stop in front of 20/20, Toddy's business/home. The old house was normal-looking from the outside, a faded green two-story, but another world waited inside the front door.

"What in the –"

"Whoa."

"Pretty weird, eh?" Toddy smiled, thrilled at their surprise – thrilled to have someone to surprise.

Standing in what had once upon a time been a den, they were surrounded by what could only be described as the North Pole. Fake snow, giant candy canes, grazing reindeer, fuzzy snowballs and glistening gumdrop-coated pine cones filled the room. Toddy flipped a power switch. The place lit up like FAO Schwartz on Fifth Avenue. Plastic evergreens sprouted from the floor-boards, neon green. Walls were glistened with cascading icicle strands.

"What is this place?" Lost-and-Found asked.

"Why, it's Christmas," said Toddy.

They moved through the house in bewilderment. Glass menageries filled with holiday figurines lined the foyer. There were costly Fontanini sets, Aurora Angels, Tuscany Bible dolls, Cabernet Noel Collections, Jingle Buddies and Mother Goose statues. Nativity sets of every course and kind – sterling, wood, crystal, brass, golden and wood-crèche. Angel children. Little Piggies with ice skates on. And a dizzying collection of Santa Clauses – rainbow, Caribbean, cowboy, even a summer Santa in a tanktop with a farmer's tan. A plastic moose grinned in the doorway of another gallery-like room, greeting them with "Merry Moosemas!" and a wave.

The entire floor was stacked to the ceiling with boxes and crates of Christmas gear – nutcracker soldiers, garland, jewel stars, ginger bread houses, candelabras, metallic doves, rainbow cycles, holiday bears, decorative sleds, even holiday peacocks with fiber optic feathers. There was more Christmas junk than they knew existed.

"What does it all mean, Toddy?" Applejack asked. "Thought you owned some kind of truck business."

"It was all here when I came," Toddy said.

"Huh?"

"Come on up. I'll explain."

Up the staircase, the lavish ornamentation continued with garland and ribbon trimmings of plaid, golden, candy-striped and sequined. On the landing at the top of the stairs was a large winterized colonial village.

"Now these little guys – they're my favorite," Toddy said, flipping a wall switch. A colony of helper elves sprung to life.

Futureman crossed his arms defensively. "Elves," he said odiously under his breath. Ever since childhood, he had hated elves, with their waxy, mechanical, maniacally friendly smiles and their devious, beady eyes that shift back and forth, back and forth. "Elves freak me out…I hate tiny…freaking Christmas elves." He gritted his teeth.

"Cute." Applejack said.

"So, I bought a Christmas store for a house – or what was once a Christmas store. The couple who sold it to me said the price included all the decorations, said they were finally sick of Christmas. So I took it off their hands. Why not? There's thousands of dollars of merchandise here."

"Makes sense."

"But that was just a verbal agreement, and I guess – how shall I say it – their word was not as strong as oak. The lawyers soon assured me that I had no right to take what wasn't mine. Okay, what do I care? I just want a home. You can have it back. And that was two years ago."

"And the decorations?"

"I don't know why they haven't come to get them but I'm bound by law not to touch the valuables until this is settled. So that is the magical story of how I came to live in a Christmas store – at least there aren't any customers."

Toddy opened the door to one last room. "And now, if you please-my neck of the woods."

In compliance with his legal guidelines, Toddy had cleared this one all-purpose room. He lived here.

It wasn't Christmas, but it wasn't exactly normal either. Gnarled root-rack candleholders stood in the corners, melted candles dripping down like stalactites. The center beam of the room was decorated with tangled, wooden vines. A cowboy hat, a small bow and arrow, a dream catcher and a Celtic cross were tied to it. The walls were hand painted by Toddy himself. A montage of images haphazardly scattered – the silhouette of a wolf raising his snout to a tie-dyed moon, a desert cactus, a lion, an Acacia tree, a monkey in a vest, a little girl with red shoes. An elephant bedizened in Indian saffron stood by a pyramid.

"You like it?" Toddy asked.

Applejack was confounded. "Uh, sure."

"I know. You think it's weird because it is. That's why I painted it. It is the mural of Toddy."

They sank into the couch struggling to grasp the meaning of Toddy the mural, while Toddy the man went to the fridge to fetch some drinks.

"That wall is, shall we say, collections from Toddy's darling mind," he said, popping off the bottle caps. "My curiosities have painted what you see here. Emanations of things that I find beautiful or intriguing –"

"What is the meaning of your paintings?" Lost-and-Found interrupted.

Toddy shrugged.

Lost-and-Found sat upright, with sudden uncharacteristic animation. "So you think your picture is just random?"

"Let's have a look-see here. We got a coyote howling at the moon and Dorothy staring at a giant worm on a mushroom. Pretty random if you ask me. But isn't the whole process of thinking somewhat random? I paint it to try to make sense out of it."

"No. Nothing is random," Lost-and-Found said sternly.

Toddy laughed, "But you see my point."

"No, I do not. I cannot believe life is random."

"*Life*, he says. Well now, we've entered an entirely new realm, my friend. Please, say what's on your mind."

Lost-and-Found leaned forward, eyes glazed and bulging. "Haven't you ever thought that in spite of all the seeming chaos and meaninglessness, your whole life was leading somewhere, leading you to a specific moment in time- to this one thing?"

"Generally, I think that everything-"

"No! One thing! Not everything. And when it happens – you're done. Gone."

"Are you talking about death?"

"No…Life." His long fingers interlocked to form a circle. "No one knows what it is until it happens, but every now and then you get hints of it, like you almost understand…."

Lost-and-Found had risen to his feet. "It's a design. When it's time, it's time. And there's nothing anyone can do about it." Lost-and-Found was staring out the window. Rapture was on his face. He yearned for the firmament.

"OK! Thank you very much." Toddy clapped his hands together and charged toward the kitchen. "Who's ready for another?"

Deep in the night Futureman awoke, his bladder painfully full. He had been putting it off for hours and couldn't hold it any longer. He was going to have to face them, even now with a vulnerable imagination, having just dreamed. The bathroom was on the other side of that blasted elf village.

"This is ridiculous," he mumbled to himself, passing through the hall. "They're not real. They're just toys. You know, your imagination doesn't always have to get the better of you. Relax."

Okay, it's time. Face the elves. Do it. He sighed and turned back.

"So, it's just you and me, little buddy," Futureman said, bent down at eye level with one of the elves. "Hard time sleeping, huh? Yeah, me too. So tell me, was it just the one, or is dentistry a common aspiration among your kind?"

At that very moment, by some act of divine comedy, the little elf, nose to nose with Futureman, sparked to life – head shivering, eyes blinking open.

"Ohh-ohh-ohh!" Futureman buckled and fell backwards onto another Christmas helper. Tiny hands seemed to grab at the back of his head. He peed himself just a little before he could get the bathroom door locked.

"Sometimes they do that," Toddy explained the next morning at breakfast. "I guess electric currents get caught in their little bodies and they just twitch.

It's great, isn't it? I'm gonna miss those little guys when they finally come take them away."

X
You said in your heart, I will ascend to heaven;
I will raise my throne above the stars of God;
I will sit enthroned on the mount of assembly,
On the utmost heights of the sacred mountain.
I will ascend above the tops of the clouds;
I will make myself like the Most High.
But you are brought down to the grave,
To the depths of the pit.
-The book of Isaiah, chapter 14, verses 13-15

The high places of the world have long called out to us. Symbols of a power that is beyond our imagining, the mountains have, like the ocean, put words of folly on the tongues of the wise. We long to meet God on the mountain.

The Hindus and Buddhists had their mighty Himalayas to contend with. Deep in the heart of these giants, they envisioned Mount Meru – 84,000 miles high. The center of the universe, home of the gods. Surrounding it were seven concentric ranges around which revolved the sun, the moon and the planets. To the east, the Japanese looked to Sengen-Sama, the goddess of Mount Fujiyama. From her high place, she ruled the land below and even today, tourists and religious faithful climb to greet her from afar, where she stands in the sun. In the western world, Mt. Olympus was the home of deity, rising 9,000 feet above the Aegean, forever untouchable. The ancient Greeks believed it was the highest mountain on earth, where the gods, according to Homer, "tasted of a happiness which lasts as long as their eternal lives."

Where there were no high places, people built them. In ancient Babylon as early as 3200 BCE, we find the *axis mundi* – "navel of the earth." An early blueprint for the pyramids, the axis mundi was believed to be a portal that connected humanity to deity. Often, at the top of the structure, a room was built and furnished with a fine bed and table – accommodations befitting a divine king.

And then there are Sinai and Golgotha, two mountains that pale in comparison to the stature and magnitude of the others, but it was on these that something different happened. Yahweh himself came down from his throne to meet humankind in unprecedented ways, and it is against these two humble peaks that all human folly must be weighed.

Somewhere among the terrene strands of Christmas, rain had collected again – a vestige of the northern storm – dumping for sixteen straight hours, the day before. As Applejack awoke, breaking his limbs apart, he expected to see that same blanket dripping down but, emerging from the shelter, he saw instead a smooth column of light, pure and heaven-bold, arriving to rouse them.

He tapped Futureman and Lost-and-Found. "Wake up, light's with us – and none too soon. Today, we're walking the Highlands."

Preserved by state parks and ranchers reluctant to modernize, the Grayson Highlands and Lewis Fork Wilderness unveil miles of high, open veldt. The Highlands are like rolling Wyoming plains with a sea of shrub and berry bush, goldenrod and purple aster.

The Trail charted over the high steppe for miles. For too long had it wound under thick forests of hackberry and sourwood, tunneled through rhododendron and heavy patches of yellowwood and witchhazel. Now before them, a broad dome of sky-meets-land swallowed the ground they walked on.

Applejack lagged behind, dobbering with the dandelions, in danger of drifting away in the wind. Lost-and-Found had taken to his normal quick pace and disappeared from sight. Futureman, walking meditatively under the aurous sun, soon vanished as well.

My thoughts, questions and dreams seep too easily from my pores. I've got loose boundary skin. My words disappear into the air. Is it that the air is too thin or is it the words themselves? Will I hear His voice, here in the highlands? Finally, at last? As clear as a cedar cracking. So, how am I now? This high enough? Time for some answers? Give them to me. Let me know your thoughts.

Early in our human history, the people of the world (with one language) conspired to build Babel, a tower to reach heaven. They wished to make a name for themselves but this is not what they had been commanded to do. The Lord desired that humankind have dominion throughout the world, so he wiped his hand over the tower, scattering the people over the face of all the earth. One language became many.

The east – the west – the north – the south – sprawled outward in all directions, great distances between the outermost points of sight. This is what they had been looking for – open uncharted spaces – but something didn't make sense. Tiny clouds were clinging to the horizon. A chill infused itself into the air. Winter was drawing near. The distances of season and cloud were connected by a cold, inevitable wind. It would surely be upon them soon.

Futureman felt heaviness in his chest as he waited for answers. The heights were not as free as he'd hoped them to be, the air not as thin. *I think I'm afraid of God* – like Job, he realized. Job, a righteous man who had sat among the ashes, scraping the boils on his skin with broken potsherds. Job had asked God *why*. Why his wife had died. Why his sons and daughters had been crushed by a storm, why his sheep had been slaughtered and all his possessions taken. And God responded to Job with a few questions of His own. Questions Futureman now began to consider.

Where were you when I laid the earth's foundations?
Who laid its cornerstone while the stars sang and the angels shouted?
Who shut up the sea behind doors?
Have you journeyed to the springs of the sea?
Walked in the recesses of the deep?
Have the gates of death been shown to you?
Have you comprehended the vast expanse of the earth?
From whose womb comes the ice?
Who gives birth to frost from the heavens?
Can you raise your voice to the clouds?
Do you send the lightning bolts on their way?
Who endowed the heart with wisdom?
Who gives understanding to the mind?

By day's end, the sky had closed like a retractable roof. Rain would be here again, tonight. Wind stirred up the dust. It stung Futureman's bare legs. He wanted to curl up on the ground but, for now, he needed to walk. This was his place in the world for now, and there would be many more miles before his legs would fade into the ground, his life remembered no more. Yet it was just a breath away. He prayed as he walked. Maybe for the first time in his life.

I cannot fathom foundation. I cannot bury the wicked in dust, for dust will be my gravesite as well. I cannot resound like thunder, neither can I send the lightning back to its home. The behemoth eats me. The leviathan swallows me down. I cannot command the snow. I cannot call existence out of nothingness. I cannot climb into the sky and trampoline on the clouds. Not really. I have darkened your counsel, Lord. I am a man and nothing more. Why do you even give ear to my cries? Why did you breathe life into my lungs? I'll shut my mouth now. I will listen. May your will be done, on earth as it is in heaven.

The men caught up with one another in a mountain hollow on the edge of another numbing Virginia squall. They pitched their tarp against the besetting wind, cast their things down and fell quickly asleep inside the mighty grip of the storm.

XI

It had been dark for so long, dawn had to be near. Applejack rolled over on his back and scanned the black dome for that hushed glow behind hills that signifies the rising sun. But there was no glow, only the brush of a high wind as it rocked the cradles of birds in treetops and squirrels asleep in their gaudy nests. He waited. The glow didn't come. The birds weren't even squawking their ungracious reveille, yet. It was very early. Shortly after midnight, he guessed.

His mind had snapped on like fluorescent hospital lights, with a crystal clear acuity that only comes when no one else is awake. There was no moon. *Has it gone down already?* He turned to the southwest. *No. It's new. Stars above. A thousand restless generations, watching. It's clear. The storm's gone.*

Applejack unzipped his worn bag and leaned forward, grabbing the sore nubs on the tips of his feet. Stretching never felt good anymore. Body was too battered and the cloudy mists of Virginia that he'd worn like a cloak for so long had made his bones swell with an old man's ache. The dark mass that was Futureman did not stir when Applejack rose and walked onto the knoll. Frost hadn't come yet and the grass was soft but frigid on his bare feet. He stared into the humming creation as it circled above him in a unison so well-orchestrated, so perfected that a million years of practice could never see such a thing done.

The noise of the wind died away and the shape of the hills dropped below his vision as a funnel of stars drew down from Polaris directly above. A spiral enclosed him so immediately that his breath seemed to fog the translucent sheen. Applejack felt like he had walked out onto a precipice. Space seemed all around him. He had no more memory of sleep or grass or ground. Stars surrounded him. He was submerged in the belly of a churning creation that no longer dreamt of autonomy. Galaxies and galaxies spun in the near distance, facing away from him. They bowed before the Great Light. Applejack looked skyward, witnessing the nightly genuflection of heaven.

Proxima Centauri burned its teeming supply of gases, green and white and blue, stretching forward arms and legs in a joyous dance. As a token of praise, it sent spare tendrils of energy toward Earth, 25 trillion miles behind. At the speed of light, over four years pass before these blazing rays arrive dimly in the eyes of earth's lonely watchers.

There was a Heaven beyond and above the heavens that flashed silhouettes of rapture through the celestial matter of this universe. Applejack could see shapes of bright beings penetrate through the curtain of planets and suns before him. Apparitions, seraphic angel-fire, enclosed the Great Light beyond the curtain, attesting to its ineffable power – the power of a hundred million nuclear storms, the power of the One who explodes the Crab Supernova into a trillion pieces, the One who spins the Orion Nebula like a thimble in his palm, who shoots Hyakutake the Comet across the galaxies so that it will one day return to his hand. The apparitions shuddered behind the curtain of creation like a flash of lightning into a mirror. The One of the Greatest Light dwelt beyond them, commanding their worship, beckoning forward the stars, conducting meteorite fields and wandering pulsars in a deafening symphony of color and orbit and void. The Universe contracted and expanded, gasping in awe, flinging itself down at the speed of light.

Ashen light of a lunar eclipse drew Applejack's eyes. He heard the powerful geyser-jets of a comet, the bend of solar winds trailing behind it. Its great luminous bulk sprang to his eye, splintering purple veins with fury, casting a sky full of supernal carvings down his spine – sculpturing far too great to be handled by human words. The distant dying Butterfly Nebula surged forward from behind a wave of opaque nothingness, its twinjets emitting pink and emerald refuse at supersonic speeds. It spoke of Restoration in its last hours. A halo of fire-red orange and magenta flicked rarefied hydrogen away from its core. Clusters of ghostly dust were illuminated by ultra-violet radiation, making shapes like thumbs poking through sheets across the fabric of chaos. Hands the size of solar systems stretch out of them toward interstellar space.

Applejack became *unaware* of himself. He no longer remembered his condition of flesh and bone. The crippling beauty of what he had seen squeezed his mind and consciousness, ringing the drops out on the earth far below. It is an enlightened catatonia. Worship of the Dayspring. Daystar.

The globe of sky beneath him pushed outward towards a corona of far-off clusters. They came near. Galaxies pulsed before him – galaxies shot so full of red giant stars they are mere degrees away from exploding simultaneously and incinerating an infinite quadrant of the universe. Their white-hot masque shook, exulting in the One Beyond – millions of light-years away from the grainy plug of Earth. No one, no thing, can know where He dwells.

Even the Universes beyond our own, quake and revel at his feet. Only He sees them as they are.

The cold, damp grass prickled Applejack's feet as he craned his head upwards. Orion's belt lashed together the arms of the spinning Milky Way. He strained to see Charon circling Pluto. Couldn't. He squinted to spy Io-Jupiter's giant volcanic moon. He could not.

Futureman and Lost-and-Found slept on, motionless on the ground. Across the berm, Applejack crawled inside his dewy sleeping bag and closed his eyes in the barred, spiraling darkness.

You are there in the void. And you fill it beyond infinity. Oh, Great Light. Oh, Maker. Oh, God.

The birds began to squawk their irreverent alarm.

XII

Futureman spent a chilly hour sitting on a rock. There were no trees on the grassy bald to shield him from the wind as it pulled mist over the terrain. The outer rim of his beard was beginning to develop something that resembled frost. He couldn't tell what time it was. Nothing had changed since he first woke. The sky was as dim as six o'clock, but it was surely getting late and neither Applejack nor Lost-and-Found had shown any sign of stirring.

"Hey. Yo." He kicked the edge of Applejack's mat and rapped on Lost-and-Found's tent. "C'mon. Time to get up."

Applejack scooted out, boots first into the dismal maw. "Now, this is more like it. Another day in paradise."

"Yeah, this weather system's got our number," Futureman said. "Gives us one day of clearshot then starts right up again with its mischief."

"Yep. Must've caught up to us this morning."

"This morning? Don't you remember what a time we had staking the tarp yesterday evening and then the rain all night long? You don't remember that?"

"Huh. If you say so. I could have sworn it was clear last night, though," Applejack shook his head.

"Clear as mud. What do you say we get down into town and get something warm into our stomachs?"

"Sounds good. State line's down there in Damascus. Then, no more Virginia."

"I say good riddance."

And so, in the half-light the three men crossed the wooly mountain in their ragged summer clothes, leaning into the gale and shielding their eyes. The cow path underfoot would carry them to cover in the bundled firs.

Winding around the mountain slowly, it led them through a change as the cow track consorted with the westward slope, and suddenly they found themselves in a funny cleft of mountain like the small of a back, a quiet little sanctuary. Rain let up. Fog cleared away. New sorts of plants were growing in warmer air on this west side of the mountain – paper birch, eastern cottonwood, hickory and perhaps mandrake. They looked around, uncertain of what it all meant, surprised by this tiny new ecosystem. Warm fattened drops splattered down from sunlit hardwood leaves above them. They knelt down to get a bite to eat.

"Applejack didn't you live around here when you were a kid?"

"Yeah, not far. We moved here from the farm in West Tennessee."

"What's this mountain called?"

"Hard to tell for sure, but I think we're just beneath Whitetop. On a clear day, we could see her from our back porch. My mother told me a trail crossed over the mountain and I always imagined what it would be like to go to the top and look out over the whole world. Guess that'll have to wait for another day."

Fog like a rimy poncho enveloped them again a couple hundred feet down, and they picked up the pace, leaving their temperate little hiding place behind. At the bottom of the mountain they linked up with the Virginia Creeper Trail, an old graveled rail bed, and followed it into town, praising it for its flat grace all the way in.

People say that Damascus is the friendliest little town on the AT. Host to Trail Days – the huge spring AT gathering – and home to a dozen little stores, cafes, parks and tourist spots, Damascus had shriveled up to nearly nothing in the late October chill. The hostel run by the Methodist church was out of commission. Black plastic covered the windows. They were putting on some sort of 'Judgment House' for Halloween, their little way of reaching out to the community.

After fruitlessly knocking on the door of three churches and one darkened café, the three men found themselves across the street from Mount Rogers Outfitters in a vacant hostel with only a little warm water left in the pipes. They drew straws for first shower. Applejack won. The steam loosened his mind, as if he were bathing in memory itself.

Applejack was a strange man and before that, he'd been a strange little kid – an odd mixture of bookworm, baseball fanatic and country boy. He had always been a pond swimmer, builder of fires, vine swinger, ravine jumper, friend to animals, tree hugger, forder of creeks, adventurer, dreamer and displaced cowboy. As a lonely child on a West Tennessee farm, he'd thought himself to be an expatriate of a lost and forgotten time when manifest destiny was not something cursed but lived. To his mind there had been no question about which way a young man was to head. There was only wide-open country. But the furor which drove those men of yore to subdue the land and push back the wildest of animals and noblest of natives was the same furor that drove them into extinction as well, leaving a frontier littered with broken souls and riddled with lost ghosts.

Many things were stirred up and undone in Applejack's heart here in the bunkhouse shower in Damascus – at the dawn of his manhood, just beyond the cusp of his greatest failure. Other truths were yet to be cast – but which ones? What? Once upon a time, things – the world – had been different, right and true. He knew that much. And even now, despite his falterings along the way, Applejack felt sure that same goodness would be returned to the earth – to humankind. Restored, somehow. Was it his job to bear this message of hope, to attest to these things? He had always hoped so. To speak of beauty, to

presage that somehow – some way – the spirit of a pure world, guileless frontier, would breathe again. Wide-open spaces begging still to be charted and
known.

That was why he had always wanted to walk from Maine to Georgia. That
was why he had always wanted to hike the Appalachian Trail. He wanted a
frontier, even if it was only a rock toss away from busy streets.

To a point, he could thank his parents for his grandiose notions of explo-
ration and message bearing. On the farm, they had never seemed to mind
much when he disappeared to the north thirty to fashion a "rather sturdy" lean-
to out of chicken wire, cedar boughs, dead pines and manure. They nodded
when he insisted that he'd explored the bobcat cave. They had even encouraged him to drag his brave little sister, Jenna-Clare, along on his forays to the
far corners of the farm, where together they scrolled out the geography of the
fields and gullies.

To tell the truth, it was they who had placed that tiny germ of irreverent
dignity into the boy's character. In between their own after-dinner crow shooting sessions and barbed wire crawling, the two of them couldn't say a whole
lot to their son about his weird perambulations and suspicious activities.

After a few blissful country years, Daddy had decided to leave their pretty
cow farm in West Tennessee and transplant the family to a little southwest Virginia town called Abingdon, the oldest town west of the Appalachians – *a
new frontier*, thought Little Applejack.

For the next few years, instead of shooting crows and chasing cows, the
foursome explored the southern Appalachians, camping along the Blue Ridge,
cabining beneath Roan Mountain, driving the mountain roads and visiting hidden places like Blowing Rock and Grandfather Mountain. They met people
who actually knew real live Cherokee Indians or had climbed to the tops of
big peaks like Clingman's Dome, Mt. Mitchell or Big Bald. Matter of fact,
from their very own back door they could look out over Abingdon and see the
rows of azure foothills, hills that seemed to the growing boy like diving boards
bobbing up and down on the far ranges.

Little Applejack never got over those silly cow pastures and stands of
knobby cedars back on the farm, but here there were mountains that got bluer
the higher he went.

He had fallen in love with the Trail on a green spring day at the age of ten.
The family of four had jumped into the car and headed towards the deeper
hollows and ridges around Damascus. The town had become one of his
favorite spots, partly because he could get away with swearing when he said
its name (Damn-ass-cuss) but mostly because that swear word was beautiful –
sitting there in the valley, fat lazy river running through the domain of the
sovereign Dairy King, ice cream castle in the middle of town.

He loved that stupid little town and that darn river and would often daydream of thundering down the mountainside on his trusty steed to overthrow the Dairy King in a mighty battle – claiming his rightful crown and announcing the golden age of his reign, a new pax romana.

His daydream ended when the car stopped on the outskirts of town. They were in a park. Momma and Daddy had a secret to tell Applejack and Jenna – "you have a baby sister coming soon." In a fit of boyish joy, little Applejack ran through the park, jumping and singing, and that's when he discovered it. Across one edge of the little park, a nearly invisible footpath ran, trickling down from the icy Far North, seeping south all the way past infinity. It blew his mind like a flying dream. Little Applejack could sense that the path had a life of its own.

This is a magic trail. And one day, I'm gonna walk it and follow it past infinity.

At long last, warm and clean, the men set out for the Dairy King to visit Applejack's boyhood nemesis. And over an ice cream cone or two, Applejack recounted his story, bringing them into this circle that had finally come full.

"You and your secrets," Futureman said. "All this time and you've never told me that this is how you discovered the AT."

"Now you know."

"Well, it makes sense to me now, why you've always wanted to walk it so bad."

The bell clanged over the door. It was Terranaut, dripping wet and plastered with that annoyed Harvard smirk.

"Where in hell have you guys been? I haven't seen you since before…"

"The hole," Futureman said.

"*The hole*, he says. Well that explains everything, doesn't it?"

"Take a load off. We'll explain it over a milkshake."

Every Friday night, come hell or high water, the local hippies, hikers and stragglers of Washington County gather in front of the MRO bunkhouse, build a bonfire and sit for beer drinking and tale telling. There's really nothing else to do. Sometimes the guitars and grills come out, too.

It happened to be a Friday when Futureman, Terranaut, Lost-and-Found and Applejack had been forced down out of the hills into Damascus, and there on Laurel Avenue, they found themselves surrounded by some of the most amiable and pleasant mountain folk they had ever met, smiling right through the drizzle.

"Sure is a shitty night," a stout, middle-aged woman observed.

"S'posed to break some time first of the week," a fellow with a pipe came back.

"Got those steaks goin, Denny?"

"You bet."

"S'posed to be a rough winter 'cording to the Almanac," a grizzled fellow by the name of Lone Wolf said. He could have been twenty-five. He might have been forty. He had gray in his beard.

"Pass me a Warsteiner, Chief." Most of the folks had their beers lying around on the ground. The evening chill kept them cool.

"Chet said he saw Big Boy over by Konnarock, yesterday-week."

"Been a while since anybody come back down a'sayin' that. Glad it weren't me." A snaggle-toothed, old-timer grinned and slapped his knee. His breath twisted around the smoke, delicately.

"I really don't believe there's anything up there. Maybe a big black bear but nothin' more."

"Fellas, I don't mean to be rude, but what in the world are you talking about?" Terranaut asked. "Is this Big Boy a person or something?"

"Yep."

"Naw, he ain't a person."

"Yes and no," Lone Wolf clarified. "You've heard of Bigfoot, course. He's usually spotted out west, and sometimes afar north. Well, there's talk from folks down 'round Waynesville in Haywood County, N'Carolina. They speak of a similar creature up 'round Eagle Nest Mountain. Call him Boojum. Say he's half-man, half-bear or some such."

"More man than bear."

"Not true. He's furry as a bobcat's ears."

"Well, anyway. Story tells 'at a pretty girl named Annie fell in love with him in spite of herself and she goes around callin' out for him in the night, like an owl. That's where the term *hootenanny* come from, they say. Anyway, some of 'em from these parts – like'iss old-timer here – says they seen the same type beast from time to time up in the highlands. Personal, I think it's just a big ole' black bear ruttin' around like usual."

"You'll say that til he comes at'chee." The old man gummed his lips and looked sternly around the circle.

"Those steaks ready, Denny?"

"Not 'less you gone French on us and taken to eaten 'em bloody."

"Ain't gone French on ye, Denny. Pass me one 'em Spatens." These were simple people, but they knew their beer.

"Y'all's getting t'wards Georgia, ain't ye?"

"Won't be long. Just hoping to dodge the bullets and the cold," Applejack said.

"Yeah, know what you mean. I been up and down the Trail m'self a few times." Lone Wolf had the beard to show for it.

"All the way?"

"Yep. North and South. I p'erfer the way y'alls is doin' it, though. What you all think of our little town here?"

"I like it, a lot." Futureman said. "Seems a little sleepy this time of year, though."

"Yep, everything idles back come late fall. Don't shut down like up in Maine, but idles back a little."

"We stopped by a restaurant that was locked up," Futureman said.

"Yeah. And the Methodist church had their hostel closed off, too. Seemed like they were getting ready for some –"

"See, that there's piss poor." Lone Wolf shot a stream of beer at the blaze.

"How do you mean?"

"Them churches! They's piss poor 'round here."

"Oh yeah?"

"Yeah. Not one of us could set foot in one of them churches without bein' scooted right back out the door." Agreement came from around the fire.

"That's a shame."

"Now, I don't have no problem with Christians, per se." Lone Wolf twisted his ruddy face toward them. "Any of you all Christian?"

"Yeah."

"Like I say, don't have no problem with Christians. It's just their damn churches I wanna burn down."

"Why's that?"

"You look up and down this here street? How many churches you count? Most of 'em different dee-nominations. There could be two and they'd still be a'cuttin' at one another's throats. Makes me sick." He spat into the fire again.

"Don't seem right," a long-hair spoke up from over by the grill.

"No. It doesn't seem right," Applejack agreed. "What do you think the problem is?"

"People get together inside of them churches an' they get to talkin' and gossipin' and thumpin' 'ere Bibles and usually end up not knowin' they ass from a hole in the ground – that's whut I think."

"Well, there's a whole lot of people saying they're Christian that don't follow Jesus," Futureman said.

"At's it right there, my friend."

"At's right."

"Right on, brother."

"Far as I can remember, Jesus talked about love, not 'bout dee-nominations and slanderin' one 'nother," Lone Wolf added.

"Yeah. And he talked about justice, too. Talked about setting people free from their sin."

"Well, I could dig on some of that, my friend, know what I mean? I got some sin that's got a real hold on me – but it'll be a cold day in hell a'fore I set foot inside one of them god-forsaken buildings agin. Say, Denny, how them steaks comin'?"

They got back to telling stories and warming their hands by the fire. The weather front blew out of Damascus that night. The next morning, Lost-and-Found disappeared, muttering cryptically about some sort of meeting or gathering. And so the new/old trio laced their boots up, put their freshly laundered clothes on and set off yet again, passing through Applejack's favorite little park on their way out of town.

BOOK III

EL CAMINO DE VIDA

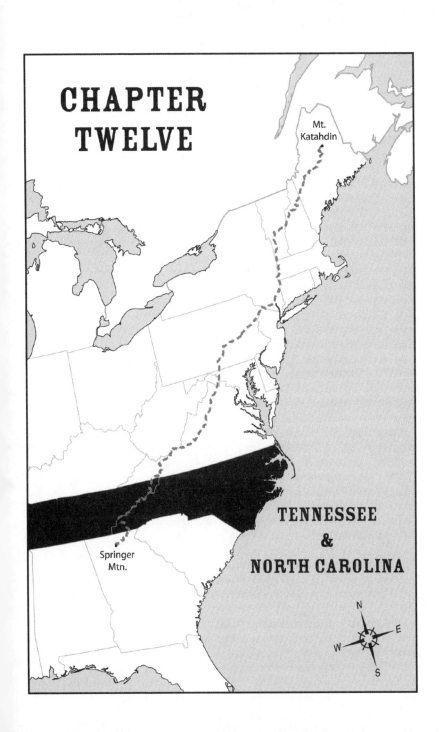

CHAPTER TWELVE

Mt. Katahdin

TENNESSEE
&
NORTH CAROLINA

Springer Mtn.

N
E
W
S

Old man and his whittled fiddle rambled somewhere in the Tennessee woods just beyond Damascus, playing his tunes there. Songs of yawning days. Around him lay hills and mountains and rugged country, old and familiar. Oh, the South. The Deep South. The place where Applejack and Futureman first felt the ground beneath their tender feet. Here, they walked with sturdy feet, hushed to listen with no expectation of grandeur. No grand band to strike up *Dixie*. They had learned their watershed lessons at the Maine/New Hampshire border and at Harpers Ferry. No, there was just old man and his finger picked melodies that pluck the leaves off the trees. The tulip poplar fell alongside silverbell – like the handshake of old friends. They were home again.

I

Trail-walkers had lessened by the day for weeks now. Spacious silence, with only the harrowing rifle report, had become the norm. Shafts of gray light were beginning to pierce the autumn canopy as they walked along together in the diverse Appalachian wood.

The rich topography and climate of the mixed Appalachian timber characteristic of East Tennessee, nurtures several different forest communities in the same soil (boreal, northern hardwood, oak-hickory, beech-maple, northern riverine and Appalachian cove among them). Tree diversity here is among the most varied on the planet – cottonwood, tamarack, hemlock, buckeye, ash, black willow, elm, maple, cherry, hawthorn, sassafras, birch and flowering dogwood, just to name a few. Indeed, the resplendent Appalachian array is evident even among its exotic salamanders. Twenty-seven different species of them – including the brown seal, the orange-cheeked Jordan, the yellow-brown two-line, the orange and red backed yonahlossee, the pink and red speckled spring, and the seven-and-a-half inch black-belly. If you're paying attention, you'll see them everywhere, lounging, watching passersby pick their way through the trees.

Terranaut had grown tired of whistling.

"So Applejack, you said we're visiting one of your old college friends?"

"That's right, in Bristol down the mountain. He has a place big enough for us."

"We're not in Manhattan anymore, that's for sure. We're in the Deep South! And you guys offered to give me the tour, remember?" Terranaut raised an eyebrow. "So, let's get on with it!"

"What do you wanna know?" Applejack said.

"Whatever you have. I mean – *whatern ye gots, yuns!* Is that the proper dialect?"

"Not really. How about writers?" Applejack offered. "The South's got great literature."

"Interesting approach," he said. "Like who?"

"Like Twain, like Faulkner, Carson McCullers, Shelby Foote, Zora Neale Hurston, Truman Capote. And don't forget Harper Lee – *To Kill A Mockingbird*. Then there's Cormac McCarthy. He's one of the newer guys on the scene."

"Okay, you've made your point," Terranaut said. "The South has some writers. That's not surprising considering all the juicy material – what with the pig farmers, crawdad eaters, gun lovers and banjo picking inbreeders."

"Lies." Futureman shook his head. "Ugly lies."

"So tell me, what is it about the South that you guys *love* so much?"

"Well, it's like Walker Percy said, it's always hard to generalize about the South – but we'll give it a shot," said Applejack.

"There's the obvious stuff," Futureman started. "Sweet tea, country fried steak, fried okra, fried cornbread, fried pickles and fried chicken and taters for Sunday dinner – which is lunch, of course."

"So fried heart attacks, basically. What else?" Terranaut said.

"You got four distinct seasons – spring, summer, fall and winter – all about three months each – well, at least that's usually how it is in Tennessee."

"Also, there's a strong sense of place, as the writers say," Applejack nodded. "Something about the way the air feels and the ground you're standing on. Heck, just driving down the street and waving to people on the sidewalk is different. People are genuinely proud to be Southern."

"You always know when you run into a Southerner, too – even if the accent doesn't give it away," Futureman added. "There's a real bond you feel when you run into another Southerner – especially when you're in a far away place. Like Ohio." He grinned.

"Of course, it's not all good." Applejack squirmed out of his shoulder straps and plopped down on the ground.

"Now we're getting to the good stuff. That other crap bores me." Terranaut made a stool with his pack. "Give me the dirt."

"First off – the humidity is miserable. We eat it like pie around here in the summertime."

"And allergies, too. Every spring, I threaten to chop my nose off," Futureman said.

"Yeah. The flowers are gorgeous but pollen's everywhere. Then there's country music. Everybody knows country hasn't been good for decades."

"The whole front porch thing doesn't exist much anymore, either – except in really small towns. But that's probably the case everywhere in the world. People are more closed off."

"What else?"

"Well, certain things haven't really been left behind. Racism is still simmering in places. It can run deep, both ways, like it's built right into the atmosphere, but it's usually real subtle." Applejack was poking little twigs into the moist dirt. "There's a layer of shame that's…buried…underneath all of it. The past lurks around. You can feel it in neighborhoods, hospitals, even churches. People hide."

"So, what's the deal with Southern hospitality."

"That world famous Southern hospitality. Yeah, it can be great, but it's also a great way to keep people from digging too deep," Futureman said.

"Like a façade, eh? Perhaps you should think about relocating to the northeast – home to the palest skin, shortest conversations, longest winters and highest suicide rate in the country."

"Everybody's conflicted about home," Applejack said.

"Hold up…ya'll hear that?" Futureman asked.

"Hearing your coyotes again?" Terranaut said.

"No. Music. And they were coyotes, I'm telling you."

"Wait, I hear it," Applejack said. "It's a song. Coming up the Trail."

"Females?" Terranaut raised an eyebrow.

There were several voices. It was a rich, full, natural sound with alto, soprano and in-between, built on the rhythm of walking. "Cause I ain't wastin' time no more. Time rolls by like hurricanes…and pourin' rain…" On it went.

"Rollin' after a subway train…" a big lady belted, coming around the corner. "Oh! Wull hey thayer, fellas. Y'all taykin' a rest?" A pleasant-faced lady of fifty or so appeared. She was wearing khaki shorts and boots.

"Yes ma'am," Applejack said.

"Perty day, ain't it?"

"Sure is."

"…Lord, I ain't wastin' time no more – Oh, well, howdy-doo! Looks like we got ourselves a little hikin' convention." Another smiling woman drew alongside them, with two more friends just behind. They waved, grateful for an opportunity to catch a breath.

"What're you ladies up to on this fine day?"

"Just gettin' some fresh air. Sometimes we like to walk to Abingdon Gap Shelter just to eat lunch and have us a look see. We been doin' it fer years now. Where you fellers headed?"

"Started in Damascus this morning, trying to get to Georgia before it snows."

"Well, my goodness, that's a mighty big task!"

"Feels small now, we've come such a long way." Applejack said.

"What's a long way?"

"Maine."

"Stars and garters. That there's the whole dern pantry! Are y'all from around here?"

"We're from Tennessee," Applejack said.

"Not me – I'm a Yankee," Terranaut said.

"Sweetie, we won't hold that against you – at least, not for long. Well, it's a momentous day for you boys."

"Yes ma'am, we're headed home," said Futureman.

"Boys, you ARE home! Didn't see the sign? You crossed over a couple miles back."

"You don't say."

"Yessir! Hallelulah! Ring the dinner bell, Betsy. Our boys have come home. Mighty fine to have y'all back!" She smiled as wide as Dixie. "Bet you'uns have sure missed it." She grabbed them roughly for a mama bear hug.

"Ma'am, you have no idea."

II
Fire burns the same, both here and in Persia.
                    -Aristotle

On a wind-stripped knob half a mile above US 421, Terranaut, Futureman and Applejack came across a family of five out for a Saturday afternoon walk – a father, a pregnant mother, two girls and a boy. Between them they had three guns. It was obvious they weren't planning on doing any serious hunting, but they'd brought the guns along just in case they saw anything to shoot at. For instance, there were plenty of soda cans and beer bottles strewn across this particular knob – target practice. The boy came along first. He was carrying a Super Comanche rifle and a Bowie knife. Yellow-dressed little sister trotted behind trying to keep up. Mama was in her last trimester. A Winston and a Diet Pepsi were helping her take her mind off the misery. Teenaged Big Sister's face betrayed her heart's desire to be grown and rid of this family pastime. And Daddy, at the rear? Well, he had two guns. What he carried in hand looked like a Browning 410. The other was tucked under his belt. Only the little girl said hello as the scraggly-looking men passed by.

Southern people love guns the most. It's a sure fact. Data from a stratified, random sample collected by DMI in 1975 of 1,538 "non-institutionalized" adults in the United States indicated that the cultural component of "Southern-ness" does indeed affect one's attitude toward gun control. 1) Those most opposed to gun control are Southerners. 2) Those most opposed to permits and handgun bans are Southerners. 3) Most people that have a shotgun rack in their back window are Southerners. 4) Most people who shoot dogs in lieu of a vet bill and 5) most people who equate enlisting in the U.S. Army to signing up for a Holy War? You guessed it – Southerners.

Incidentally, most Southerners are Christians of some sort. Southern Christians (or is it Christian Southerners?) generally tend to see religion and politics as one and the same, war and prayer being equally beneficial to humankind. Most can't define Manifest Destiny, but they sure believe in it. *This is God's Land. It says it right here on my dollar. Look!* To be Southern is to be Christian is to be an American patriot. To be an American patriot is to own a gun. Yet as bent as the understanding of faith, politics and vocabulary might be, most Southern gun owners really are just good old boys who like to eat fried foods, re-work old Chevys, spit tobacco into empty Mountain Dew bottles and brag about the quality and quantity of the animals they've shot. Typically, they are not murderers or violent crime offenders.

These are, of course, gross generalizations and unforgivable over-simplifications. The average person you talk to in Charlotte or Atlanta these days has come down from Akron to work for Coca Cola or Dell and prefers drinking non-fat mochas at Starbucks to sport of any kind.

[Note: We must be very careful in our advanced, post-post-modern multi-culture not to be intolerant or insensitive. Stereotyping is an *evil* thing (if one may use the word evil without being guilty of moral coercion). As we aim for a society that is boundary-less, without stratification or division, without fanaticism or rigid conviction, without class, race or socio-economic barbed wire, then we must actively avoid (would it be too much to say *eliminate*) stereotypes and the hasty application of harsh labels on each other. That future, that de-cultured culture would be free to shape its own heroic, visionary, new world. It would be free to forge the first "world culture," a global community – a planet extricated from the myopic totality of tribalism, of harmful religious zealotry. It could redeem the devolving course of humanity – it could create worldwide harmony at last. But, let's be honest – if there is one category of humans that cannot be maligned enough, it is the gun toting, church attending, Anglo-Saxon Southerner. Who really cares what becomes of him? He refuses to change. His world is gone, and good riddance. He will contribute nothing to the millennial, globalized, garden salad American technocracy of the future. After all, his existence reminds the western world of everything it wishes to leave behind – a long and ugly history of oppressive, Caucasian chauvinism. Sound about right?]

Though, in the end, who can refuse the sweet-sounding exclamation of the twelve-year-old Southern gun-boy, after the first firing of his new *Super Comanche*:

"Mane, this hare gern's awlsome! 'Is 'ud blow der poo outer 'at twenty pointer I seen up on nat ridge."

"I've just gotta say that, so far, I'm really impressed with your neck of the woods," Terranaut said. "I mean, wow. You are Tennesseeans – and who wouldn't wanna be! Go Vols! This is rich, between Boojum and hootenanny and tobacco spittin' and that pistol-packin' welfare family back there. I totally get it now. That Southern mystique you guys have got goin' on – OK, for a while, I bought it. Swallowed it whole. But, now? Now, it's all around me, at my very fingertips – this wonderland. Yes! I see what all the fuss has been about. Why would you want to be a part of the Union when you could have all of this?!"

"I miss Lost-and-Found," Futureman muttered.

"Until now I've been a little envious of you two. You got the laid-back accents and the nice families and the stories about your yeoman grandparents and all. It's very charming, really, but I have to tell you that this is not exactly what I've been picturing in my head. It's more Flannery O'Connor than *Steel Magnolias* – and that's not a good thing. Boy, am I glad I caught up with you two – right at the Tennessee border, too. Seriously, I'm all in. You are my guides, so lead the way. Show me what you got."

"Alright then, Terranaut. Let's begin," Applejack suggested. "What you're gonna do first is climb up to the top of that hill, break a couple of branches off a tree, stick them on your head and count to a thousand. If you hear anything that sounds like gunshots, don't worry – you probably won't feel a thing."

Applejack's college buddy, Brandon – now an English teacher at the old alma mater – was leaning against his red Subaru when they came out of the naked sweet gums.

"Hey there, old man."

"Hey yourself. You've met Futureman, I believe."

"Trail names, huh?" Brandon said. "Bunch of pagan hippie tree huggers." He smiled wryly.

"And my other pagan friend here goes by Terranaut," Applejack said.

"I'm just an observer, Brandon. Here to find out what the South is all about."

"That's a tall order," Brandon said. "Better get started."

Bristol, Tennessee was a colorful place to go to college. On the small side of a city, it is big enough to afford the opportunities to explore and act out that a young man needs, but small enough to keep tabs.

Bristol had been a hopping railroad town, years ago. Now there is little industry and little growth. Aside from the regular professionals, a sizable portion of the proximal population would be considered backward by outside standards, yet despite their disadvantages, hillbillies are a kind and intuitive folk. Their way of life changes little, regardless of Wall Street vacillations or White House foreign diplomacy. Hillbillies may come into a town such as Bristol to buy groceries and other supplies once a week, or even once a month. They lead simple lives. In addition, Bristol has a surprising number of homeless people wandering its streets and condemned buildings.

Downtown Bristol is a physical symbol of the town's uniqueness. Main Street is State Street, where the double yellow line divides Tennessee from

Virginia. On the Tennessee side, a huge mural covers one of the buildings – a coronation, proclaiming Bristol as the birthplace of country music. It is the site of the famed Carter family sessions. Incidentally, some claim that Bristol was the last place that Hank Williams was seen alive.

Brandon and Applejack had been drawn together by their love for music – bluegrass, mountain, folk, blues and most importantly, the Beatles. Sleepy by most standards, Bristol held its own when it came to local music. So whenever their attentions strayed from their studies, Applejack and Brandon naively followed the music – encountering a bizarre cast of banjo-pickers, boxcar willies, burnt-out singers, vagabonds, drunken prostitutes and yes, even midget wrestlers there on State Street. They'd wasted a lot of time and had little to show for it, but their adventures were as hair-brained and idiotic as they were rich and deep.

"After you fellas get cleaned up, I thought we might go over to a friend's house for some dinner. Applejack, you know some of these guys." Brandon was taking his time steering through the streets.

"Sounds good."

"Fine by me."

"Brandon, are there going to be any young ladies there?" Terranaut wanted to know up front.

"Doubtful, but a couple of the guys have girlfriends. If that's not a problem for you, then – yeah, there will be some young ladies."

"We had a saying in the Navy – gotta get in to get your feet wet," Terranaut said.

"The Navy, huh?" Brandon asked. "How was the Navy?"

"About what you'd expect – a bunch of guys stuck on a boat, afraid to get their feet wet."

Brandon's friend, Robbie, lived in a beautiful stone house above downtown. He'd recently finished his Master's of Divinity and was in the final stages of ordination in the Episcopal Church.

"Come in! Glad to have you! Come in!" Robbie greeted them at the door. Music blasted through the house as they followed him in. "Meet my girlfriend, Delores." Robbie said, staggering a bit as he led them into the kitchen where several people were gathered around a small beer keg.

"Help yourselves. *Mi casa es tu casa*. Now, if y'all would excuse me, I need to check on something." Robbie filled his mug and slid out of the kitchen.

Brandon lowered his voice, "Rob's going through some hard times, lately."

"Oh yeah?"

"You know he just went through seminary. Well, in order to get ordained as a clergyman in the Episcopal Church, you have to pass all these tests and be approved by the session or committee or whatever, right? Rob's a brilliant guy. He did really well in school and was cruising through the whole process when, I don't know, something happened."

"What?"

"Not sure. I think he messed up on one of his tests or something."

"Can't he just take it again?"

"I don't think so. It's not looking like they're going to ordain him." Brandon shook his head.

"After all that? That's too bad."

"He's not handling it real well. Doesn't know what to do with himself."

"I can understand."

"Anyway, so tell me about the Trail – what have your experiences been like?"

"Well, we met this guy who lives in a Christmas house and –"

"And we got kicked out of a bowling alley –"

"And we almost got sprayed by a skunk."

"Oh, uh, that's very interesting, guys." Brandon looked absently around the room. "Hey, has anybody seen Rob? Where's he gone?"

"Father Rob is right here, Brandon."

They turned and beheld a horrifying sight. There stood their host in the doorway, pint of beer in hand – black pants, black coat, black shirt, white collar. He'd gone into his room and donned a clerical outfit. Now, he looked just like a priest – close-trimmed beard, cigarette – all of it.

"Robbie – what are you doing? Where did you get that?"

"It's Father Rob, Brandon, and I bought it. Figured if they weren't going to give me one, then I'd get one. So I did. That's exactly what I did. I walked right up to the counter and I paid for it. Actually I paid about thirty thousand dollars for it – if you count tuition and books."

"Robbie, come on, buddy – why don't you go take it off. Everything's gonna be fine, man –"

"Father Rob, Brandon, and what are you afraid of? It's just a piece of cloth. That's all it is. Cotton and polyester – or whatever the heck they make it from." Robbie smiled, walked to the keg and filled his mug again. "I want to propose a toast. Everyone! That's right. Father Rob wants to make a toast. Gather round." Folks were coming to the kitchen to see what all the commotion was about.

"Oh Rob, not now." Delores pressed her hand to her brow.

"Robbie, you don't want to do this."

"Brandon, we do what we have to do and I have to make a toast – right here, right now. Lift your glasses, one and all, to the Episcopal Church." He tossed his mug back. "To my mother, the church. Here-here! The mother who didn't want me."

"Oh, God – Rob stop." Delores moved toward him.

Rob hoisted his glass again. "To the church that didn't think that I was good enough for it – here-here! To the church that loved me enough to send me away – tough love! Here-here!" He drained his glass.

The room was so utterly devoid of sound that Futureman could hear electromagnetic particles colliding somewhere around the coffee pot.

"I'm going to join the Army." Rob set his mug on the counter and walked out of the room.

Two days later, Terranaut, Futureman and Applejack were standing in front of the Grindstaff Monument, a few miles from Iron Mountain. A lone chimney juts from the ridge, commemorating the solitary life of a hermit named Nick Grindstaff.

"Thanks for taking me into Bristol. I had a really good time." Terranaut seemed strangely earnest, a bit overwhelmed by the palpable sadness of the monument.

"It's our pleasure. So, what do you think of the South, so far?"

"The way I see it, people are basically the same – anywhere you go. I've been all over the world and people seem to want the same things. They want to be loved and they want to love –" Something was caught in his throat. "They want to figure things out. Why they're here, who they are. Ultimately, I guess you could say, they want to know God. And they're just trying to figure that out."

"Sometimes, I wonder if here in the South we're so surrounded by religion that we can't hardly find God," Applejack said.

"Prophet without honor?" Terranaut looked through the trees.

"What was that?"

"*A prophet is not without honor, except in his own country*. A great teacher said that." Terranaut smiled. "Just the same, I guess that desire really is sin in people. I'm starting to see it – maybe even feel it a little bit."

"Fire burns the same, both here and in Persia. A great teacher once said that." Applejack smiled.

"We're more alike than we let on. Who needs the Mason-Dixon line, anyway?" Terranaut grinned.

"So, this weekend Futureman and I are meeting my family at Roan Mountain. You should come."

"That sounds really nice." Terranaut paused again and looked off toward the hills. "But I think I need to keep moving. Winter's coming."

"True. Winter comes hard sometimes, even this far south."

"Then, I suppose the grand tour is over." Terranaut reached out to shake goodbye, real emotion coming through those New England blueblood hands.

"See you on down the way," Futureman said.

"Sure thing." He moved to the fringe of forest, turned back toward them. "See you at Springer."

III

Spirits were rising. They felt recharged. It had been a good weekend with Applejack's family. In fact, it was the very same cabin at the foot of the mountain they'd spent many summer nights in years and years ago. They enjoyed some of Momma's good country cooking and Daddy prepped Applejack for the date he'd lined up for him back home. Brave little Jenna wasn't there. She was married and grown. But Abbie was – the little surprise from Applejack's favorite park – with her golden hair and firefly smile.

They tossed baseball and took walks through the crisp morning air. At night Daddy built his overgrown fires in the stone pit, until they filled the cabin with smoke and sent everyone gasping out onto the front porch. The visit was enough to soothe the homesickness for a while.

But the time had come for Applejack and his friend to leave once more. Applejack's mother looked nervous when they finally got out of the car and stepped onto the frozen ground. She had a moment of regret, there at the top of Roan Mountain. *I encouraged this. I told him not to quit when he had the heat stroke. I told him not to worry about the hunters.* It was bitter, by far the lowest noontime temperature of the year. Branches were sharp and brittle, cold like knives hanging in the air. The sun seemed to be setting already. *But I have to let them go, to finish what they started.*

Roan, the first mountain taller than 6,000 ft since Washington in the Presidentials, is one of the famous southern balds – grassy, treeless summits. Unlike the Appalachians of the northern Trail with their bare-gray, sprawling ranges stretching for miles above treeline, southern balds stick out of the thick deciduous forest like swollen thumbs. No one knows why. A great deal of speculation and research has gone into the examination of these anomalies, but with little result. Theories and legends proliferate. Many have suggested that lightning fire scoured these mountaintops centuries ago, and perhaps over-grazing cattle intensified the problem. One theory proposes that the surface layer of fecund soil is thin, pressed too close by bedrock underneath for sufficient growth. Some guess that natives cleared the land, possibly for spiritual ceremonies; some blame the incessant assault of wind; others insist that the vegetation has been burnt away by the white-hot righteousness of God passing by. At any rate, these balds are the crop circles of the southern ranges and have captivated the Appalachian imagination for two centuries or more. But the mysteries of Roan Mountain are of particular interest.

As he walked, Applejack's mind was running back over the time he'd spent with his mom, dad and baby sister. *She's not such a baby anymore. Actually, she's going to be a beautiful woman very soon. And Daddy seemed more relaxed than I've seen him in a while. Work must be going well – but why does he keep talking about this girl? Eliza or Elisha? He wouldn't stop. How many times did he insist that I ask her out when I get home? I don't know, we'll see. Anyway, it was real good to see them. But it's not the same without pretty little Jenna – not like the old days.* He moved quickly and lightly across the mountain, into a thin veil of leaves. At this altitude winter comes early, drawn in by November westerlies. Pushing quickly over the southernmost promontory and down, a good half-hour had gone by before Applejack realized that he hadn't seen Futureman in quite a while.

Roan Mountain was the prize possession of the Catawba Indians through much of the 17th and 18th centuries. Though the neighboring Cherokees were the dominant tribe for most of that period, the Catawbas clung to the bald mountain as the symbol of their nobility. Many times they invited their enemies to the meadow-summit to battle for supremacy, under the watchful eye of the Great Father and the pantheon of earth spirits – drawn close to the sacred mountain to see the valiant feats and heroic deaths of the Catawba braves. In late spring, beautiful rhododendron blossoms break forth with lush pink blooms, but if you look closely, you might see blossoms of a slightly darker shade – a rich red, said to have been drawn from fertile soil stained with the blood of the fallen. And even on a pleasant day in late spring with the rhododendrons unfurled around, it is nearly impossible to miss hearing the peculiar sound of strident wind as it strips the dome bare. Of course, wind is capable of creating many interesting noises – a jump-start for the imagination – whether it's the whir of a lazy breeze or the howl of a storm, but there is something exceptional about the wind over Roan Mountain. It sounds like baleful singing.

Futureman stood on the east side of an open field, hands clenched like claws in the frigorific wind. He couldn't find blazes anywhere. Every second, his eyes mislead him, everything in sight, icy and white. He had no memory of losing the Trail and couldn't exactly recall where he'd come from. *Was there a split somewhere? Is this a side trail? I've got to get down off this mountain pretty soon or I could be in trouble – did I come from the north side of the bald or the west side – what? Oh, there. Voices. People talking. I bet Applejack is looking for me.* Futureman walked northwest across the mountaintop, headlong into the wind, catching faint bits of speech out of the gale, until he came to a brown dead-end of oaks at the base of a small gully. Nothing but branches scratching and rapping against each other. *I came the wrong way. There. There they are again. Yeah, of course. The wind is from the northeast.* Leaning forward like a straining pack mule, he marched across to the other side of the mountain, only to find a strange pile of rubble and gray stones- nothing, no one. *There they are again. What am I hearing? Where are those voices coming from? There's nowhere else to go up here. Is someone laughing? Surely not in this squall. Or – no – it's singing. Definitely singing. That's got to be Applejack.*

It was common, in the settling years of the 18th and 19th centuries, for more optimistic herdsmen and farmers from the valley to tell their frightened children that the voices on Roan Bald were the strange harmonies of an angelic choir. They said, like the Catawba, that this stark high mount was where God drew closest to the earth. But many disagree. Anyone who has ever spent much time there can verify that the voices often sound more like the mournful baying of an animal caught in a trap than the soothing noise of a heavenly choir. As far back as 1799, we have writing that refers to the wailing of the mountain as evil wind. There are reports from that era that suggest the sight of clouds spinning in a circle over the bald would have been a common one. Cattlemen who grazed their livestock nearby insisted that the devil himself made music there by driving the wind and rain into a vortex above the rocks. However, scientists are hesitant to confirm that any rock formations which might produce such a sound are found on the mountain.

But, evil weather or no, the view from Roan Bald is thrilling in any direction. In the late 1800s a man named Colonel John Wilder sank his fortune into the construction of a resort hotel (he called it *Cloudland*), resting directly on the Tennessee-North Carolina state line. It was said that the wind pounded the hotel so fiercely that, at times, the guests feared it would be dislodged from its foundation. From time to time, the occasional thrill-seeker would stay at the resort, and head out in search of the wicked wind's source. Accounts varied. Several times the clamor was described as the great humming of bees or flies – long after the insect season had passed. Henry Colton of Knoxville reported to the newspaper that he'd heard a distinct sound in the wind, like the piercing rattle of glasses clanging against one another.

But perhaps the most famous testimony is that of a young adventurer named Libourel. On an especially murky, fog-laden day, against the advice of Colonel Wilder, Libourel set out to find the origin of the wind. The Colonel and his guests waited through the violent storm for his return. When he finally reappeared haggard, panicked and speechless, his clothes hung from his body in tatters. He wordlessly packed his bags and left the mountain, refusing to speak of his ordeal. It wasn't until many years later, in his old age, that Libourel disclosed what he had seen. Seeking shelter from the storm under an outcropping of rock on the south edge of the bald, he claimed that at the height of the storm a gust of wind blew him into a cave hidden behind him, and in that hole he saw and heard the wailing and singing of a ghostly choir. Libourel swore that an assembly of damned souls surrounded him, their bodies torn open by torture, teeth clacking like brittle bones.

Half an hour before dusk, just beneath the south edge of the mountain, Future-man finally heard his name called.

"Applejack! That you?"

"Futureman!"

He descended a couple hundred feet to a hollow bowl, sheltered below the bald.

"Am I ever glad to see you, Applejack. Thought I was going to be lost in the dark." He dropped onto a log.

"What happened to you? Where have you been for the last two hours? I looked everywhere. I even went back over the mountain." Applejack stood over him.

"I don't know, man. I don't know how I got off the Trail. I kept walking in circles," he said breathlessly.

"What do you mean? How did you lose the Trail?"

"I have no idea. Spent twenty or thirty minutes just sitting on the founda-tion of some old building on top – didn't know what else to do. How long have you been shouting for me?"

"Not long. I didn't think it would do any good in the wind. Why?"

"Well, I – I kept hearing voices. At first, it was just talking. Then there was –"

"Voices?"

"And then singing. Pleasant at first, like a real song, but it grew worse."

"What do you mean worse?"

"Well, it got strange. It was bizarre – like someone in pain."

"Probably just the wind howling."

"No. I know I get spooked sometimes – but this was different. It definitely didn't sound like just wind."

Applejack sat in silence for a minute, straining to hear something. "What was it, buddy? What do you think you heard?"

"I don't know. I just want to get down off of here."

They walked in silence – Applejack straining to hear, Futureman struggling to forget – until at last they came upon Clyde Smith Shelter. And, in what seemed a safe hollow, they fell asleep in the still darkness.

IV

Somewhere along the way, Johnny got a bad rap. Like that kid, Dale, who pooped his pants on the playground in the third grade and was still catching hell for it on graduation night. OK, one time, maybe fifty times, Johnny got drunk and yelled at some hikers. So he's that miserable no-good drunk that owns a hostel on the Appalachian Trail. Maybe most of the items in his hostel (including toilet paper), or maybe all of them, cost something – so he's that *capitalist* pig! Maybe one time, maybe it was ten, he broke Janet's heart (she owns a hostel, too) – so Johnny's a male chauvinist pig of the worst kind, the object of all female hiker loathing.

There wasn't any room left on the anti-Johnny bandwagon but if nothing else was clear about the world of the AT, one thing was: Johnny was a vile human being who owned a hostel in Erwin, Tennessee, and "you should never – *ever* – stay there!"

It was great for business.

With all the bad press, Applejack and Futureman had no choice but to stay with him when they rolled into Erwin – to see what kind of creature he really was.

A particular chill – winter throwing knives – traveled in the wind. Fall's busy preparation for the cold had given the mountains an ache, a groan from deep down; nightcaps out, they were about to snooze. The clouds were shifting, stretching, thinning, and stacking – layer upon layer, as winter's gray-white afghan began to fill the sky, while the wood smoke of chimney fires combed through the air.

Erwin is like any small town in northeast Tennessee: a few streets, dead ends, one or two stoplights, a couple of family-owned diners and a library with children's books, thirty-year-old encyclopedias, and a collection of King, Grisham and Rice novels.

"There it is – Johnny's place," Applejack said, pointing across a small bridge.

"Looks pretty cool," Futureman said.

The hostel sat on the A.T. at the edge of town, along a bend in the Nolichucky River. It was essentially a compound of sorts with campsites and a fenced-in village of tiny cabins huddled inside. A series of wood-lined, pebbled paths connected each one. The main house where Johnny lived guarded the front of the property. A light was on. Smoke billowed from the chimney.

Inside they found a hiker store stocked with all kinds of useful equipment – compasses, knives, headlamps, socks, gaiters, orange plastic shovels (so no one will shoot you while you're pooping), pots, stoves, etc. No one was behind the counter. Beside the store they found a den. A pot-bellied stove sat in the corner.

"Hello?" Applejack called.

A voice rang from the den. "Ugghhh. Hang on just a – eerrragggh – just a minute." A rickety reclining chair rattled, and a man appeared, closing the door behind him. He was in blue jeans and flannel shirt, with thick salt-and-pepper hair pulled over with a smidgeon of tonic, five-day old gruff on his face, big gut, and eyes a little bloodshot. "Sorry. Been a little quiet around here lately. I get to dozin' off sometimes. I'm Johnny. You need a place for the night? Pretty cheap. Good deal."

Unfortunately, he looked exactly as they had imagined. "Yeah, we'll need a place, getting cold outside."

"Perfect whiskey weather. Somethin' hot to keep you goin," Johnny said, ruffling some papers for the boys to sign. "Need any gear? Batteries? New poles? Them poles look a little beat down."

"Naw, just a room."

"Take a slack pack? Go up and over Big Bald tomorrow, twenty-one miler, come back and warm up in the cabin. Like you say, it's gettin' cold. Got heaters in each cabin. Do it for real cheap. Good deal." He had that pushy disinterested sales persona – the kind that works.

"We'll see, Johnny."

The hostel was empty. The translucent outer shells of last spring's northbounders (once green) clung to the walls like katydid exoskeletons. The bunkhouse was cozy, a wooden box-frame shack just big enough for a double bunk, a heater and a pale green TV.

Futureman got the rabbit ears straight enough to catch two stations.

"...no, no, over, just a little bit to your left, there, that's it."

It was an old movie, *Magic*, a ventriloquist murder mystery starring Anthony Hopkins in his early years. They watched for a while, until the credits came.

"Can you imagine pitching this idea to the studio execs," Applejack commented. "OK, here's the premise: a shy, split personality – uh – ventriloquist, kills his wife and is haunted by his own murderous dummy..."

"This is the kind of stuff that's missing in Hollywood today," Futureman said.

"Exactly. See what else is on."

Buzzing in – Oprah, of course. Demigod, queen of feline daytime hearts. She emerged from the corridor, striding into her vast empire. Her entrance incited an eruption – a torrid lava flow of emotions, a pyroclastic cloud of tears and dreams. One lady melts as Oprah touches her on the wrist. Another faints (eunuchs with smelling salts stand by). The show was interesting as usual: a fill-in-the-details happy hour about fulfilling destinies, reminding viewers that *you are unique and special* and that *it's healthy to cry, a lot, because we're saving the world one heart, one diet and one book at a time.* (After the commercial break, seat number 35 wins a sexy houseboy named James.)

Johnny was in the den sipping some scotch and reading a newspaper. A crackling fire glowed through the iron grate, as coals popped and shot cinders onto an old green rug. Johnny's dog nursed her new litter in the corner.

"Hey, Johnny, how's it going?" Futureman said, entering the room uninvited.

"Oh, hey." Johnny shifted in his lean-back, startled by the breach of his sanctuary. "Uh, just readin' the paper. Can I help you with somethin? Need anything in the store?"

"I don't need anything. I was just wondering what you were up to. Nice place you got here. I really like it. You build it?"

"Uh?"

"Wow, those puppies are cute. May I?"

"Easy now, mother," he said quietly. "She's a little testy with strangers."

Futureman rubbed the dog's head until he was sure it was alright to hold one of her pups, and sat down beside the fire with the puppy in his lap. "You named 'em yet?"

When Applejack came in a half-hour later, Futureman and Johnny were rolled back in laughter.

"– so I reached across the fire to see if my socks were dry, and drug the bottom of it right through those flames! Ignited right here, middle of my chin." Futureman pulled his beard down to reveal the gap.

"No kidding!" Johnny said, heaving. "That was real stupid of you."

"Well, I'm pretty stupid."

"But funny. Stories like that are always good after the fact, you know? Something to get you going. I do stupid things all the dern time."

Applejack was standing in the doorway, a puzzled expression on his face. *Johnny's having a good time?*

"Come on in, Applejack. Take yerself a seat," Johnny said.

"Al – alright."

"So, you two sure you wanna slack over the mountain tomorrow? First real cold snap of the year. It could be real bad on top."

"Yeah. Applejack, we're slacking over the mountain tomorrow. First real cold snap of the year." Futureman nodded.

"OK," Applejack said.

"And be sure to say hello to Hog Greer for me while you're up there, would ya?"

"Hog Greer?"

Shrill wind whipped through the compound, while glowing coils cast heat into the corners of the room. The base of Big Bald started its ascent twenty yards across the Nolichucky from where they sat, rising 5,516 feet into the midnight blue sky. The same orange heat would be there again tomorrow night, waiting for their return.

Sometime in the late 1700s, a young German immigrant named David Greer (sometimes seen as Grier) settled in the mountains of western North Carolina. According to legend, David had set his sights on the daughter of Colonel David Vance, an esteemed gentry man and veteran of the Revolutionary War. She was clearly beyond the reach of the young laborer and when she refused his attentions, he stormed off into the wilds searching for isolation – the only cure for his broken heart. Greer drove straight for the highest point on the horizon and sometime in 1802, he settled on the Higgins Creek side of Big Bald. Holing up in a cave against the harsh weather, David closed the open end with shale and mud, made himself a vent for smoke and lived, for a time, inside the cavern – comfortable as a wild animal.

But Greer was no fool. A man of some education, he set up a kingdom government for the mountain – a hand-written set of laws and articles recognizing that he alone was the Sovereign of Big Bald Mountain.

The legend of Hog Greer is rich – relaying the life of a man who openly defied the government by carrying a loaded gun into court to plead his case (Greer was acquitted on grounds of insanity); a man who fed the mountain animals with the crops of his own field: beardless rye, potatoes and corn; a man who wanted to be near the Higgins Creek spring, so he built a cabin over it; a man who mutilated stray cattle to amuse himself; a man who ambushed Holland Higgins and shot him dead over the property rights to an orchard; a man who narrowly escaped many attempts on his life – and never forgot a single one of them. Hog Greer was not a man to be trifled with. In fact, the valley folk were so 'afeared' of him, that mothers threatened their disobedient children into submission by the mere mention of his name: 'Be good or Hog Greer will git yuns.'

In the spring of 1834, Greer came down to town to leave some broken tools at the shop of smithy George Tompkins. When Greer returned at the agreed-upon time and saw the tools lying unrepaired on a table, he absconded to a nearby hollow with his ever-ready rifle and commenced to build a blind of elderberry – the vantage from which he intended to deliver Tompkins his deathknell bullet. But Tompkins was no fool either. He waited Greer out and when a frustrated Hog turned from the blind to retire to his mountain kingdom, Tompkins strode forth and shot him in the back. The mountainfolk considered it an appropriate death for the demon-eyed scoundrel – no charges were pressed on Tompkins.

Hog Greer ruled the high country for over thirty years, but the king's body returned to the earth unmarked. Two centuries later, his violent echo can only be heard in the lore of the mountainfolk song and verse – and, some say, in the shrieking evergreens of Big Bald Mountain.

"Futureman, this is bad. I'm st-starting to lose the feeling in m-my hands and feet," Applejack said, huddled under a tree. The rain had pulled in hard that morning on the tail of the wind. Strong gusts, filled with sleet, pummeled the top of the bald – white fog everywhere, grasping at the branches and bushes, shock frosting the wooden grass.

"Hands? What ar-ar-are those?" Futureman's clumsy fingers wouldn't tear the wrapper off his beef jerky snack. He put it back into his pack.

"We're going to have to ru-run this thing and get back to Johnny's. This is b-b-bad hypothermia weather." Shorts and rain shells were all they had to protect them from the elements. Their daypacks were nearly empty, containing only a few snacks and icy water.

Like skydiving in infinity, they moved through the mist across Big Bald. The ground was frozen. Grass blades crackled under their feet. At the wall of the forest on the opposite lip of the bald, white gusts surged together, a bending spine of wind, and crashed down onto the frosted deerberry. The trees pulled apart and snapped together like bear traps. *I wonder where Hog Greer's cave is,* Applejack thought as he listened to the shrieking evergreens. *Wish I had time to look for it.*

But they didn't. The wind chill was in the teens and they had no overnight gear. Thinking singularly of hot bunkhouse showers fifteen miles away, they trotted on. A blood rush was the only thing that could keep them going.

The scalding hot steam filled the bathhouse stalls. They stood, grunting under the high-powered showerheads. Their bodies moaned and cracked like winter pipes heating up in an old house. Fingers uncurled one by one, beards melting, as the words still trapped on top of the bald began to fall out of their mouths.

"Futureman, that's the last time we hike up into a cold sky without any gear."

"No, it's not. We're stupid. We'll do it again."

"Yeah, you're right. We'll do it again."

A knock rapped on the bunkhouse door. Daylight was barely trickling through the windows out of a rain-black sky.

"I guess Johnny's ready for dinner," Futureman said as he went to the door.

Lost-and-Found was standing on the other side, sopped to the bone and shivering, "G-g-guys, g-good to s-s-see you again."

"Hey there, buddy. Sit down and get yourself warm."

After a few minutes, the heater set his stutter at ease.

"Where'd you hike from?" Applejack asked.

"I hiked forty-three miles to get here. I read your Trail logs and figured you would be here at Johnny's or just beyond. It's awful lonely out there. I haven't seen anyone in days."

Some bodies are simply made of a different kind of material. They experience no arch failures, back problems, neck pains or curvature of the spine their entire lives. They defy chiropractors, run iron man races at sixty, thruhike at seventy, dance the cha-cha at ninety. These bodies understand that escalators don't break – they just turn into stairs. Anomalies, freaks of nature, trophies of physicality. Yes, they too will turn to dust in the end with the rest of humankind – but a finer grain.

Applejack and Futureman had always marveled over the abilities hiding in Lost-and-Found's adamantium frame. Back packing forty-three miles would kill some people. It is manageable for only a handful of hikers. Lost-and-Found was one of them.

When Lost-and-Found emerged from the shower, Applejack and Futureman were in the den. Johnny had ordered pizza for everyone on account of, "Why the hell not?"

"Yeah, me and Janet have had some rough waters in the past. We were together years ago, but had a bad break. She started that hostel over there. I had mine, and we've kinda been fighting ever since, but the bad blood's been calming down. She came over the other day, and we actually had an intelligent conversation. What d'ya know?"

"So this is good business for you?" Applejack asked.

"Aw, not really. I make enough to keep the place running. I figure it's a good life. I guess I don't know what else I'd do. The season comes and goes with the hikers. Nice to meet people. I've always been a little closed off – and yeah, I got a drinking problem. You guys have probably heard. But my new woman's helping me out with it. She's a real angel. Together, we'll get there."

How many times has Johnny made these confessions? Is he really opening up, or is he just burning the bull?

A bad rap is hard to break. It can take years. Sometimes it takes changing locations, or even hair color. Sometimes, it takes becoming the rap. And then sometimes, it takes getting up and realizing that everyday is brand new – no matter how much mud is left on yesterday's boots.

As usual, they got up early the next morning, preparing their minds for the cold, but the winter sky had folded into the forest near the bald. The sun was out again, rising to balance the chill. Johnny shook their hands at the trailhead south of Big Bald. He didn't charge them for the ride. Their next brush with civilization would be a place called Hot Springs, but to get there, they would have to pass world's end.

V

Conspiracies come in all shapes and sizes. They are not always far-reaching, born out of subversive ambition. Neither are they always hatched in high places in the dark. Board rooms and elliptical offices are easier to soundproof, but you and I conspire daily in our own little empires, do we not? Let's be honest for a moment. We're not above the little game here and there. We make one plan to escape from another. We plot with the guy next door to get the neighbor's noisy dog into the pound. We ask Denise to bring sweet potato casserole to supper because Grandma's has that funny aftertaste. These little moral compromises don't hurt anything really, do they? They're necessary adjustments that lubricate the problem areas of life. Ultimately, they're for the benefit of the whole. Do we really want to get to the bottom of things? Do we really want to know what people are up to, what's hidden behind their words? Surely it would be easier if everyone just kept his secrets and schemes to himself.

Applejack wanted warm oatmeal for breakfast – but he wasn't of a mind to cook it.

"Futureman, since you're going down there anyway, would you get some water for me? You know, while you're at it."

"Actually, I don't need any more. I wasn't really planning on –"

"My feet are pretty sore this morning. I need a few minutes to give 'em a rub-down."

"Ok, sure."

"Hey, uh, buddy?"

"Yeah?"

"Don't you think it would be nice to heat up some tea? I've got your favorite. Cinnamon. It's a bit chilly out here, you know."

"To tell the truth, I would like to just get on the Trail and get going –"

"I think you could really use some hot tea. It might help with your sniffles."

"I didn't notice I'd been sniffling, Applejack, but –"

"Since you're up already, why don't you just go ahead and start up the stove – boil some of that water. That'd be real good."

"Uh, I guess. Alright."

Futureman, being the decent and loyal friend that he was, sparked up the Whisperlite and brought the pot to a boil. He carried it over to Applejack, a cup of dry oatmeal resting beside him.

"Alright, just pour that in there and I'll be good to go. You're gonna really enjoy some piping hot oatmeal, Futureman. It'll do you right."

"I don't eat hot oatmeal, Applejack. Remember? I never eat hot oatmeal. You said we needed tea – for my cold."

"Oh. Yes, you're right. I did say that. Well, boil another pot then and we'll make some tea."

Near noon, Applejack caught up with Futureman, who had his things spread out in the sun on a mossy ledge just to the west of the Trail.

"How's it going?" Futureman asked.

"Fine. I'm a little tired of winding around all over the place. But, overall, fine," Applejack said

"They do like to steer the Trail every which way but straight."

"It doesn't make sense to me. Remember back a ways when we walked around the whole circumference of that mountain with the fire tower on top. Why can't we just walk straight to the top, get out in the sunlight a little bit and enjoy a nice view? Apparently they – whoever *they* are – have decided that we should walk as far as possible, in order to see as many anti-climatic places as possible. They mock us."

"Are you referring to the ATC?" Futureman asked.

"I guess. Whoever routes and re-routes these trails. Oh, I suppose it's to help preserve the land and all. I reckon that's good."

"I doubt their reasons are as simple as that," Futureman said.

"Huh?"

"Don't be naïve, Applejack. Those guys are getting rich off the Trail."

"What?"

"Believe it. I heard some dude in Damascus talking about this guy he met, said they re-routed the trail near his house, and then two weeks later an oil company bought the land and made a fortune."

"Please. An oil company?"

"Rest assured, those ATC guys aren't in it for nature. Nobody's that nice. It's all about money."

"Futureman, don't you think that maybe you're reading a little too much into –"

"He said the government's in on it too. They put pressure on the ATC to appease Washington lobbyists, and get this – most of them are already secretly employed by the same gigantic corporations that want to exploit the land to begin with."

"That doesn't make any sense at all."

"Yeah, I know. I don't really believe it but it's pretty interesting to think about."

"If you say so. Actually, the ATC Board is probably just a few rangers and a couple of friendly doctors and businessmen that like the outdoors. Since when did you start feasting on conspiracy theories?"

"I don't know. Sometimes I just start to go a little crazy out here."

"Me too. Let's get a move on."

Ahead, stirring in the forest, Champagne paced back and forth, waiting for them, waiting for anyone.

Futureman, hiking head down along the narrow path, nearly plowed into the rail-thin man before he saw the white sneakers and dumbbells underneath his nose. The sun was at an angle and cast a slanted light on the snaggle-toothed stranger that stood before him. A skipper hat was pulled down to his eyes.

"Oh. You scared me," Futureman said.

"It's not me you should be scared of, son," the stranger said. His gray beard looked like feathers poking out the sides of his face.

"It's not?"

"Are you carrying a short wave radio?" the man asked.

"No. What do you mean? Why should I –"

"We've been gutted. The country is in ruins."

Futureman's face lost its color. "They did it again? The terrorists!" His thoughts went immediately to his family, to Sarah in New York.

"Yes. They've been doing it for a long time now. They've pulled the wool over our eyes and you need to know."

"Oh, God help us. I've been out here and completely missed it."

"You need to get down to a town as soon as possible and get on the phone to your loved ones, boy."

"What happened? You've got to tell me what's happened."

"They've infiltrated every strata of society and are pulling it down around our ears – but it's not who you think. My name is Champagne." He put one of the dumbbells under his arm and extended his hand.

"What are you talking about? Who? Please, tell me." Futureman was frantic.

"The true power players of society – of the nations."

It suddenly dawned on Futureman what he was dealing with here, and color came back to his face. His lip tightened. "With all due respect, sir. I have to get going." He tried to step around but Champagne blocked him with a firm hand.

"The truth has been right under our noses the entire time – and we refused to see it. I've only recently put the pieces together myself."

"OK, I don't have the time for this. I have a long way to –"

"You think you don't have time until it's too late."

I'm not going to get out of this, am I? "Alright. What's been right under our noses? What have you discovered?"

"They've been meeting in a secret board room to determine the fates of the nations. This clandestine group has been setting the economic patterns and running the machinery of the world for centuries now. They control everything."

"See, I thought you were talking about another 9/11. I was really worried."

"That's just the tip of the iceberg, my friend." Champagne's eyes bulged. "Sugar in the coffee! It's going to be a whole lot worse the next time, guaranteed. Islamic terrorists weren't responsible for 9/11. That's what *they* want you to think. They control the government. The CIA was actually responsible for the fall of the World Trade Towers. And there's nothing we could have done to stop it. That's how powerful this group is."

"How did you come upon this amazing revelation?"

"The answers are hidden in the KJV."

"The King James Bible?"

"Yes, hidden between the lines, it's all there. I've committed myself to a rigorous course of study. It has taken precious time but now I see the truth. Your entire health as a human being is determined by whether or not you see the truth. The fabric of reality is predicated by the grid through which you view the world."

"I see that."

"I had to remove myself from the chaotic settings of the so-called normal life. They want to keep us distracted. They don't want us to see the fabric! Only after I came here to the mountains have I pieced it together, the TRUTH, over at the study center – bit by bit. Bit by bit." Champagne squinted into the trees.

"There's a study center out here?"

"Yes, not far away."

"And why, if I might ask, are you carrying dumbbells?"

"I have a demanding exercise regimen. Must keep sharp."

"Well that's nice. It probably helps to –"

"I've uncovered the root of all disease!" Champagne's eyes grew wide.

"The root of disease?"

"Of ALL disease!"

"So – what is it?"

Champagne leaned in close and whispered. "Guilt."

"Guilt," Futureman repeated. "What about bacteria?"

"How do you view reality? Bacteria – viruses – cancer – they feed on guilt. It's in the grid. The degree to which you are healthy is not determined by bacteria."

"Well thank you, very helpful, I'll try not to feel guilty as much. Now, I really must –"

"Get the radio."

"And I'll be sure to get a radio."

"Excellent!" Champagne said as Futureman walked away. "If you want to look at my research, contact me...Champagne!" His voice echoed around the corner. "P.O. Box..." Futureman picked up his pace. "King James!"

VI

Futureman moved fast through the trees. His mind was mixing words. *Conspiracy plus monotony equals monospiracy.* Laughing but not really, he pounded on the shanks of the path, almost running now. *Got to get there. Thoughts and curves and that ATC! They did this! Making me walk like their pawn around these endless endless endless curves!*

The trees were bemused.

"What's he rushing towards?" Southern Red Oak asked.

"Who knows, who ever knows?" Mockernut responded.

"You want to know what I'm rushing towards? Do you! You want to know?" Futureman stammered.

"If you'd be so kind," Oak said.

"Because...because...I'm trying to get away from...because the curves, they..."

"Yes, little one?" Oak nudged.

Futureman gave up. "I don't know."

Oak balked, a creak in the tops. "Ahh, legs."

"What about legs?" Futureman asked.

"Always moving with them. Always going somewhere."

"What's wrong with moving?"

"What's wrong with standing in place?" Mockernut asked.

"But the point of having legs is to use them – to move," Futureman said. "We don't exactly have roots like you."

"Is that so?" Oak said.

"Yes, that's one of the things that makes us different from you."

"Hmm, interesting. We learn something new everyday, don't we?" Oak said.

"We sure do," said Mockernut.

"I know, I know," Futureman said. "You think I'm too fast-paced, that I don't take time to slow down and be quiet, but you don't understand. I've hiked here from Maine."

Oak's laughter shook the ground.

"Well, that's very special," Mockernut said. "And how are our tree friends doing up in Maine? We keep meaning to visit, but we can't go anywhere, you see. We've got roots."

A small patch of eastern redbuds giggled – little squeals.

"Seriously, I know what it's like. I've embraced the quiet peace of the far ranges!" Futureman demanded.

"Far ranges, eh? Then why are you running?" Oak asked.

"Wh –?"

"Where are you going, he means to say?" Mockernut clarified.

"To the city."

Oak balked again. "Ahh, the city."

"You have something against the city?" Futureman asked.

"Well now, I've not ever seen a city. What do you think about it?"

"The city? Uh, hard to say really," Futureman said. "I don't like it all that much. Crowded, kind of ugly and loud."

"But you're running there now?"

"Yeah."

"Why?"

"Uh, I don't know…"

"Let me ask you, how far do you have to go before you get there?"

"About six miles I'd guess," Futureman said.

"Oh. It's gotten much closer." Tall Oak frowned and shook its branches in the tops. Leaves fell through the forest. "But what do I know about miles? I'm a tree."

"Is something wrong?" Futureman asked.

"I'm shedding. Gonna go to sleep soon," Oak said.

"Hah – shedding, he says," said Mockernut. "At least you still have leaves. I'm already naked."

The little redbuds squealed.

"Winter's coming, huh?" Futureman asked.

"Ah, winter," Oak said. "Wind up there on top of the canopy – it's quite cold."

"Stop your complaining," Mockernut said. "At least you *have* a canopy."

Oak took a deep breath and burrowed into the decaying loam, cinching its beams for winter. "Okay, my boy. Away with you now. Run along to the city."

"Wait, tell me what you meant by –"

"Off you go now."

VII

When he got to Hot Springs, Futureman immediately found the Sunnybank Inn, a historic bed and breakfast that was cheap and friendly to hikers. When the proprietor opened the door, he made no attempt to hide his sagging face or teary eyes. Something told Futureman that more than gravity was pulling him down. Sunnybank was quiet, as though death was in the corners.

The Inn was elegant, a 19th century manse with simple rooms, simple square frame ways, striders in the floorboards, and in every plank a rusty nail. One room connected to another, each with a life all its own – filled with antiques. A music room with Woody Guthrie sheet music, guitars, violins, banjos and mouth harps. There was a sitting room with an oriental rug, circle backed chairs, green felt poker table and a marble chess set. A parlor showcased a gorgeous white mantelpiece, and a cast-iron wood rack with graying logs; an old bellows leaned against the stone, rocking chairs draped with fading quilts. There was a library with old hardback classics – *Moby Dick, Far From the Maddening Crowd, The House of the Seven Gables.* A steep, narrow stairway led upstairs. The boarder's rooms were separated by colors and paintings on the walls that told stories. The bathrooms had legged washbasins with porcelain handles, oval mirrors and yellow-brown stains around the drains.

The man leaned against the crooked doorframe, elbow crushed, face following the wood seams.

"Is this not a good time?" Futureman asked.

"No, no – come in, come in. You're always welcome here. I'm Elmer." He held out his hand and forced a smile. He'd been preparing a gourmet vegetarian dinner. The kitchen air was filled with the crisp smell of plants.

"This place is yours as long as you want to stay here. Play music in the music room, chess or cards in the sitting room. Not that there's anybody to…well, it's kind of empty right now." Tears began to well up again. His chest filled with sorrowful breathing. He took his glasses off and wiped them. "Please, uh, read a book in the library, sleep in if you want. This home is yours. I do ask, though, that you join us for dinner tonight at seven. It's kind of a tradition around here."

"Certainly, sir."

Elmer retreated to his cooking. He grabbed a sweet onion, some peppers, mushrooms, and began to slice them.

There was a beautiful hound – old boy, shiny brown coat tinged with gray – sleeping on a mat next to the radiator in the stairwell.

Futureman inched up the stairs and chose the crimson room. A picture of a river, predominantly dull yellow in color, hung on the wall. The window opened to the backyard under a setting sun. A rusted iron gating, bent in places, surrounded the lawn. Two large oaks shadowed the grass. There were tombstones of the families that had lived here. Futureman stared out the window as the sun sank low into the sky.

He heard voices downstairs and went to check. Another man was in the kitchen speaking with Elmer. He waved at Futureman in periphery then mentioned to Elmer that he had taken care of arrangements.

Elmer nodded.

"Maybe I should come back later. I can come back later," Futureman said.

"No, no," Elmer said. "I'm truly sorry for all the awkward silence, my friend. But you have managed to come in the time of a death." He put his eyes to his sleeve again. "Ernie, would you –"

"Sure," Ernie said. "Elmer's fourteen year old hound is about to be put down. I've just placed a call to the vet and he's coming over."

"I am so sorry," Futureman said. "What is his name?"

"His name is Rufus," Elmer said, lifting his head.

Futureman looked at Elmer soberly. "Did you say *Rufus*?"

The very same day that Futureman had pulled himself out of the Wilderness, too beat up to deal with reality, he had called home to hear some familiar congratulatory voices, ones that would console his raw heels.

Bobby answered.

"Bobby! I'm alive, made it out of the Wilderness."

"Great, great, that's – good," Bobby said, a reticence in his voice.

"Something wrong?" Futureman asked.

"I don't know how to say this."

"Say what?"

"Uh, your sister – she – she had a miscarriage."

"N-no. That can't be right, Bobby. She –"

"Found out a few days ago. I'm sorry to tell you like this."

It was her first child. Futureman had been praying for the baby. It was the one thing that picked him up off the smoldering Wilderness floor.

Bobby cleared his throat a second time. "And also buddy, I'm sorry – but your dog, Rufus – he had to be put down yesterday. His lungs just couldn't hold out anymore."

"Is my sister okay?"

"Yeah, she's doing good. Doctor says she can get pregnant again."

"And Ben?"

"She and Ben are fine. Your parents are with them. They said they are all trusting in God's will."

A mysterious will. "Thanks, Bobby. Hard things to say, and did you say that Rufus…"

A lost child takes precedence over a dead dog. Sorrow for Rufus had remained hidden in the hollows of the Maine forest. Futureman had grieved for the child, but not for Rufus. He realized now, in Elmer's kitchen, that he'd never said goodbye.

Big Rufus had a paw on Elmer's knee, head on his master's lap, struggling to breathe. Dark mucus hung from the end of his snout, pink infection collecting in his eyes.

"Elmer, do you mind if I…"

"No, please." Elmer offered.

The dog clung to the weight of Futureman's hand, staring up into his eyes. *My own dog.* "Goodbye, buddy."

When the vet came, Futureman was waiting at the top of the stairs, arms crossed. Elmer rubbed the dog gently and nodded as the man set his things on the kitchen table.

"Thank you, my dear old friend for the fourteen years you gave to me," Elmer said. Rufus raised his head for the last time, and laid it back down on Elmer's lap.

Ernie and Elmer wrapped him up in his mat and carried him to the back yard. Futureman watched through the window as they buried the old hound in the black earth under the second tall oak.

Dinner was exquisite. Friends of Elmer's and hikers past gathered in the dining room around a huge antique table. Applejack and Lost-and-Found had come from the woods in time for the vegetarian feast. Elmer shared his grief, unabashedly, but having these people around the table brought him a balanced joy. His toast spoke of redemption, "To those we will always remember..." and the shared stories – of pain made right.

VIII

Next morning at the Smoky Mountain Diner, Lost-and-Found was fidgeting in his seat, breaking apart the half-eaten Benedict mound on his plate with the tip of his fork.

"Taste funny?" Futureman asked.

"No. It's fine," Lost-and-Found said, looking out the window.

"Everything okay?" Applejack asked.

Lost-and-Found avoided eye contact. "Of course."

"You sure?"

"It's fine."

Lost-and-Found stood to pay his bill. "I've got some stuff to do around town, guys – so – I'll catch up with you tonight."

"Stuff?" Futureman asked.

"Yeah, just some...a new pair of shoes...and other stuff."

Applejack glanced down at Lost-and-Found's shoes. They were a little worn but certainly didn't warrant a new pair.

"And make some calls and things," Lost-and-Found added. "Go on ahead."

"We'll wait. We're not in a hurry. You, of all people, should know that."

"No – go!" he said emphatically.

"Alright. We'll meet up with you tonight at Roaring Fork Shelter, just

below Max Patch?" Applejack looked at Lost-and-Found intently. "Okay?"
"Roaring Fork, got it," Lost-and-Found said, halfway out the door.
"Something's fishy," said Futureman. "What do you think he's up to?"
"I don't know. He is Lost-and-Found, after all."

Once an old homestead clearing where sheep and cattle grazed, Max Patch is now a 4,629-foot high, USFS-protected grassland in the sky – a bald surrounded by thick-growth eastern redbud, birch, ash, magnolia and silverbell. Standing abreast of the high plains, the sky is unfettered above. The blue-pitched Smokies wait to the south and misty Mount Mitchell to the north.

The luster of fall was fading. Crimsons, yellows and oranges were now browning on the saprogenic forest mat – offering carious life to the unseen creatures below. Vast amounts of organic materials from the fallen leaves, needles, branches and moldering tree stumps make up the base of the litter-soil food web, playing a crucial role in the biochemical cycle of life in the forest. Amazingly, when it seems that everything is going to sleep, the majority of forest species are coming out to play – the *cryptozoa*, billions strong in the damp dark alcoves of the soil, feed on the decay. Mites, springtails, ants, termites, roundworms, earthworms, potworms, isopods, centipedes, millipedes, spiders, false scorpions and beetles – creep, crawl and writhe underneath. A microscopic horror.

By high noon, Applejack and Futureman were seated on the lip of the mountain. They had hiked sixteen miles in four hours and hadn't even rushed. It was just one of those days where a soft path and a lukewarm breeze makes the air light enough to slice right through. Roaring Fork Shelter was hidden deep in the forest on the hook of a stream. A large fire pit was dug out in front. Charred log thumbs scattered around it.

"Should we hike over Max Patch today? We could do another ten before nightfall," Futureman said, pumping his heel against the dirt, understanding – these days should be taken advantage of.

"I know. It's a perfect day to go long, but we gotta wait for Lost-and-Found."

"You're right. Anyway, how long has it been since we had a good fire?"
"Too long."

Two hours later, they had a burn pile that was shoulder-high – comprised of box-elder legs, hemlock chunks, chinkapin knots and dead buckeye stems with sawdust trunks. They'd pulled off and dragged in anything and everything that looked like it might burn – from hangnail kindling to corkscrewed green branches. Then, they set to cracking the thickest logs with heavy rocks from the stream, enthralled to watch the broken pieces catapult through the air.

The blue heat of the fire burned it all, even the 'unburnables' they had collected for entertainment. Wet branches sizzled. Water in the xylem and phloem klongs boiled and hissed. Even the wet decay of rotten stumps disappeared, their fat knuckles turning to vapor.

It burned all afternoon and into the night, pushing back the inky black. The dancing fire entranced them, blue-black white-hot pocket of coals bringing sweat to their foreheads. All noises fell indistinctly into the rhythm of the popping wet wood. Syncopation, tapping, rustling...

When suddenly, it broke through – the sound of a walker.

"Something's coming," Futureman said.

Applejack looked out from the glare of the fire ring. A flicker on the trees, there it was, creeping by like a large curious animal – and gone.

"What is it?"

"I don't know."

"Is it Lost-and-Found?"

"Maybe. He should have been here by now, that's for sure. But he would have seen our fire and come over here."

"Lost-and-Found! That you?" Futureman called.

No answer. The moon spotlighted a bend in the trail. A human figure broke into it and was gone.

"I think that's him. It's lanky enough to be him," Futureman said.

"If it is, he's walking awful fast. Even faster than usual."

"Surely he saw the fire."

"Course he did. C'mon, let's go check it out," Applejack said.

They put their boots on and moved as quickly and stealthily as they could. It was a mile before they caught sight of the hiker – black spindle clicking through the branches.

"Turn off your light," Applejack whispered.

"Why?" Futureman asked.

"I want to figure out what he's up to."

"We don't even know if it's Lost-and-Found. Whoever it is could be hiking all night for all we know. Besides, all our stuff's back at the shelter."

"C'mon, you're always up for this sort of thing. And it *is* Lost-and-Found – nobody else glides like that. Let's at least follow him up to Max Patch. It'll be gorgeous up there, anyway," Applejack said, his pupils dilating.

"Fine."

Something had never been quite right about the boy Lost-and-Found. His strange look, his hangdog laughter, his erratic mood swings and vague talk of destiny; and, of course, there was the midnight star ritual Futureman had seen back in New York. It all added up to something and Applejack wanted to get to the bottom of it.

Under the full moon, the Trail came into a wide path that broke through the sparse piedmont surrounding the Max Patch bald.

"Hey, wait. You feel that?" Applejack asked.

"Yeah – the static? Tons of it – it's raising the hairs on my skin."

"What is it? There's no storm. And it's too cool to be heat lightning."

Hiding in a small selva patch, they looked out at Lost-and-Found as he made his way up the steep northern slope and onto the thick grassy cone, tripping and clawing at the ground as he went along.

"What on earth is he doing?" Futureman asked.

"I don't know, but there's something on top of that Patch, and he's trying to get to it."

Finally, the boy paused in the middle of the summit, his long body profiled against the moonglow. He slung his pack down, broke apart a bundle of sticks and, jabbing them vertically into the ground, formed a circle around himself.

"My word," Futureman whispered, as Lost and Found took off his shoes, threw them into the bushes and pulled another pair from his pack.

"Well, I'll be – he *was* getting new shoes in town," Applejack said.

The boy then took three of the sticks and slid them together to form a staff, fastening what appeared to be some sort of medallion piece to the top.

"What. In. The. World." Applejack uttered, as Lost-and-Found held the make-shift scepter up to the sky.

Futureman was about to comment himself, when the medallion turned on and shot a neon rainbow into the firmament.

And that's when the spaceship came down.

Applejack and Futureman did not – no longer – not now – have the ability to make intelligible sentences concerning the matters of what they were seeing.

Applejack tried: Nomgong to meet up masters on a purpose.

To which Futureman responded: Space balls with lighted flesh booms.

It was huge. It covered the whole top of the mountain and blotted out the moon. It was made of a non-earthly metal with glow dots, divots and dents all over it.

It made an awkward squealing noise as it parked itself in the air over Lost-and-Found's circle. Then it opened in the middle and shot a beam of light down. This, of course, set Lost-and-Found's twigs on fire. The staff with the medallion went up into the alien vessel first; then followed the man-child Lost-and-Found. He clasped his hands together in the center of his chest and rose into the light, at the last moment, unlatching them to wave goodbye.

The craft moaned and jostled, tilting down on one side, and banged into some trees before cometing up through of the earth's atmosphere.

And it was gone.

"Starkind the moops," Applejack said.

Futureman waved. "Glowind a comet blimp."

(Aliens are real. Pass it on.)

IX

"He is a man of mystery. The great world outside his mountains knows almost as little of him as he does of it; and that is little indeed. News in order to reach him must be of widespread interest as fairly to fall from heaven; correspondingly, scarce any incidents of mountain life will leak out unless they be of sensational nature, such as the shooting of a revenue officer in Carolina, the massacre of a Virginia court, or the outbreak of another feud in "bloody Breathitt.""

-Horace Kephart, 1913

In those days, it was another world right next door, beyond the green fortress walls of the great Appalachians. As foreign as the tribes of pygmies under the canopy of the Congo, as unknown as the ranges of the Hindu Kush were *the people of the hills*, nestled in a sea of waving mountains wherein and beyond were Cherokee. The landscape acted as a natural barrier to development in those days, with rushing rivers, waterfalls, chasms, ravines, wild forests, tangled laurel jungles a hundred miles thick and trees larger around than ten men grasping hands. As impregnable as a thousand castle walls were the Southern Appalachians.

"Our typical mountaineer" wrote Kephart "is lank, he is always unkempt, he is fond of toting a gun on his shoulder, and his curiosity about a stranger's name and business is promptly, though politely, outspoken."

He speaks a unique dialect. He says, "Suzie hain't mean nothin by it, she's jes lettinown." He sometimes turns his long *a*'s to *e*'s: "Tut far was blezin som'in fierce." His short *u*'s to *i*'s, "Hain't no sich thang." He adds a hard *h* to his short *i*'s: "Hit's a long ways from hur." *Done* is *daun*, *ask* is *ax*, *caught* is *catched*, and *grew* is *growed*. His possessive pronouns are *hisn, hern, yourn* and *theirn*. He says, "I used to could," "I might should," "I needs taught all yourn a lesson," and "They's (meaning five or so) done landed een jail agin." Finally, his speech will be so colored with archaic English (not found since Chaucer) and half-bred terms so confounded by Gaelic and Anglo-Saxon diction, that any attempt to find a pure linguistic ancestor is as unlikely and arduous as the journey of a pack mule through a summer tangle of mountain laurel: "You-unses been lettinon a meal from nawt a sound a meat. Ye gots hate ter eat."

Above all things, the mountain man is a storyteller. As James Robert Reese puts it, "A good everyday tale teller can walk to the local store, buy a sack of six-penny nails, talk to a few persons along the way, return home, and make the rest of the family envious of his or her wondrous adventure." The storytellers are dying out, though. Those remaining are eighty, ninety and one hundred years old – left to tell about them gooder days.

Mountain folk were a resourceful people of simple and primitive ways, accustomed to the kind of brawn that brutal year upon brutal year develops. They made cabins out of logs, mud and horsehair. They turned fallen trees into churches, brooms, tools, schools and barns. They used creek beds for roads and patiently cleared small patches of jungle thicket to plant seed and harvest on. But in the wake of industry and the pace of modern development, little by little, these skills started to wane.

When the giant lumber companies of the North heard about the great trees in the southern Appalachians it was just a short time before they were cutting them down. Worlds collided.

"Inderstry's what dern it. 1920 then was," Jep from Seldom Seen Hollow says, standing in his yard. Beyond him are coalmines, railroad warehouses, lumber piles, sawdust pyramids, metal cranes and boxes stacked up thirty feet high. "Use to there was this'n tree, it'd be huge granpappy oak b'now, 'twixt all the houses, served as a droppin' point – letters, clothes, marmelade, boots, things left thar from all rackets a'goods. If Aunt Loo come o'er mine house and left hern shoes, I's juss set 'em under that'n tree. And when a faller come long an' sawred 'em as Aunt Loo's, he'd pile 'em up and take 'em straight on back to Aunt Loo." Jep grasps his suspenders. "But tain't like that now. Ey God, no sirs. First boy that sawed 'em shoes now'd throwed 'em straight over'n that thar crick, and poor Aunt Loo'd have ter go 'round wet-footed. Folks now frettin' about this'n done or that'n done, men's featherin one'nother with lead, ain't nary bitty sense in it. Hat's after 1920, see. Inderstry's what dern it."

Modernity pulled the mountain out of the man and reset his place not at the hill's foundation, a child in awe of the heights – but on her peak, a man on the throne of his new domain. The people in the hollows between the green crown tops of Hallelujah set out a'walkin along the short hand of society toward bigger, brighter and better, and now most of the true mountain folk of the American past are stayed only in memory. But a few – a very few – remain, still hidden just beyond the laurel.

Danny stood on the trail with a gun, looking into the gray forest, his ears toward noises – the clutter of awkward birds: wild turkeys, grouse and bobwhites. Davenport Gap, Applejack and Futureman's final destination before dark, lay beyond Danny and his gun. The natural spring where they could refill their water bottles (since they were now out and quite thirsty) – beyond Danny and his gun. The peace and quiet of the trail, the lonely bends and curves along the carpet paths to Georgia – beyond Danny and his gun.

The man had a long beard that might as well have been tucked into the waistline of his pants. His face had seen hard winters, grit stained into the folds of his cheeks, deep crow's nests around his eyes, eyebrows thick and bristly. He was gnawing fat on a chaw. Its black juice leaked out the side of his mouth onto his beard, and he made no attempt to steer it otherwise, content that it follow that yellow streak down for hours, perhaps days, months or years. Danny rested his gun at the shoulder. He said he'd heard them coming before they woke up that morning.

"Howdy der fallers, whur you-unses goin ter?"

"Down the Trail a bit," Applejack said.

"Whacha' doin out hur?"

"Hiking. What are you doing, sir?"

"Muh? Mern jiss hunnin grass."

"Hunting?"

"Mmm."

"Grass?"

"Yarp. Grass."

Grass? Not grass. "Oh, grouse?"

"S'what are said. 'Em bobtails floutin heres and theres, seen 'em times in the hunrits. They's flarin heres all'oer, thick ees molarses, usual."

"You shot any yet?" Futureman asked.

"Hain't seen non yet. Thick ees molarses, usual." He squinted at them. "Lerks you-unses nide warder. Cabins gotty warder. Ye find it d'reck'ly."

"We were planning on getting some at the next –"

"You-unses foundin warder o'er my way. Cabins gotty warder. Jessa holler down around na bin." Danny trudged through the thick rhododendrons lining the trail. "Faller mern leeyud fellers." He disappeared, crashing into the thick growth.

"Eeeeeeeeeeee," Futureman said.

"Yeah, what do you think?" Applejack said.

"I don't know."

"Well, he said there's water, and we need a place to camp tonight."

"What if he's not right in the head, though? I mean the dude has a gun –"

"I guess we're about to find out."

Applejack bounded into the dense laurel and disappeared. Futureman plunged in after him. The coarse branches pulled at their faces and legs.

"I can't believe we're doing this," Futureman said.

"What's gotten into you lately. You been actin' like a school girl."

"I know, but…"

The rhododendrons melted away and opened into a hidden patch valleyed in the middle of the forest.

"Har sheen is." Danny opened his arms, brown pocket overalls pulled his heels up.

It was an old homestead. The grass was green, tall and clumpy, scattered with shepherd's purse and common yarrow. Three springs gurgled water into a small delta. On the far end stood an old, ransacked smoking barn. Across from it sat a shotgun shack superincumbent on cinder blocks, its dilapidated door held shut by a wire nailed to the outside. There was a fire ring to the east of the cabin with plenty of chopped wood.

"Now, this'n warder's better'n any I e'er tested. Fillern up an enjoyn."

"Thanks a lot, Danny. We'll be on our way soon," Applejack said.

"Nawp. You-unses er stayin hair."

"Well, we appreciate it, but –"

"S'place is a good fren-er-mines. Been hisn family hunrits a years. Loddy time go it were a homestead. Now's jess sittin hur rottin. Use it all a time when I's out hunnin. Figgered he wun't mind if you-unses used it too."

"I don't know, Danny. You sure he won't care?" Futureman asked.

Danny rustled his brow. "S'what are said, weren't it?"

"Alright, we'll take you up on it. And again, it's awful kind of you to –"

"Yen fallers jess watch at for 'em shrews. They's little sucks, bite mean though. Pison too!"

Applejack wasn't sure he heard him right. "Excuse me, did…did you just say poisonous shrews?"

"I'll tell you-unses now." Danny put the butt of his gun on the ground and leaned on the other end of it. "I hain me a cuzin, title a Frubby Dinson. Year yester last, he's out cawlin dogs and cornerin bars, when he run 'crost a batch a'em pison shrews. Dartin here to there." Danny scoured the ground with his eyes. "They's mean like, 'em shrews. Frubby musta scared 'em up cuz one come featherin' up hisn leg, layed right into him. When Frubby done comed home 'at night, he'uz all puffed up like a pregnated hawlg, stayed sickly in bed far as a season's holler. Tell you-unses now, 'em shrews'r pisons likey king cobra."

"King cobra? You said they're as poisonous as a –"

"Po Frubby D, hat sumbitch now afeared a'any critter at moves. 'Em pison shrews messed him up good, I'll tell you-uns a'what." He put his gun back on his shoulder. "Well, reckon I's a'settin on now, gotter get me one a'em grasses. They's thick ees molarses 'round here, usual."

"Thank you, sir, for the cabin, the water, and the…shrew warning," Futureman said.

"I aren't a sir, jessa regu'ole one-man fool. Cabin's yourn as much mine." Danny turned and spoke over his shoulder, "Jiss don' ferg it up." And he disappeared into the rhododendrons.

The blue cupola sky turned to black, stars out in plain view above the clearing. The fire was a simple one, the steady flicker of uniform logs.

"Futureman, it's pretty amazing that we're sitting here. How many people have walked right by this place on their way to Hot Springs or Davenport?"

"Couldn't say."

"This homestead could be two hundred years old. We're sitting on a real piece of history here, and Danny? He's the real deal, a true-blooded mountain man frozen in time. This place is hidden from the world."

"Mm." Futureman gazed at the underside of the burning logs, diagonal lines of black coal – like a tiger skin. "It kind of makes me wonder."

"About what?"

"About what else is hidden."

"In these mountains? What do you mean?"

"Inside, in our own chests."

A pocketed coal burst, a word burning in the fire. The sparks rose, blue to orange, a confession. Futureman whispered it.

"Say again."

"Confession."

"What do you mean?"

"Freedom from sin, resolve for guilt. Forgiveness for the road ahead. That's what's in my chest." Futureman rustled a log. The spark ran up his arm.

"Bobby shaved his beard, you know," Applejack said.

"I've been thinking about that."

"I don't get it. After all those miles, after your blisters, my chafing and that thousand-mile tunnel of doubting between New York and Pearisburg – and he goes and shaves his beard."

"Don't seem right."

"And yet it does."

"Yeah, I know."

"I'm sorry, Futureman. I'm sorry for letting you down. For not encouraging you when you needed me. For not digging down deep."

"I'm sorry too. And not just for that, but for the times before that. And for tomorrow – because I know I'll wake up and let you down again."

Slowly, the wind died down, and the darkening, oxygen-deprived flames turned to a smolder that recommended sleep. There were other words caught in the fire, in a pocket of coals buried underneath the slow burn.

It was dark when Applejack woke up to the sound of a hound ruffling and baying in the laurel nearby. He sat up. *Every hound has an owner.*

"Futureman, get up. Get up." He shook at Futureman's shoulder.

Futureman was sleeping hard.

"Futureman!"

Futureman moaned and turned his face down.

"Mountain men are coming."

Futureman sat upright, as if he'd never been asleep. "Where! How many! Weapons!" he said, peering wide-eyed into the trees.

Applejack crawled to the door.

A human voice sounded in the forest.

"They're probably just hunters, wouldn't you say? Probably hunting coon,"

Applejack said.

"Or hikers," Futureman said.

Half a dozen voices differentiated in the nearby brush, accented, loud, laughing.

"I don't like this – not good, not good at all," Futureman crouched on his knees.

"Hold on –"

"We gotta make for it!"

"Take it easy."

Futureman pulled on Applejack's shirt. "C'mon man."

"I'm scared, too. Just settle down!"

Two other hounds appeared in the tall grasses of the clearing, followed by four men. They shined their lights into the cabin.

"Har dar, fellers," one of them hollered. "Yaw daun warry 'bout dyem dawgs, they's harmless as a tree'd bar."

"It's us you-unses should warry bout!" another one said.

Uuhhhhhhh. "Excuse me?" Applejack shouted. "We don't want no –"

"Don't mine Jimmy! He's a bit loosed up on the shine!" a third said.

Moonshine?

"You frenz a Po Po's?" the first man shouted.

Applejack stuck his head out a bit more. "We, uh, Danny…brought us back here and said –"

"You say Danny?"

"I guess so. Yessir."

"Ole Danny! He's a good ole faller – freyund a Po Po's. If you-unses frenz a Danny, then you-unses frenz a Po Po's. And if you-unses frenz a Po Po's – then hell, you-unses're frenz a eres!"

Applejack waved stiffly. "Thank you – thanks, then. Hope you get a raccoon."

"Yep. Yall's is welcome ter stay h'yeer long as y'ont to. Jiss don ferg it up."

X

The path spiraled off Snowbird Mountain and drained down into the Pigeon River at Davenport Gap. They emerged from a forest of American elm and sourwood onto a bridge over Interstate 40. Down below, lying on the highway was the carcass of a deer, half-eaten by crow.

"Applejack, why is it that the only time we ever see a dead animal is when we cross over a highway?" Futureman asked.

"Because cars drive on highways."

"It was a rhetorical question."

"I know."

The rotiform thumping of tires (rubber clown faces smashing-smashing-smashing-smashing) and the charred smells of effaced tread dissipated, as they etched their way up the dirt road that turned into mountain trail once again, swallowed whole by the arms of undraped rhododendron.

They had come to it at last, their own backyard. Rows on rows of mountain upon mountain. The huge old-growth trees had been cut back centuries prior, but even still, they seemed to twist upward endlessly through the disappearing greens – up, up, up to the very knuckles of the Smoky Mountain peaks. The backs of their hands.

"The Cherokee called it *Shaco-nagee*."

"What?"

"Land of the Blue Mist."

"Ah, land of the blue mist. Yes."

So it was that Applejack and Futureman finally returned home, climbing up the precipitous torso of the range, switching back and forth along its contoured frame. Engulfed by the cold blue veil just a hundred feet in, they trod upward into the misty mountains.

According to the Cherokee people, in the heart of Shaco-nagee, there exists an enchanted lake – *Atag-hi*, "place of water birds." It is somewhere below the tallest mountain, near the headwaters of Deep Creek, but Ataghi, the magical lake, cannot be seen by human eyes. It is concealed by a shroud of balsam, hemlock and twisted rhododendron. By the decree of the Great White Bear, no human can behold it. But this was not always so.

The enchanted lake teems with birds, reptiles, fish and beasts of every kind. But it is bear – the wisest and most revered of all creatures – that guard the lake as their most sacred treasure. Bears, blessed by the Great Creator with high intelligence and even the gift of speech, discovered long ago that a dip into the waters of Ataghi would cure all disease and heal all wounds. A place of life, the lake is engulfed day and night by the beasts of the mountain as they drink and play and thrive. A great crowd of birds circle over the waters, awaiting their turn.

For thousands of years, the Great White Bear – leader and medicine man, has kept the lake hidden from the eyes of men, but legend has it that there was once a young brave whose heart was pure. Not wishing to use the lake or take it for himself, his only desire was to see it with his own eyes. For days he fasted and prayed, and one morning the lake appeared before him-the broad vale of amethyst-colored waters swarmed with creatures of every imaginable size and shape: eagles, wolves, rabbits, deer, hawks, ducks and mice. From the heavens, a violet waterfall pounded down over the rocks, filling the lake with medicine water. The young man was overwhelmed. As the vision faded, he marked his place with a pile of stones, hoping to return to paradise, to Ataghi.

The young brave was greatly admired among his people for finding the lake. Spring grew into summer, and summer passed into fall. A harsh winter came down from the north, freezing the hunters' fingers and destroying the storehouses. Even the forest animals cowered in their holes. There was no food anywhere to be found. As a last resort, the starving people sent out the young man to retrieve game from the 'place of the water birds.' Not wishing to see his family die, he finally agreed to return to the valley and find his stone marker.

All through the icy night, near death, he sang his prayers and cried out to the Great White Bear. At dawn, the wind died, the sun shone down over the snow and the magical waters appeared before him again. Without hesitation, the young brave pulled back his bow and shot a bear. Sacred though it was, this creature would feed many people. As the bear fell he turned to the young man and spoke. None of the other creatures heard his words. All fell to silence. The shrieking of birds ceased. The howling of the coyote ended and the multitude of animals waited, as the Great White Bear descended from his den to administer justice.

Days later, after the blizzard broke, a search party found the body of the young brave. It lay on the ground, ripped apart by bear teeth. There were no tracks in the snow.

Since that day, neither man nor woman has seen the enchanted waters of Ataghi. The Cherokee say that, even still, small tokens of the magical lake are scattered here and there – reminders of paradise. If you are silent and watchful, you may notice them. Hunters have claimed that the furious beating of wings can be heard around Deep Creek spring. Some insist that a strange mist hovers above a small valley there in the fleeting moments of dawn, and many years ago, an old-timer returned from the hills carrying a water lily he'd picked somewhere in the heart of Shaconagee. Most of the good people of the valley laugh at these notions, yet the Cherokee maintain that the sacred lake is there still, paradise on earth. But it is hidden – lost to humankind, buried in the earth beneath the broken trust and treacherous blood of good intentions.

Applejack stepped out onto Sunup Knob. At five thousand feet, the knob is normally a perfect perch to watch the sun rise over a blue valley, but for Applejack, it was too late in the year and too late in the day. Winter was pulling her cloak over the shoulders of the mountains. Applejack's diving boards were still. Unmoving distant ridges blended into the solitude of harnessed heights. Hoar frost had come. At this elevation, fog and mist hang so long in the air that the moisture freezes, coating the branches of the trees and spindles of rhododendron with layer upon layer of razory ice.

"If we fell off this perch, we'd get cut into a million pieces," Futureman said, looking down.

"Beautiful, though, isn't it?"

"Beautiful like confession."

"Nobody's around. No noise. No nothin'."

Futureman looked to the north. Pale light crept through a graveyard of skeleton poplars, stripped bare by the cold. Their blood was freezing, hiding their life away.

"This is the most visited park in the whole country. Now, it's just us and a handful of others."

Applejack crouched, resting against the frozen rubble. "It's silent now, but something stirs."

"We'll see. Just keep quiet enough to listen."

On the wind, was it a dying breath or the patient abiding sigh of the resilient mountain folds? They couldn't tell.

"I beheld with rapture and astonishment a sublimely awful scene of power and magnificence, a world of mountains piled upon mountains...an amazing prospect of grandeur," wrote William Bartram of the late-18th century wild lands. One of the first botanists of the new world, his plant collecting had taken him to many places-among them, the Great Lakes, Canada and Florida.

Commisioned by the wealthy (including King George himself), Bartram was well financed as he came to study and explore, but Captain John Stuart – superintendent of Indian affairs in the southern colonies – advised against it. A few traders with permits from the Crown had found their way into the deeper hills but, by and large, white men tended not to fare well there. Since the beginning of European arrival, settlers had violated British law, entering into unauthorized lands in search of rich, habitable land. And as contact between the two great cultures of 'civilized' Europe and 'native' Cherokee became more frequent, dissonance grew – from a curious flirtation to an epic clash. By the time Bartram arrived, bad blood was already brewing.

But the botanist was a Quaker. He took a rather simple approach concerning the matter. "I have no intent to shed theirs, so why should the Indians want to shed my blood?" When Bartram came to the edge of the Blue Ridge Divide, he stepped across it, entering the hazy blue heights three days after the first shot of the American Revolution was fired.

Inside, he found Eden.

Scientists agree, the richest and most diverse forestland in all of North America is found in the Great Smoky Mountains National Park. 19th century scholar/explorer Horace Kephart wrote, "Whether one be seeking ferns or fungi or orchids or almost anything else vegetal, each hour will bring him some new delight." The famous naturalist John Muir commented, "[The Appalachian forests] however slighted by man, must have been a great delight to God; for they were the best He ever planted."

The entire canon of Appalachian species – from Georgia to southern Canada – can be encountered on a casual day hike through the Smokies. Elms, gums, holly, butternut, magnolia, cucumber, willows, persimmons, basswood, beech, birch, sourwood, box elders, red cherry, black spruce, aspen, species of oaks, hickory, dogwood, pitch pine, chestnut and tulip poplars – and this is only the beginning. There are over 130 tree species within the borders of these mountains. In Bartram's day, the oaks were six feet wide; the chestnuts nine feet; and the great tulip poplars eleven feet across, with heights towering into the hundreds – their lowest limbs could be spotted eighty feet up.

Spring in the Smokies sets the hills alight with a blooming carpet of over fifteen hundred floral types: red cardinals, pink turtleheads, Turk's cap lily, purple-fringed orchids, bee-balm, jewels, goldenrod, sunflowers, mountain gentian, monk's hood and coneflowers among them. The sweet Joe Pye weed grows into ten-foot tall purple umbrellas. Bright yellow tendrils of the spice-bush move over the ground like veins. Mountain laurel and rhododendron bloom as far as the eye can see. And then, there are the flame azaleas, of which Bartram wrote,

> The epithet *fiery* I annex to this most celebrated species of azalea, as being expressive of its flowers; which are in general the color of the finest red-lead, orange, and bright gold, as well as yellow and cream color…the clusters of the blossoms cover the shrubs in such incredible profusion on the hillsides that suddenly opening to view from dark shades, we are alarmed with apprehension of the woods being set on fire.

In these mountains, precipice, bald and rock outcropping are an oddity, but their occasional discovery opens up an undulating view of waves, layers of speckled greens breaking through a blue mist that hangs almost always beneath the mountain's many crowns. In the early winter, the sight is beautiful but unnerving as dead leaves float down to the valley like ashen flotsam wafting from a fire.

Atop Old Black, Applejack and Futureman looked out over the hills, spare and wistful. They sat on a black stump to rest, near day's end.

"I have to say these mountains surprise me," Applejack said.

"How so?"

"They're just powerful. I guess I've underestimated them. I had it in my head that nothing could compare to the Mahoosucs or the Whites. Our own Smoky Mountains give 'em a run for their money, don't they? But, now that it's nearly winter, they make me sorrowful for some reason. It's almost as if they're speaking."

"Speaking, eh? I thought I was the only one who heard voices. So, what do you think they're saying?" Futureman asked.

"I don't know yet…but I'm listening. Well, two miles to go til supper. I think we should build another fire tonight."

"Good idea. Maybe, there are more words to hear in there."

They stood and stretched their muscles, stinted fast by the cold.

Applejack stared long into the valley once more before picking his walk back up. In the distance, there it was again, as in the Wilderness before. A red wind rising.

"Futureman, why do we not listen?"

There was no response. Futureman had gone.

People come from all over the world to visit the Smoky Mountains. Automobiles fill its roads in droves. In the Newfound Gap parking area, you'll see license plates from Ontario, British Columbia, New Mexico, Maine, Montana and Washington. You'll hear accents from Sydney, Rio, London, Amsterdam and Moscow. A festive atmosphere of international vacation rings in the air, but this is a stark contrast to the world Kephart described in 1913,

> The southern highlands themselves are a mysterious realm. When I prepared, in 1904, for my first sojourn in the Great Smoky Mountains, which form the master chain of the Appalachian system, I could find in no library a guide to that region. The most diligent research failed to discover so much as a magazine article, written within this generation that described the land and its people. Nay, there was not even a novel story that showed intimate local knowledge. Had I been going to Tenerife of Timbuktu, the libraries would have furnished information a-plenty; but about this housetop of eastern America they were strangely silent; it was *terra incognita*.

During the first forty-two years of his life, Horace Kephart was a librarian and a father. But in 1904 he left everything and wandered into these southern mountains in search of what he referred to as the 'Back of Beyond.' He did not reemerge until 1913. His wife waited for him.

Kephart spent the rest of his life in Bryson City fighting for what he had found, But another force had come onto the scene, driven by a power just as compelling as the imagination of the wonderstruck explorer – but one with very different intentions. Foresting.

The loggers came as soon as they could. The bandsaw arrived in the 1880's, and with it the big lumber companies. They'd started up in Michigan, Wisconsin and Minnesota, and when all the white pines were gone, they moved to the flatlands of Mississippi and Louisiana, replacing the old pines there with young oak, rattan and briers.

The lumber companies hired tree scouts to find the best trees, and when they caught wind of the hardwood diversity existing on the southern heights, they began purchasing acreage from speculators by the tens of thousands. In those days, the forests were pristine beyond our imagining, bursting with oceans of tulip poplar, black walnut, cherry, hickory, white oak and yellow poplar. These trees brought high dollar on the wood market. Logging tycoon extraordinaire, Colonel W. B. Townsend, claimed he could get 40,000 board feet from just one acre of southern highlands hardwood. A single tulip poplar, the giant of the forest, might yield 18,000 alone. The first trickle of loggers quickly turned into a flood, as they were sent by the Ritter Lumber Company, the Scottish Carolina Timber and Land Company and many others. Before long, the Smoky Mountain forests were so festooned with timbering that the hired hands became known as 'lumber herders,' and a cry echoed through every wildwood:

> "If your tonnage is too great for a narrow-gauge railroad, you need a standard gauge. But if it's not large enough for a narrow gauge, you need a mule team. If it isn't large enough for a mule team, get an ox team; if there is not enough for an ox team, then pack it out on your back."

It was a frenzy of cut and build, slash and earn. When talk came of preservation, the lumber companies pushed to have the Smokies declared a free-range national forest, seeking shelter behind the bureaucratic guise of reforestation ethics. Against this action, Kephart wrote, "If the Smoky Mountain region was turned into a national forest instead of a national park, the 50,000 to 60,000 acres of original forests that are all we have left would be robbed of their big trees. They would be the first to go. Why should this last stand of splendid, irreplaceable trees be sacrificed to the greedy maw of the sawmill? Why should future generations be robbed of all chance to see with their own eyes what a real forest, a real wildwood, a real unimproved work of God, is like?"

By 1940, the logging companies had cut away ninety-three percent of the forestland of the South and eighty-five percent of the Smoky Mountain timber country.

The 200-foot tulip poplars and majestic black walnuts, the magnificent cherries and yellow poplars had become apparitions. Their mighty roots, now only clenched stumps, littered the gouged-out womb of the oldest forest on earth.

Applejack and Futureman left early the third day from Mount Collins on their way toward Clingman's Dome, the highest point on the Appalachian Trail. The higher they climbed, the more ice covered the branches. Everywhere, the trees were nodding off, falling asleep – dreaming the innocent dreams of the young. Beneath them, the ancient land waited. Most of the year, her sorrow went unheard, dulled and drowned out by the human activities of summer and the new growth of her baby trees, but with the coming of winter, her widowed whispers of mourning resurfaced, rattling through the bare branches of naïve timber.

Applejack and Futureman approached the crown of the range – literal apex of their long journey – in the morning light, sun fighting through the white blanket. It is now called Clingman's Dome, named after Brigadier General Thomas Lanier Clingman (explorer, soldier, antebellum politician, mining expert and scientist, the first to record the height of the mountain). Before that, it was called Mt. Buckley and Old Smokey. But before that even – beyond our own forgotten past – it was *Kuwahi*, 'the mulberry place,' home of the Great White Bear.

The wind froze their mouths. The chill burned their eyelids. Atop the Dome they stood, shivering at 6,643 feet above sea level. Down on planet earth it was only autumn, but up here in the high country – *God's country, by God!* – it was winter, the brittle bane of breath.

Unsure of how to deal with the forlorn story before them, Applejack and Futureman slapped each other on the back with the joking and cornball ribbing of two haggard old friends, and hobbled down from the cranky pinnacle, re-submerging themselves in a forest of adolescent spruce, a gaping wilderness of swollen secrets. Somewhere nearby, the remains of a bear-torn brave lay, still, his blood slowly seeping into the ground.

> "It seems to be a good book-strange that the white people
> are not better, after having had it for so long."
>   -Drowning Bear, on the Bible

Up until to the final moments before the 1830 death march known as the Trail of Tears, the white man's dealings with the Cherokee had retained, at least, a veneer of best wishes.

Before the Revolution, the Indians of the southern Appalachians had remained relatively unharrassed by European imperialism. The English King ruled in favor of off-limits policy regarding Indian lands. This, of course, infuriated the colonial land speculators who wanted to capitalize. As John Ehle wrote, "One might go so far as to wonder if 'Give me liberty or give me death, but in any case give me Kentucky,' was the battle cry in some circles."

By the 18th century, the Cherokee nation spanned forty thousand square miles east to west from South Carolina to Alabama, south to north from Georgia to Virginia. According to the tribe, the land of Kentucky was holy and magical. It was sparsely populated, wild and fertile, where herds of buffalo roamed and where deer and other small game existed in great bounty. These were the sacred hunting grounds of the Cherokee.

After the Revolution, land speculators and contractors began to gain favor in political circles and the age of expansion got underway. Roads to the West were unfurled by the decree of a "manifest destiny" and the stage was finally set for the conquest of the mountains-an expansion built more on trust in gold than in God.

In 1828, an Indian boy gave a piece of the fabled aurous metal to a white trader. This proved a fatal mistake. In a letter penned to his children in 1890, soldier John G. Burnett – a mountain man who had grown up hunting and fishing with the natives – explained, "That nugget sealed the doom of the Cherokee." It was the gold rush of the east. Prospectors flooded the hills, many claiming to be government agents. They confiscated lands, built small forts and set up mining colonies, razing many Indian villages along the way. All sense of land contract was broken, and the blood ran thick.

That same year saw Andrew Jackson become President. The new President had enjoyed a good relationship with many native tribes – especially with Chiefs John Ross and Junaluska, the respected heads of the Cherokee nation. In fact during the 1812 Battle of Horseshoe Bend, it was Junaluska himself who had saved Jackson's life. Junaluska had taken five hundred of his best warriors to help the White General. During the battle, Jackson fell into the hands of the fierce Creek and, as a warrior was about to take Jackson's life, a tomahawk flew through the air and buried itself deep in the brave's skull. It was the tomahawk of Junaluska. Jackson won the battle and later rode the victory into the Whitehouse.

With high hopes for the new President and their old friendship, Chief John Ross sent Junalaska to Washington DC to plead the Cherokee case against the sins of the gold brigands. Junaluska found a cold reception. Seated at the very same dinner table, Jackson ignored his presence and sent away the man who had saved his life, without recognition of any kind. And so it was that the deaf ear of the American government condemned the Cherokee, banishing them to the arid lands of the West.

In May 1838 General Winfield Scott led four thousand regulars and three thousand volunteers into the Smoky Mountains. It was a brutal operation. The soldiers executed unruly chiefs, dragging men and women from their villages to the stockades. Many elderly, too weak to travel, found the end of a bayonet. Women were forced to leave their babies to die. Along the way, many dead were left unburied or thrown into unmarked graves, and through it all, the Cherokee were given no explanation. The white soldiers spoke in a language they could not understand, and translators, like Burnett, were few. Grief-stricken by the fate of his people, Junaluska cried out, "Oh my God, if I had known at the battle of the Horseshoe what I know today, American history would have been differently written."

The operation haunted Burnett until the day he died. As an old man, he finally recounted his past to his children, concluding the letter, thus:

Murder is murder, whether committed by the villain skulking in the dark or by uniformed men stepping to the strains of martial musick. Murder is murder, and somebody must answer. Somebody must explain the streams of blood that flowed in the Indian Country in the summer of 1838. Somebody must explain the four thousand graves that mark the trail of the Cherokees to their exile.

I wish I could forget it all, but the picture of those six hundred and forty-five wagons lumbering over the frozen ground with their cargo of suffering humanity still lingers in my memory. Let the Historian of a future day tell the sad story with its sighs, its tears, dying groans – let the Great Judge of all the Earth weigh our actions and reward us according to our works.

Children, thus ends my promised birthday story.

This December –
The 11th 1890 –

Private John G. Burnett
Captain McClellan's Company – 2nd Regiment
2nd Brigade Cherokee removal 1838-39

The land had spoken. On their fourth day, from the top of Shuckstack Mountain, Applejack and Futureman beheld an unbound view that dispersed across the wide Tennessee valley. Through the thin air, they could see that the lands, farms and rivers, houses and buildings were naked, though their specific details were blurred.

"I think I can hear what they're saying now, Futureman."

"Yes, the voices. What?"

"Blood is everywhere but our sins are hiding. Ours, theirs. We hide but the blood remains. In the ground, in the wind, in the trees. Everywhere. When winter strips away the scar tissue, we are able to see the truth – but down in the valley, it's never really winter. And the noise of the world covers over our guilt."

"We tell ourselves that we don't have to remember anymore..." Futureman's words trailed off.

"So, what's left?" Applejack stared into the white sky.

"Only confession."

"Ah. Confession."

As they left their voices to walk along the ridge again, their words were picked up by the wind and carried toward heaven, where the man Jesus uses them to plead for mercy from the Great Judge who waits, ready to freely give it. The Judge who sees all sin – sin on the mountains and sin in the valleys, sin named and un-named, known and unknown.

The small tract of land now set aside as the Great Smoky Mountains is preserved – a feeble enclave of what once was. There is blood in the soil and sorrow in the air. The towns surrounding it – Gatlinburg, Pigeon Forge, Townsend – offer everything the world of man has to offer. And the sins of the past are covered over, like tracks in the snow.

XI

Futureman spoke to Oak. "Hello, Old Man. I want to ask you a question."
    Oak said nothing.
    "Mister Oak! You awake?"
    Oak stood still, snoring. Winter had come.

Death and life, this is the anatomy of a tree. The dirge of leaf's parting. The bud-scale scar at the end of one season's growth and the lenticels of next year's (waiting) bloom. But death comes first, visible life in dormancy until the awakening of Spring.

At its very core, you can see the tree's occupation with the cycle of death and life. Beneath the bark, there are two types of wood, the heartwood and the sapwood. The heartwood is the skeleton. It is dead. The sapwood surrounding it is the tissue. It is alive. The vibrant cambium (xylem and phloem) sings with the movement of water and minerals from the decayed soil. In order to find the age of a tree, you count its seasons. Every season leaves a scar (mark of sleep – mark of death). Ring upon ring shows its growth (mark of waking-mark of resurrection). The concentric rings are not all equal. Some seasons yield more growth than others. Drought and stress make for thinner rings. Heavy rains and rich decay provide for thicker growth. Occasionally a ring will be singed blackish where a fire has burnt through the bark and consumed the cambium. Counting the age of a tree takes patience, a deciphering of its experience with life and death.

Winter forest is quiet. The song of the lone cello. The reedy groan of the bassoon. The high-altitude whir of piano's sustained *sostenuto*. The tunneled green path of spring, summer and fall is now a flowerless channel through the twisted laurels. The woodland spreads wide, wooden columns holding up the melancholic sky. Voles, lemmings and hares scamper through the open under-story, precariously, nervous eyes toward the unseen clutch of the great gray owl.

Other than southbounders, there are few personages on the Trail in winter. There is the solitary day hiker aiming to leave his or her prints in the virgin snow. There is the random group of overnighters sipping on Jack and looking for the kind of scary stories that like to hang out around fires and, of course, there is the young shivering Boy Scout troop trying to earn their winter badges.

Matt was at Fontana Dam below the far end of the Smokies. A former student of both Applejack and Futureman, he was now a friend. When they'd said their goodbyes five months ago, dozens of people had promised – "If you make it down south I'll come out and hike with you guys." Besides Bobby, Matt was one of the few who meant it. Waiting in shorts and a polyester hiking shirt, Matt stood shivering seventeen miles from his parents' car. Up from the valley, he wasn't expecting this day of all days to be the one when winter officially arrived.

The fortuitous snow had been building for weeks, a casserole of wet feathers, and now it began to fall – corpulent snowflakes – covering everything in a vestal white.

It blanketed the eastern ridge within the hour.

"Winter's wonderland! We've been waiting on the snow for weeks now," Futureman said.

It collected on the toes of Applejack's boots – small pyramids. He dug his poles into the freshly fallen blanket and catapulted clumps into the air. "White beauty always makes the cold bearable."

"Well, personally I'm freezing!" Matt said.

"Maybe you shouldn't have worn shorts," Futureman said.

Matt was an outdoor adventurer, without a doubt. But he was a *summerist*. A mountain biking, kayaking, rafting, skiing, canoeing, repelling and rock-climbing summerist. A summerist is someone who actively denies that it is winter. Cutting a hole in the arctic ice and jumping into it in a Speedo for a polar club swim, this is something a summerist does. Pulling a naked ski run in Aspen on Spring Break or snowshoeing a 5K in a tuxedo for charity, these are the activities of a summerist. But walking seventeen miles over a mountain ridge contemplating the falling snow and quiet wingspan of the great gray owl, these are things he does not comprehend.

"Why didn't you guys tell me it was this cold out here?" Matt said, hugging his chest.

"It's winter time. I guess we thought you'd figure it out." Applejack said.

"It's not winter in the valley. It's still fifty degrees in Knoxville."

"We're not in Knoxville."

"How come you guys aren't cold? You're wearing shorts, too."

"We're cold."

"You sure aren't acting like it."

"What do you want us to act like?"

"Me!"

"Okay, let's run then."

Running, the snow looked as if it were falling horizontally, hitting their chests.

"Hyperspace!" yelled Futureman.

"Gorgeous!" Matt said. "I feel like I could run a marathon out here. Bet you guys could run a marathon after all the walking you've done. Let's all run a marathon after you finish – ooh, like that volcano run in Hawaii. Geez, it's cold. I gotta speed up!"

"Go on ahead, but we're gonna stay back and enjoy the –"

Matt was already around the corner.

Contemplation comes easy in the falling snow. It mesmerizes. Questions and the intention of answers are given their respected place, given time. Time. Time, to consider. Each flake was patient with its descent, falling down from above as thoughts, memories, dreams and propositions. Faces coming down. *Dad. Ben. Bear. Blackbeard. Mama.* Onto the ground. *Ann Marie. Bobby. Jenna Clare. Derek. Shadow. Abbie and many others.* Blending into the snow, voices in the flakes. *"I miss you." "This is going to hurt." "Don't wait forever." "Will you go out with me?" "I like you, you know." "Daddy, watch!" "I'm lost." "I don't know how to say this." "Your grandpa is gone." "This is where I end and you begin." "Begin what?"* They meandered through the air, drifting slowly.

Mulled-over questions – some resolved, most not – fell down through the sleeping trees. Robust flakes. Patient. The alabaster blossoms of winter settled over their doubts. Where solitude gave room, only the important questions would stick to them now. All others fell to the ground, joined to the burnished blanket.

The question – *"Who put wisdom here?"* – landed on Applejack. He pondered it around the bends.

It's too vast to manage, to comprehend. The answer is underneath the bark of the trees, waiting in the foundations of the mountains, and yet somehow imprinted on my bruised soul. What words have I to offer for such a question? Nothing but that God is wisdom. Should I not be known more by my questions than by my answers? God is great enough for my questions. Is it possible that I am a man and a child at the same time – always?

Futureman trudged along, building mounds of snow in front of his feet, watching it climb up his legs, calves red and numb, blue shins, black knees, as he thought.

I am like a tree, one of the saplings. This journey, like seasons. Leaves start fat and green – Maine, New Hampshire, Massachusetts – forest alive, joy oozing – mixed with life and pain – grow tired in the draught of heat – New York, New Jersey, Pennsylvania – I begged for answers – why, how, what, when? – and then on and on still still still always – Why? Why have to die? The color of questions (Virginia) – vivid, demanding, wild, capricious. And death – end before end (now), the illusion of retirement. Like the tree's scar, only sleeping. Under the cold snow now, dreaming. Purging. This is how I wait for resurrection. I wonder what will happen when the sun comes back out?

The light had grown faint. They found Matt in the snow ten miles up, pacing back and forth, tree to tree, doing jumping jacks, hopping, kicking his legs up like a Rockette – anything to keep his blood from the process of petrification, five miles from the trailhead, from his parents' warming car.

"How long have you been here, man?" Futureman asked.

"Aba-aba-bout two-two-ten, yeah, ten hours."

"Why did you stop?"

"Because I c-c-came out here to hike with you guys, so that's just w-what I'm-I'm going to do. And then-then-then we can go to Hawaii and sit in the la-la-la-la-lava."

"Thanks, buddy. That means a lot. Now let's run," Applejack said.

Matt's parents were sitting in their car, heater running, fog lights on. It was nearing total darkness and snowing heavy, hills and roads coated. Futureman emerged from the wood, first in line, and walked into the dull yellow light. From Cindy's perspective – an apian that had been shoved forward in the evolutionary process by a monolith he found on Cheoah Bald Mountain. They had not seen him in a long time. His beard was almost a year thick now, encased in frozen breath and snow.

Cindy clutched her husband's arm. "Glen, honey – what is that coming out of the woods?"

"Well, now I do believe that's our friend, Futureman."

"Futureman?" Cindy asked.

"Matt said they go by 'Trail names' out here. He told me on the phone."

"Oh, that's fitting – I guess," said Cindy. "Let's be nice, now Glen."

"Honey, I was planning on it."

Matt and Applejack emerged from the woods behind Futureman.

The blue-black dusk of the early evening brought cold weather just as sinister – but grinning. Single digit wind ripped through the valley on this west side of the ridge. They climbed into the back seat to warm up a bit.

"Are you sure you don't want to come back to Knoxville with us?" Cindy asked. "You're going to freeze out here. Where will you stay?"

"We'll find a shelter," Applejack said.

"No!" A protective tone. "You've got to get inside – somewhere. Glen, tell them."

"Honey, I'm sure that they are perfectly capable of –"

Cindy nudged him with a pointy wrist bone.

"On second thought, it might be a good idea –"

"We are going to find you a cabin. We insist, and Glen is going to pay for it," Cindy said.

Glen raised an eyebrow. "Y-yes, why don't you, uh, let me get you a cabin?"

A scouring wind pressed against the side of the car. White drift cloud swirled across the road.

"Sleep in a heated room at least. Will ya'll please do that for me?" pleaded Cindy.

"If you insist. We're not in the habit of turning down angels," Applejack said.

"Well, thank the Lord for that," Cindy said.

A local ma and pa store was still open. A cardboard sign in the window read: *caBin foR hirE*. They knocked. Pa got out of bed. Glen paid.

"See ya in Hawaii, Matt," Futureman said.

"Right after Springer."

The cabin was spare, one bed with a double thick, hand-sown quilt, a wall heater and an old shortwave radio on a small wooden table. The dials on it were large and bronze, like cracker-jack pinwheels. Futureman fooled with it. A dim yellow light bulb hung above it (chord stapled to the ceiling) and flickered. Applejack leaned in to listen. Futureman turned the knobs through the high-pitched fuzz. Songs and voices broke in and out, a banjo tune, a rockabilly song, the call of a preacher –

"Wait," Applejack said. "Turn it back a little. It's a mountain preacher. This could be good."

The fuzz clicked, shrieked, broke away and picked back up again.

"There, what's he saying?"

The preacher was in a spirit run, hidden in these southernwoods, tucked away from the modern world – a mountain song tongued with an old deep-south rhetoric. Zion radio buzzing the gospel through the valley – the voice of the apocalypse, echoed inside the wooden-walled booth. Feet pounded on boards as the listener's wailed and clapped their hands, issuing shouts of sorrow and salvation.

"Glawwwry's comin. On biways and skyways, thatn horse is comin in. On saddleback wit' judgment rack, thatn Rider's ridin in. Thar thee men in yonder's wind. Watch yeeself, Olllle Black Sin, Son a Main's a-comin in!" The wooden floors pounded in the background. The people wailed above the heeled cacophony.

Outside the cabin, lustral winds picked up speed and whipped through the black bends along the Nantahala River, and the preacher sang on.

"Yon' dry bone valley, Lawd's comin' fur mee. Ya'll'n in black sin shoes, Lawd's comin' for you's." Layfolk shouted and pounded their heels on the wood floors of Zion – down, down, up, down, down, up.

The red pine walls of the cabin rattled as the wind tore at the corners of the roof, and the light bulb swung – back, forth, back, forth – casting across the old radio.

"...eeesh comin' dowwwn, tain't pay no feeee. Eeesh glawwwry sound, git yond' humbled knee." Merciful cries clung to the static.

The canyon walls rose blue above the valley high into the night air, into a calm ether – easy, thin, where there was almost a clear sky, moon creeping through the torn, white/gray curtain, while the valley below grew darker. A new wind came now from the west, through the black bends. It pulled the skin off the trees. It split the branch tips and shattered the frozen cones. Come to purge the land.

The scarlet oaks cracked against the cabin walls. Applejack and Futureman jumped, startled. There was fear outside the cabin, beyond the door, creeping in through the cracks.

"Thatn Rider come soon, tain't none to hide they's doom – nary a one! Yond bitten sinner's ear, lay salvation's womb. Hisn crimson sea, thatn crimson blood set yun free. Git yond on bended knee, thine Lord, Jesus be. Get yond on bended knee, yuns be set free."

And the mountain choir began to sing,

"Thou sinner come, come all to me. Thou sinner come, to thy crimson sea. On yonder shore, your sin no more. Thou sinner come, come home to me."

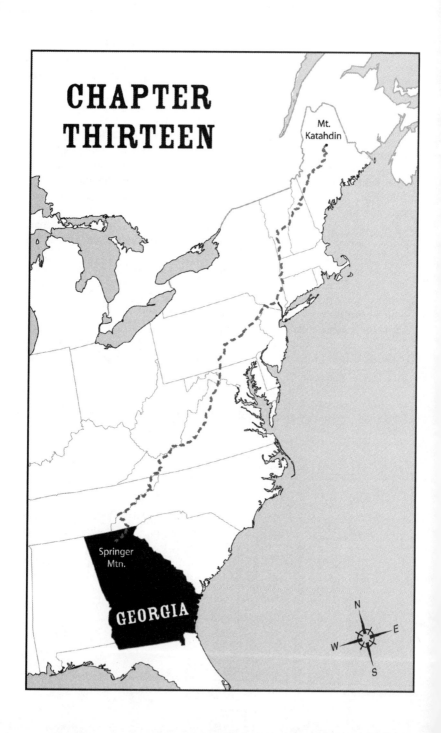

CHAPTER
THIRTEEN

Mt.
Katahdin

Springer
Mtn.

GEORGIA

They saw the green truck coming through the black bends. They watched him put his feet down onto the Georgia soil. They watched him slam the door, eyes fixed in a wide stare. Face clean-shaven, a tangle of emotions clung to it instead. They spoke to one another. Friends. Their words and tears fell onto the ground, rolled down the slope and plunged into the river. They floated through bends and feeds and intersections. Traveled waterways out to sea and tossed above the deep. Pulled up from the surface of the Atlantic, Baltic and Pacific, they found jet streams and channels through the sky and crossed the globe. Finally caught in a wintry mist moving into the valley 3,500 feet below Copper Ridge Bald where the three men stood. A cold, crisp air filling their lungs.

I

Bobby was buzzing with nerve. "Okay, so." He bent down and shuffled through a plastic zip-bag full of papers. "I've been looking at the topo map – was thinking that we could head up to Copper Ridge tonight and camp on top. What were you guys planning?"

"We weren't. Wherever is fine. We're just glad you're here, Buddy," Futureman said.

Bobby worked eagerly, snapping buckles and cinching belts, talking excitedly, "Wow, finally here, yessir," clipping karabiners, "gonna be a great ten days to Springer," refolding his bed mat, "can't imagine…what you're feeling…" putting his Nalgene bottles into… "pockets… schedule changes… youth night and all…" picking up his pack, "yall've come… two thousand miles… Katahdin … achievement… homestretch… Springer… back then… now it's…" on his shoulders and ready to go.

"Shall we?" Bobby said.

Futureman and Applejack had been following a broad-winged hawk through the sky. It descended rapidly to the ground. The white underbelly of a deer mouse flashed between its claws as it rose up toward the north ledges. Applejack swished water through his mouth and held the bottle up to the light. Futureman pressed the balls of his feet against a rocky ledge. *Oh, they're spreading out, feels so nice.* He smiled.

Bobby notched his thumbnail with the point of his index finger. His nostrils fanned. For some reason, he couldn't swallow very well. *Why are we standing around like this?* Quiet worries burned inside. *I haven't hiked two thousand miles. What if I can't keep up with them? No – I'm gonna keep up with them if it kills me. All this time, I wanted to be out here, to sleep on the ground and wake up at dawn to boil coffee and smoke my pipe under the trees? Yeah, I'm gonna do this if it kills me.*

"Guys? Don't you wanna go?"

(Hawk barely visible in the distant horizon) Applejack nodded. "She's there already, Futureman."

Stone by stone, together they climbed up out of the hollowed-out ravine, into the thick of an old rolling world and a new narrow path.

It was growing again – it grew whenever he thought about it – the headache. All the blood from his body collected in his head as though gravity had been reversed. With every step it pounded against his skull. Bobby stopped walking. He stabbed his poles into the ground and drove his knuckles into his temples. *Where is this coming from? Feels like I need to pop it open and let it drain out. Is this the first one I've ever had or – did I have one yesterday? No, that was this morning. We've climbed 5,000 feet. Deez! They just keep going, all day. What are they? Gotta stop soon, drain this pulsating bloodbomb out of my head. No – you came out here to hike – with them – and that's what you're going to do, even if it – unless it kills you.*

Bobby was in a Wilderness of his own. He swallowed the last four ounces of water in his bottle and crossed Rocky Bald in the failing light. *I'm there, finally – to the bald. Wait – aw crap, this isn't Copper. How can this not be...the mountain?*

Applejack and Futureman had pitched their tarp on a shelf of Copper Bald that overlooked the valley. Futureman still searched the sky for that hawk long gone. Applejack picked his way over the ledge – grab a limb and swing down, grab and swing, rocks and rubble – chips of stone falling, tumbling down.

An hour later, Bobby made a rustling coming out of the forest and climbed up to the shelf, his head gathered like a balloon on a string. He nodded slightly, built his tent, said two words, they dribbled out onto the ground. And before giving the moon time to break through the heavy pink/white/royal blue mist, he fell inside and began to snore, babble and snore, babble and snore.

At seven o'clock, rouge appeared in the sunset, as well. And along with it, some short trippers, their accents broad and lazy, moneyed. Not hillbilly. Deeply, richly Southern.

"Hey theyuh, bowez," a man, thirty-something, scrambled up the ledge. "Hope we ain't int'ruptin' yo-uh quiet time up heah."

"Oh no, on the contrary. We've had our fair share of that lately." Apple-jack rapped the slab of stone beside him. "Come on up."

"Don't mind if I do. Name's Dean." He extended his hand.

"Good to meet you. I'm Applejack, and this here's Futureman."

"We 'preciate you lettin' us sit fo' a spell," Dean said.

Another fellow grunted his way up the outcropping, struggling to maintain his dignity. "Hey. Erruggh. I'm Darryl." He was bald, setting sun on the crown of his head. He plopped down beside Futureman.

"You all been out here long?" Dean asked.

"Long enough to get good and cold," Futureman said.

Dean pulled a silver thermos out of his pack, unscrewed the top and passed it to Futureman. "See if this'll straighten ya out."

"Whoa, Chester!" Futureman shook his head like a wet dog.

"Yessuh. That there is first rate Nor' Ca'lina moonshine," Dean said. "Got me a neighbuh brews a batch for me at the start of e'ry winter." The smile of a proud papa.

"That's got some kick to it."

"I look fo'ward to this from Jan-wary own. We don usually see nobody, though. I's a bit s'prised to run into long hikers. It's a nice s'prise, though."

"Say now," Darryl said, "I got somethin' else you might be int'rested with, if'n you don't have a taste for the other." He passed a mason jar around. "My own personal aperitif, ever so sweet and smooth if I do say so myself. An apple brandy I like to call *applejack*."

Dean raised an eyebrow. "Oh. Darryl – this here fella goes by that very name."

"I'll be," Darryl said. "That true?"

"Surely is," Applejack said.

"You b'lieve in coincidences?" Darryl asked. "Cause if'n so, then apparently you should reconsiduh."

As they sat and sipped, a moon the size of the great globe itself drove up from the horizon into the high-ceilinged sky. Not far away under the rocking black oaks, Bobby slept, his dreams turning to sighs that faded meekly into the chilly *Nor' Ca'lina ayer.*

II

Bobby arose the next morning with the same headache, but it was accompanied by a wooden resolve that grew as he sipped his coffee. The North Carolina boys were sleeping soundly, their snoring contributing to the mist, as the three pushed on into the Georgia landscape.

That afternoon, on a fifty-three hundred foot tower of rock that tops Wayah Bald above the purged Nantahala valley, Applejack fell asleep on warm stones. Momentary lapse of cold – sunlight clawed through a tear in the clouds. His thoughts reeled together without effort.

What a gorgeous day. Couldn't be more different than those days at the beginning, that death march out of the Wilderness. March. March. 'Beware the Ides of March', my Latin teacher used to say – Jenny Buckner, what a gal she was. And what was it she had over her door? 'Sic transit gloria mundi.' Can't remember what it means, anymore. Guess it's part of that puzzle that will never be completely solved, still sitting there on the table in Brooklyn, pieces lying under Sarah's feet, hidden underneath the ratty couch Futureman slept on. But that's part of the beauty, isn't it? Can't make all the pieces fit. They don't ever work out quite the way we want them to. We're just not clairvoyant, and that's fine. It's usually more magnificent than we ever dreamt anyway. Dream. Dreaming in Shaw's House as Mike peeled his orange, dreaming as the pollen in Bombadil's heart burst forth to bloom, dreaming of a girl named Elisa, a girl I've never seen but love. I dream of Eternal Peace in a golden town called Damascus, like Paul. The Apostle. This is my Road to Damascus. This has been my dream all along, your dream, APPLEJACK, as you march toward the last blazing step op that last golden hill, march, march on – APPLEJACK – marching – "Hey, Applejack!" I'm still marching...

"Wake up, buddy. C'mon. Let's eat some lunch. Bobby cooked up some gumbo. It's got garlic and everything." Futureman stood above him, in that moment of slow waking. The same moment from years ago, the same moment from Monson, the same moment of tomorrow and tomorrow and tomorrow.

"Guess I fell asleep for a minute." The back of his neck was warm. He swung his feet down onto the stone steps, shining to him in the sunlight like white-hot coals.

That night the chill came back, but into the morning, in the cold-blooded spiracle of rocks below Siler Bald, the fire simmered.

"Fire?" Futureman said, rubbing his eyes.

"I kept it going all night," said Bobby, stirring coffee.

"Didn't a rain come in last night?"

"It was hardly a rain," Bobby said.

(Water falling from the sky-is this not rain?)

"Mmm. I smell coffee." Applejack said, waking.

"Want some?" Bobby asked.

"Sure."

Warm coffee in a mountain shelter in wintertime, there is no better place for it.

"God bless you, Bobby. Now, tell me again why you couldn't come with us in the first place?"

Over spans of Trail, Bobby had been working with his hiking poles, trying to find a place for them in his stride – *weight here, weight there, drag now, lift every three steps, no – four, now two, not again for three – now one – oop, my neck! Where's the galldarned rhythm?*

Terrain rolled, root curled, erosion and run-off, earthy unschooled stairs. *Tap. On that rock. On that root. On that leaf – Ah, I see – let them rest and move involuntarily. Gently here, strong there, slide it over this stone, set it in the groove of that root. The same tempo as the body itself traversing. This one wants to rake the ground, this one wants to poke that decayed log – they are extensions of my fingers – don't work so hard to figure them out. They'll move enough on their own.*

An opaque mist settled comfortably on the hillsides, as it often does in the late Appalachian fall, trapping a portion of the sun's daily gift close to the ground.

"Maybe it won't get too cold tonight," Futureman said to no one.

The trail turned into a halo of rhododendrons. Vines of slumbering, swollen-knuckle leaves tangled thick, creating the illusion of a vulpine labyrinth winding through the hills for hours. It spit them out for a late lunch at Rock Gap Shelter.

The hopefully warm conditions worsened, producing horizontal Edinburgh winds and chilly humidity. Winter hiking in summer clothes: good for motivation, bad for resting and eating. Bobby stood by the rickety table, map spread out before him. [Some hikers pay attention to maps – topography, water sources, directions, forest boundaries, names of parks, peaks and pied a terre. Some don't. Sometime after Damascus, Applejack slipped off the topo edge. *Journey* had swallowed him up. Futureman never did care – "Let's just see where the wind blows." *A date with fate*, he called it.]

"So, Firescald Ridge would be," Bobby pointed... "southwest from here, and Hurricane Top...there, to the northeast."

Strands of sunlight pierced the fog. Futureman and Applejack stared into it, entranced while Bobby talked. His words echoed.

"Another twelve miles to Carter – " *(37th President, nice smile)* " – Gap shelter, and we're pacing at about three miles" *(inches)* "per" *(year)* "so we should make it there, oh, I'd say by – " *(eternity).*

"Sounds about right," Futureman said.

"We're sitting at 4,000 feet right here," Bobby continued. "Guess the temperature" *(of the sun)* "is about 38, 39 degrees" *(of separation).* "What do you guys think?"

"That's right, distance is insignificant, but we still can't get away from the sun," said Applejack.

"Huh? What –"

"Sounds terrific. I'll lead us to Jimmy Carter – he's old now," Futureman said.

Bobby shook his head and fell in line.

Bobby brought out the map again after two miles of nowhere walking. Somewhere in there, Futureman had gotten off the Trail and now they were bushwhacking through a patch of overgrown ragweed beside a stream.

"Where the heck are we?" Bobby said. "Where's the blazes?"

"That's a good question. I must have zoned out for a bit," Futureman said.

"Let's have a look," Bobby said. "We came from…and now we're…is this Kimsey Creek? No, can't be…I don't get it, Futureman. How did you lose the Trail? I thought you were supposed to be in the lead."

"I don't know," Futureman said, grinning. "But it looks like we got ourselves a date with fate." Bobby continued grappling with the map.

"Wait a sec. We might be here, on Kimsey Creek. So this could be –"

"We'll just keep going," Applejack said. "Woods are pretty cool, anyway. Looks like nobody's walked through them in a decade."

"What if we get lost," Bobby said.

"We *are* lost. We'll find it eventually."

"Deez nuts. Who needs maps anyway?" Bobby shoved it back into his pack. "Let's date fate. I got a tent."

Four hours later, Granddaddy Mountain spit them back onto the A.T., patting their little behinds. Temperature had dropped down into the teens.

"Well, lo and bee-hold, mountain men! Somehow we got to Muskrat Creek shelter," Futureman said.

"Good. Shelter's got a fire pit and we're gonna rage it," Applejack said.

"Guys, did you guys see that owl back there flying through the woods? Didn't know their wings were that huge." Bobby said, nice and warm.

"Good grief, man. When did you put all that junk on?" Futureman asked.

Bobby was wearing biking pants, a pair of long underwear, flannel sleepers and rain pants; a biking shirt, a Mountain Hardwear silk weight, a smart-wool fleece liner, his $270 Archteryx weather shell, a neck warmer, an ear muff headband and (the weak link) some red, dollar store, magic stretch gloves.

"Just now," Bobby said, "while we were standing here."

"Really?"

"Let's rage that fire!" Applejack said.

"Good idea, my hands are pretty cold," said Bobby.

III

The great gray owl waits on the perch of the elm. You won't see him if you aren't looking, so still his patience. And you won't see him even if you are, so cunning his ferocity. A watcher in the woods. The owl sees all, hears all. His flight comes with intention – a path of consummate death pervading evenly throughout the forest. In winter with the leaves gone, his steady patrol can be followed as he scours the loam below, eyeing his prey, listening – a vole mouse, a lemming, a rabbit, a squirrel. Even at night, from a hundred yards, if he can't see, owl hears the movement of the tiniest of feet and stages a precise intersection. His claws are razors, his beak a barlow. The grace of the owl is seen in the juxtaposition of these two qualities: patience and ferocity. This is why he is considered wise.

IV

The eyes are only sensitive to light for a moment. A cold nose only stings until it's numb. The freefall delirium of a skydive is crippling – at first.

Waking up is singular. Nothing else is like it, the precarious moment of becoming. It means that life has returned, at least once more; that the lungs are full of breath, for now. In the fleeting half-glow, we realize again who we are and who we are not. We look around, and as the light of day casts itself across the features of the room, recognition of place and past descends. Then, as the moment wavers on the edge, it poses its only question: *Now that I am here, what will you do with me?* And if we do not see it there or if the answer is too long in coming, the cares of the world crash in and bear us away. More often, we fear its open stance – the broad sloping plain of possibility beyond, too freeing, too dangerous to embrace – and so we refuse to answer, hiding between the sheets in restless anxiety. Truth is – wild things scare us, night or day.

But in the out-of-doors, things are a little different somehow. The change is too slight to notice at first-like the growth of a baby's tiny toes. Maybe, Applejack had never before seen it there on the cusp. As the New England summer passed, waters trickling and flowers opening around him, his first thoughts of the day strayed far into the future – towards Springer. By early October, his sleeping bag had grown thin and the bright birds of summer were far away. But still, it lingered for him, unnoticed.

On a morning in late November, when the cold dawn called an end to a night of shivering misery, Applejack saw the day for what it was – a new mercy.

He looked around. His boots were frozen solid, rigid as boards. Yesterday's sweaty clothes hung, hard like window glass, from a tree. The gray fire pit was completely lifeless, too cold even for a mound of Bobby's hot coals to last through the night. The trees were wedded, woven together by the gossamer cloth of ice and frost, the silver fingers of a white oak clasping the snow-weighted limbs of a maple. Strands of light trickled down through the crystallized air. A sky not hollowed by death; but one purified by its Master.

Bobby sat upright in his puffy bag. A nose and two eyes poked out of an opening the size of a small pickle jar.

"Eeesss purrrrdy cullllllld!" Bobby said, hesitant to reemerge into the raw, single digit wind.

One huge mummified foot stretched out to kick a boot upright. Hard as rock. The laces stood stiff in the air like petrified spaghetti.

"This is going to hurt."

"This is funny," Futureman said, shorts on, daggered nipples, hopping up and down, chewing on his lip. "I can't even put my feet into my shoes, they're so frozen. Have to tie 'em down the Trail after they thaw out."

"I'm glad we're going into town for resupply, tonight," Applejack said.

"Hold up, guys, I gotta fire up my stove for some coff –"

"Get outta that cocoon. I'm dying here! Who wants coffee? More like a couple shots of *Hot Damn*!" Futureman hollered.

"Gonna be a hard hitch, on these lonely mountain roads. Let's throw for who has to be the thumber," Applejack said, as he scurried towards the path.

"Just keep holding it out, Bobby. You're doing real good," Applejack called from his enclave of relative warmth at the edge of the woods.

Bobby snarled from the highway, "You're not the one standing out here in this damn wind! Which happens to be the only thing that has come by in the last forty-five minutes."

"How much longer?" Futureman yelled from inside a rhododendron bush.

"Shut up," Bobby yelled back.

"Maybe ten more seconds, maybe two more hours. You just never know," Applejack offered.

Thirty minutes later, Bobby couldn't tell if he was still alive or not. "Someone wanna switch with me?"

No.

"WILL someone switch with me?"

"Hey, you lost the paper-rock-scissors war – fair and square."

"Please, I'm freezing my deez off out here in this wind. My thumbs are black. Stupid magic gloves! And my eyeballs are frozen. Please. You BAS-TARDS!"

"Okay, I'll come out there. Quit your whining," Futureman said.

"Bless you. Now you'll see how cold it really is."

Bobby jogged to the trees, crumpled up into a ball and started to breath on his fingers.

As soon as Futureman stepped to the edge of the road a truck pulled up.

"You fellers need a ride?"

"Hiawassee?"

"You betch-y'uns. Jiss git in the back 'ere, getchyall outta this wind!"

"You gotta be kidding me," Bobby muttered.

V

Today, the affluent population of Hiawassee is tucked away in resort homes beside the turquoise waters of Lake Chatuge. The Cherokee called this lake "place where water dogs laugh." The mountains surrounding it were the "great blue hills of God." Five waterfalls feed the Lake. In the forest are ancient stones with Native American creation stories etched on them. They are thought to be over ten thousand years old.

"Y'uns take her easy now," the driver called and drove away. The streets of Hiawassee were quiet, emptied by the cold. The men set out to accomplish what they came for. A warm room, a re-supply and a bottle of whiskey.

When making preparations back home in Knoxville, Bobby had suggested bringing something for a toast on their final night before Springer. Four times Bobby made mention of the bottle, on account of – "to make sure we have it." Four times Futureman countered, assuring him – "why carry the extra weight when we can just pick some up in Hiawassee?" Futureman had won the argument and now they were out in the cold.

"So I've noticed," Bobby said as they walked through town, "that there are no package stores."

"Yeah, um…" Futureman began to get nervous.

"Do you think that this might be a dry county? I only ask because you insisted we would pick some up here, remember?" Bobby said.

"Yes. We'll ask," Futureman said.

The grocery store clerk confirmed their fears.

"All we want is a small bottle."

"Sorry," the clerk said. "They's still a prohibition on in these parts. If y'uns want some hot sauce, gotta drive four counties over."

"Geez, I'm sorry guys," Futureman said. "Maybe we should find a used car lot."

It wasn't funny.

"I mean, if I had known…I didn't know."
Bobby and Applejack remained silent. And cold.

As cold as it was, they were forced to open the windows that night in the hotel room. Bobby's fresh b.o. added to the cloud of long-dead fish scales piled in the corner around their gear, and after twenty minutes of warmth, they could take it no more. They slept in their bags. A sixty dollar shelter.

Unicoi folded in the morning light, merging the wintry white with the gray umbra of the sheer gap. Climbing upward out of town, they came to a forest inhabited by a tangible sorrow, one too deep for whiskey to drown.

"This place feels haunted," Bobby said.

Futureman turned to Applejack. It was that same blood cry from the wintertime Smokies. They felt it here, under the stones that littered the ground.

According to the Cherokee legend of *Nu na hi du na tlo hi lu i*, as tears shed by braves and mothers fell along the Trail of Tears, they turned into roses. Mothers wept over their lost babies. Braves wept because there would be no people to continue their race. The elders prayed to *Ye ho waah* for strength, and *Ye ho waah* answered by turning each tear into a rose with seven petals, representing the seven Cherokee nations. The rose's center was gold, symbolizing the lust that had driven them from their homes. In time, the roses turned to stone – a mark of memory and coming judgment. The flowers still grow to this day in Oklahoma, at the Cherokee journey's end.

Bobby was sore, but his legs were holding together, building strength. *They'll make it to Springer,* he thought, *to watch my friends find that final blaze. I hope they notice my beard is growing back.*

After a midmorning bite, he and Futureman made for Henson Gap. Applejack stayed behind at Blue Mountain Shelter. He'd found something, a tattered logbook – run over by water and wind – so chewed up by mice and signs of time that it was barely there. Some of the pages had been ripped out and used as fire starter by boozed up Rasputin followers.

Carefully flipping through it, Applejack pieced together, among the broken markings, names of hikers and their recordings – accounts of the first grueling northbound days, already ancient from early spring. On the back cover he found a note with an address. It read,

After this here book is full of your stories and howdy-do's, please return it to me.
Have a good hike and take care of those ounces,
                        Reggae

He couldn't believe it – *Reggae*, from just below Katahdin – the first thruhiker he and Futureman had seen on day one of their journey. (He was strong, worn but not haggard.) "Well lookee here – he's a Tennessean, from Milan, not twenty miles from the old cow farm. It may not be much to look at, old boy. It's fell on some hard times, but you're gonna get your book back."

Applejack stuffed it into his pack. "What a world – what a wide, small, wonderful little world," he said, and set out through the pine and elm, picking his way toward the Gap.

Home. Reggae's there already, farm country Tennessee. He's been there – since I was green, Wilderness – green as June grass, dumb on childhood dreams – the disconnect of imagining. There we were, me and Futureman, running south – stick-legged and stiff-necked through the skeltered woods, walking the lines headlong into a blurry nightmare so lost from joy that I can't even remember those hellish miles – hundred-yard-stare, a thousand-mile-yarn of hell-worn Wilderness. But home – coming soon you say? – ready to swallow me up in sheets and clothes, clean as a whistle I'll be, too – good as new, and yet, I feel as though I'm lookin for home all over again this time – like I was when I was there yesterday. I know it's not here, on this bald globe-from this dirt I came, pages ripped out and layin' in the ashes – but to the feet of the carpenter I'll return. Home, Son of Man, we're coming indeed – ready to lay down these brittle bones at your feet, feet like bronze glowing in the furnace – never tire, we're coming, marching toward the sound of that Voice. And there will be no pain on that day. Voice – the sound of mighty rushing waters. And we shall sing again, a new song. Home – the seven stars of his right hand. Home – eyes like blazing fire. Home – face like a million shining suns. Home – where the long night of winter ends. Home. And the people of earth's broken-clay bones are mended. Home. Home, I'm coming. Might be today.

Applejack found Futureman in the gap, resting on the ground, looking up at a particularly complex section of trees.

"What are you doing?" Applejack asked.

"Looking at the branches," Futureman said.

"For any reason?"

"Incredible."

"Mind if I?" Applejack asked.

"Please."

Looking up, back dropped by the white sky, the branches were suspended in an intricate web, circles and arcs spiraled, rectangles and octagons and elephant stands clumped together in no particular order that could be seen. Small skinny branches springing from the bundle like a million stick bugs moving in the wind, so complicated it strained the eyes after a few seconds.

"Pick one piece of the mess and follow it down," Futureman said.

Applejack found an empty leaf stem and followed it from twig to branch to trunk, down to the base of the tree where it met earth.

"Pretty simple, huh?" Futureman said.

"Yeah, pretty simple."

"Like everything – find the base, and it's not so overwhelming," Futureman said.

"Man, I love it out here," Applejack said.

"Me too."

"What's gonna happen when we go back in a few days?"

"I don't know. I guess we'll have to find the bases when we get there."

"And what about the things that don't have a base?"

"I suppose they'll just drift away in the wind, like leaves do in the fall."

VI

"I didn't think we'd see anyone out here," he said. He had carefully-sculpted hair. He didn't like wearing his Scoutmaster hat, so he had one of the Scouts carry it.

"We're out here," Futureman shrugged.

"Dirk's my name. Normally, we don't see anybody else out here. Perry and I been bringing the boys out for seven or eight years now and I don't think we've ever seen anyone else out here this time of year, have we Per?"

"Willie, I'm gonna have to ask you to put that down," Perry said, bringing up the rear. At six and a half feet tall, he towered over the boys.

"Hey! Willie!" Dirk shouted.

Willie had a stick and was preparing to jab the boy in front of him in the rectum.

"In seven or eight years I don't guess we've ever seen anyone else out here," Dirk repeated. "We try to do some hikes with the boys in the winter – hey, Willie and Brad! Cut it out." Willie and Brad were sneaking rocks into an unsuspecting boy's backpack. "So, we do winter hikes with them, don't we Per? And teach them about trees and mountains and different kinds of trees and things. It's a good time." Dirk gave the death stare to Frank Rogers' kid. "Yes-sir-ree-bob, surprised you fellas are out here.

You homeless? Joking, joking, with the beards and all –" He began counting his troopers, one, two, three…

"What *are* you guys doing?" one of the boys asked. "I mean, where ya goin?"

"Buddy, we're hiking this trail here. The Appalachian Trail. Comes all the way down from Maine and ends here in –"

"Zach! Get up. This isn't a rest break. We're leaving in just a second." Perry stooped down to help the boy onto his feet.

"Maine is, like, two thousand miles from here," the boy said.

"Bradley Wedge, I swear to the holy – stop it, give me –" Dirk snatched Bradley's infrared pointer keychain from his hands.

"Brad brought it to see if he could fry Robbie's retinas off!" Timmy Rogers shouted.

"Now that's enough!"

Dirk turned back to Futureman. "What did you say you were doing out here?"

"We've been doing the App –"

"Scotty!"

"What was that again, sorry?"

"We're –"

"You see, Perry and I like to get out into the Great Outdoors and show the boys how it's done, right Per? Teach them about different kinds of mountains and things and how to make fires out of – well, see this right here?" Dirk reached up and broke off a limb. "This here is what's called a sweet gum oak."

"Sir, the book said sweet gums are maple trees –"

"Robbie, don't bother these guys. And Zach, don't you sit down again. Zachary! Stand up! I see you sitting down!"

"Dirk, it's like this – we live in the woods from April until November," Futureman said. "Then we go work at the mall until Christmas time." Dirk was tucking in his shirt. "I'm a Santa Claus."

"Mister?" Robbie raised his arm. "You mean you sit in one of those…"

Futureman winked at the boy.

"Stevie Mac – Drop it! Drop that. Disgusting. Wait until your mother…" Dirk gripped the boy by the elbow. Stevie had a poopy hand. "So, you men shot anything, yet? Any good bucks or partridges or elk or – Brad!" He gave Bradley the eye.

"Tons," Applejack said. "I'm his elf." He pointed to Futureman. "We do okay at the mall. I mean, it's not six figures or anything, but it's steady income for at least one month a year. And the kids just love this guy. Taxidermy helps pay the rent in the off season."

Robbie raised his hand again.

"Zach! Up! Are you guys doing a weekend hike or something, then?" Dirk pushed a branch away from his face.

"Mr. D, they just said –"

"Robbie, stop interrupting these men. Get in line. There you go. Thank you for always being so helpful. Robbie here's my best scout."

Applejack nodded. "Sometimes people don't like to have the animals in their Christmas pictures, so we just Photoshop them out. Problem solved."

"That's great – tighten up that formation in the rear. Behind Robbie, everyone! We're moving out, momentarily. Robbie, I need my hat now."

"I work in the candy store across from Sears," Bobby said. "That way we can all ride to work together."

"Mr. D? These guys are saying some weird stuff –"

"Step to it, scouts," Dirk said. "Like Whitman says, we have miles to go before we sleep."

"Sir, don't you mean…" Robbie started to say.

"Step! Step! Step!"

"See ya, boys! Enjoy it out here," Futureman said.

"Thanks," Robbie said. "Good luck on the rest of your journey."

"Keep an eye out for those oak maples," Bobby said as the line marched past.

"Will do. Enjoy Springer – wiseguys." Perry grinned and turned back toward the trop. "Pick it up, now. Four frosty miles to go before we sleep. That's it. There you go."

They pulled into Walasi-Yi Center in Neel's Gap – the northbounder's Monson. Bull Mountain sits on one side, Blood on the other. If you're walking north toward Katahdin, Walasi-Yi is your first sign of civilization, where you ponder the important question – *do I really want to be out here?* If you're walking south, Walasi-Yi is just a building made out of brick, wood and stone.

The hiker hostel below was empty and filled with a musky air.

"I'm starting to get this place, I think," Bobby said, looking around the room.

"How so?" Futureman asked.

"Everything is used here. It's all old stuff. Old gear, old shoes, old clothes. People just leave things and move on, and this place is made from what's left behind. The sheets have holes. The lampshades don't match. The wall is painted three different colors. Even the hinges on the door are all different."

"You're attention to detail has always amazed me, Bobby."

"And I was reading this Trail register here." Bobby opened the brown book. "Some pretty interesting entries. Like this one, from a guy named Blackbeard."

Futureman straightened. Applejack dropped his gear.

"Who'd you say?"

"Uh...let's see, his name's Blackbeard. He finished almost three weeks ago. Do you guys know him?"

"Read it."

"Out loud?"

"Yes. Please. Would you?"

November 5
Alone in the hostel. Hiked in from somewhere. The miles and places have been blending together for a while now. So are the days. What are days, anyway? Just periods of time. What is time? Just a collection of moments we give a name to. Can you bend time? Yeah, it's bending all the time. Can you change it? Yeah, moments are always changing. It's bending and changing right now as I write. I'm alone. Yesterday, I was with Little Moose and Fred Baby. A few days ago, I was on Katahdin. The day after that, I was in the Whites. And the day after that, back in New York with my family in the Hamptons. Now I'm here. Tomorrow, or the day after − who knows, I might be back in Maine. I'm starting to suspect that the sign at the top of Springer is the same one I saw on top of Katahdin. What's the difference anyway? All you people who know me, I leave youse a kick in the ass (that's me hugging you). Yeah, I'm still the same pent-up New Yorker I always was. Or maybe I'm not. Everything's changing.
                    Peace in the Hamptons,
                    Blackbeard

"So you guys know him?"

"Yeah, we know him," Applejack said. "We raised some hell together up in Maine."

VII

Night drummed the roof. Their dreams rose lightly around sounding beams and through cracks. Like grace, they drifted upward, past the screen of clouds, into the deep cobalt, past the exosphere, onward beyond Jupiter and Charon, past Orion, past Scorpius and Sagittarius, into the unknown. Attached memories tried up through the atmosphere as well. Too heavy for space, they fell back down toward the earth. Some of them burned up during reentry. Some made it, changed.

The men slept fast til morning, lightly breathing the smoldering bits of fallen grace into their lungs.

The top of Blood Mountain was cropped with patches of boulders and inlets of granite. Its foundation laid into the rock, a stone hovel rested in the center, with three rooms and a foyer.

The day was lenient, a low bearable wind, patient. Thoughts could wander, taking their time if you let them.

"This place would make a good monastery," Futureman said, standing in the doorway.

"Springer is just a couple mountains that way," Applejack said, pointing out one of the windows. "I don't know…if I'm ready for that."

"I'm trying not to think about it," Futureman said.

Bobby came in. "You guys are almost at the end!" His words echoed off the stonewalls.

"The end – what's to say Springer is the end?" Applejack said.

"A plaque," Bobby said. "The plaque on Springer says – southern terminus of the Appalachian Trail."

"A plaque," Futureman said pathetically.

"He's right, there are no blazes past Springer."

"And once upon a time, there were no blazes at all," Futureman said.

Accomplishment came hollow to Applejack and Futureman. The A.T. suddenly seemed to them like a petulant child skipping irreverently across mountains too old to fathom. And they, having not accomplished even this small path, were more naïve still.

"Nevertheless, we move on – to this end before end," Applejack said.

"Ah, how poetic."

"It sure would be nice to have that bourbon," Bobby said, again.

"Okay, I know," Futureman said. "I know you asked me eight times before you came out, but for the last time, how was I suppose to know it was a dry county?"

"You seemed pretty sure of yourself," Bobby said.

"Hey, no hard feelings," Applejack said, breaking up the fighting of two boys on a farm. "It is just an inanimate bottle of whiskey, after all. But – he's right, Futureman, it sure would have been nice."

Futureman stayed behind at Blood Mountain Monastery, on account of pondering the light. Bobby and Applejack disappeared off the peak into the laurel.

It was patient and seemed lonely. *But light is not lonely. Light uncovers sin and makes the wrong things of this world right. Right? Light is connected to Word and Word to truth.* Futureman closed his eyes and began breathing deeply. *I could be a hermit up here, I think. Linger in the air like the butterfly flapping its wings in the sunlight, that butterfly in the wilderness.*

Suddenly, a rough voice broke his meditation. "Hey there, guy."

Startled, Futureman unfolded.

"Nice day, isn't it?" The man said. He had short hair, just a bit of

growth on his face. There was something vaguely familiar about him –
somewhere back in…

"You're almost done," the man said.

"About two days now, I guess, but who's counting?" Futureman said.

"The whole world is counting, my friend." He spoke with experience.

"So, have you…"

"Northbounder. I finished up at Katahdin a couple months ago. I live
just down the road here."

"You miss it – the Trail?"

He peered into the valley. "Yeah. I have some regrets, but I do miss it.
Kinda like to do it again. You know, second chance and all – I'm sorry,
where are my manners? I didn't even introduce myself." He leaned down
and held out his hand. "I'm Yukon Rasputin."

A B-52 bomber may as well have dropped the name down from the
sky. *Yukon Rasputin!* Enemy of conscience, haranguer of Tom from Dalton, Kraken from the deep. Futureman formed and passed a kidney stone
before he was able to speak.

"Ahh. Of course. We met once before. You're Yukon Rasputin."

"Yes, I am."

"You're a legend on the Trail, you know. Like a bad legend."

"Yeah. Sometimes, I can't handle myself and it just kind of comes
out."

Somehow, a profound truth had been uttered.

"Yeah, I guess it does."

"The past is never really through with us." Rasputin looked across the
valley, toward his home. "Say, you got anything to toast the last night
with? All these dry counties around here and all."

"Uh, well. Funny you should mention that."

"Will this help?" Rasputin held up a bottle of Jim Beam. It flickered in
the light.

"Are you serious?"

"Of course, anything for a fellow hiker. But if you don't mind, I'd like
to take the first swig?" He threw back a hearty draught, closed with a
long sigh. "Yessir, easy does it. Well, here you go, friend. And don't get
there too fast."

They had another night to be out in the woods but Futureman couldn't
help himself. As their fire burned under Gooch Gap Shelter, the clouds
parted and the stars set their brilliance adrift into the Milky Way.

"I'd hoped to save it, but on a night like tonight, we should have a
toast," Futureman said.

"With what, water?" Applejack said.

Futureman tossed the bottle to Applejack. "How about some redemption – *Yukon Rasputin* style."

Appeljack was speechless.

"You'll never guess who I ran into on Blood Mountain after you guys left."

"You didn't…"

"The one and the same."

Applejack let out a holler. "Could it be any other way?"

"Who's Yukon Rasputin?" Bobby asked.

"Bobby, my friend – his is a story sixteen hundred miles in the making."

VIII

She heard them coming around the bend, beating strong against the ground. A tap. A click. A jab. Echoing, moving fast, in a distinct rhythm. Poles (extensions of fingers) vaulted off the roots and grazed across the padded earth. Their shoulders and heads appeared out of the brown tangle. They stepped fluidly without effort. Their stride had been forged over time.

They had long hair and massive beards. Eyes intense, far off. Their shirts were ragged. Their packs were folded and cinched. They wore black nylon creek-gaiters, torn to shreds, lying loose around their ankles. They used their hiking sticks carelessly and without thought. They were strong. Worn but not haggard.

"Those guys have walked here from Maine," the girl said. She was on a practice hike, an early run for the upcoming spring season of northbounders. In just over three months, she would be setting out on her long walk toward Katahdin. She had all her gear with her – heavy-laden pack, poles and new, unscratched, boots not yet broken in.

"They're about to finish. They're a day away from Springer. I won't get in their way." She stepped aside.

They stopped. "There she is," they said, first sighting of Springer, in view above the thick sassafras. They hardly noticed the greenhorn standing before them.

"Any advice?" she asked.

"Sure," said Futureman. "Get rid of the Nalgenes. Use Gatorade bottles instead. Saves a pound."

"And learn to stay put before you go anywhere," Applejack said. "A wise man told me that."

"Alright." *Not exactly what I was expecting but,* "Thank you."

And they were gone.

As they made their way down Sassafras Mountain, they spotted a plane
flying with intent. It was dropping water over the trees. The smoke of a
forest fire rose into the sky. Billows thinned and turned to strings, played
by the wind. From their perch, it seemed peaceful, not the ravenous
chomping of flame on bark – ignited by the tiniest of sins, a thrown
cigarette or unattended camp stove.

"Is there a fire over there?" Futureman asked.

"It's pretty obvious there's a fire," Bobby said.

"You think it'll come over this way?"

"I doubt it. Looks like they got it contained."

"Good, cause we're about to uncontain one tonight," Applejack said.
"It is our last fire, after all."

Fire grabbed at the oxygen, singing it orange. Pure blue flame seeped
from the base of the core logs and clawed down into the coals, digging up
hidden words. Dross simmered with the dance of sparks, dissipating into
the mountainous regions, nameless, wide and echoing, timeless and still,
while everywhere through the valley, smoke rose.

Bobby pulled out a pair of old Birkenstocks. Years had ripped the cork
apart and flattened the soles to little more than paper. He set them on the
combusting logs. "I've been meaning to burn these for a long time." The
cork began to turn black. "There's a lot of stories in those shoes." The
rubber boiled and dripped down into the coals. "Stories I'm not too proud
of. Jesus said how blessed are they whose feet carry peace. These shoes
have carried anything but peace, and I'm burning them, here and now,
with my brothers in the presence of our Master. As a confession of my
sins."

Once released, words are free to do as they please. Tonight, it pleased
them to drift away, toward heaven with the cinders of the evergreen. Last
fire on the Appalachian Trail.

IX

Applejack and Futureman awoke to the smell of sugar and oats. Bobby
was crouched at his stove, dropping chocolate chips into the pot. A sterling thermos of coffee waited beside him on the ground, along with three
silver cups. He grinned through the steam.

"You know what today is?"

"Wednesday?" Applejack said.

"It's your last day. Springer's just over that hill."

"I suppose it is."

"You know what tomorrow is?" Bobby asked.

"Thursday?" Futureman said.

"Tomorrow is Thanksgiving."

"By gum, you're right." Applejack pulled a thin flannel blanket from his pack and wrapped himself in it. "Appreciate the breakfast, Bob."

"Call it a going away present," Bobby said, offering them each a bowl of chocolate chip oatmeal.

"Thanks, buddy. We wouldn't be here if it weren't for you," Applejack said.

"Oh, Bob. I don't eat hot oat – uh, nevermind. Thanks," Futureman said.

Applejack gathered his things with warm hands and a full belly. Futureman cinched up his laces and turned toward the woods. Bobby sat on a log. Smoke rings drifted up from his pipe. His gear lay unpacked on the ground.

"Hey, Bobby. You gonna be ready to head out soon?" Applejack asked, picking at a patch of moss with his pole.

"You fellas go on ahead. I'm taking my time this morning – taking it all in. I'll catch up."

"We don't mind waiting."

"Go on, now. I ain't gonna tell you twice." Bobby smiled and turned back toward the valley.

Applejack and Futureman wound through Fryingpan Gap in the mist, past Long Creek Falls, over Three Forks and Stover Creek. Midmorning, they came to a flat cove. Spruce, elm and black oak pushed back from the path. Hoar frost covered the lost whittled-down branches, no clear sun today.

USFS 42 trickled by in front of them, a gravel track leading to nowhere. No sound of engine or busy highway followed it in. The wind came steady and firm – but all alone. Futureman looked down. The dirt under his feet hurdled the service road and pushed up into the brush. Springer Mountain was beyond it. He took a deep breath.

"Applejack, we've come far to get here."

"Feels far."

"So, now what? Is this where we make some sense of it all?"

"What can be said, Stephen – but that this little Trail proved to be a great road. And I'm mighty proud I walked it with you."

"I'll never be sorry you asked me to come along, Colin."

"I'm glad about that." The smell of fresh winter pine stirred on the hill ahead. "But I didn't ask you." He smiled.

"No matter. Well, shall we?"

"Not so fast there," Bobby said, trotting into the clearing. Steam rose off his shoulders. "You two think you can be rid of me that easy?" One by one he pushed his hiking poles together, compressing them between his hands. Broken arrows.

"No, Bob. We weren't figurin' on leaving you. We knew you were right behind."

"I've been with you since the day you left – every step of the way. Sweating and bleeding and all of it. I want you to know that – and something else, too. If you didn't notice, my beard's growing back." He looked up at the mountain. "You are my brothers. I love you. Your sins are my sins. My failures are your failures. Here we are together. There's no going back, only forward. See you on top." And with that, Bobby fastened his poles to his pack and walked into the ascending forest.

A wave of mountain fog covered over his tracks, stone cold above the frozen ground, and he left them standing there, waiting. On those frost-colored hills of sunnygold.

Suggested Reading

Barnett, Janet and Randy Russell. *Mountain Ghost Stories and Curious Tales of Western North Carolina*. John F. Blair, 1995.

Bartram, William. *Travels and Other Writings*. New York: Princeton University Press, 1976.

Bonhoeffer, Dietrich. *Life Together*. New York: Harper & Row, 1954.

Bruce, Dan "Wingfoot." *The Thru-hiker's Handbook*. Georgia: Center for Appalachian Trail Studies, 1994.

Bryson, Bill. *A Walk in the Woods*. New York: Broadway Books, 1998.

Coggins, Allen R. *Place Names of the Smokies*. Tennessee: Great Smoky Mountains Natural History Association, 1999.

Drake, Richard B. *A History of Appalachia*. Kentucky: University Press of Kentucky, 2001.

Emblidge, David, editor. *The Appalachian Trail Reader*. Oxford: The Oxford University Press, 1995.

Fisher, Ben C. *Mountain Preacher Stories: Laughter Among the Trumpets*. North Carolina: Appalachian Consortium Press, 1990.

Harrison, P. *Seasons of the Coyote: The Legend and Lore of an American Icon*. New York: HarperCollins Publisher, 1994.

Higgs, Robert J. and Ambrose N. Manning. *Voices From the Hills: Selected Readings of Southern Appalachia*. New York: Frederick Ungar Publishing, 1975.

Higgs, Robert J. and Manning, Ambrose N. and Miller, Jim Wayne, editors. *Appalachia: Inside and Out*. Volumes One and Two. Tennessee: The University of Tennessee Press, 1995.

Kephart, Horace. *Our Southern Highlanders*. Tennessee: The University of Tennessee Press, 1976.

Kricher, John and Gordon Morrison. *Eastern Forests: A Filed Guide to Birds, Mammals, Flowers and More*. New York: Houghton Mifflin, 1988.

Laccarriere, Jacques. *Men Possessed By God: The Story of the Desert Monks of Ancient Christendom*. New York: Doubleday and Company, Inc., 1964.

Luxenberg, Larry. *Walking the Appalachian Trail*. Pennsylvania: Stacjpole Books, 1994.

McPherson, James. *Battlecry of Freedom*. Oxford: The Oxford University Press, 1988.

Merton, Thomas. *Wisdom From the Desert*. New York: New Directions, 1960.

Mooney, James. *Myths of the Cherokee and Sacred Formulas of the Cherokees*. Tennessee: Charles Elder, 1972.

Mueser, Roland. *Long Distance Hiking*. Maine: Ragged Mountain Press, 1998.

Petersen, Lee Allen. *Edible Wild Plants: Eastern/Central North America*. New York: Houghton Mifflin, 1977.

Schlosser, Eric. *Fast Food Nation*. New York: Harper Collins, 2002.

Setzer, Lynn. *A Season on the Appalachian Trail*. Menasha Ridge Press, 1997.

Shackleford, Laurel and Weinberg, Bill. *Our Appalachia: An Oral History*. New York: Hill and Wang, 1977.